Ignasi Navarro i Ferrando (Ed.)

Current Approaches to Metaphor Analysis in Discourse

Applications of Cognitive Linguistics

Volume 39

Current Approaches to Metaphor Analysis in Discourse

Edited by
Ignasi Navarro i Ferrando

DE GRUYTER
MOUTON

ISBN 978-3-11-076432-1
e-ISBN (PDF) 978-3-11-062946-0
e-ISBN (EPUB) 978-3-11-062597-4
ISSN 1861-4078

Library of Congress Control Number: 2019941310

Bibliographic information published by the Deutsche Nationalbibliothek
The Deutsche Nationalbibliothek lists this publication in the Deutsche Nationalbibliografie; detailed bibliographic data are available on the Internet at http://dnb.dnb.de.

This volume is text- and page-identical with the hardback published in 2019.
Typesetting: Integra Software Services Pvt. Ltd.
Printing and binding: CPI books GmbH, Leck

www.degruyter.com

Contents

Ignasi Navarro i Ferrando

Metaphor analysis in discourse. Introduction

1 Cognition, metaphor, and discourse

By now, humans have explored the planet entirely, have unveiled the secrets of life to the extent of clone production and DNA manipulation, have developed technology so far to allowing interplanetary travelling, and have "guaranteed" the species' survival by the implementation of renewable energy. At this point, the scrutiny of human cognition – the working of our brain and mind – is one of the most exciting challenges for the 21st century. Human cognition and communication can be analysed from many perspectives as well as with diverse instruments and methodologies. Psychology, Neuroscience, Artificial Intelligence, Anthropology, Philosophy, and Linguistics ally in this campaign of enormous scope. All in all, cognition is still a mystery in its many facets, metaphor being one of the cognitive devices in the eye of the hurricane.

As early as the 4th century BC, Aristotle used the term "metaphor" to define a rhetorical strategy, employed by poets for language embellishment, consisting of either mere name transference or analogy (*Poetics* XXI, in Butcher 1902). Since then, a large corpus of literature has expanded the analysis of this (now envisaged as a) cognitive mechanism (see Barcelona 2003; Dirven and Pörings 2002; Gibbs 2008; Hampe 2017; Ortony 1993; Semino and Demjén 2017). Morevoer, an additional multiplicity of semantic transfer types, like hyperbole, metonymy, and others have been further scrutinized (see Ruiz de Mendoza and Galera Masegosa 2014). At present, a metaphor is conceived more narrowly as a set of conceptual analogical correspondences. In fact, a scientific view of human thought needs a deep account of this cognitive resource, to the extent that research interest in cognitive science focuses on its transcendental role in cognition (Cuccio 2018; Cuccio and Steen 2019/this volume; Feldman 2006; Hampe 2017; Lakoff 2009; Lakoff and Johnson 1980, 1999). As a result, the assumption that humans think metaphorically is already fairly spread. Consequently, we generally assume that much of our conceptual system, our knowledge and many domains of our experience are metaphorical so that we understand our existence and communicate with each other on the grounds of metaphorical models to a large extent. Given

Ignasi Navarro i Ferrando, Institut Universitari de Llengües Modernes Aplicades / Department of English Studies, Universitat Jaume I, Spain

https://doi.org/10.1515/9783110629460-001

that discourse is the most obvious external manifestation of human thought, conjoining metaphor analysis with discourse analysis turns out to be irredeemably necessary.

In this context, the expression "domain of experience" can refer to a complex knowledge configuration, i.e., expert scientific knowledge about sophisticated areas, including new disciplines such as nanotechnology, genetic engineering, space engineering, astrophysics, etc.; all these, both old and new, areas of knowledge obviously display their idiosyncratic forms of language (discourse), which may reveal itself as highly metaphorical. Likewise, "domain of experience" can also refer to laymen's everyday bundles of knowledge like the virtual internet, home activities, sport or cooking. Given that experts need to communicate their knowledge to the community, they normally use language that activates or evokes everyday life models, metaphors being necessary to carry out social interaction. In short, metaphor allows for the optimization of a set of shared embodied models to understand whatever new fragment of reality, or a new conception of it, which only a few can access directly. A grounded model of experience taken from everyday life or our physical environment can facilitate our understanding of more abstract chunks of experience, such as emotions, i.e., as we may say that desire is a poison or hope is a medicine (on cultural diversity of emotion metaphors see Apresjan 2019/this volume; Oster 2019/this volume).

At this point, as Åhäll and Borg (2013: 198) assert, the world – including the social world, i.e., science, economy, politics, religion, and other social spheres – does not exist intelligibly outside the meaning that human beings ascribe to it. In this sense, discourse is constitutive of "reality" because it helps to configure a conventional collective representation of reality (Durkheim 2008[1912]). In this line, Searle (1995) remarks the distinction between intrinsic and observer-relative world features, being the former ontologically objective and the latter ontologically subjective, though the latter may be socially sanctioned (epistemologically objective). Thus, physical atoms being the intrinsic features of a screwdriver, its observer-relative characteristics include the interactional functions it has been designed for. This example illustrates how human beings assign non-ontological roles to world entities. Moreover, once these assignments become conventional and agreed upon, they turn into epistemologically objective agreements, thereby grounding social facts and objects. Money, marriage, academic careers, games, and social institutions emerge as epistemologically objective social entities, even though they lack ontological existence – because they are not intrinsic properties of the world. On these grounds, Searle describes the notion of social reality, where language, discourse – and also metaphor – thereby emerge as the overt manifestation of epistemologically objective entities that lack an ontological status.

Even so, cultures may differ as for their social reality, and therefore their worlds also do so. In this respect, Moscovici (2008) coined the term *social representation* and described how the community's way of thinking affects and influences the individual's conceptualizations. Thus, representation being an act of thought, the world, society, and culture only exist in the subject's mind. Accordingly, as individuals confront new information that does not fit into their previously assumed worldviews, a conflict arises which, in Moscovici's view, is resolved either by *anchoring* or *objectification*. The former relates new information to already known schemas by integrating it into mental models, while the latter turns abstract concepts into something concrete in immediate reality. This constructionist approach, thus, conceives of social reality as a subjective creation on which a social group establishes a consensus. In this context, human beings, though spatially, temporally and cognitively limited, address the world with the purpose of knowing and explaining it through both their individual and social experience, and consequently, concepts like absolute truth or absolute reality become evanescent (Lakoff and Turner 1989). Discourse emerges as the repository of human knowledge configurations that build up our social knowledge and, as overt knowledge manifestation, offers the framework for the set-up of social reality.

2 On the interdependence of metaphor analysis and discourse analysis

In the light of the construct of social reality, it seems plausible to suggest that discourse development needs knowledge organization and content coherence. Given that a diversity of discourse types, genres and modes create meaning, they also create our experience of reality. Humans as intelligent organisms build abstract cognitive domains, as opposed to and in addition to grounded ones. Humans think metaphorically, and discourse emerges as the material, external manifestation of human thought. Discourse comes about everywhere, and so does metaphorical thinking and knowledge. Thus, to make generalizations about conceptual mappings in our mind, we need to detect concrete realizations of metaphorical language in real discourse (Charteris-Black 2004; Musolff 2004). The intimate link between the expression of metaphor and its discursive realization can be illustrated through the distinction between the individual and supra-individual levels of metaphor analysis (Kövecses 2010, 2015, 2019/this volume; Silvestre-López 2019/this volume). The individual level reveals actual uses in real communicative situations, where particular speakers may activate creativity mechanisms, like target-induced versus source-induced – either internal or external – creativity

(Kövecses 2010: 289). In addition, other context induced creativity mechanisms, such as the physical setting, the interlocutors' knowledge about discourse participants, the cultural context, the social environment, and the linguistic context may play a role (Kövecses 2015: 99). As a consequence, variation and creativity in the use of metaphor in discourse become apparent at the individual level. At that level, analysts search for how and why users select metaphors for particular communicative purposes, how their online thinking flows with metaphors, how the context constraints or enhances metaphor usage, or how metaphors provide coherence to texts. On the other hand, the subindividual level defines universal grounding mechanisms, whereas the supra-individual level configures the static and conventionalized systems of mappings in particular cultures (Kövecses 2010: 305–309).

It is an assumed fact that metaphors contribute to discourse coherence (Ricoeur (2003[1975]). Furthermore, Kövecses has shown how metaphor provides coherence to discourses not only intratextually but also intertextually (Kövecses 2010: 285–287; 2015: 54–55). From another perspective, van Dijk and Kintsch (1983) remarked the role of metaphors as discourse strategies showing that text coherence is ineluctably bound to cognition and therefore to mental representations (analysis of text macrostructures only allows for a psychological approach). How do metaphors – as a discourse strategy – help build discourse? Which models are used to present events metaphorically? How are individuals characterized, regarding their role, their attitude or their position within the metaphorical model employed? If a metaphor appears recurrently in a particular discourse – or put it differently, in different texts on the same topic – what is the consequence for the comprehension and conceptualization of the domain of experience that these texts refer to? What is the role of an ICM or metaphor in signalling the dominance of a perspective or how does it suggest a particular viewpoint? Finally, what is ruled out because the models used leave it out?

More and more answers to these questions lead to the conclusion that metaphors help create our experience about the meaning emerging from discourse. Musolff (2004: 32–33) illustrates how political metaphors constitute integral aspects of argumentative reasoning typically aiming to prove a contested issue and therefore to legitimize a particular course of action (see Dilai and Serafin 2019/this volume; Porto and Romano 2019/this volume; Sánchez 2019/this volume). Musolff argues that if metaphors can lead to conclusions that bind politicians and states' decisions they must function as warrants in an argument, i.e., they offer valid justification for using particular premises to arrive at a specific conclusion.

All our data in metaphor and discourse analyses consists of what people say, write, paint, film, play, etc. and we can access what they mean on the grounds of careful analysis. There are no alternative channels to our institutionalized social reality. As a consequence, metaphor comprehension and interpretation is necessarily bound to its examination in discourse (Kövecses 2015: 7–11). To illustrate this idea it may be useful to look at how discourse may influence society and power relations. Foucault (1979) developed the tactical concept of the *microphysics of power*, advocating that subtlety of any form of manipulation is in direct proportion to its impact. Discourse is not just a way of speaking, writing, filming or painting, but rather it is bound to social and institutional practice through ways of regulating society. Therefore, discourse structures, social structures as well as cognitive structures, i.e., conceptual systems, go hand in hand. For instance, the creation and maintenance of ideology (van Dijk 2015) imply social cognition related to discourse to the extent that what we refer to as social context is mental representations of society rather than society itself.

A crucial issue here is the Cognitive Linguistics assumption that metaphorical models constitute a fundamental component of human knowledge (Lakoff and Johnson 1999; Lakoff and Turner 1989). In the light of the ideas suggested above, the postulate that knowledge is partly metaphorical is perfectly compatible with accepting the role of metaphor as a cognitive discursive strategy. Discourse production constantly activates mental models, which can be grounded models based on image-schematic knowledge or complex ICMs rooted in the community culture, or even elaborate structural metaphors shared as commonly accepted wisdom, as far as we assume that metaphors configure socially shared knowledge in the epistemic community. At this point, whereas grounded knowledge comes from direct experience, other kinds of knowledge originate only through discourse, and inferences drawn therefrom, which are, in turn, interpreted on the basis of shared models (Silvestre 2019/this volume). Interpretation, therefore, results in much more vivacious mental spaces than what is explicit as text. Clear evidence of this assumption is shown by multimodal analyses of metaphor (Cöegnarts 2019/this volume; Górska 2019/this volume; Porto and Romano 2019/this volume). It follows that to produce and understand discourse we need a large amount of previous knowledge, conceived – beyond the classical objectivist view – as epistemically justified, shared beliefs in the linguistic, cultural, epistemic community (van Dijk 2015). Accordingly, operational discourse interpretation requires epistemic appropriateness to the situation, understood as shared mental representations, presuppositions, implications, and inferences. All in all, any interpretation resulting from a discursive fact is relative, contextual (cultural and communicative situation) and determined by the knowledge criteria of an epistemic community (cf. Cai and Deignan 2019/this volume).

Conceptual Metaphor Theory posits that metaphors are common ground in communication as part of a shared conceptual system that provides knowledge structures for mental representations of particular situations, furnishes rich settings for presuppositions and supplies tools for both realizing implications and drawing inferences. In addition, more and more evidence shows that metaphors constitute a store in long-term memory as multimodal mental models offering common ground for discourse interpretation. Discourse, rather than just language, is necessary because the same linguistic text used in different contextual situations or communities may result in different readings (see Cuberos et al. 2019/this volume; Sánchez Ruiz 2019/this volume). Creating fear, hope, or focusing on specific aspects of knowledge through the use of metaphors implies multimodal communication because what we remember from communicative facts lies in the emerging mental model, rather than the text (for illustration of diverse metaphorical modes see Górska 2019/this volume; Coëgnarts 2019/this volume; and Porto and Romano 2019/this volume). Conclusively, semiosis works simultaneously through diverse modes.

Human inferential activity and reasoning responds to diverse modes of stimuli emerging from everyday experience as well as models and beliefs thereof rather than from the standards of formal logic. Accordingly, our inferential processes tend to eliminate those mental models that require more cognitive effort and to employ instead those most cognitively fluent, either because they belong to previous knowledge (conceptual system) or due to their effortless perception and processing (Johnson-Laird 2006). Discourse may reveal the rhetorical force of an expression, a picture or a film scene, but to what extent can an analyst discover what the author's intention was, the degree of intentionality or awareness in the moment of actualizing a particular expressive device? Discourse multimodality responds to these premises, and consequently, the analysis of modal diversity is, at present, one of the growing areas of study both in metaphor as well as discourse studies (Forceville 2019/this volume).

3 Approaches to metaphor in discourse. This volume

The goals of research on conceptual metaphor in discourse are at present remarkably multifaceted, from describing specific social, pragmatic, rhetorical, aesthetic, and discursive functions in real discourse data, through assessing metaphor entrenchment in the cultural and conceptual system, to identification methods as well as criteria for metaphorical mapping description and classification. The volume the reader is about to explore provides a broad panorama of perspectives tackling diverse aspects of metaphor analysis, including a wide range of topics such as the levels of source domain knowledge configuration, new target domain knowledge, conscious usage, metaphor identification procedures, communicative functions, linguistic metaphor, visual modes of metaphorical expression, corpus processing, trans-modal metaphor, among others. One of the assets of this collective work consists in showing how the scrutiny of metaphorical connections in multimodal discourse reveals the conceptual nature of metaphorical thinking. The book is organized in three parts, each one focussing on certain aspects of metaphor analysis in discourse. The first part emphasizes the description and characterization of metaphorical knowledge. The chapters offer a view on knowledge configurations like image schemas, frames, scenarios and domains that configure particular kinds of discourse and knowledge. The second part puts the stress on communicative aspects, particularly on the analysis of author/speaker intentionality and the tools to measure intention and effect in metaphor usage. Finally, the third block in the volume delves into the intricacies of disclosing metaphorical codes in non-linguistic modes of semiosis, be it cartoons, film, or other visual media.

The first chapter in part I is an important, well-argued attempt to bridging the gap between different approaches to metaphor, namely the frame-based and mental-space-theory approaches, as well as the deliberate vs. non-deliberate distinction. The proposal goes a long way into understanding the various frameworks from the perspective of their goals and methodologies and seeks to establish a degree of complementariness among them. Kövecses (2019/this volume) examines crucial issues in CMT from a multi-level view of conceptual metaphors, ranging from image-schematic structures to mental spaces. The author raises the issue of "deep" vs. "superficial" metaphors and their ontological status. He suggests the term "deep metaphors" for metaphorical knowledge configurations at the frame, domain or schema level, while superficial ones appear in online discourse at the level of mental spaces. Secondly, Kövecses raises the question of whether "deliberate" metaphors are purely deliberate. He proposes that deliberate metaphors come with a large non-deliberate part, in that they evoke frame-, domain-, and schema-level metaphors. Third, he discusses the issue of methodological "rivalry" between theories of metaphor, suggesting that the different methodologies and approaches apply to varying levels of metaphor, all of them being useful in doing their respective jobs. Kövecses offers a valuable and useful contextualization for the reader to grasp how diverse perspectives can be compatible and complement each other in particular research projects, as can be appreciated in this volume.

Oster (2019/this volume) provides a cross-cultural description of several emotion words from the domain of anger in Spanish and German (*ira, rabia, enojo* vs. *Zorn, Wut, Ärger*). The author evaluates differences and similarities regarding the regulation and expression of these emotions in these languages. First, she undertakes a descriptive analysis, combining fundamental notions from cognitive semantics, such as conceptual metaphor and metonymy, with a corpus-based methodology that makes use of fundamental corpus-linguistic notions like semantic preference and semantic prosody (Oster 2010, 2014, 2018). The author evaluates the resulting data in the light of semantic foci, which helps organize and group the detailed data obtained in the first phase of the analysis in order to paint a broader picture of how different cultures conceptualize given emotions and which aspects they foreground. The results offer both cross-linguistic evidence of similarities and differences between languages/cultures and an intra-linguistic evaluation of how near synonyms differ from and complement each other in each language.

Cai and Deignan (2019/this volume) show the interaction between quantitative and qualitative analytical procedures providing significant findings for their research. The study is indicative of the value of using both reasonably large corpora and detailed discourse analysis techniques. The authors remark the correlations generally found between particular functions of metaphor and the genres and registers where they are employed. They observe that specific metaphors found in economic discourse support the development of new knowledge and theory, play a pedagogic function, or are useful in persuasion and topic framing. In a comparative study between Chinese and British economic press, they show cultural differences and similarities in metaphor usage and function.

Isaeva and Burdina (2019/this volume) address the issue of knowledge transfer and acquisition, which may lead to implications in the intensification and specification of separate scientific fields and the reinforcement of interdisciplinary links. Their hypothesis states that deliberate conceptual frame creation provides a solid ground for adequate specialized knowledge transfer, leading the authors to delve into the issue of term semantic transformation in different discourses. Evidence of both etymological and metaphorical consistency of the term *virus* in medical, pharmaceutical, and computer science discourses shows the invariability of conceptual frames of the term *virus*. Subsequently, specialized knowledge transfer enhancement can be explained through conscious, intentional term usage in frame creation, coherent with both background and scientific knowledge.

Apresjan (2019/this volume) focuses on syntactic metaphor, which appears in metaphorical mappings across syntactic domains, or in metaphor-driven constructional polysemy. Syntactic metaphor underpins the diversity of the morphosyntactic expression of thematic roles. More concretely, while nominative or dative grammatical cases usually code the Experiencer role in Russian emotion verbs, there is no regular expression for the Stimulus role. Different emotion types require specific Stimulus expressions, such as dative for 'to rejoice', instrumental for ‘to be proud’, genitive for both ‘to fear’ and ‘to be ashamed of’, and finally prepositional constructions for different types of ‘JOY’, ‘SADNESS’ and ‘ANGER’. The author employs corpus methods to show that all the constructions used to encode Stimulus in Russian psych verbs are predominantly used to express other semantic roles. The author suggests that, in each case, the role of Stimulus is the result of a metaphoric mapping from the domain of another semantic role, the latter determined by the type of emotion and the event structure of the corresponding psych verb. Thus, the Stimulus in radovat'sja ‘to rejoice’ becomes a syntactical Addressee (dative) metaphorically, because it implies overt manifestation of positive feeling directed at the stimulus. Anger involves a violent reaction; hence the Stimulus in serdit'sja ‘to get angry’ is syntactically expressed as Patient of aggressive physical actions through the ‘at’ construction. Other metaphoric mappings between semantic roles include PRIDE IS ATTRACTING ATTENTION, SADNESS IS THINKING, and others. The paper also shows that conventionalized syntactic metaphor can give rise to novel metaphors which occur spontaneously in discourse, such as SILENCE IS AGGRESSION.

Esbrí et al. (2019/this volume) explore users’ interaction with online genres and navigation patterns, paying special attention to the role of semantic frames and metaphors. The authors analyse the most common words and expressions in the social network ‘Facebook’ and in ‘Amazon’ to identify semantic frames for further metaphor identification following the MIP Procedure (Pragglejazz Group, 2007). The analysis of conceptual frames configuration and subsequent description of the metaphorical mappings and inferences between digital frames (contextual frame) and literal frames constitutes an improvement in metaphor identification procedures. Their findings suggest that semantic frames have been adapted into virtual semantic frames. Dissimilarities between literal and contextual semantic frames lead to consider the appearance of ’Metaphorical Transference’. The results help to unravel the role of metaphorical frames as knowledge configurations providing coherence to cybergenres.

Dilai and Serafin (2019/this volume) apply recent advances in Conceptual Metaphor Theory to political discourse analysis. In particular, the authors analyse the metaphorical framing of the Ukrainian Euromaidan discourse viewed as a communicative situation during a range of demonstrations and civil unrest in Ukraine (November 2013–February 2014) ending up in a series of violent murders and change of political power. Their analysis reveals how the social and political reality of those days was conceptualized in the minds of millions of Ukrainians. Moreover, by treating metaphor as an integral part of a culture (see Kövecses 2005), the study provides an insight into the understanding of the Ukrainian picture of the world and conceptualization system. The study unveils the cognitive models underlying metaphorical expressions in Euromaidan discourse, their target and source domains and the emerging mappings that guide discourse interpretation.

A refreshing and challenging chapter by Cuccio and Steen (2019/this volume) opens the second part of the book, devoted to consciousness issues in metaphor usage. The authors delve into the analysis of recent evidence of the connection between language and neurophysiological activity related to sensorimotor experience. Their results suggest that language expressing particular actions activates related areas of the motor cortex even if no physical action is carried out. This mechanism, known as Embodied Simulation (Gallese and Sinigaglia 2011), has been shown to be a widespread mechanism in the brain, also characterizing the control of emotion and perception, as well as the processing of metaphor mappings. The authors review the literature on this issue and propose a novel definition in interaction with the distinction between deliberate and non-deliberate metaphor usage (Steen 2008, 2015, 2017). They aim to explain the role of conscious intentionality in the use of metaphor, its correlation with the mechanism of Embodied Simulation, and how this affects the resulting mental representation of a metaphor in working memory.

Antonio-José Silvestre-López (2019/this volume) reveals an array of deliberate metaphor uses based on specific comparison devices, e.g., similes, analogies and explicit metaphor formulae in a selection of Buddhist writings on meditation. These uses are associated chiefly with explanatory and reconceptualization functions (Goatly 2011), together with the (re)creation of vivid scenarios that help the writer communicate experience in direct, lively ways. The author remarks the role of deliberate metaphor usage in instructional settings, where the instructor needs to explain the essential procedures of meditation in simple and clear terms. As a result, deliberate metaphor usage may well be a key parameter in the discourse about meditation since it fulfils particular communicative intentions and needs. The study concludes considering source domain genericity-specificity preferences in deliberate and non-deliberate usage and addresses the ways the conscious use of metaphor may constitute a useful resource in instructional settings for the therapeutical applications of meditation practice (Silvestre-López 2016).

The study by Cuberos *et al.* (2019/this volume) explores the occurrence of developmental patterns in the use of metaphors by native and non-native speakers of Spanish. The authors assume that intentional use of figurative language is a communicative choice on the part of the speaker-writer. The authors aim at determining the effect of some variables such as age, L2 proficiency level, discourse genre and modality of production in the production of deliberate metaphorical expressions by the two types of speakers (native versus no-native). The chapter constitutes a good attempt to provide a developmental framework for deliberate metaphor production in discourse. All in all, the study shows valuable insights into how creativity and transfer have an impact on metaphor usage in non-native discourse.

Sánchez Ruiz (2019/this volume) combines various methodological approaches (Conceptual Metaphor Theory, Contemporary Theory of Metaphor, Critical Metaphor Analysis and MIPVU) in a fascinating survey on the influence of metaphor usage on the communication of ideology. The author shows how figurative language constitutes a fundamental tool in the political arena as it allows speakers/writers to present, mask, restructure, share or reject, ideas, opinions, values and beliefs either positively or negatively. The study explores the impact of figurative language on society as it persuades the reader and reproduces ideology. As a result, the chapter offers a view of the role of figurative language in the construction of an alternative reality for ideological persuasion in political writing. On the other hand, it analyses the ideological implications of persuasive devices identified in such context.

The third part of the book explores some fields of inquiry related to the manifestation of metaphorical thought and discourse through non-linguistic modalities. The studies included here focus on various examples of the immense diversity of possible multi- and trans-modal instantiations of metaphorical communication.

Górska's (2019/this volume) minutiose analysis of cartoons shows that visual representation carries a huge load of image schematic inferences. From a multimodal approach to metaphor (Cienki and Müller 2008; Forceville and Urios-Aparisi 2009), the author analyses the spatialization of abstract concepts (such as HAPPINESS, LOVE, WISDOM and STUPIDITY) in cartoons. The analysis illustrates how the image-schematic source domains highlight particular aspects of abstract concepts. In addition, the study claims – and provides supportive evidence for it – that spatialization of abstract ideas in the visual medium may be independent from their linguistic expression. Her findings reinforce the view that metaphor, as a conceptual mechanism, manifests in multiple modalities beyond natural language. Since cartoons also rely on the linguistic medium, the author advocates for the suitability of multimodal analysis of abstract concepts for unraveling the dynamic mechanisms of metaphoricity.

In an illuminating chapter, Coëgnarts (2019/this volume) discusses the notion of conceptual metaphor regarding the visual manifestation level of films. Firstly, the author tackles the problem that iconicity seems to block the metaphorical analysis of film, as an issue he considers inherent to the visual mode. Then, he proceeds to discuss metaphorical analysis in film in three phases. Firstly, he illustrates how image schemas may be elicited in visual images through the implementation of various filmic stylistic techniques (e.g., camera movement, editing). Secondly, he focusses on the importance of metonymy in representing target domains in film. Finally, in a meticulous display of rigorous analysis, the chapter illustrates how stylistically motivated image schemas may be mapped onto the inferential logic of metonymically represented target domains.

Porto and Romano (2019/this volume) elaborate an innovative proposal for the analysis of transmodality in metaphorical discourse. The authors suggest that "transmodal metaphors are those which have migrated from one mode (verbal, visual or sonic) to another, often as a consequence of a change in the medium, which affects both the modes and the discursive practices involved" (Porto and Romano 2019/this volume: 321). As the authors illustrate, this migration process may bring about new mappings, meanings and functions. The chapter scrutinizes the effects of transmodality in the emergence and development of one of the metaphors that have been prominent in recent years' Spanish protest discourse, THE TIDES metaphor (*LAS MAREAS*). The analysis of a combined corpus of textual, pictorial and musical realizations of the metaphor in various media serves for an explanation of the evolutionary mechanisms by virtue of which the metaphor is subsequently used in diverse media and acquires different nuances depending on the socio-political, cultural and physical contexts where it is used. The study shows the validity and usefulness of the notion of transmodality in order to explain the evolution of a metaphor as it is instantiated in different modes and contexts acquiring new semantic, pragmatic, rhetorical and affective values.

Let us note here the connection between this study and Steen's distinction between deliberate and non-deliberate metaphors. The fact that metaphor makes use of different sets of correspondences across modes is suggestive of this type of metaphor being eminently deliberate, where deliberateness would have a connotational rather than a denotational value.

Starting at Multimodal Theory (Forceville 1996, 2002) and Multimodal Metaphor Annotation (Bolognesi et al. 2017; Šorm and Steen 2018), Muelas-Gil (2019/this volume) analyses multimodal metaphor in printed media discourse. More concretely, the study surveys metaphor frequency in multimodal elements complemented by headlines and their interpretation by groups of subjects. The data reveal that while visual metaphors tend to convey the metaphor on their own, the combination of image and text (i.e., multimodality) facilitates a most accurate understanding and interpretation of the metaphor.

Finally, Forceville (2019/this volume) provides an insightful comment on the chapters in the last part on multimodality together with an enlightening view on the evolution of research on the multimodal character of metaphorical discourse. Forceville remarks that the affordances characterizing modes other than language enable them to metaphorize in ways that are difficult, or even impossible, to achieve in verbal form. This view opens a vast range of possibilities for discovering the manifold ways in which human cognition may express itself. Forceville's response to the chapters emphasizes their ground-breaking standpoints on that panorama. His outlook on the future evolution of figurative thought and communication studies announces a flourishing proliferation in the field of rhetoric, where not only metaphor and metonymy but the whole set of tropes promise to be protagonists. Forceville argues for the need to expand present-day research to all tropes, to promote further investigation into the (still somewhat unexplored) multimodal genres and subgenres (e.g., film, art), to adapt and readapt models depending on the nature of the data to address, and to embed the analysis of tropes in a theory of both communication and cognition.

This volume is the result of a long process since its inception. Originally, it was conceived as a collection of selected papers from the *4th International Conference on Metaphor and Discourse* at Universitat Jaume I, in December 2015. Fortunately, three invited chapters have been added to the resulting set, the ones by Cai and Deignan, Coëgnarts, and Forceville. I am deeply indebted to these authors for their generosity in accepting to participate in the project. I also owe all the contributors special gratitude for their patience and effort, and both De Gruyter Mouton as well as the series coordinators for believing in this project and for their constant support. My honest hope looks forward to fulfilling the participants' expectations in making this contribution worthy of the field of metaphor and discourse studies.

Acknowledgements: This research has been financed by FEDER/Spanish Ministry of Science, Innovation and Universities, State Research Agency, project no. FFI2017-82730-P and by Universitat Jaume I, project UJI-B2018-59.

References

Åhäll, Linda & Stefan Borg. 2013. Predication, Presupposition and Subject-positioning. In Laura Shepherd (ed.), *Critical approaches to security: An introduction to theories and methods*, 196–207. London & New York: Routledge.

Apresjan, Valentina. 2019/this volume. Metaphor in grammar: mapping across syntactic domains. In Ignasi Navarro i Ferrando (ed.), *Current approaches to metaphor analysis in discourse*, 111–130. Berlin & New York: De Gruyter Mouton.

Barcelona, Antonio (ed.). 2003. *Metaphor and metonymy at the crossroads*. Berlin & New York: De Gruyter Mouton.

Bolognesi, Marianna, Romy van den Heerik, & Ester van den Berg. 2018. VisMet 1.0: An online Corpus of Visual Metaphors. In Steen, Gerard J. (ed.), *Visual metaphor. structure and process*, 89–114. Amsterdam: John Benjamins Publishing Co.

Butcher, Samuel H. (ed.). 1902. *The Poetics of Aristotle*. London: Macmillan and Co. Ltd.

Cai, Dongman & Alice Deignan. 2019/this volume. Metaphors and evaluation in popular economic discourse on trade wars. In Ignasi Navarro i Ferrando (ed.), *Current approaches to metaphor analysis in discourse*, 57–78. Berlin & New York: De Gruyter Mouton.

Charteris-Black, Jonathan. 2004. *Corpus approaches to critical metaphor analysis* Houndmills, UK: Palgrave Macmillan.
Cienki, Alan & Cornelia Müller. 2008. Metaphor, gesture, and thought. In Raymond W. Gibbs (ed.), *The Cambridge handbook of metaphor and thought*, 483–501. Cambridge: Cambridge University Press.
Coëgnarts, Maarten. 2019/this volume. Analyzing metaphor in film: Some conceptual challenges. In Ignasi Navarro i Ferrando (ed.), *Current approaches to metaphor analysis in discourse*, 295–320. Berlin & New York: De Gruyter Mouton.
Cuberos, Rocío, Elisa Rosado & Joan Perera. 2019/this volume. Using deliberate metaphor in discourse: native vs. non-native text production. In Ignasi Navarro i Ferrando (ed.), *Current approaches to metaphor analysis in discourse*, 235–255. Berlin & New York: De Gruyter Mouton.
Cuccio, Valentina. 2018. *Attention to Metaphor. From neurons to representations*. Amsterdam: John Benjamins Publishing Company.
Cuccio, Valentina & Gerard Steen. 2019/this volume. Deliberate Metaphors and Embodied Simulation. In Ignasi Navarro i Ferrando (ed.), *Current approaches to metaphor analysis in discourse*, 185–203. Berlin & New York: De Gruyter Mouton.
Dilai, Marianna & Tetyana Serafin. 2019/this volume. Metaphorical conceptualization in the Euromaidan discourse. In Ignasi Navarro i Ferrando (ed.), *Current approaches to metaphor analysis in discourse*, 155–181. Berlin & New York: De Gruyter Mouton.
Dirven, René & Pörings Ralph (eds.). 2002. *Metaphor and metonymy in comparison and contrast*. Berlin & New York: De Gruyter Mouton.
Durkheim, Emile. 2008[1912]. *The elementary forms of the religious life*. Mineola, N.Y.: Dover Publications.
Esbrí-Blasco, Montserrat, Carolina Girón-García & María Luisa Renau-Renau. 2019/this volume. Metaphors in the digital world: The case of metaphorical frames in 'Facebook' and 'Amazon'. In Ignasi Navarro i Ferrando (ed.), *Current approaches to metaphor analysis in discourse*, 131–153. Berlin & New York: De Gruyter Mouton.
Feldman, Jerome A. 2008. *From molecule to metaphor*. Cambridge, Mass. & London, England: M.I.T. Press.
Forceville, Charles. 1996. *Pictorial Metaphor in Advertising*. London and New York: Routledge.
Forceville, Charles. 2002. The identification of target and source in pictorial metaphors. *Journal of Pragmatics* 34 (1). 1–14.
Forceville, Charles. 2019/this volume. Developments in multimodal metaphor studies: a response to Górska, Coëgnarts, Porto & Romano, and Muelas-Gil". In Ignasi Navarro i Ferrando (ed.), *Current approaches to metaphor analysis in discourse*, 367–378. Berlin & New York: De Gruyter Mouton.
Forceville, Charles & Eduardo Urios-Aparisi (eds.). 2009. *Multimodal metaphor*. Berlin & New York: De Gruyter Mouton.
Foucault, Michel. 1979. *La microfísica del poder*. Madrid: La Piqueta.
Gallese, Vittorio & Corrado Sinigaglia. 2011. What is so special about embodied simulation? *Trends in Cognitive Science* 15 (11). 512–519.
Gibbs, Raymond W. Jr. (ed.) 2008. *The Cambridge Handbook of Metaphor and Thought*, NY, USA: Cambridge University Press.
Goatly, Andrew. 2011 [1997]. *The language of metaphors*, 2nd edn. London & New York: Routledge.
Górska, Elżbieta. 2019/this volume. Spatialization of abstract concepts in cartoons. A case study of verbo-pictorial image-schematic metaphors. In Ignasi Navarro i Ferrando (ed.),

Current approaches to metaphor analysis in discourse, 279–294. Berlin & New York: De Gruyter Mouton.
Hampe, Beate (ed.). 2017. *Metaphor, embodied cognition and discourse*. Cambridge: Cambridge University Press.
Isaeva, Ekaterina & Olga Burdina. 2019/this volume. Transdiscursive term transformation: the evidence from cognitive discursive research of the term 'virus'. In Ignasi Navarro i Ferrando (ed.), *Current approaches to metaphor analysis in discourse*, 79–109. Berlin & New York: De Gruyter Mouton.
Johnson-Laird, Philip N. 2006. *How We Reason*. New York: Oxford University Press.
Kövecses, Zoltán. 2005. *Metaphor in culture: Universality and variation*. Cambridge: Cambridge University Press.
Kövecses, Zoltán. 2010 [2002]. *Metaphor. A practical introduction*. 2nd edn. Oxford & New York: Oxford University Press.
Kövecses, Zoltán. 2015. *Where metaphors come from*. Oxford & New York: Oxford University Press.
Kövecses, Zoltán. 2017. Levels of metaphor, *Cognitive Linguistics* 28 (2). 321–347.
Kövecses, Zoltán. 2019/this volume. Some consequences of a multi-level view of metaphor. In Ignasi Navarro i Ferrando (ed.), *Current approaches to metaphor analysis in discourse*, 19–33. Berlin & New York: De Gruyter Mouton.
Lakoff, George. 2009. *The Neural Theory of Metaphor*. Report: January 2009. University of California at Berkeley. http://www.neurohumanitiestudies.eu/archivio/SSRN-id1437794The_Neural_Theory_of_Metaphor.pdf.
Lakoff, George & Johnson, Mark. 1980. *Metaphors we live by*. Chicago: University of Chicago Press.
Lakoff, George & Johnson, Mark. 1999. *Philosophy in the Flesh*. New York: Basic books.
Lakoff, George & Turner, Mark. 1989. *More than Cool Reason* The University of Chicago Press.
Moscovici, Serge. 2008. *Psychoanalysis: Its image and its public* [1961]. Cambridge: Polity.
Muelas-Gil, María. 2019/this volume. Visual metaphors in economic discourse. An analysis of the interaction of conventional and novel visual metaphors in *The Economist*. In Ignasi Navarro i Ferrando (ed.), *Current approaches to metaphor analysis in discourse*, 347–365. Berlin & New York: De Gruyter Mouton.
Musolff, Andreas. 2004. *Metaphor and Political Discourse*, Houndmills, UK: Palgrave Macmillan.
Ortony, Andrew (ed.). 1993[1979]. *Metaphor and thought*. 2nd edn. Cambridge & New York: Cambridge University Press.
Oster, Ulrike. 2010. Using corpus methodology for semantic and pragmatic analyses: What can corpora tell us about the linguistic expression of emotions? *Cognitive Linguistics* 21 (4). 727–763.
Oster, Ulrike. 2014. Emotions between physicality and acceptability. A Contrast of the German Anger Words Wut and Zorn. *Onomázein* 30. 286–306.
Oster, Ulrike. 2018. Emotions in motion. Towards a corpus-based description of the diachronic evolution of anger words. *Review of Cognitive Linguistics*. 16 (1). 191–228.
Oster, Ulrike. 2019/this volume. Cross-cultural semantic and pragmatic profiling of emotion words. Regulation and expression of anger in Spanish and German . In Ignasi Navarro i Ferrando (ed.), *Current approaches to metaphor analysis in discourse*, 35–56. Berlin & New York: De Gruyter Mouton.
Porto, M. Dolores & Manuela Romano. 2019/this volume. Transmodality in metaphors: TIDES in Spanish social protest movements. In Ignasi Navarro i Ferrando (ed.), *Current approaches to metaphor analysis in discourse*, 321–345. Berlin & New York: De Gruyter Mouton.

Pragglejazz Group. 2007. MIP: A Method for Identifying Metaphorically Used Words in Discourse. *Metaphor and Symbol* 22(1). 1–39.
Ricoeur, Paul [1975]. *La métaphore vive*. Paris: Éditions du Seuil. (Engl. 2003. *The rule of metaphor* London: Routledge).
Ruiz de Mendoza Ibáñez, Francisco J. & Galera Masegosa, Alicia 2014. *Cognitive modeling. A linguistic perspective*. Amsterdam: John Benjamins.
Sánchez Ruiz, Raquel. 2019/this volume. George Ridpath's use of metaphor, metonymy and *metaphtonymy* during the Peace Campaign (1710–1713) of the War of the Spanish Succession. In Ignasi Navarro i Ferrando (ed.), *Current approaches to metaphor analysis in discourse*, 257–276. Berlin & New York: De Gruyter Mouton.
Searle, John R. 1995 *The Construction of Social Reality*. New York: The Free Press.
Semino, Elena & Zsófia Demjén (eds.). 2017. *The Routledge handbook of metaphor and language*. New York, USA: Routledge.
Silvestre-López, Antonio José. 2016. The discourse of mindfulness: What language reveals about the mindfulness experience. In Pilar Ordóñez-López & Nuria Edo-Marzà (eds.), *New insights into the analysis of medical discourse in professional, academic and popular settings*, 173–198. Bristol: Multilingual Matters.
Silvestre-López, Antonio José. 2019/this volume. Deliberate metaphors in Buddhist teachings about meditation. In Ignasi Navarro i Ferrando (ed.), *Current approaches to metaphor analysis in discourse*, 205–233. Berlin & New York: De Gruyter Mouton.
Šorm, Ester & Steen, Gerard J. 2018. VISMIP. Towards a method for visual metaphor identification. In Steen, Gerard J. (ed.), *Visual Metaphor. Structure and process*, 47–88. Amsterdam: John Benjamins Publishing Co.
Steen, Gerard J. 2008. The paradox of metaphor: Why we need a three-dimensional model for metaphor. *Metaphor & Symbol* 23 (4). 213–41.
Steen, Gerard J. 2015. Developing, testing and interpreting Deliberate Metaphor Theory. *Journal of Pragmatics* 90. 67–72. https://doi.org/10.1016/j.pragma.2015.03.013.
Steen, Gerard J. 2017. Deliberate Metaphor Theory: Basic assumptions, main tenets, urgent issues. *Intercultural Pragmatics* 14 (1). 1–24.
van Dijk, Teun A. 2015. *Discourse and knowledge*. Cambridge, UK: Cambridge University Press.
van Dijk, Teun A. & Walter Kintsch. 1983. *Strategies of discourse comprehension*. New York: Academic Press.

Part I: Metaphor and knowledge configuration in discourse

Zoltán Kövecses

Some consequences of a multi-level view of metaphor

Abstract: Based on my multi-level view of conceptual metaphors (Kövecses 2017), I examine three issues in Conceptual Metaphor Theory (CMT): First, I raise the issue of "deep" vs. "superficial" metaphors and their ontological status. It can be suggested that deep metaphors are those that are at the frame, domain or schema levels, while superficial ones are at the level of mental spaces. Second, I take up the issue of whether "deliberate" metaphors are purely deliberate. I propose that deliberate metaphors come with a large non-deliberate part, in that they evoke frame-, domain-, and schema-level metaphors. Third, I discuss the issue of methodological "rivalry" between theories of metaphor. I suggest that the different methodologies and approaches apply to different levels of metaphor and that they are all useful in doing their respective jobs.

Keywords: multi-level metaphor, deep vs. superficial metaphor, deliberate metaphor, methodological approaches to metaphor

1 Introduction

In the past few years I have proposed a "multi-level view of metaphor" within the framework of Conceptual Metaphor Theory (Kövecses 2015a, 2017). In essence, the proposal was that the four types of conceptual structure relevant to the study of metaphor, such as image schemas, domains, frames, and mental spaces, can be regarded as occupying different levels in what I called "schematicity hierarchies." Schematicity hierarchies have these conceptual structures arranged in vertical hierarchies on different levels of schematicity – from most schematic to least schematic. Specifically, we can distinguish *four* levels of schematicity at which the four types of conceptual structures can be placed. The four levels go from the most schematic to the least schematic, as represented in the diagram below:

Zoltán Kövecses, ELTE, Budapest, School of English and American Studies

https://doi.org/10.1515/9783110629460-002

The upward arrow in figure 2.1 indicates increasing schematicity, whereas the downward arrow indicates increasing specificity.

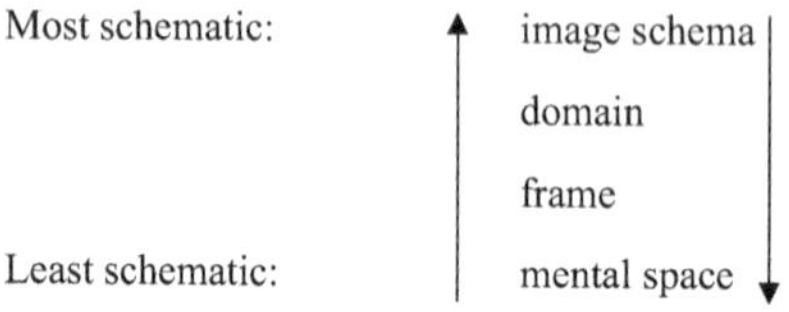

Figure 2.1: Schematicity hierarchy for four conceptual structures.

I also suggested that three distinctions apply to these four levels. The first distinction from the top is between image schemas and the three lower levels. Image schemas are analogue structures in the brain/mind, while domains, frames, and mental spaces are not (they are propositional). The second distinction is between mental spaces, on the one hand, and frames, domains, and image schemas, on the other. The basis for the distinction is that whereas frames, domains, and image schemas are structures in long-term memory, mental spaces are operative in working memory (see Fauconnier 2007). The third distinction is between the level of *linguistic* utterances used in actual communication and those of the *conceptual* structures mentioned. Figure 2.2 displays the various distinctions:

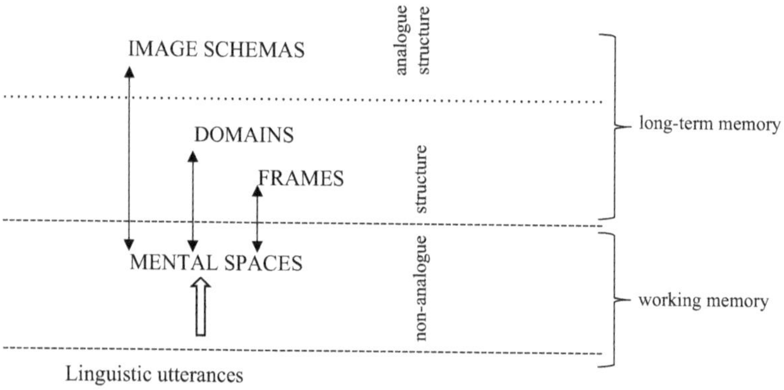

Figure 2.2: The multi-level view of conceptual and linguistic structures.

Furthermore, I claimed that the multi-level view of metaphor helps us resolve, or at least clarify, some issues in conceptual metaphor theory. In particular, I raised the following issues (Kövecses 2015a): (1) Which linguistic expressions related to a source domain are used metaphorically in relation to a target? (2) What is the appropriate conceptual structure that participates in metaphorical conceptualization? (3) At which level of generality should we formulate conceptual metaphors? (4) Do the mappings always go from source to target? (5) Are all linguistic metaphors systematic? Given these questions, I argued that the issues are not independent of each other but are closely related. They all have to do with how we think about our conceptual system: in particular, how we think about its essential structures in terms of their schematicity and what kind of distinction(s) we postulate regarding its operation in our attempt to account for the functioning of the system.

In the present paper, I wish to examine three *consequences* of the new, multi-level view of metaphor in relation to (1) a proposal by George Lakoff, (2) a distinction emphasized by Gerard Steen, and (3) a fundamental issue in the methodology of studying metaphor within a CMT framework. In particular, they are as follows:

- What are "deep" vs. "shallow" or "superficial metaphors? What is their ontological status in the metaphorical conceptual system?
- Do "deliberate" metaphors exist independently of "nondeliberate" ones? How best can we characterize them in a multi-level view of metaphor?
- What is the "best" method to study metaphors out of the many available ones in the various disciplines that deal with metaphor?

In what follows, I address the three questions and attempt to examine them in light of the multi-level view of metaphor.

2 Deep vs. shallow metaphors

In a 1995 paper, George Lakoff distinguishes two different kinds of metaphor: "deep" and "superficial." He explains the basis for the distinction in the following way:

> The metaphors I have discussed so far in the paper have been both conceptual in nature and deep, in the sense that they are used largely without being noticed, that they have enormous social consequences, and that they shape our very understanding of our everyday world. It is important to contrast such deep conceptual metaphors such as Morality is Strength and The Nation is a Family with superficial metaphors, which are only of marginal interest but which often lead analysts astray. (Lakoff 1995, http://www.wwcd.org/issues/Lakoff.html)

In other words, conceptual and deep metaphors are used without being noticed, they have enormous social consequences, and they shape our understanding of the world. Given this characterization, we can ask what the ontological status of deep and superficial metaphors is – especially in relation to the four-level hierarchy as described in other publications (Kövecses 2015a, 2017). How do deep and superficial metaphors fit into the schematicity hierarchy defined by the conceptual structures of image schemas, domains, frames, and mental spaces, as shown above?

The particular example Lakoff uses to demonstrate superficial metaphors is that of the *safety net*. He illustrates the metaphor from a newspaper article: "Senator Phil Gramm told a college commencement audience that the social safety net erected by government by the New Deal and the Great Society had become a 'hammock' that is robbing the country of freedom and virtue" (from Lakoff 1995, http://www.wwcd.org/issues/Lakoff.html). Lakoff offers an interpretation of the metaphor along the lines of his book *Moral Politics* (1996). He states that "[t]he tightrope is straight and narrow – a moral path." This is based on the well-known conceptual metaphor MORAL IS STRAIGHT. Given the metaphor, walking the tightrope corresponds to working and falling off to losing your job.

In addition to this interpretation, several other metaphors seem to be equally possible in understanding the passage. One of these would be the conceptualization of actions in general as motion. Another would take into account the balancing act of the tightrope walker. Furthermore, we can think of the movement of the tightrope walker as a life-related metaphor having journey as its source domain. Finally, we can interpret the situation depicted by the sentence as a combination of controlling and life-action metaphors, in which controlling life amounts to keeping a job. The set of conceptual metaphors according to this interpretation would thus be:

- ACTION IS MOTION
- CONTROL IS PHYSICAL BALANCE
- LIFE IS TRAVEL
- LEADING A LIFE IS JOURNEYING
- KEEPING ONE'S JOB IS KEEPING ONE'S BALANCE WHILE WALKING ALONG A TIGHTROPE
- LOSING ONE'S JOB IS LOSING ONE'S BALANCE WHILE WALKING ALONG A TIGHTROPE

The last two metaphors are the most specific ones, given the schematicity hierarchy mentioned above. They occupy the level of mental spaces. These highly specific metaphors go together with some everyday knowledge that is carried over from the source to the target:

> The tightrope walker needs a safety net so as not to injure himself if he falls.
> People need social support in case they lose their jobs.

The knowledge provides the basis for the social support of working people.

More importantly for the argument here, the conceptual metaphors identified above (i.e., CONTROL IS BALANCE, ACTION IS MOTION, etc.) can be found at four different levels: the levels of image schema, domain, frame, and mental space in the following way:

Image schema:
- ACTION IS MOTION
- CONTROL IS PHYSICAL BALANCE

Domain:
- LIFE IS TRAVEL

Frame:
- LEADING A LIFE IS JOURNEYING

Mental space:
- KEEPING ONE'S JOB IS KEEPING ONE'S BALANCE WHILE WALKING ALONG A TIGHTROPE
- LOSING ONE'S JOB IS LOSING ONE'S BALANCE WHILE WALKING ALONG A TIGHTROPE

The schematicity hierarchy works in the following way in this case: Actions in general are metaphorically understood as (self-propelled) motion (image schema level). Life is a kind of action and travel is a kind of motion (domain level). It is a major aspect of life that we live (lead) it, which is understood through journeying (the activity aspect of travel; see Framenet, https://framenet.icsi.berkeley.edu/fndrupal/frameIndex) (frame level). A part of leading a life is having (or not having) a job, which is understood as walking along a tightrope (mental spaces level). The MOTION and BALANCE source domains are conceptually integrated (blended) at the level of mental spaces in the image of "walking the tightrope" (on blending, see Fauconnier and Turner 2002). As can be seen, both the target and source domains are more specific elaborations of higher level metaphors, as we go down the hierarchy.

This organization of the metaphors tells us about what the distinction between "deep" and "superficial" metaphors actually means. The deep metaphors would be the image schema-, domain- and frame-level ones. The superficial metaphor would be the one at the level of mental spaces. In other words, we can reinterpret and reconceptualize Lakoff's distinction between deep and superficial metaphors in terms of the schematicity hierarchy shown above. The deep metaphors are the ontologically most schematic ones, while the superficial ones are the least schematic. His terms "deep" and "superficial" are metaphorical construals of the three "higher" (image schema, domain, frame) and the "lowest" (mental space) levels.

3 Deliberate vs. non-deliberate metaphors

Actually, what Lakoff means by superficial metaphors, such as *safety net*, corresponds to or at least greatly overlaps with what Gerard Steen (2013) refers to as "deliberate" metaphors. Steen defines the latter as follows:

> Deliberate metaphor affords conscious metaphorical thought, but is not identical with it (Steen 2011b). Instead, deliberate metaphor can be defined as the instruction for addressees to adopt an 'alien' perspective on some target referent in order to formulate specific thoughts about that target from the standpoint of that alien perspective (Steen 2008, 2010, 2011a). This is typically achieved by some form of explicit and direct metaphor, such as simile. (Steen 2013, https://www.academia.edu/363751/Deliberate_metaphor_affords_conscious_metaphorical_thought)

He offers the following example for this kind of metaphor:

> Imagine your brain as a house filled with lights. Now imagine someone turning off the lights one by one. That's what Alzheimer's disease does. It turns off the lights so that the flow of ideas, emotions and memories from one room to the next slows and eventually ceases. And sadly–as anyone who has ever watched a parent, a sibling, a spouse succumb to the spreading darkness knows–there is no way to stop the lights from turning off, no way to switch them back on once they've grown dim. At least not yet. (Steen 2013, https://www.academia.edu/363751/Deliberate_metaphor_affords_conscious_metaphorical_thought)

Clearly, in this case, the metaphor is not confined to a single word. It is an extended description of how we should imagine Alzheimer's disease. As Steen points out, in comprehending the metaphor, our view of the disease changes; we adopt a new perspective on it. How can the multi-level view of metaphor outlined in the paper enrich this understanding of deliberate metaphors?

First, let us note that the example is based on the notions of light and darkness – basic schematic perceptual experiences. We understand a number of related abstract concepts in terms of the image schema of LIGHT: RATIONALITY, KNOWLEDGE, INTELLIGENCE, TRUTH, MORALITY, and maybe some others. They all have to do with reason, yielding the metaphor REASON IS LIGHT. They all have a positive evaluation, as opposed to their antonyms, EMOTIONALITY, IGNORANCE, STUPIDITY, FALSITY, IMMORALITY, etc., which are all negatively valued. In other words, we are dealing here with the image schema metaphors of REASON IS LIGHT and LACK OF REASON IS DARK.

Second, the bodily experience of light turning into darkness and darkness turning into light is used to conceptualize the human mind. The metaphor that elaborates on the REASON IS LIGHT image-schema metaphor is that of MENTAL FUNCTIONING, or more simply, THINKING IS USING LIGHT. The THINKING IS USING LIGHT metaphor covers a variety of mental activities, such as imagining, speculating, observing, considering, etc., which are understood in terms of ways of using light: *vision, envision, visualize, observe*, and, etymologically, *specere* 'to look,' *considerare* 'look at closely,' etc. from Latin (see Sweetser 1990). The general domain within which this metaphor functions is that of the mind; hence the MIND AS BODY metaphor (see Johnson 1987), of which THINKING IS USING LIGHT is an example.

Third, a specific case of mental functioning, or thinking, is understanding. A well-known conceptual metaphor for understanding is: UNDERSTANDING IS SEEING (Lakoff and Johnson 1980). This is a frame-level metaphor, where the specific mental activity of understanding is conceptualized as the specific sensorimotor activity of seeing – a specific version of making use of light (with the help of the eyes).

Fourth, the example paragraph for deliberate metaphor spells out the specific details of the frame-level metaphor. Normal mental functioning corresponds to having the lights on in a house, whereas its lack corresponds to darkness in the house. In short, the metaphor at the mental-space level is: LACK OF NORMAL MENTAL FUNCTIONING / LACK OF UNDERSTANDING (i.e., HAVING ALZHEIMER'S DISEASE) IS NOT HAVING THE LIGHTS ON IN A HOUSE.

If this analysis is on the right track, we can suggest that deliberate metaphors come with a large non-deliberate part at the image-schematic, domain, and frame levels. The deliberate metaphor that is presented at the least schematic, most experience-rich level (the level of mental spaces) is accompanied by and actually assumes a set of systematic "higher-level" (in Lakoff's sense, "deeper") conceptual metaphors and image schemas.

Another example that comes from my own work (Kövecses 2015b) and points in the same direction can be offered. An article from USA TODAY is about cyclist Lance Armstrong's confessions concerning his doping, and tells us that his confessions up to that point had not been sufficient to redeem himself and clean up the sport of cycling. Several (crisis) experts who were interviewed thought that additional steps must be taken by Armstrong to achieve this. One specialist in crisis management said this in an interview: "To use an analogy from the Tour de France, he's still *in the mountain stage*, and will be for some time" (2013, USA TODAY, 6W Sports, Weekly International Edition, my italics, ZK).

What we have here is that the specialist has extensive knowledge about the topic of the discourse, which is Armstrong's doping scandal. That knowledge includes that as a cyclist Armstrong participated in several Tour de France events and that this race has several "mountain stages." I suggested that the topic of the discourse primed the speaker to choose a metaphor to express a particular idea; namely, that, in order to come completely clean, Armstrong has a long and difficult way to go. This idea was expressed by the metaphorical linguistic expression *in the mountain stage* – a deliberate metaphor. The metaphor is based on the mapping "impediment to motion → difficulty of action (making full confession and being forgiven)" in the ACTION IS MOTION conceptual metaphor. The action is further specified as a RACE and at the mental space level we have AN UPHILL BICYCLE RACE. Thus, the metaphorical layers are:

Image schema level:
- ACTIVITY IS MOTION

Domain level:
- COMMUNICATION IS (FORWARD) MOTION

Frame level:
- CONFESSIONS ARE BICYCLE RACES

Mental-space level:
- THE LENGTH AND DIFFICULTY OF CONFESSING WRONGDOINGS IS THE LENGTH AND DIFFICULTY OF BEING IN THE MOUNTAIN STAGE OF THE TOUR DE FRANCE

The two examples I have briefly looked at above indicate not only that deliberate metaphors have a large non-deliberate part at the image-schematic, domain, and frame levels. They also show that the deliberate metaphors *are actually based on* metaphors that are non-deliberate, and the deliberate and non-deliberate parts are inseparable, they work jointly within the same schematicity hierarchy of metaphorical concepts. Moreover, it follows that the metaphors that are termed deliberate *are really both* deliberate and non-deliberate at the same time.

One could argue, of course, that some deliberate metaphors are truly isolated on the mental-space level; that is, unlike the previous examples, they do not come with a large background conceptual package. Let us consider a potential example for this possibility. We can take an example used by Steen, sonnet 18 by Shakespeare.

> Shall I compare thee to a summer's day?
> Thou art more lovely and more temperate:
> Rough winds do shake the darling buds of May,
> And summer's lease hath all too short a date;
> Sometime too hot the eye of heaven shines,
> And often is his gold complexion dimmed;

One could say that in the sonnet there is a single, isolated deliberate metaphor: "Shall I compare thee to a summer's day?" and that there are no deep metaphors that would unconsciously guide the way we understand and appreciate the poem. However, a closer look reveals that the various layers of metaphors that characterize the other examples can be found here as well.

Image schema:
- INTENSITY IS HEAT / COLD

Domain: EMOTION:
- INTENSITY OF EMOTION IS DEGREE OF HEAT / COLD

Frame:
- LOVE IS FIRE: LOVE'S INTENSITY IS THE DEGREE OF HEAT OF FIRE

Mental space:
- THE INTENSITY OF THE POET'S LOVE IS THE DEGREE OF A SUMMER DAY'S HEAT

The HEAT-COLD image schema is well-known in the cognitive linguistic literature in the conceptualization of emotions (see, e.g., Kövecses 2000). It can be found in such conceptual metaphors as LOVE IS (HEAT OF) FIRE, ANGER IS (HEAT OF) FIRE, AFFECTION IS WARMTH, FRIENDLY IS WARM, UNFRIENDLY IS COLD, etc. In the sonnet, Shakespeare turns the HEAT OF FIRE metaphor into a very specific heat-related metaphor: the kind of heat we feel in a summer's day (but then he argues against it). Actually, the emergence of and the motivation for these metaphors is even more complicated if we consider how our bodily experiences of body heat as metonymy turn into heat of nature (as from fire and the sun) as metaphor. (On this, see Kövecses 2013).

But the main point of the discussion above is that deliberate metaphors come with a large non-deliberate conceptual package: the conceptual metaphors that are presupposed by the most specific level of metaphorical conceptualization – at the level of mental spaces.

4 Methodology

There are a number of different approaches to the study of metaphor within a general conceptual metaphor theory framework. These different methods sometimes compete with one another and claim superior status in the field. Lakoff and Johnson's (1980, 1999) work was later seen as an "intuitive" approach to the study of metaphor. The label was used because Lakoff and Johnson and their followers were believed to rely on their own intuitions in identifying metaphors and grouping them into sets of examples to demonstrate the existence of conceptual metaphors. Corpus linguists argue that to find all or most of the conceptual metaphors in a language, one needs to take advantage of large corpora, such as the BNC (British National Corpus) or COCA (Corpus of Contemporary American English) (see, e.g., Charteris-Black 2004; Deignan 2005; Stefanowitsch 2006).

They emphatically point out that our linguistic intuitions are not adequate for studying metaphors. More recently, Kövecses and his co-workers (Kövecses 2015c; Kövecses *et al.* in press) proposed to revive the older intuitive method. Following Kövecses' (1986) initial suggestion, I call the revised method the "lexical approach" and show that the lexical method has advantages that the corpus-linguistic method cannot ignore. Other metaphor scholars place emphasis on the social-pragmatic uses of particular metaphorical expressions. They typically work with smaller databases than corpus linguists, and study the communicative functions of metaphors in authentic discourses (e.g., Cameron 2003; Musolff 2006; Semino 2008). Some scholars pay attention to how frames and metaphors are related and study various metaphorical constructions (see, e.g., Sullivan 2013). They often make use of the Framenet project that was developed by Charles Fillmore.

Psycholinguists and cognitive psychologists study metaphors as a conceptual phenomenon and the embodied nature of metaphorical conceptualization (see, e.g., Boroditsky 2001; Casasanto 2009; Gibbs 1994, 2006; Gibbs and Colston 2012). This work is largely experimental – in the form of either "in vitro" or "in vivo" experiments (see Kövecses 2005, on this distinction). Neuroscientists take advantage of the most recent brain imaging techniques and try to identify the neuronal activities that underlie the use of conceptual metaphors in the brain (Gallese and Lakoff 2005; and see, Coulson 2008, for an overview). Finally, groups of scientists are working to build computational models of how humans use conceptual metaphors for a variety of purposes (see, e.g., Feldman 2006; Narayanan 1999).

Thus, we have at least the following approaches dedicated to the study of conceptual metaphors:
- Intuitive approach
- Corpus linguistic approach
- Lexical approach
- Discourse analytic approach
- Framenet type approach
- Psycholinguistic experimentation
- Neuroscientific experimentation
- Computational modeling

There are no doubt other approaches, but even this set shows very clearly the variety of methods for the study of conceptual metaphor.

How can we pair off the different approaches with the different levels of metaphor described above? The following pairing of approaches with the levels is suggestive, rather than definitive. Most of the approaches can be used to study several different levels. I suggest that the particular approaches attach primarily to particular levels of metaphor, as shown below:

IMAGE SCHEMAS	-	Psycholinguistics; Neuroscience
DOMAINS FRAMES	-	Intuitive approach; Lexical approach; Framenet
MENTAL SPACES	- - -	Discourse analysis; Computational modeling Corpus linguistics Psycholinguistics; Neuroscience

Figure 2.3: Approaches to metaphor and the schematicity layers to which they apply.

What lends significance to these pairings of levels and methods is threefold: First, there is no single approach that can be used to study all levels of metaphor. Second, several distinct approaches can be used to study the same level(s), but they can contribute complementary insights to it/them. Third, certain approaches may be better fitted to study a particular level than others.

To demonstrate the first point in the previous paragraph, I will briefly look at the "lexical method" and corpus linguistics. Researchers using the lexical method search for various lexical items or other types of information that are related to the general topic, or concept, under investigation (such as particular emotions indicated by particular lexemes: e.g., *anger*, *fear*, *surprise*). These include synonyms, antonyms, related words, various idioms and phrases, collocations, and, importantly, even the definitions of the lexemes (see Kövecses 2015c; Kövecses *et al.* in press). The most likely sources for these types of information are dictionaries: monolingual and bilingual dictionaries, thesauri, collocation dictionaries, idiom dictionaries of various sorts, and, in general, any collections of words and phrases related to a concept. Very importantly, researchers prefer and tend to use dictionaries that offer example sentences and usage notes (about register, frequency, provenance, etc.) for the linguistic expressions (words, idioms, collocations, etc.) that they contain for the lexeme in question. Since it is not possible to find all of this information in a single dictionary, several different dictionaries of various kinds must be consulted before one can collect (possibly) all the lexical information that characterizes a lexeme under investigation.

The various lexical items that belong to a particular concept, or domain, are dominantly *types*, not tokens. The linguistic expressions that are identified by the dictionaries represent lexemes. In this method (that is based on mostly dictionary data), it is not possible to gage the actual frequency of the tokens, which is a drawback of the method. Furthermore, since the lexical method deals with types, that is, with linguistic expressions that have become lexicalized, the types provided by the dictionaries represent the most conventionalized linguistic expressions of a language related to a domain. The types that are identified are at the image schema, domain, or frame levels, that is, the level of *decontextualized language,* which Kövecses (2010a) calls the "supraindividual" level, as opposed to the mental-spaces level, that of *contextualized linguistic usage* (of the types) by individual speakers who use tokens. This level was referred to by Kövecses (2010a) as the "individual" level.

We shoµld note here that corpus linguistics, as another method, was proposed in the study of language, including metaphor research, to correct the deficiencies of work at the supraindiviual level; specifically, to draw attention to contextualized linguistic usage in real discourse, i.e., the individual level (see, for example, Deignan 2005; Semino 2008; Stefanowitsch 2006) and to be able to do quantitative analyses of tokens. Both of these are legitimate proposals. But they work at a level that is different from the level where the lexical approach operates. The lexical approach works with types attaching to frames and domains, while various corpus methodologies work with tokens (as well as types) at the level of mental spaces.

The lexical approach can uncover the most conventionalized metaphorical linguistic expressions related to a target domain (i.e., the types) on the basis of which researchers can hypothesize the existence of systematic conceptual correspondences between two domains – the conceptual metaphors. The conceptual metaphors can be assumed to be shared by speakers of a language who have acquired the metaphorical expression types relating to a target. Experimental studies indicate that this is indeed the case (see, e.g., Gibbs 1994, 2006; Gibbs and Colston 2012). Thus the lexical approach can reveal a considerable portion of the shared metaphorical conceptual system in a linguistic community, though not the metaphorical conceptual systems that particular individual speakers possess.

By contrast, corpus linguists suggest that the lexical approach does not work for the individual level of metaphor analysis. This criticism is valid. But it should be kept in mind that the lexical approach was not designed to capture contextual variation in the use of metaphors and the individually variable metaphorical conceptual systems of individual speakers (on these issues, see Kövecses 2005, 2010b, 2015b). There are several other more specific criticisms coming from corpus linguists (see, e.g., Kövecses 2011, 2015b), but the discussion so far suffices to draw attention to the issue of relationship between the multi-level view of metaphor and the various methodologies that are employed in metaphor studies. Most important of these, in my view, is the following: The different levels of metaphor are associated with different goals and these goals go together with different methods. If we want to characterize how individual speakers use metaphors in context, we use corpus- and discourse-based approaches; if we are interested in making hypotheses concerning our shared metaphorical conceptual system, we can legitimately employ the lexical approach.

5 Conclusions

The multi-level view of metaphor has several implications for conceptual metaphor theory. Of these, three were discussed in the present paper. First, concerning the issue of "deep" vs. "superficial" metaphors and their ontological status, it can be suggested that "deep" vs. "superficial" metaphors can now be given a more precise ontological status. Deep metaphors are those that are at the frame, domain or schema levels. Superficial ones are those that function at the level of mental spaces, that is, typically unconventional metaphors in discourse that can activate a number of conceptual metaphors at all of the "higher" levels. Second, regarding "deliberate" metaphors, I proposed that deliberate metaphors can be reconceptualized as manifesting entire schematicity hierarchies of concepts. That is, deliberate metaphors, as we saw, come with a large non-deliberate part. They evoke frame-, domain-, and schema-level metaphors. Given this, the metaphors that are taken to be deliberate are also non-deliberate in their conceptual background. In the view presented here, the two kinds of metaphors (deliberate and non-deliberate) are inseparable. Third, and finally, I discussed the issue of methodological "rivalry" in relation to the question of what the "best" method is to study metaphors. Here, the suggestion was that different methodologies and approaches apply to different levels of metaphor and that they are all useful in doing their respective jobs.

All in all, it seems that by applying the multi-level view of metaphor we can gain a great deal of coherence and uniformity in the description of a variety of different phenomena in the study of metaphor.

References

Boroditsky, Lera. 2001. Does language shape thought? Mandarin and English speakers' conceptions of time. *Cognitive Psychology* 43. 1–22.
Cameron, Lynne. 2003. *Metaphor in educational discourse*. London: Continuum.
Casasanto, Daniel. 2009. Embodiment of abstract concepts: good and bad in right- and left-handers. *Journal of Experimental Psychology* 138 (3). 351–367.

Charteris-Black, Jonathan. 2004. *Corpus approaches to critical metaphor analysis*. Basingstoke and New York: Palgrave-MacMillan.

Coulson, Seana. 2008. Metaphor comprehension and the brain. In Raymond W. Gibbs (ed.), *The Cambridge Handbook of Metaphor and Thought*. 177–194. Cambridge: Cambridge University Press.

Deignan, Alice. 2005. *Metaphor and corpus linguistics*. Amsterdam: John Benjamins.

Fauconnier, Gilles. 2007. Mental spaces. In Dirk Geeraerts & Hubert Cuyckens (eds.), *The Oxford Handbook of Cognitive Linguistics*, 371–376. Oxford: Oxford University Press.

Fauconnier, Gilles & Mark Turner. *The way we think*. New York: Basic Books.

Feldman, Jerome. 2006. *From molecule to metaphor*. Cambridge, MA: MIT Press.

FrameNet. https://framenet.icsi.berkeley.edu/fndrupal/frameIndex.

Gallese, Vittorio & George Lakoff. 2005. The brain's concepts. *Cognitive Neuropsychology* 22 (3–4). 455–479.

Gibbs, Raymond W. 1994. *The Poetics of Mind. Figurative Thought, Language, and Understanding*. New York: Cambridge University Press.

Gibbs, Raymond W. 2006. *Embodiment and Cognitive Science*. Cambridge & New York: Cambridge University Press.

Gibbs, Raymond W. & Herbert Colston. 2012. *Interpreting Figurative Meaning*, Cambridge & New York: Cambridge University Press.

Johnson, Mark. 1987. *The body in the mind*. Chicago: The University of Chicago Press.

Kövecses, Zoltán. 1986. *Metaphors of anger, pride, and love. A lexical approach to the study of concepts*. Amsterdam: John Benjamins.

Kövecses, Zoltán. 2000. *Metaphor and emotion*. Cambridge & New York: Cambridge University Press.

Kövecses, Zoltan. 2005. *Metaphor in culture. Universality and variation*. Cambridge & New York: Cambridge University Press.

Kövecses, Zoltán. 2010a [2002]. *Metaphor. A practical introduction*, 2nd edn. New York: Oxford University Press.

Kövecses, Zoltán. 2010b. A new look at metaphorical creativity in cognitive linguistics. *Cognitive Linguistics* Vol. 21 (4). 663–697.

Kövecses, Zoltán. 2011. Methodological issues in conceptual metaphor theory. In Sandra Handl & Hans J. Schmid, (eds.), *Windows to the mind: Metaphor, metonymy and conceptual blending*, 23–39. Berlin & New York: De Gruyter Mouton.

Kövecses, Zoltán. 2013. The metaphor-metonymy relationship: correlation metaphors are based on metonymy. *Metaphor and Symbol* 28 (2). 75–88.

Kövecses, Zoltán. 2015a. Distinguishing levels of metaphor. Unpublished ms.

Kövecses, Zoltán. 2015b. *Where metaphors come from. Reconsidering context in metaphor*. Oxford & New York: Oxford University Press.

Kövecses, Zoltán. 2015c. Surprise as a conceptual category. *Review of Cognitive Linguistics* 13 (2). 270–290.

Kövecses, Zoltán. 2017. Levels of metaphor. *Cognitive Linguistics* 28 (2). 321–347.

Kövecses, Zoltán, Laura Ambrus, Dániel Hegedűs, Ren Imai, & Anna Sobczak. In press. The lexical vs. corpus-based method in the study of metaphors. In Marianna Bolognesi, Mario Brdar, & Kristina Despot (eds.), *Fantastic Metaphors and Where to Find them. Traditional and New Methods in Figurative Language Research*. Amsterdam: John Benjamins.

Lakoff, George. 1995. Metaphor, Morality, and Politics, Or, Why Conservatives Have Left Liberals In the Dust. Retrieved from http://www.wwcd.org/issues/Lakoff.html – First published in 1995 *Social Research* 62 (2) 177–213.
Lakoff, George. 1996. *Moral politics*. Chicago: The University of Chicago Press.
Lakoff George & Mark Johnson. 1980. *Metaphors we live by*. Chicago: The University of Chicago Press.
Lakoff George & Mark Johnson. 1999. *Philosophy in the flesh*. New York: Basic Books.
Musolff, Andreas. 2006. Metaphor scenarios in public discourse. *Metaphor and Symbol* 21 (1). 23–38.
Narayanan, Srini. 1999. Moving Right Along: A Computational Model of Metaphoric Reasoning about Events. In Proceedings of the *National Conference on Artificial Intelligence (AAAI '99)*, Orlando, Florida, July 18–22. 121–128. AAAI Press.
Semino, Elena. 2008. *Metaphor in Discourse*. Cambridge: Cambridge University Press.
Steen, Gerard. 2013. Deliberate metaphor affords conscious metaphorical cognition. https://www.academia.edu/363751/Deliberate_metaphor_affords_conscious_metaphorical_thought (accessed 12 March 2019).
Stefanowitsch, Anatol. 2006. Words and their metaphors. In Anatol Stefanowitsch & Stefan Th. Gries (eds.), *Corpus-based Approaches to Metaphor and Metonymy*, 64–105. Berlin & New York: De Gruyter Mouton.
Sullivan, Karen. 2013. *Frames and constructions in metaphoric language*. Amsterdam: John Benjamins.
Sweetser, Eve. 1990. *From etymology to pragmatics*. New York: Cambridge University Press.

Ulrike Oster

Cross-cultural semantic and pragmatic profiling of emotion words. Regulation and expression of anger in Spanish and German

Abstract: This paper provides a cross-cultural description of several emotion words from the domain of anger in two languages. It aims to evaluate differences and similarities regarding the regulation and expression of those emotions. The paper employs a combination of two approaches. First, it undertakes a descriptive analysis of emotion words, combining fundamental ideas drawn from cognitive semantics, such as conceptual metaphor and metonymy, with a corpus-based methodology that makes use of key corpus-linguistic notions like semantic preference and semantic prosody (Oster 2010). The paper then goes on to evaluate the resulting data in the light of Ogarkova and Soriano's (2014) concept of semantic foci. These foci are used to organize and group the detailed data obtained during the first phase of the analysis in order to paint a broader picture of the ways in which different cultures conceptualize given emotions and which aspects they foreground. The paper carries out a contrastive study on anger in Spanish and German (*ira, rabia, enojo* vs. *Zorn, Wut, Ärger*). The results are interpreted on two different levels: crosslinguistically, i.e. in terms of the similarities and differences between languages/cultures; and intralinguistically, i.e., by evaluating the ways in which different emotion words from the same category in each language differ from and complement each other.

Keywords: Emotion words, anger, corpus-based approach, semantic and pragmatic profiling, Spanish, German

1 Introduction

The conceptualization and expression of emotions is one of the most researched topics in Cognitive Linguistics since Kövecses' seminal works (e.g., Kövecses 1986). The initial assumption, within conceptual metaphor theory, of largely universal

Note: This study has been supported by research projects FFI2015-68867-P, funded by the Spanish Ministry of the Economy and Competition, and P1-1B2013-44, funded by Universitat Jaume I.

Ulrike Oster, Universitat Jaume I, Facultat de Ciències Humanes i Socials, Spain

https://doi.org/10.1515/9783110629460-003

conceptualizations of emotions due to their embodied nature has since been nuanced by a series of studies. These highlight variations in emotion conceptualization across different cultures and languages (cf. Yu (1995) as one of the pioneering contrastive studies, and Ogarkova, Soriano and Lehr (2012), a recent comprehensive research project in several European languages). Such research has led to a more refined view of universal embodiment, in which "embodiment and culture naturally come together in a mind that is simultaneously embodied and acculturated" (Kövecses 2006: 6). Cross-cultural variation can occur because "people do not use their cognitive capacities in the same way from culture to culture" or "because of differences in such factors as social-cultural context, history, or human concern that characterize these cultures" (Kövecses 2015: 13).

The vast body of linguistic research dedicated to the description of emotions and emotion words includes many studies that have adopted a cross-cultural or cross-linguistic approach. It would be impossible to provide a general overview of this enormous and diverse field. I will therefore only briefly mention the research this paper builds upon with respect to anger in the languages it discusses. Soriano and her colleagues have provided most of the scholarship on Spanish language concepts of anger, both from a cognitive linguistic and, more recently, from an interdisciplinary perspective (Barcelona 1989; Ogarkova and Soriano 2014; Ogarkova, Soriano, and Lehr 2012; Soriano 2013; Soriano et al. 2013; Soriano-Salinas 2003). German anger concepts have attracted a greater diversity of authors and approaches (Durst 2001; Fries 2004, 2013; Ogarkova, Soriano, and Lehr 2012; Oster 2014; Weigand 1998).

In addition to providing detailed results on specific emotion concepts across many different languages and cultures, the accumulated evidence of these and other studies has led to a growing consensus that emotion conceptualization is subject to the combined influences of embodiment, cognition and culture, and that the combination of these factors accounts both for common universal patterns and culture-specific divergent aspects. However, the crucial question remains: what is the origin of these divergences? Or, to put it in Emanatian's (1995) words, "[w]hat (beyond trivially obvious aspects like geography and climate) is the nature of these cultural influences? A look outside language at the links evident in ritual, architecture, or religion, for instance, may give us clues..." (Emanatian 1995: 180).

In an attempt to find causes for the differences in emotion expressions between languages and cultures, some researchers have sought to trace specific metaphorical conceptualizations back to theories about the body prevalent in certain cultures and/or time periods, such as those stemming from Chinese traditional medicine and its theory of yin/yang, the theory of the five elements (Yu 1995) or the influence of the humoral doctrine on emotion conceptualization in post fifteenth-century English (Geeraerts and Grondelaers 1995; Gevaert 2005). Other scholars, influenced by Hofstede's theory of cultural dimensions in cross-cultural communication (Hofstede 1980, 1991), have attributed the differences to their societies' more "individualistic" or more "collectivist" characteristics. This approach has proved especially fruitful when applied to the so-called self-conscious emotions. For example, both Lewandowska-Tomaszczyk and Wilson (2014) and Krawczak (2014, 2015) analyse the concepts of shame and guilt by comparing an individualistic culture (English) with a collectivist culture (Polish).

Ogarkova and Soriano (2014) also apply the same dichotomy (individualistic vs. collectivist) to anger words in English, Russian and Spanish. This has enabled them to confirm a series of hypotheses derived from prior psychological research: negativity, controlled expression and enhanced regulation are more salient in Russian and Spanish, which are both collectivist cultures, while unrestrained manifestation is more salient in English (Ogarkova and Soriano 2014: 111). The rationale behind this assumption is that "in collectivistic compared to individualistic cultures, anger is predominantly viewed as more negative and socially-disruptive, an emotion that challenges social order and harmony, and thus, should be regulated with regard to its expression and one's acting on the feeling" (Ogarkova and Soriano 2014: 111). In addition, their findings corroborate the existence of cultural differences as to the saliency of physiological aspects of the emotion (somatization), which are reportedly more prominent in Chinese, Russian and other similar cultures than in a US American context (Ogarkova and Soriano 2014: 97, 111).

This combination of a corpus-based approach involving "metaphorical profiling" with a concentration on a limited number of key aspects (semantic foci) of emotion conceptualization seems very promising. This paper therefore sets out to ascertain whether Ogarkova and Soriano's concepts of regulation and expression of emotion can provide useful tools for the better understanding of the meanings of emotion words: not only with regard to the contrasting descriptions of anger in collectivist vs. individualistic cultures, but also within cultures. It therefore aims to establish the following points, at two different levels.

- With regard to the distinction between collectivist and individualistic cultures: can existing results regarding the expression and regulation of anger be reproduced with other languages? Following Ogarkova and Soriano's line of thought, we will hypothesize that a) expressions emphasizing the control of anger are more salient in Spanish than German and b) those emphasizing lack of control over the emotion are more salient in German than Spanish.
- On an intralinguistic level: is the approach suited to distinguishing different emotion words from the same domain, i.e. near-synonymous lexemes expressing different facets of the same emotion category?

2 Method

2.1 Methodological foundations

The approach adopted here is a corpus-based description of emotion lexemes that is closely related to Kövecses' lexical approach and methodologically similar to Stefanowitsch's corpus-based "metaphorical pattern analysis" (cf. Kövecses 2019/this volume, for a discussion of the scope of both approaches and their differences). It applies fundamental ideas from cognitive semantics, namely metaphorical and metonymical conceptualizations, together with key corpus-linguistic notions, such as semantic preference and prosody (Oster 2010). The approach uses detailed co-occurrence analyses to allow us to access qualitative and quantitative data on the metaphorical and metonymical conceptualizations of each emotion. It also sheds light on additional factors, such as conceptual proximity (i.e., the relative position of the emotion word both within the conceptual domain and with respect to other emotion concepts); syntagmatic relations (which provide information on prototypical causes, consequences or experiencers of the emotion) and information about the ways in which the emotion is described and evaluated (semantic prosody).

This kind of analysis permits a very fine-grained description of the conceptualization of each emotion word. The present study, however, requires a less complex set of parameters in order to be able to characterize the emotion words contrastively (both cross- and intralinguistically) in broader terms – without neglecting more detailed semantic analysis. An attempt was therefore made to reduce the aspects under consideration to a manageable number and to create coherent groupings of several different types of conceptualizations and expressions, in accordance with Ogarkova and Soriano's (2014) concept of semantic foci. Employing an approach they call "metaphorical profiling", Ogarkova and Soriano distinguish two dimensions of the emotion – regulation and expression – each of which features two opposed semantic foci. On the one hand, there is a dichotomy between enhanced regulation (the attempt to retain control) and unrestrained manifestation (loss of control). On the other, there is a distinction between the free expression of an emotion (e.g., visible anger) and internalized emotion (e.g., internalized anger). The latter constitutes a somatized vision of the emotion in which the emphasis is on the emotion's location inside the body, and the physical effects it has on the person experiencing it.

This study adopts Ogarkova and Soriano's approach and will employ a very similar terminology. The first dimension will be Regulation. This includes the opposed semantic foci Control and Lack of Control. The second dimension is related to Expression, with semantic foci Visibility and Internalization. The approach presented here employs a corpus-based methodology also very similar to that of Ogarkova and Soriano, although it is somewhat more comprehensive with regard to the aspects it takes into account. It discusses metaphorical expressions, as Ogarkova and Soriano's approach does, but also includes information on the physical manifestations, the consequences of the emotion and its description (as illustrated by semantic preferences) as well as the evaluation of the emotion (semantic prosody). This is explained in more detail in section 3.

2.2 Corpora and procedure

The first step, i.e. the comprehensive semantic and pragmatic description of the emotion words, has been carried out using the same procedure for both languages. First, corpus queries have been performed to provide data for analysis in the form of lists of co-occurrences with access to concordance lines.[1] The semantic and pragmatic nature of the analysis restricted the choice of corpus in two ways. On the one hand, sufficiently rich and reliable results for this kind of analysis can only be obtained from very large corpora, permitting enough instances of rather infrequent co-occurrences of the emotion words to be retrieved. On the other, facilities for querying the corpus and organising the results must fulfil certain minimum requirements to enable us to frame complex queries.[2] The following freely accessible on-line corpora have therefore been used as sources.

The main German resource used was *Deutsches Textarchiv* (DTA, cf. Geyken et al. 2015),[3] in combination with the *Digitales Wörterbuch der deutschen Sprache* (DWDS), both compiled by the *Berlin-Brandenburgische Akademie der Wissenschaften*. Spanning a period from the 17th to 19th centuries, the DTA contains 140 million tokens, whereas the *DWDS Kernkorpus* (encompassing the 20th century) contains 100 million tokens. The collocation database CCDB was used as a complementary source during the first phase of the analysis.[4]

1 More details on the exact procedure for COCA and Corpus del Español can be found in Oster (2010) and for the German corpora in Oster (2014).

2 Unfortunately, this ruled out the corpora of the *Real Academia de la Lengua Española*, CREA and CORDE.

3 The corpora are accessible through these links: DTA: http://www.deutschestextarchiv.de/; DWDS: https://www.dwds.de/; CCDB: http://corpora.ids-mannheim.de/ccdb/; Corpus del Español: http://www.corpusdelespanol.org/hist-gen/2008/.

4 CCDB allows us to access the collocation profiles of approximately 220,000 node words (lemmas). The collocation profile of a lemma shows which other words it is most often combined with. CCDB is based on a 2.2 billion word subset of the German Reference Corpus DEREKO, compiled by the *Institut der Deutschen Sprache* (IDS).

For Spanish, we selected the *Corpus del Español* (Davies 2002). Although there is a very recent, extremely large version of this corpus (containing 2 billion words collected from the WWW in 2013–2014), that version exhibited some problems with verb lemmatization. We therefore deemed it advisable to use the smaller 2001–2002 version, which comprises 100 million words, spanning the period from the 13th to the 20th centuries. Its smaller size also means that this version of the corpus is more comparable to the main corpus used for German.

In order to retrieve as many relevant co-occurrences as possible, we had to use several different queries for each emotion word. Since the corpora's search interfaces are rather different, the query process had to be adapted to the possibilities offered by each corpus. For example, the following useful features help to rationalize the search process and are afforded by most corpora: searching by lemmas; differentiating each query by the part of speech (POS) of the search lemma or co-occurring word; selecting specific sub-corpora in accordance with genre or time; searching for compounds containing the search word (i.e. *rabia, rabia*); grouping results by lemmas; establishing a minimum co-occurrence frequency or a maximum number of hits, etc. (cf. Oster 2010: 734–736). Following the core procedure defined by the Pragglejaz Group (2007), the relevant items can be identified from the resulting lists of co-occurrences, and can then be classified according to one or more of the aspects under analysis (conceptual metaphor or metonymy, descriptive or evaluative aspects, etc.).

The second step was to select the co-occurrences indicative of a conceptualization in accordance with one of the semantic foci. One of the most important features of the DTA's search interface was indispensable to this endeavour: the possibility to combine queries and search for a number of different search words simultaneously. Additional queries were thus run in the relevant sections of the DTA/DWDS, using the lists of expressions for each semantic focus that resulted from the initial study. Due to the query syntax, each of these combined searches had to be performed twice: by first searching to the left of the main search word (the emotion word, in our case) and then searching to the right. For example, here are the two queries for the semantic focus of control for the German anger word *Zorn*. String a) will find any co-occurrence of *Zorn* with any form of any of the search terms in brackets within four words to its right, and string b) will perform the same action on words to its left[5]:

5 The number of possible alternate search words is not unlimited. In this case, the longest successful string contained 30 lemmas. Beyond that, the string had to be split in two or more separate queries. Cf. http://www.deutschestextarchiv.de/doku/DDC-suche_hilfe for instructions on how to use the query language.

a) "*Zorn* #4 /(unterdrücken|verhalten|zügeln|Zaum|zähmen|bändigen|kanalisieren|herunterschlucken|hinunterschlucken|hineinfressen|-bremsen|zurückhalten|besiegen|bekämpfen|bezwingen|runterschlucken|hinunterspülen|beherrschen)/"
b) "/(unterdrücken|verhalten|zügeln|Zaum|zähmen|bändigen|kanalisieren|herunterschlucken|hinunterschlucken|hineinfressen|bremsen|zurückhalten|besiegen|bekämpfen|bezwingen|runterschlucken|hinunterspülen|beherrschen)/ #4 *Zorn*"

As a result of the query, DTA displays a histogram showing the frequencies per one million tokens for each of the chosen time periods. The results of search string a) can be seen in Figure 3.1, for example. In this example, the time interval was set to 50 years. If no periodization is required, the interval can be set to 400 in order to obtain the total frequency of occurrences from 1600 to 1999.

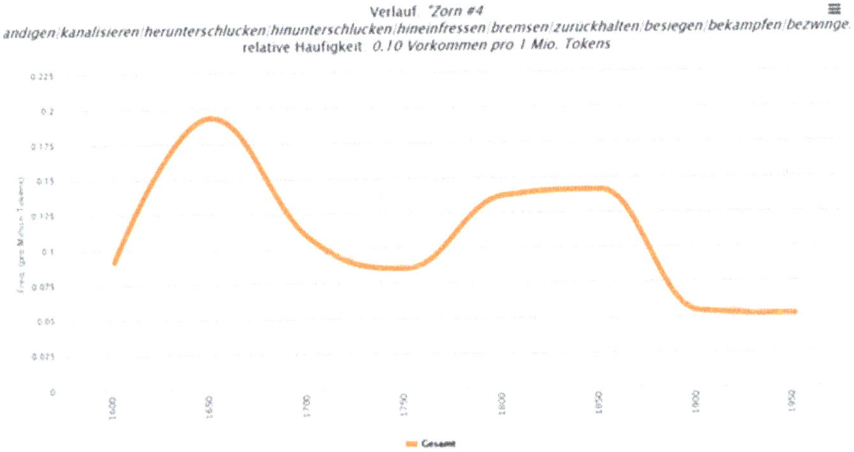

Figure 3.1: Histogram in the DTA.

3 The classification of co-occurring expressions with regard to the four semantic foci

Using Ogarkova and Soriano's (2014) approach involving semantic foci (cf. section 1), two dimensions were used to characterize the emotion words: Regulation (Control vs. Lack of Control) and Expression (Visibility vs. Internalization). Before comparing the results of the quantitative analysis, however, let us examine some examples of the co-occurrences that can be interpreted under the rubric of one of the four foci.[6]

The most productive aspects analysed included a series of conceptual metaphors and their subtypes or entailments; the expression of physical manifestations (as traces of conceptual metonymy); part of the information on semantic preference (consequences of the emotion); and semantic prosody (evaluation). In some cases, the entire group of expressions found for a metaphor or metaphor subtype/entailment can be interpreted as expressing one of the foci. However, the selection was made manually and only includes those expressions that clearly reflect a conceptualization of one of the four semantic foci. For example, only some examples of the metaphor subtype A STRONG EMOTION IS A BOILING SUBSTANCE are classified under the semantic focus Lack of Control, namely those that refer to the moment at which the substance boils over, i.e. can no longer be controlled. All these examples happen to be from German. Other instances of the metaphor which merely concentrate on temperature (such as the boiling point) are subsumed under the heading "Physical reactions: Rise in body temperature" and therefore classified under the dimension of Expression (Visibility of the emotion).

a) Regulation: Control

In the semantic focus of Control (cf. Table 3.1), we mainly include expressions of the following metaphor types: THE EMOTION IS AN ENTITY IN A CONTAINER (THE BODY), THE EMOTION I AN OPPONENT and THE EMOTION IS AN AUTONOMOUS FORCE. A number of expressions found through the analysis of the semantic preferences of the emotion words, i.e. some of their typical consequences, are also relevant to this category. In this particular case, the relevant actions are designed to elude confrontation with others and can therefore be interpreted as attempts to control the emotion.

Table 3.1: Regulation: Control.

THE EMOTION IS AN ENTITY IN A CONTAINER (THE BODY)	
– Retaining control means keeping the emotion inside or down	'to suppress' → Sp: reprimir la *ira*, contener la *ira*; G: *Zorn* unterdrücken
	'to swallow' → Sp: tragar la *ira*; G: *Zorn* herunterschlucken;
THE EMOTION IS AN OPPONENT	
– Something you fight back against	'to defeat' → Sp: vencer, dominar, resistir la *ira*; G: *Zorn* bezwingen, widerstehen, *Wut* besiegen;

6 A more detailed presentation of this classification can be found in Oster (2018).

Table 3.1 (continued)

THE EMOTION IS AN AUTONOMOUS FORCE	
– A beast you try to keep under control	'to keep a rein on' → Sp: domar, refrenar la *ira*, poner rienda; G: *Wut* zügeln, *Zorn* im Zaum halten
– A natural force: water	'to channel' → G: *Ärger* kanalisieren
– Consequences of the emotion	
– Actions that avoid confrontation with others	'silence' → Sp: silencio 'to stand back' → Sp: apartarse, levantarse

b) Regulation: Lack of control

The metaphor types detailed above, together with those that conceptualize the emotion as illness or madness, give rise to expressions that reflect a diametrically opposed idea: that of losing or lacking control of the emotion (cf. Table 3.2). Once again, the emotion's characteristic consequences are also productive. In this case, the consequences include acts of aggression or destruction.

Table 3.2*:* Regulation: Lack of control.

THE EMOTION IS AN ENTITY IN A CONTAINER (THE BODY)	
– Losing control is the substance going out of the container	'to burst' → Sp: reventar, estallar de *rabia*; G: platzen, zerplatzen, zerspringen vor *Wut*
	'to come up' → Sp: vomitar la *rabia*, desbordar; G: *Wut* steigt hoch, steigt auf
	'outbreak' → G: Ausbruch von *Wut*, *Ärger* bricht hervor
– A strong emotion is a boiling substance (intensity is heat):	'to boil over' → G: aufwallen, überschäumen vor *Wut*, *Zorn* kocht hoch
THE EMOTION IS AN OPPONENT	
– An attacker or something that dominates	'to attack' → Sp: la *rabia* invade, ataque de *ira*; G: der *Zorn* packt, überkommt, schüttelt 'to dominate' → Sp: dominado por el *enojo*
THE EMOTION IS AN AUTONOMOUS FORCE	
– A destructive force	'raging' → G: rasende *Wut*, *Zorn* tobt
– A natural force: water	'to surge' → G: *Ärger* brandet
– A natural force: fire	'to go up in flames' → Sp: ardor, abrasar; G: eruptiv, lodern, aufflammen, auflodern
– A natural force: wind	'storm' → Sp: tormenta, torbellino, huracán de la *ira*

Table 3.2 (continued)

– A beast which is out of control	'fierce' → Sp: fiero, feroz, desatar la *ira*; G: wild
	'reinless' → Sp: desenfrenado, desbocado; G: zügellos, ungezügelt, unbändig, blind
THE EMOTION IS A PHYSICAL OR MENTAL DISEASE	
– Madness	'mad' → Sp: loco, locura, perder el seso, delirio de *ira*; 'beside oneself'[7] → G: außer sich vor Wut, sich vergessen
– Drunkenness	'drunk' → Sp: embriaguez, emborrachar, embriagado; G: trunkene *Wut*
Consequences of the emotion	
– Acts of aggression or destruction	'to act violently' → Sp: arremeter, despedazar, disparar; G: zerschmettern, zertrampeln, einstechen auf
	'weapons' → Sp: cuchillo, espada, lanza
Conceptual proximity: other feelings, states or attitudes	
– Feelings of aggressiveness	G: mordsüchtig, Rachbegierde
Description of the emotion	
– irrational	G: sinnlos, heillos, unreflektiert
– disproportionate	'boundless', 'uncontrollable' → G: maßlos, grenzenlos, unkontrollierbar

c) Expression: Visibility

The emotion becomes visible (cf. Table 3.3) when it is forced out of the body or displayed like a physical object, when it is perceptible because of its physical manifestations, such as trembling, crying or blushing, or when it is evident from the subject's verbal responses.

Table 3.3: Expression: Visibility.

THE EMOTION IS AN ENTITY IN A CONTAINER (THE BODY)	
– Losing control means that the substance leaves the container	'to yell out' → G: *Ärger* herausschreien, hinausschreien
THE EMOTION IS AN AUTONOMOUS FORCE	
– A natural force: electricity	'lightning' → Sp: relámpago de *ira*, fulminar, relampaguear

7 These expressions are clearly related to the "split-self metaphor" (Lakoff 1996), in which a Person is split between a Subject and a Self. They are included here under the heading of 'madness', since what they describe is a similar state of alienation of the experiencer.

Table 3.3 (continued)

THE EMOTION IS A PHYSICAL OBJECT	
	'to show' → Sp: manifestar, mostrar su *enojo*
Physical manifestations	
– Agitation	'to tremble', 'to stomp', 'to gnash one's teeth' etc. → Sp: temblar, trémulo; G: zittern, stampfen, Zähneknirschen
– Screaming or crying	'cry', 'tears', etc. → Sp: gritar, llorar; G: Träne, weinen
– Visibility in the face	'face', 'eyes', 'to glare', etc. → Sp: cara, rostro; G: Gesicht, Augen, Blick, funkeln
– Change of colour	'redden', 'dark red', 'blush' etc. → Sp: enrojecer; G: gerötet, hochrot, erröten
– Contraction	'to clench', 'to distort' → G: ballen, verzerren
– Rise in body temperature	'hot' → Sp: hervir; G: kochen, glühen vor *Zorn*
Consequences of the emotion	
– Verbal responses	'to insult' → Sp: maldecir, insultar, blasfemia

d) Expression: Internalization

Conversely, Internalization (cf. Table 3.4) is typically conveyed through expressions based on the metaphor THE EMOTION IS AN ENTITY IN A CONTAINER (THE BODY). On the other hand, perhaps surprisingly, there are physical manifestations that can be interpreted as internalizations in which the emotion affects the body by reducing expressiveness, as in *stumm* ('mute') or *blass* ('pale'). In this group, we have also included expressions such as *verhehlen* ('to disguise') which demonstrate that the emotion is being evaluated as something potentially shameful.

Table 3.4: Expression: Internalization.

THE EMOTION IS AN ENTITY IN A CONTAINER (THE BODY)	
– Something inside the body	'full of' → Sp: lleno de, interno; G: voll, voller, innerlich
	'body', 'heart', 'soul', etc. → Sp: corazón, alma; G: Leib, Bauch, Herz, Seele
– Something that comes from the outside	'to fill' → Sp: llenar de, engendrar, infundir; G: erfüllen
– An emotion that is strong is deep inside the body	'deep' → G: tief

Table 3.4 (continued)

Physical manifestations	
– It affects the voice	'mute' → G: sprachlos, stumm
– Change of colour	'pallor' → Sp: pálido; G: blass, bleich, erblassen
Evaluation (semantic prosody)	
– The emotion is potentially shameful	'undisguised', 'unadmitted' → Sp: disimular, encubrir; G: keinen Hehl machen aus, unverhohlen, uneingestanden

4 Results of the contrastive study

In this section, we compare anger words in Spanish and German with each other and with equivalent words in the other language. We selected three of the most basic anger words in each language, in accordance with the studies mentioned in section 1. In pursuit of the paper's first two aims, we begin by focusing on a comparison between the overarching emotion categories of anger in the two languages (represented by *ira, enojo, rabia* in Spanish and *Zorn, Wut, Ärger* in German). We then study contrasts between these near-synonyms with respect to the dimensions of Regulation and Expression.

4.1 The category of anger in Spanish and German

The overall distributions of the semantic foci for anger in Spanish and German instantly reveal considerable differences between the two languages. Judging by the observed raw frequencies alone (Table 3.5, column AF, i.e. absolute frequencies), Control and Visibility are more important in Spanish than in German, whereas Internalization is more prevalent in the German anger words than in the Spanish ones.

As the German corpus is larger than the Spanish one, however, it is important to look at relative frequencies. In this case, there are two ways of calculating relative frequency. We can calculate the "number of expressions of focus x" relative to:

a) the total number of foci-related expressions co-occurring with the emotion word(s) in the corpus, or
b) the total number of tokens of the emotion word(s) under consideration.

Both approaches are interesting and provide slightly different information. For methodological reasons, I will use a combination of both approaches, choosing the most appropriate approach for the type of comparison I wish to make.

Table 3.5: Absolute and relative frequencies for the four semantic foci in Spanish and German.

		Spanish			German		
		AF*	T-RF*	F-RF*	AF	T-RF	F-RF
Regulation	Control	333	29.1	8.6%	162	7.8	4,9%
	Lack of Control	916	80.0	23.7%	980	47.3	29,8%
Expression	Visibility	2136	186.6	55.4%	1182	57.0	35,9%
	Internalization	472	41.2	12.2%	968	46.7	29,4%
Total foci-related expressions		3857	337.0	100%	3292	158.9	100%
Total tokens (ira+enojo+rabia / Zorn+Wut+Ärger		11445				20720	

* AF: Absolute frequency; T-RF: Relative frequency per 1000 tokens of the emotion word; F-RF: Foci-related relative frequency.

a) Converting the observed raw frequencies into relative frequencies against the total number of foci-related expressions (F-RF in Table 3.5) focuses the comparison on the internal distribution of the four semantic foci, but does not take the number of co-occurrences per token of the emotion word into account. Foci-based relative frequency has been used for crosslinguistic comparisons for the following reason. Despite efforts to select corpora (and corpus sections) in such a way as to maximize their comparability, differences between corpora and their internal makeup and search facilities are inevitable. This can influence the number of expressions that can be found. For example, Table 3.5 shows a striking difference between Spanish and German in "frequency of expressions per 1000 tokens of the emotion word" (T-RF): 337.0 vs. 158.9, i.e. in Spanish there are more than twice as many instances per 1000 tokens than in German.[8] Given that different corpus properties might be partially responsible for such differences, thus distorting the crosslinguistic comparison, it is preferable to express this type of comparison in relation to the total number of foci-related expressions in each language, i.e. as a percentage.

b) Calculating relative frequencies with respect to the total number of tokens of each emotion word (T-RF in Table 3.5), on the other hand, provides additional insights into how expressively each emotion word is used, since it shows the frequency of the foci-related co-occurrences for each emotion word. This is of

8 It might of course be the case – and this would make for an extremely interesting finding – that Spanish *ira, rabia* and *enojo* are used in a much more expressive way than German *Zorn, Wut* and *Ärger*. To validate this claim, however, we would need to conduct further studies with a different research focus and design.

particular interest when comparing different emotion words in the same language, which is unproblematic since such comparisons rely on data from the same corpus. We therefore will use token-based relative frequency (T-RF) to compare each set of three terms – *ira/rabia/enojo* and *Zorn/Wut/Ärger* – with each other (cf. 4.2).

To study the differences between Spanish and German, on the other hand, we use foci-based relative frequency (F-RF). As Figure 3.2 shows, the visible expression of anger takes up much more space in Spanish (55.38%) than in German (35.91%). Internalization, on the other hand, is rather marginal in Spanish (12.24%), but very important in German (29.40%), as is Lack of Control (29.77). In both languages, Control is the least frequent item, far less common than the other three.

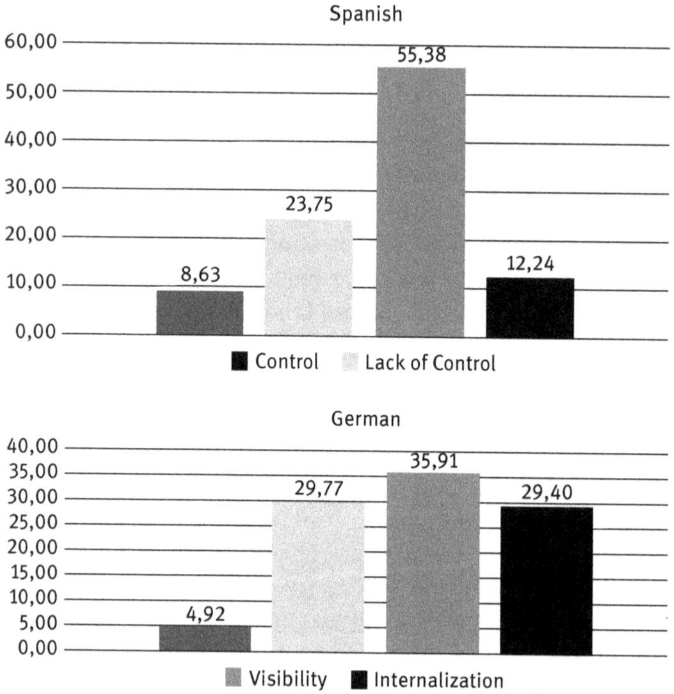

Figure 3.2: Percentage of the four semantic foci in both languages (F-RF).

When we examine the two dimensions (Regulation and Expression) separately, the picture becomes even clearer. In both languages, Lack of Control is emphasized over Control (first vs. second column), and Visibility takes up more space than Internalization (third column vs. fourth). However, there are clear differences between them in these areas, too. Spanish anger demonstrates a far greater predominance of the free expression of anger over its internalization (a difference of more than 23% in Spanish and only 6% in German), whereas German places greater emphasis on lacking control instead of keeping a handle on the emotion (a difference of 22% in German and only 14% in Spanish). This means that the hypotheses formulated in section 1 are confirmed: In our corpora, expressions emphasizing the enhanced regulation of anger have proved to be more salient in Spanish than in German. Conversely, expressions emphasizing loss or lack of control over the emotion are more prominent in German than in Spanish. Both findings were confirmed by a Fisher exact test at $p<0{,}001$.

It is also interesting to note that the Visibility-Internalization dichotomy does not run parallel to that of Control-Lack of Control. We might have expected a stronger emphasis on Lack of Control to lead to more open displays of the emotion. On the contrary, however, the corpora reveal that the (relatively) stronger Spanish need to keep the emotion under control is accompanied by a greater freedom to express it than in German. This might be tentatively explained by another of Hofstede's cultural dimensions, namely that of Indulgence/Restraint, added to the four original dimensions in the 2010 edition of Hofstede (1991). Although Hofstede's concept is more oriented towards the satisfaction/restraint of **positive** human desires,[9] the degree to which a culture's emotions – whether positive or negative – are expressed may correlate with the culture's score on this dimension. In our case, at least, this appears to be true. With a score of 40 (i.e. towards the "Restrained" end of the scale), Germany scores lower than any of the Spanish-speaking countries (Spain 44, Argentina 62, Chile 68, Colombia 83, Dominican Republic 54, Mexico 97, Peru 46, Uruguay 53, Venezuela 100).

4.2 Intracategorical distribution of Spanish and German anger words

Ira and *Zorn* on the one hand and *rabia* and *Wut* on the other are usually described in bilingual lexicography as each other's closest direct equivalents. The frequency distribution in the two corpora (cf. Table 3.6) supports this view from a purely numerical point of view, but also provides the first hint that there might be more to it than that. Occurring at similar frequencies, *ira* and *Zorn* are the most frequent emotion words, while *rabia* and *Wut* each reach less than half that number of tokens per million words. In Spanish however, the third anger

9 This is Hofstede's definition: "Indulgence stands for a society that allows relatively free gratification of basic and natural human desires related to enjoying life and having fun. Restraint stands for a society that controls gratification of needs and regulates it by means of strict social norms" (Hofstede 2011: 15).

word, *enojo*, is almost as frequently used as *ira*. The incidence of *Ärger*, on the other hand, is very low.

Table 3.6: Frequencies of the anger words in the Spanish and the German corpus.

Corpus del español (100 million words)	***ira***	***enojo***	***rabia***
tokens	4837	4342	2226
tokens per million words	48.37	43.42	22.26
DWDS-DTA (240 million words)	***Zorn***	***Wut***	***Ärger***
tokens	12970	5382	2386
tokens per million words	54.04	22.43	9.94

When we examine the ways in which anger words are distributed among the four semantic foci, we can easily detect distinct patterns in each language. In both languages, there is one word that co-occurs more frequently than the others with expressions denoting one of the semantic foci. Figure 3.3 shows that Spanish *ira* scores much higher on all the semantic foci except Internalization. On the whole, however, the differences between the Spanish anger words seem to be primarily differences of intensity rather than divergences in semantic focus, since the most important semantic focus for all three words is Lack of Control and the least frequent is Control. Overall, the semantic foci display a similar frequency pattern for all three emotion words, *ira* being the most frequent and *enojo* the least.

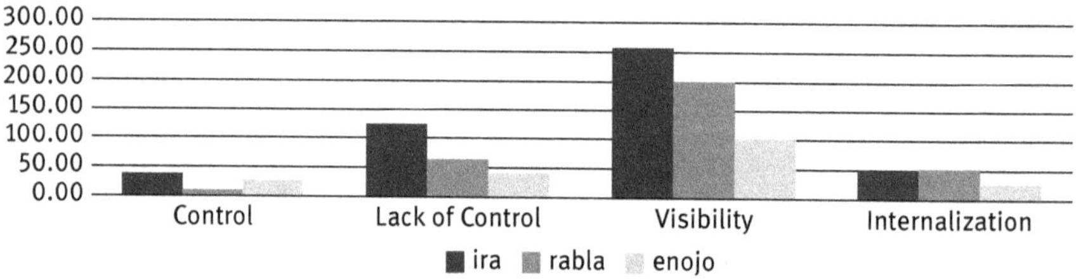

Figure 3.3: Distribution of the semantic foci in the Spanish corpus.

In German (cf. Figure 3.4), the most expressive emotion word is *Wut*, especially with regard to Lack of Control and Visibility and to a lesser extent for Internalization, too. This combination suggests that, as an emotion, *Wut* is overwhelming in its effects: both on the body (Internalization) and on the experiencer's reactions (Lack of Control and Visibility). The pattern for *Zorn* is similar – at a lower level and with a much weaker emphasis on Lack of Control. Instead, the most important

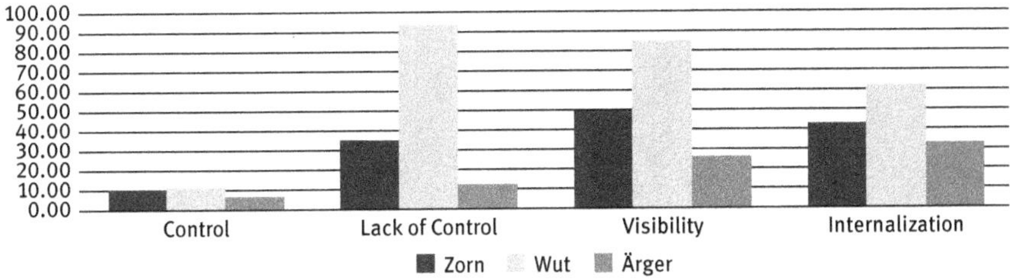

Figure 3.4: Distribution of the semantic foci in the German corpus.

aspect of *Zorn* is Visibility. At the other end of the scale, we found that *Ärger* is the most neutral word, since it is far less frequently used in combination with metaphorical and metonymic expressions. The most relevant semantic focus for *Ärger* is Internalization, although this is mostly due to its lack of representation in the other, more outwardly directed semantic foci. By contrast with their Spanish equivalents, therefore, each of the German anger words has a dominant semantic focus: Lack of Control for *Wut*, Visibility for *Zorn* and Internalization for *Ärger*.

Radial diagrams provide an alternative way of expressing the data (Figure 3.5 and 3.6). The dimension of Regulation (the semantic foci of Control and Lack of Control) was plotted on one axis and the expression-related foci Visibility and Internalization on the other. This resulted in quadrangles of different shapes and sizes, which offer interesting additional insights through their visual representations of the major differences between the words.

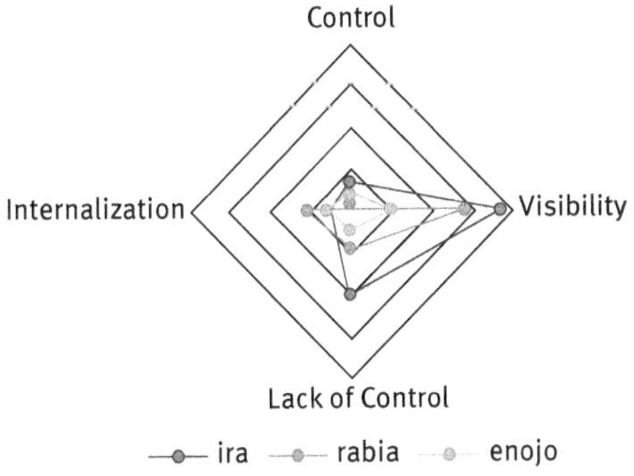

Figure 3.5: Radial diagrams for ira/rabia/enojo.

The Spanish quadrangles for *ira/rabia/enojo* are distorted towards Visibility in a very pronounced way, while Internalization is scarcely represented and Control even less so. Since the shapes are similar, size is the most important differentiating factor here. And size is clearly related to what we might call expressiveness, i.e. the words' tendencies to be combined with expressions denoting one or more of the semantic foci. The more expressive the word, the bigger the quadrangle.

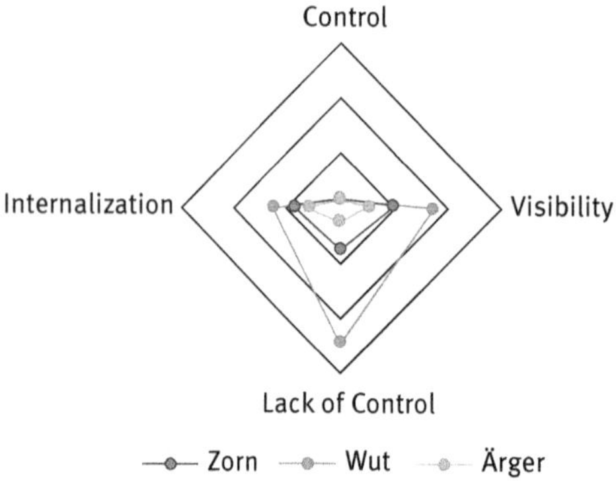

Figure 3.6: Radial diagrams for Zorn/Wut/Ärger.

The smallest (i.e. least expressive) quadrangle is that of *enojo*, which displays a tendency towards Visibility. The same trend, in a far more marked form, is evident with *rabia* and *ira* and those two words are also characterized by the predominance of Lack of Control over Control.

The diagram for German, on the other hand, reveals a distortion of a different type (cf. Figure 3.6). While all three anger words are more or less balanced on the Visibility-Internalization axis, they are very much tilted towards Lack of Control on the Regulation axis. The sizes of the quadrangles confirm that *Wut* is by far the most expressive of the three and *Ärger* the most neutral. The diagram's shape, on the other hand, clearly shows which aspect is most prominent for each word (Lack of Control for *Wut*, Visibility for *Zorn*). The stronger the aspect, the more the almost perfectly rhomboidal shape that characterizes *Ärger* (because of its near-balance between Visibility-Internalization and Control-Lack of Control) becomes distorted into a kite shape that gives more weight to the other semantic foci.

5 Conclusions

The research presented here has pursued objectives at two levels: first, a contrastive description of the concept of anger in two cultures, one commonly characterized as collectivist (Spanish-speaking countries) and the other as individualistic (Germany); secondly, the intralinguistic description of near-synonymous emotion words.

As far as the first aim is concerned, the comparison between Spanish and German anger words has confirmed the hypotheses that expressions emphasizing the control of anger are more salient in the Spanish corpus than in the German one, and that those highlighting lack of control are more prominent in German. Additionally, regarding the dimension of Expression, we may conclude that anger is more freely expressed in Spanish texts than in the German corpus, while the German corpus contains many more co-occurrences expressing Internalization of the emotion. Hofstede's (2011) investigations into the cultural dimension of Indulgence/Restraint may explain these results. According to Hofstede, Germany has a more restraint-oriented culture than any of the Spanish-speaking countries. However, more research, including investigations into other emotion concepts and language combinations, is needed to substantiate this finding.

Applied to an intralinguistic comparison of near-synonymous emotion words, our approach has also demonstrated its capacity to highlight and visualize major differences in the conceptualization of emotion terms. In this specific case, the approach has revealed that the three Spanish anger words *ira*, *enojo* and *rabia* are quite similar in their distribution of semantic foci, with a pronounced inclination towards Visibility. The differences between them lie more in the intensity of the emotion – *ira* is the most intense and *enojo* the most neutral – than in divergences in semantic focus. In German, however, the difference in intensity (*Wut* is by far the most intense, followed by *Zorn* and *Ärger*) is not the most important aspect. Instead, each anger word can be characterized by its specific combination of the four foci: *Ärger* is almost centred between the two axes of Regulation and Expression, whereas Lack of Control predominates for *Wut* and Visibility for *Zorn*.

As with every corpus based study, the results must be viewed in the context of the corpora from which they have been obtained. In this particular case, two main limitations must be taken into consideration. One is the loss of comparability when using different corpora for each language, corpora that have been compiled according to different criteria and procedures. Efforts have been undertaken to enhance comparability as much as possible through the calculation of foci-based relative frequency. The second limitation is that the Spanish corpus (Corpus del Español) includes texts from Spain as well as from a number of Latin American countries. While other large reference corpora for Spanish, such as CREA and CORDE, also adopt this approach, which enhances the linguistic diversity found in the corpus, this may mask regional preferences for certain emotion words or specific usages. Even more importantly, perhaps, it may be somewhat risky to assume cultural homogeneity among such diverse countries simply on the basis of a common language, a potential pitfall illuminated by the large differences in Hofstede's data on different Spanish-speaking countries (cf. section 4.1). Future studies might therefore consider limiting the scope of the investigation to a more culturally homogeneous subset of the corpus, even if this reduces the empirical basis of the study in question.

References

Barcelona, Antonio. 1989. Análisis contrastivo del léxico figurado de la ira en inglés y en español. In AESLA (ed.), *Actas del VI Congreso Nacional de Lingüística Aplicada*, 141–148. Santander: Universidad de Cantabria.

Davies, Mark. 2002. *Corpus del Español: 100 million words, 1200s-1900s*. Available online at http://www.corpusdelespanol.org/hist-gen/.

Durst, Uwe. 2001. Why Germans don't feel "anger." In Jean Harkins & Anna Wierzbicka (eds.), *Emotions in Crosslinguistic Perspective*, 115–148. Berlin & New York: De Gruyter Mouton.

Emanatian, Michele. 1995. Metaphor and the Expression of Emotion: The Value of Cross-Cultural Perspectives. *Metaphor and Symbolic Activity* 10 (3). 163–182.

Fries, Norbert. 2004. Gefühle, Emotionen, Angst, Furcht, Wut und Zorn. In Wolfgang Börner & Klaus Vogel (eds.), *Emotion und Kognition im Fremdsprachenunterricht*, 3–24. Tübingen: Gunter Narr.

Fries, Norbert. 2013. de ira. *Linguistik online* 13 (1/03). 103–124.

Geeraerts, Dirk & Stefan Grondelaers. 1995. Looking back at anger: Cultural traditions and metaphorical patterns. In John R. Taylor & Robert E. MacLaury (eds.), *Language and the Cognitive Construal of the World*, 153–179. Berlin & New York: De Gruyter Mouton.

Gevaert, Caroline. 2005. The ANGER IS HEAT Question: Detecting Cultural Influence on the Conceptualization of Anger through Diachronic Corpus Analysis. In Nicole Delbecque, Johan van der Auwera & Dirk Geeraerts (eds.), *Perspectives on Variation: Sociolinguistic, Historical, Comparative*, 195–208. Berlin & New York: De Gruyter Mouton.

Geyken, Alexander, Matthias Boenig, Susanne Haaf, Bryan Jurish, Christian Thomas, Frank Wiegand & Kay-Michael Würzner. 2015. Zeitliche Verlaufskurven in den DTA- und DWDS-Korpora: Wörter und Wortverbindungen über 400 Jahre (1600–2000). *Conference at Jahrestagung DHd 2015: Von Daten zu Erkenntnissen: Digitale Geisteswissenschaften als Mittler zwischen Information und Interpretation*, February 23 to 27, Graz. http://www.deutschestextarchiv.de/files/Thomas_DTA-DWDS-Histogramme_Graz2015.pdf (accessed 2 March 2019).

Hofstede, Geert. 1980. *Culture's Consequences: International Differences in Work-Related Values*. Beverly Hills / London: SAGE.

Hofstede, Geert. 1991. *Cultures and Organizations: Software of the Mind*. New York: McGraw-Hill.

Hofstede, Geert. 2011. Dimensionalizing Cultures: The Hofstede Model in Context. *Online Readings in Psychology and Culture* 2 (1). 1–26.

Kövecses, Zoltán. 1986. *Metaphors of Anger, Pride, and Love: A Lexical Approach to the Structure of Concepts*. Amsterdam: John Benjamins.

Kövecses, Zoltán. 1990. *Emotion Concepts*. New York: Springer-Verlag.

Kövecses, Zoltán. 2006. Embodiment, Experiential Focus, and Diachronic Change in Metaphor. In R. W. McConchie, Olga Timofeeva, Heli Tissari & Tanja Säily (eds.), *Selected Proceedings of the 2005 Symposium on New Approaches in English Historical Lexis (HEL-LEX)*, Somerville, MA: Cascadilla Proceedings Project. http://www.lingref.com/cpp/hel-lex/2005/paper1341.pdf (accessed 2 March 2019).

Kövecses, Zoltán. 2015. *Where Metaphors Come From. Reconsidering Context in Metaphor*. Oxford: Oxford University Press.

Kövecses, Zoltán. 2019. Some consequences of a multi-level view of metaphor. In Ignasi Navarro i Ferrando (ed.), *Current approaches to metaphor analysis in discourse*, 19–33. Berlin & New York: De Gruyter Mouton.

Krawczak, Karolina. 2014. Shame, embarrassment and guilt : Corpus evidence for the cross-cultural structure of social emotions. *Poznan Studies in Contemporary Linguistics* 50. 441–475.

Krawczak, Karolina. 2015. Negative self-evaluative emotions from a cross-cultural perspective : A case of "shame" and "guilt" in English and Polish. In Krzysztof Kosecki & Janusz Badio (eds.), *Empirical Methods in Language Studies*, 117–136. Frankfurt a. M.: Peter Lang.

Lakoff, George. 1996. Sorry, I'm not Myself Today: The Metaphor System for Conceptualizing the Self. In Gilles Fauconnier & Eve Sweetser (eds.), *Spaces, Worlds and Grammar*, 91–123. Chicago: University of Chicago Press.

Lewandowska-Tomaszczyk, Barbara & Paul Wilson. 2014. Self-Conscious Emotions in Collectivistic and Individualistic Cultures: A Contrastive Linguistic Perspective. In Jesús Romero-Trillo (ed.), *Yearbook of Corpus Linguistics and Pragmatics 2014: New Empirical and Theoretical Paradigms*, 123–148. Cham / Heidelberg / New York / Dordrecht / London: Springer-Verlag.

Ogarkova, Anna & Cristina Soriano. 2014. Variation within universals: The "metaphorical profile" approach to the study of anger concepts in English, Russian, and Spanish. In Andreas Musolff, Fiona MacArthur & Giulio Pagani (eds.), *About Metaphor and Intercultural Communication*, 93–116. London: Bloomsbury.

Ogarkova, Anna, Cristina Soriano & Caroline Lehr. 2012. Naming feeling: exploring the equivalence of emotion terms in five European languages. In Paul, A. Wilson (ed.), *Dynamicity in emotion concepts*, 3–35. Frankfurt a. M.: Peter Lang.

Oster, Ulrike. 2010. Using corpus methodology for semantic and pragmatic analyses: What can corpora tell us about the linguistic expression of emotions? *Cognitive Linguistics* 21 (4). 727–763.

Oster, Ulrike. 2012. "Angst" and "fear" in contrast: A corpus-based analysis of emotion concepts. In Mario Brdar, Ida Raffaelli & Milena Žic Fuchs (eds.), *Cognitive Linguistics between Universality and Variation*, 327–355. Newcastle upon Tyne: Cambridge Scholars Press.

Oster, Ulrike. 2014. Emotions between physicality and acceptability. A Contrast of the German Anger Words Wut and Zorn. *Onomázein* 30. 286–306.

Oster, Ulrike. 2018. Emotions in motion. Towards a corpus-based description of the diachronic evolution of anger words. *Review of Cognitive Linguistics* 16 (1). 191–228.

Pragglejaz Group. 2007. MIP: A method for identifying metaphorically used words in discourse. *Metaphor and Symbol* 22 (1). 1–39.

Soriano, Cristina. 2013. Conceptual metaphor theory and the GRID paradigm in the study of anger in English and Spanish. In Johnny R. J. Fontaine, Klaus R. Scherer & Cristina Soriano (eds.), *Components of emotional meaning: a sourcebook*, 410–424. Oxford: Oxford University Press.

Soriano-Salinas, Cristina. 2003. Some Anger Metaphors in Spanish and English. A Contrastive Review. *International Journal of English Studies* 3 (2). 107–122.

Soriano, Cristina, Johnny Fontaine, Anna Ogarkova, Claudia Mejía Quijano, Yana Volkova, Svetlana Ionova & Viktor Shakhovskyy. 2013. Types of anger in Spanish and Russian. In Johnny J. R. Fontaine, Klaus R. Scherer & Cristina Soriano (eds.), *Components of emotional meaning: a sourcebook*, 339–352. Oxford: Oxford University Press.

Stefanowitsch, Anatol. 2006. Words and their metaphors: A corpus-based approach. In Anatol Stefanowitsch & Stefan Thomas Gries (eds.), *Corpus-Based Approaches to Metaphor and Metonymy*, 63–105. Berlin & New York: De Gruyter Mouton.

Weigand, Edda. 1998. The Vocabulary of Emotion. A contrastive analysis of ANGER in German, English and Italian. In Edda Weigand (ed.), *Contrastive Lexical Semantics*, 45–66. Amsterdam / Philadelphia: John Benjamins.
Yu, Ning. 1995. Metaphorical Expressions of Anger and Happiness in English and Chinese. *Metaphor and Symbolic Activity* 10 (2). 59–92.

Dongman Cai and Alice Deignan

Metaphors and evaluation in popular economic discourse on trade wars

Abstract: Metaphor is used for different functions, including supporting the development of new knowledge and theory, communicating this, and persuading or framing its topic. All of these functions have been noted in economics texts. Analyses of popular economics texts have found that the same metaphor vehicles can be exploited in different ways to present different evaluations of their topic. For instance, both the Eurosceptic British press, and the Europhile Italian press framed the introduction of the Euro using a BIRTH metaphor, but used it very differently to convey their views (Semino 2002). We study the metaphors used to write about Sino-EU trade disputes in two popular newspapers, from China and the UK, in two corpora of approximately a third of a million tokens each. We find that similar metaphor groupings are used, notably FIGHT/WAR, but with differing frequencies and in different ways. The Chinese texts used FIGHT/WAR metaphors to write about protectionism, which tended to be personified and was rarely associated with a specific country. The UK texts used similar metaphors about free trade, which was characterised as the victim of assaults and in need of defending. As well as these qualitative findings, we found the quantitative data suggestive, though larger corpora would be needed for robust statistical conclusions.

Keywords: metaphor; evaluation; ideology; economics; trade disputes

1 Introduction

The following quotation about China's participation in international trade, reporting its readiness to morph into a market economy, is from the Chinese English language newspaper "The China Daily":

(1) ... *More remarkable is China's readiness to dance with "wolves" fed by the global free trade system.* (Xinhua 2016)

Dongman Cai, University of Leeds
Alice Deignan, University of Leeds, School of Education

https://doi.org/10.1515/9783110629460-004

Corpus evidence[1] suggests that the idiom *dance with wolves* is not frequent (except when citing the 1990 film by Kevin Costner), but that it has an established meaning, something like "to be involved with unpredictable, untamed, possibly dangerous forces", connoting bravery and skill. In this context, it seems that China refers to its courage in opening up its trade to developed countries that have a stronger voice internationally, and that are familiar with the rules of the game of international trade. The citation also extends the *wolf* metaphor with *fed by*, perhaps revitalizing it.

Also on the topic of Chinese participation in trade, the following is from the "Financial Times":

(2) *When doom-mongers predicted that the Great Recession would lead to the vampire of 1930s protectionism rising from the dead, they may have been watching the wrong graveyard.* (*Financial Times* 2012)

In (2), the VAMPIRE metaphor presents a very overtly negative evaluation of protectionism and related practices, and, like the WOLVES metaphor used in the "China Daily", has been extended creatively. Both quotations use metaphor to support their ideological position. The potential of metaphor to express different ideological perspectives has been explored in the political, religious and economics domains, the latter largely within Europe and the US. This chapter contributes to the discussion by analyzing the metaphors used to present different positions on economic questions by writers in China and the UK. It asks specifically how the terms *free trade* and *protectionist/protectionism* are framed metaphorically in popular English language economic discourse by writers from the two countries, and what evaluations are conveyed through the metaphors used.

2 Context

The economies of China and the European Union are strongly interlinked. In 2017, it was reported that "The EU is China's biggest trading partner, while China is the EU's second biggest, following a dramatic increase in trade in recent years that has come along with wealth, jobs, development and innovation for both sides. In 2016, China-EU trade amounted to 547 billion U.S. dollars. EU invested 8.8 billion dollars in China in 2016, a 35.1% increase from 2015; while China's non-financial direct investment in EU stood at 7.29 billion U.S. dollars, 1 percent increase from 2015" (Xinhua 2017).

1 The Oxford English Corpus (2 billion words) and English Web 2015 (18 billion words), both searched using the Sketchengine interface (Kilgarriff et al 2014)

However, there are ongoing tensions. China joined the World Trade Organisation in 2001, with the expectation that it would be recognised as having Market Economy Status after 15 years of membership. This status continues to be disputed by the EU and US, after the 15 years have elapsed, and is an ongoing source of difficulty in Sino-EU relations.

Specific trade disputes between the two have occurred, in part due to their different economies: China is a socialist market economy system in which public ownership plays a dominant role, although the country is in the process of rebalancing the role of the government and the market. The member states of the EU have market economies driven by market forces. Three recent disputes concern Chinese exports to the EU; of solar panels, steel, and raw materials. In the first case, in 2012, the EU accused China of selling solar panels at prices below the cost of production in order to take market share, a dispute which threatened to escalate into a much wider trade war. The second case concerns the steel industry, which is central to China's economy, and is dominated by state owned enterprises, while the EU is the second biggest steel market in the world. In recent years, the EU has claimed that overcapacity in China has threatened its own steel producers, and has called for anti-dumping and anti-subsidy measures, which are seen by China as protectionism. The opposite situation holds for the third example, raw materials. China is a leading producer of raw materials including rare earths and metals, essential for a range of industries, and has imposed export duties and quotas on these, raising prices for overseas buyers. China states that the policy exists to protect its resources and the environment, while the EU claims that it gives its own manufacturers a competitive advantage. This dispute has been ongoing for some years, with measures concerning different raw materials being challenged by the EU and US on different occasions.

The trade relationship is thus important for both sides, but has been conducted against a background of very different social and economic structures, and a legacy of disputes that have not been fully cleared up. This study examines the metaphors used by writers from both positions, to convey their stances on the issues core to the disputes, of free trade and protectionism. Our corpora consist of online reportage from the "China Daily" and the "Financial Times" on the topic of Sino-EU trade disputes between 2001, the date of China's accession to the WTO, and 2017.

3 Metaphor in economic discourse

The centrality of metaphor to economic discourse was first remarked on by two economists, Henderson and McCloskey, rather than linguists. Henderson (1982) commented that many core technical terms in the field are metaphorical in origin, while other metaphors are used more deliberately and creatively. McCloskey (1983) describes some of the central metaphorical models used by economists, such as supply and demand *curves*, and *elasticity*.

3.1 Functions of metaphor in economics discourse

Both Henderson and McCloskey noted that metaphors in economic discourse serve a range of functions. Henderson (1986) described them as follows:
1. Decorative or illustrative, that is, without a specific purpose;
2. Not specific to economics; general to all language "as a central organising device"; and
3. Metaphor as "a device for exploring specific economic problems and a basis for extending the domain of economic ideas" (Henderson 1986: 110–11).

The first and second functions are not of interest here, being irrelevant to framing and evaluation in specialised discourse. The third seems the same as that described as "theory constitutive" by Boyd ([1979] 1993), in relation to scientific metaphors. McCloskey (1983) also makes the case for metaphors having this theory constitutive function. Echoing Lakoff and Johnson (1980), he shows that metaphors are "not ornamental" (McCloskey 1983: 503) but are often fundamental to economic thought. In 1995, he tied these arguments more explicitly to Lakoff and Johnson, in his piece "Metaphors Economists Live By". Resche (2012) has argued for the centrality of theory constitutive metaphors to economic discourse, tracing patterns of ORGANISM and MECHANISM metaphors through the history of economic thought, including in the work of non-English speaking thinkers. An example of this is the source domain of GROWTH, examined in detail by White (2003). White shows that in its current sense, *growth* is a relatively recent term, not fully established even in the mid-twentieth century, but writes that it is now "totally institutionalised as an indispensable economic performance indicator" (White 2003: 133). He examines naturally occurring citations of the term, with its source domain collocates, arguing that "when economists and journalists deal with economic performance the metaphorical sense of growth is highly active and indeed more complex than what might be expected from a folk understanding of the concept" (White 2003: 135).

A second function of metaphor in specialised genres is the pedagogic. This has been recognised for some time as a function of metaphor in scientific texts (e.g., Boyd 1993; Semino 2008). Skorczynska and Deignan (2006) capture an aspect of this function in their category of "illustrating". Their examples indicate that a pedagogic function is intended, and they note that the function is very rare in research articles but more frequent in popular texts and textbooks. Resche notes that "Teachers and textbook authors naturally use exegetical metaphors to support their explanations" (Resche 2012: 94), but claims that these are always related to the fundamental metaphors underlying thinking in the field. In writing about metaphor in science, it is widely recognised that theory constitutive and pedagogical functions may be realised through the same linguistic metaphors (e.g., Deignan, Semino, and Paul 2019; Semino 2008). The same has been found to apply to economics (Alejo 2010).

McCloskey argued for another function of metaphor in economic discourse, the persuasive. He claimed that the discourse of economics is far from value free; rather, "the range of persuasive discourse in economics is wide, ignored in precept while potent in practice" (McCloskey 1982: 501). This is an almost inevitable extension of the theory constitutive function; because metaphors hide and highlight aspects of their topic, they present a non-neutral view of it. The point at which a theory constitutive metaphor might be considered persuasive or ideological will be subjective, but is certainly related to whether there exist alternative ways of talking or thinking about the topic.

Metaphors that are found widely across a discipline or genre, which give a non-neutral presentation but are not the only way of talking or writing about the topic, are often described as having a framing effect. Semino et al. (2016) describe this effect in their exploration of violence and war metaphors used to talk and write about cancer. Their corpus linguistic study of discourse around terminal cancer is informed by the views of some high profile cancer patients, and by healthcare professionals, who have said that VIOLENCE metaphors often frame the experience unhelpfully. For metaphors that are clearly non-neutral, but are only found in a small number of related texts, or in the discourse of one language user, this function is often described as persuasive (e.g., Charteris-Black 2011). Persuasive use of metaphor is a noted characteristic of the discourse of politicians (Charteris-Black 2004, 2011; Musolff 2017) and advertisers (Hidalgo-Downing and Kraljevic-Mujic 2017). Studies of the framing and persuasive effects of economics metaphors are discussed in the following sections.

3.2 Metaphors and framing in economic discourse

Koller (2005) develops a detailed argument linking Critical Discourse Analysis and metaphor theory, claiming that metaphor is strongly linked to ideology: "Metaphor [...] proves to be an interface between the cognitive structure underlying a discourse, on the one hand, and the ideology permeating it, on the other hand," (Koller 2005: 206). She conducted studies of economic discourse focussing on mergers and acquisitions (M&A) (Koller 2002, 2005), finding that "media discourse on M&A is very much characterized by a selectively used cluster of fighting, mating and feeding metaphors, which combine into a scenario of evolutionary struggle" (Koller 2005: 217).

Berber-Sardinha (2012)'s analysis also shows how metaphors present a non-neutral view of the economy. He examined the functions of metaphor in texts covering the major phases of the Brazilian economy from 1964 to 2010, during which time inflation was a constant challenge. He argues that certain metaphors have framed thinking about the economy in each of the phases, in some cases causing lasting damage. For example, the notion that the economy is a cake (Berber-Sardinha 2012: 105), which must be allowed to increase before it can be shared out, provided a rationalisation for Brazil's very unequal distribution of wealth. Arrese and Vaga-Miguel (2016) analyse metaphors of the European sovereign debt crisis, and show that in publications across a number of European countries, Greece was metaphorically described as *ill*. The illness was characterized as *infectious*, and needing *medicine* to prevent it *spreading*, with the term *contagion* (and translation equivalents) being particularly frequent, except in Greece itself (Arrese and Vaga-Miguel 2016: 145–6). Bickes et al. (2014) also found the sickness metaphor was used in this period in German publications, about Greece, Spain and Italy.

3.3 Comparative studies

There have been a number of comparative studies considering how economic issues are written about using metaphor in different countries, through contrastive analysis of corpora intended to represent national discourse. Some have found differences in metaphor which are attributed to cultural differences. Charteris-Black and Ennis (2001) compared corpora of financial reporting in English and Spanish newspapers relating to the 1997 stock market crash. They found evidence of ORGANISM, MOVEMENT and DISASTER metaphors in both languages, with some differences in frequencies and emphasis between the two. The British corpus also contained some nautical metaphors not found in the Spanish corpus; these differences are perhaps attributed to culture. Arrese and Vara-Miguel (2016) however found relatively little difference in metaphor use across a large number of European countries in writing about the European debt crisis in texts published between 2010 and 2012.

In a comparison of the UK with a non-Western context, Chow (2014) also found that culture influenced metaphor use in economic texts. She compared corpora of economic reports from "The Guardian", a British English left-of-centre newspaper with the "Hong Kong Economic Journal", focussing on bodily movement metaphors. Fukuda (2009) compared metaphors used in Japanese and US texts, finding that while both used metaphors derived from LIVING ORGANISM AND LIVING ORGANISM WITH MECHANICS, only the US used metaphors from a purely mechanical source domain. He suggests that this could be due to the different histories of the discipline of economics in the two countries. In the US, the discipline is said to have been influenced by concepts from physics, while Marxian economics, which tended to a biological rather than mechanistic model, has been a significant factor in the development of Japanese economic policy following the second world war (Fukuda 2009: 1700). This difference sits at the border between the cultural and the ideological.

A number of other comparative studies have found differences in metaphor use that seem more likely due to ideology, that is, in which metaphors frame different views of their topic. Semino (2002) examined metaphorical representations of Euro based on corpora of English and Italian newspapers over the period when Euro was introduced in 1999. She finds that most dominant metaphorical patterns are shared between the two languages but differences existed in their frequencies and linguistic realizations due to both cultural and attitudinal differences toward the topic. BIRTH was the most frequent source domain for metaphors in both languages, but the languages differed in their "uses of novel realisations" (Semino 2002: 7). In the Italian corpus, the Euro was described as *a sturdy baby* to express either neutral or positive views while in the English corpus it was described negatively as a *heavyweight baby*. Semino (2002: 4) writes that the similarities can be explained by the closely similar conceptual metaphorical systems underlying the two languages. The differences seem to be "partly as a result of differences in the nature and status of particular source domains in the two cultures and partly as a result of differences in the dominant attitudes to the Euro in the two countries" (Semino 2005: 5).

Charteris-Black and Musolff (2003) also focussed on the early days of the Euro, comparing representations of Euro trading in corpora of financial reporting from the British and German press. Metaphors of upward/downward movement were used almost identically in the two corpora, suggesting a shared conceptual map of the domain of economics. They also note that metaphor has pragmatic, ideological qualities. In both corpora, HEALTH metaphors are used, in which the Euro is personified, but in the British corpus, this occurs to a much greater extent, with a range of lexis representing the Euro as *afflicted* and *suffering*. The British texts also present the Euro as a combatant, again, personified, "that can *hit out* as well as *suffer* blows from opponents" (Charteris-Black and Musolff 2003: 174), apparently expressing and framing the British scepticism around the Euro. Rojo López and Orts Llopis (2010) found differences in the ways that the financial crisis of 2007-2008 was written about metaphorically between the British publication "The Economist" and the Spanish "El Economista". They attributed these to the Spanish authorities wishing to downplay the effects of the crisis.

Liu (2015) compared metaphors in the "China Daily" and the "New York Times", investigating how each framed a currency dispute between China and the US. He finds that the same five overarching source domains: PHYSICAL MOVEMENT, PHYSICAL CONFLICT/WAR, HEALTH/STRENGTH, VICTIM, and MACHINE are used by writers in both newspapers. These are exploited differently however, to frame the issue according to the positions taken by each newspaper, in line with the governments in their respective countries. For instance, while both newspapers use metaphors related to the theme of MACHINES to refer to exchange rates, in the "China Daily" the main lexicalisation of this is *adjust*, while the "New York Times" used the far stronger *overhaul*. To describe the fixing of the Chinese currency at a predetermined rate, both newspapers used the neutral and technical metaphor *peg* but the "New York Times" used a number of metaphorical synonyms for this, all with negative evaluations in the context they were used in: *fix*, *tie*, *lock* and *yoke* (Liu 2015: 348).

Differences are not always national or cultural. O'Mara-Shimek et al. (2015) studied coverage of the 2008 stock market crash, and found that newspapers taking a liberal stance, such as the "New York Times", tended to use animate-biological metaphors to describe the stock market more frequently than "The Washington Times", positioned to the right of centre. The writers hypothesise that this expresses a belief that the stock market should be nurtured, in contrast to the laissez-faire approach of the conservative press. In Horner's (2011) study of American public discourse about the 2008 financial crisis and the US government bailout, different metaphors were used by those favouring a bailout plan and those opposed to it.

3.4 Genres of economic discourse

Henderson (2000) pointed out that there are very significant differences between the metaphors used in texts for different readerships. He notes that "It would be unusual for an economics text-book to contain the following statement: 'Sorry to be party-poopers, but America's economy still looks horribly bubble-like'" (Henderson 2000: 169), this statement having appeared in the popular publication "The Economist" (September 25, 1999: 17). Herrera-Soler and White (2012: 2) note that "economic discourse ranges from the highly specialized journal through academic books and into journalism and broadcasting". It is established that texts written for different readerships will have different features, including metaphor.

More recently, Deignan, Littlemore and Semino (2013), summarise and develop metaphor research in genre and register. In the field of economics, Skorczynska and Deignan (2006) contrasted research and popular articles on the same topic, and found that their two corpora shared almost no linguistic metaphors.

In order to compare metaphor use between Chinese and British economic discourse on the same topic, we therefore needed to decide on a fairly narrow genre, as otherwise any differences that we found might be due to differences in the intended readership of the publication rather than to the writers' evaluative frames. We chose to focus on popular economic discourse, because of this genre's role in constructing public attitudes and shaping public opinion (Chow 2014; Happer and Philo 2013).

4 Methodology

4.1 Corpus Construction

In this chapter, we report on the metaphors that are used to frame the notions denoted by the terms *free trade* and *protectionism/protectionist*, or associated with them. This forms part of a wider study (Cai forthcoming). We examined our choice of popular economic discourse using the established register parameters of mode, tenor, and field (Halliday and Hasan 1976). Regarding mode and tenor, we had decided, as noted above, that we wanted to study written texts which are popular, and also influential. More specifically, we wanted texts written by specialised writers for educated non-specialists, or that are read by specialists as leisure material, and from publications regarded as popular but well informed. We therefore asked a sample of graduates working in the financial and business sectors in the US, UK and China to recommend periodicals, and for this study, decided as a result on the English language "China Daily" and the UK "Financial Times". Our chosen field is trade disputes, so we then identified candidate terms to automatically identify texts on the topic of trade disputes between China and the EU/US. We did this by (1) manually compiling a pilot corpus of texts on trade disputes, and (2) comparing this pilot corpus with a reference corpus to identify words key to the pilot, using the software Sketchengine (Kilgarriff et al. 2014). We then used these as query terms to identify further texts from the publications, using their websites and Nexis UK[2]. The initial query terms were: *Sino*, *China*,

2 https://www.nexis.com

Chinese, EU, European Union, trade, dispute. After further examination of our texts, we added the terms *anti-dumping, anti-subsidies, protectionism, retaliation, punitive, market economy status, trade imbalance*. Finally, we checked the texts returned for relevance. This enabled us to build corpora of 318,720 words from the “China Daily”, from 606 texts, and 351,391 words from the “Financial Times”, from 617 texts. We compiled these corpora as .txt files and analyzed them using three software tools: Sketchengine, WMatrix (Rayson 2008) and AntConc (Anthony 2018).

4.2 Metaphor identification

We used WMatrix (Rayson 2008) to semantically tag our two corpora. We then followed the methodology developed by Koller et al. (2008) to identify metaphor candidates in specialised corpora. Koller et al. used WMatrix to tag three collections of texts, including a corpus of corporate mission statements. They argue that “the domain L1 (‘life and living things’) is much less expected to be key in a collection of corporate texts than is the domain I1.1 (‘money and pay’)” (Koller et al. 2008: 150). However, WMatrix showed that ‘life and living things’ was in fact a key domain in the corpus, suggesting “that the associated lexemes may be used metaphorically” (Koller et al. 2008: 150). From the WMatrix output for our corpora, we identified vehicle groupings that were unexpected in economic discourse. One such grouping is FIGHT/WAR. Words associated with this include: *aggressive, bullets, damaging, defend, fight, gun*, and *hurt*. From the initial output, a concordance can be created. Figure 4.1 shows an extract of the concordance for terms that were identified with the semantic tag “Damaging and destroying” in the “Financial Times” corpus.

488 occurrences.			Extend context		
f the Atlantic , to have more	damaging	consequences . Taken to its lo	1	More	Full
and a trade war that would be	devastating	to EU-US relations.Only recent	2	More	Full
r the next month to check for	harmful	drugs in horse carcasses acros	3	More	Full
t subsidies in five years and	slash	its domestic subsidies by more	4	More	Full
r to what extent he wishes to	destroy	and rebuild the architecture o	5	More	Full
g that the company said would	damage	investment and job creation in	6	More	Full
, France 's trade minister ,	broke	cover in the past three days a	7	More	Full
deals that , he claimed , had	destroyed	US manufacturing jobs and depr	8	More	Full
TTIP.The consequences may be	baleful	, as John Kornblum , a former	9	More	Full
ing the idea that a deal will	damage	consumer , labour and environm	10	More	Full
universities are unrivalled .	Carnage	it is not . If any large econo	11	More	Full
ing domestic champions to the	detriment	of the single market . Now the	12	More	Full
ctive aspect of the decisions	violates	ideas of fundamental fairness	13	More	Full

Figure 4.1: Concordance citations for the A1.1.2: “Damaging and destroying”.

We analysed these concordances manually to identify metaphors, using the Metaphor Identification Procedure (MIP) (Pragglejaz Group 2007). Due to the size of our corpus, we were not able to read entire texts, as specified by MIP, but we found that given the specialist nature of the texts, we had no difficulty in establishing contextual meaning from a snippet view of the co-text. We also studied concordances of *protectionism/protectionist*, *free trade*, again using MIP to identify metaphors in the concordance citations. We classified the linguistic metaphors that we identified into vehicle groupings using the procedure developed by Cameron et al. (2009: 74–76). We did not include metaphors with general reference, following the second of the methodological options that Kimmel (2012) describes, when "a restriction to one or a small set of related domains makes sense, because the researcher wants to maintain a thematic focus. This means discarding all off-topic metaphors without interest to the study" (Kimmel 2012: 5). All metaphor counts in this chapter therefore refer to metaphors that describe or refer in some way to economics topics. We then analyzed all citations of metaphors found through both procedures, manually in context, to identify evaluative meaning. In this chapter, we focus on domain-specific metaphors that were found in collocation with the words *protectionism/protectionist* and *free trade*.

5 Findings

5.1 Quantitative findings

Numbers of each search term, and normalised frequencies (per million) for each corpus are given in Table 4.1. This shows that the words *protectionism/protectionist* together are a good deal more frequent in the "China Daily" than in the "Financial Times", while the phrase *free trade* is of similar frequency in the two corpora.

Table 4.1: Numbers of occurrences of search terms in each corpus.

	Financial Times		China Daily	
Term	**freq**	**normalised**	**freq**	**normalised**
Protectionism/protectionist	375	1,067	651	2,042
Free trade	185	526	171	536

The vehicle groupings for domain-specific metaphors used with *protectionist/protectionism* are shown in Table 4.2, with raw and normalised (per million) frequencies. These are rounded to nearest whole number hence the total is not exact.

Table 4.2: Vehicle groupings for metaphors used with *protectionist/protectionism*.

Financial Times			**China Daily**		
Vehicle grouping	**freq**	**norm**	**Vehicle grouping**	**freq**	**norm**
Fight/war	20	57	Fight/war	75	235
Movement	15	43	Direction	38	119
Physical power/contact/shape	13	37	Movement	28	87
Liquid movement	12	34	Illness/health	20	62
Direction	12	34	Liquid movement	10	31
Vehicle	7	20	Crime	9	28
Game	5	13	Machine	6	19
Fire	5	13	Direction	6	19
Plant	4	11	Vehicle	5	16
Crime	3	8	Person	5	16
Vampire	3	8	Game	4	13
Machine	2	5	Weather	2	6
Person	2	5	other	4	13
Total	103	293	total	212	665

The vehicle groupings for domain-specific metaphors used with *free trade* are shown in Table 4.3, with raw and normalised (per million) frequencies.

For the most part, numbers are relatively small, and given that the process of vehicle grouping is intrinsically subjective, we would hesitate to draw many strong conclusions on this quantitative data. Nonetheless, there are some points to note. As is standard, the normalised frequencies are calculated relative to corpus size throughout,[3] but we note that another factor is at play regarding the metaphor counts in Tables 4.2 and 4.3. We have shown that the words *protectionist/protectionism* are significantly more frequent in the "China Daily" corpus, which would lead us to expect that the counts for metaphorically used words with

3 https://www.sketchengine.eu/my_keywords/freqmill/

Table 4.3: Vehicle groupings for metaphors used with *free trade*.

Financial Times			China Daily		
Vehicle grouping	**freq**	**norm**	**Vehicle grouping**	**freq**	**norm**
Fight/war	17	48	Fight/war	10	31
Structure	3	8	Game	10	31
Direction	3	8	Animal	2	6
Person	2	5	Vehicle	1	3
Plant	2	5	Person	1	3
Game	2	5	Direction	1	3
Other	6	16	Container	1	3
Total	35	95	total	26	80

them would also be higher for that corpus. This is indeed the case. In total, the normalised frequency of metaphors used with *protectionist/protectionism* is more than twice as high in the "China Daily" than in the "Financial Times", proportionately slightly higher than the frequencies of the terms themselves would suggest. For the most frequent vehicle grouping, FIGHT/WAR, the normalised frequency of domain-specific metaphors used with *protectionist/protectionism* is five times as high in the "China Daily" as in the "Financial Times". That is, while roughly similar proportions of metaphors are used across the two corpora, "China Daily" uses a much greater number of ones that suggest conflict.

The reverse pattern is seen, though to a lesser extent, for metaphors with *free trade*. The normalised frequencies for *free trade* are nearly identical, but there are slightly fewer metaphors used with the expression in the "China Daily". Metaphors from the FIGHT/WAR vehicle grouping are more frequent in the "Financial Times", with normalised frequencies of 48 in the latter as opposed to 31 in the former. Indeed, for this publication, FIGHT/WAR metaphors dominate figurative discussion of free trade.

In both corpora, for all search terms, metaphors from the grouping FIGHT/WAR are the most frequent.

5.2 Qualitative analysis

Tables 4.2 and 4.3 show that the most frequent metaphors used with *protectionist/protectionism* are from the vehicle grouping FIGHT/WAR, for both corpora.

Citation analysis shows that there are differences within this broad pattern. "The Financial Times" uses lexis such as *fight*, *swipe*, and *battle*, in the following citations:

(3) Europe is prepared to *fight back* against economic protectionism by the Donald Trump administration with policies akin to those used to combat Chinese anti-competitive practices, according to France's industry minister.

(4) Gordon Brown has taken a thinly veiled *swipe* at French and Italian protectionism

(5) Ms Lagarde, who has been locked in a rhetorical *battle* over protectionism with Mr Trumps commerce secretary, Wilbur Ross ...

In (3) and (4), the perpetrator of protectionism is specified, while in (5), it is implied. This is in contrast to FIGHT/WAR metaphors in "China Daily", which for the most part tend to construct protectionism as an autonomous entity rather than ascribing it to a particular cause, as in citations (6) to (9).

(6) There can be no compromise in the *battle* against protectionism, wherever it resides.

(7) China and the 27-member bloc, as two globally significant economies, should coordinate their macroeconomic policy-making and jointly *combat* trade protectionism.

(8) While they promise to *combat* trade protectionism, many foreign nations do something different.

(9) China offers hope in *fight* against protectionism.

Even where a perpetrator of protectionism might be inferred, the "China Daily" tends towards being indirect, as in citations (10) and (11):

(10) During the week-long trip to Europe, he called on nations *to guard against* trade protectionism, saying China will not purposely seek a trade surplus.

(11) ... both sides should channel their political capital into encouraging mutually beneficial arrangements rather than entering into protectionist *battles*.

As well as characterising protectionism as a general, autonomous entity rather than a specific national policy, the "China Daily" seems to use metaphors more frequently to negatively characterise protectionism. There are 16 citations of *fight* [protectionism] in the "China Daily", compared with 4 in the "Financial Times". The "China Daily" uses the phrase *oppose protectionism* 13 times, compared with 2 in the "Financial Times". Even these 2 are not owned, discoursally, by the "Financial Times"; both citations are quotations from other sources, one of which is China. The "China Daily" citations include:

(12) China is ready to work with the US side to carry out comprehensive economic cooperation, jointly ease trade imbalance, advocate free trade, *oppose* protectionism.

In a number of citations in the FIGHT/WAR vehicle group, the "China Daily" uses metaphor to show China as a *victim* of protectionism. This is noticeable in citations for *victim* and *target* in particular:

(13) This is also true with China, which has been [the] *victim* of trade protectionism for more than a decade.

(14) China has been the *target* of trade protectionism since late 2008.

There are 6 citations of *victim* and 7 of *target* in the "China Daily", all referring to China, and in the "Financial Times" 1 of *victim*, which also refers to China, and none of *target*. There are 6 citations of *resist protectionism* in "China Daily", again characterising protectionism as autonomous:

(15) We need to work together to *resist* trade protectionism and stay cautious against the application of any trade restrictions.

In comparison, there are 3 citations of the expression in the "Financial Times", all of which are quotations from other sources, including China.

The second most frequent vehicle grouping occurring with *protectionist/protectionism* in the China Daily is DIRECTION. These metaphors frame the notion as a destination or as a direction of travel. Unlike the FIGHT/WAR metaphors discussed above, these tend to be associated with the policy of specific politicians or governments.

(16) EU's proposed tougher trade rules open [a] dangerous *road toward* protectionism.

(17) When Donald Trump and Bernie Sanders have helped move US trade policy in a much more protectionist *direction*.

The second most frequent vehicle group used with *protectionist/protectionism* in the "Financial Times" is MOVEMENT, which is the third most frequent in "China Daily". Citation (18) is from the "Financial Times", and (19) from "China Daily", framing protectionism as a destination and an entity respectively.

(18) ... calling for Brussels to take immediate action against China's booming clothing sector, and countries such as Sweden warning against a *return* to protectionism.

(19) CD Simon Evenett, director of the London-based Center for Economic Policy Research, indicated in a recent report that protectionism has *returned*, especially since the final quarter of 2012.

The "China Daily" also uses small numbers of metaphors from other source domains, with a similar set of meanings. In (20), a *[protectionist] pall* (a cloth draped over a coffin, used metaphorically to stand for a repressive force) is framed as if it has its own agency, unattributed to the policy of any country. In (21), protectionism is an abstract possibility, *quench* and *poisonous* framing it as a tempting but ultimately very damaging course of action.

(20) China's solar companies change horizons as a protectionist *pall* falls over European market.

(21) China has from the beginning responded to the challenges with resolute reforms to make a market economy at all costs, rather than *quench* its initial disorientation with *poisonous* protectionism.

These and other vehicle groupings in "China Daily" are too infrequent to draw generalisations but the data are consistent with an overall trend towards framing protectionism as a negative abstract entity independent of governments, with some exceptions. Nominal *move*, which we included in the vehicle grouping GAME, is the main exception to this general trend in "China Daily", in that it is sometimes associated with the US or its president, as in 23).

(22) He added that every country should work hard to maintain open trade relationships and avoid protectionist *moves*.

(23) The protectionist *move* by the Obama administration will ultimately hurt the US-China trade relations.

Both newspapers occasionally framed protectionism as a beast or a monster. Citations (24) and (25) are from the "China Daily"; (26) is from the "Financial Times".

(24) Protectionism is *raising its ugly head* in the US.

(25) For one, by viewing China as a non-market economy, Tokyo has followed in the footsteps of the United States and the European Union by denying China its deserved status, making itself the "third domino" in unleashing the *monster* of protectionism, which isn't good news for the global economy.

(26) ... lead to the *vampire* of 1930s protectionism rising from the dead, they may have been watching the wrong graveyard.

Free trade occurs less frequently in both corpora, with fewer associated metaphors. In both, the FIGHT/WAR vehicle grouping is the most frequent. In the "China Daily", this is lexicalised through *champion*, as in 27):

(27) The two sides have also sent out positive signals to the world with their resolution to *champion* free trade and globalization...

In the "Financial Times", a much wider range of metaphors from this vehicle grouping is used, referring much more strongly to free trade being under threat than in the "China Daily". The following are from the "Financial Times".

(28) German business chiefs prepare to *defend* free trade in US.

(29) But events this month – including wildcat strikes and now an *assault on* free trade resulting in the biggest clothing crisis since the second world war.

(30) There is concern that the EU remains vulnerable to anti-establishment movements that whip up public support by *attacking* free trade and open markets.

The only other vehicle grouping of any frequency used to write about free trade is GAME, in the "China Daily". This tends to compare the domain of games with free trade, and point out similarities and differences, as in the following, quoted by "China Daily".

(31) "Free trade is a win-win situation and it is not a zero sum game"

Metaphors from the GAME vehicle grouping are also used, less frequently, in the "Financial Times".

6 Discussion and conclusion

As discussed in our methodology section, we used identical query terms to select texts from these newspapers, from between 2001–2017, in order to select texts that are related to the notions of protectionism and free trade. The same series of trade disputes between China and the EU/US is discussed in both newspapers. If the coverage of these were oriented in the same way, we would predict the frequencies of the key terms to be very close, and the frequencies and types of metaphors used to be very similar. The results showed this not to be so in all cases. We have found nothing in the data itself to explain this.

One hypothesis is that the "Financial Times", founded in 1888 and long rooted in a market economy system, is very fiercely opposed to protectionism at a philosophical level; indeed, this is part of its core value system. The relatively low frequency of the term itself may reflect that it is part of the background value system and does not need to be repeatedly mentioned. Similarly, the relative lack of metaphors used to write about it in the "Financial Times" may be because protectionism is a well-established notion for its writers and readers, and thus does not require metaphors either as a pedagogic or framing tool. The "China Daily" was founded much more recently, in 1981, and has come from an economy which has undergone radical change over the lifetime of the newspaper. This could explain why protectionism is mentioned much more frequently, and why when it is mentioned, it is much more likely to be alongside an explanatory metaphor, and invariably one that conveys a negative evaluation towards it.

The data are less marked for *free trade*, which is used with similar frequencies in the "Financial Times" and the "China Daily", but is more likely to be used in conjunction with a metaphor when it appears in the latter. A possible explanation could be that free trade, again, is perceived as a long-established default in the value system of the "Financial Times", and therefore needs little explicit mention. In contrast, for China, free trade is a relatively new system. Further, the various disputes with the EU and the US over what is understood by free trade mean that it has not been unproblematic in implementation for China. We have no evidence from our data to support these hypotheses, which could only be tested through detailed discussion with well-informed language users from each community.

A pattern emerging from the qualitative data is that the "China Daily" regularly shows China as a victim of protectionism, which it often, but not always, characterises as autonomous, as opposed to the result of a particular nation or politician. This framing was not found anywhere in the "Financial Times". The "Financial Times" writes of fights against protectionism, which are often associated with other Western nations, but not of the UK, EU, or any other nation being *victims* or *targeted*. The "Financial Times" does however describe *free trade* itself as being under attack; this may explain the high proportion of WAR/FIGHT metaphors used to describe it in this newspaper. Both newspapers write of the need to *support*, *defend* or *champion* free trade, which in the "Financial Times" is *under assault* from an unnamed attacker.

Both newspapers show some creativity in metaphor use. We began this chapter by citing the metaphor *dance with wolves,* used in the "China Daily", and *vampire rising from the dead,* used in the "Financial Times". Overall, our data suggested that innovative metaphors were found more in the "China Daily" corpus. The following extract, with domain-specific metaphors highlighted, is from the same article in China Daily (Xinhua 2016) as the *dance with wolves* citation:

(32) The nation's *milestone accession* to the world's largest trading bloc has made a perfect *marriage* between the nation and the global value *chain*, as burgeoning Chinese businesses begin to go global, and international enterprises *ride on the crest* of their ambitions in the *tantalizing* Chinese market... compared with other resources, the stamina *nourished* by an inclusive and *flexible* mindset will *win* in the *race* for the *silver line* of the global free trade.

This passage is not untypical of many sections of the "China Daily" corpus and shows a creativity in figurative use that is found far less often in the "Financial Times". As was the case for the frequencies described above, we have no evidence to help us establish why this is so. Possibilities are that writers for the "China Daily" take account of many of the readers being second language speakers of English, and/or that because the core concepts of the market are more recent to this readership, more metaphor is used to explain them, and/or, that the "China Daily" has a stronger desire to be persuasive in its presentation of these concepts and the Chinese position.

This chapter has investigated how metaphors are used to frame two core, opposing economic concepts, in two comparable newspapers from nations which are very different in their history but which, in today's globalised world, interact with each other frequently. We have found a number of similarities, but some subtle differences, which we are exploring further with a wider range of corpora.

The interaction between our quantitative and qualitative findings proved to be important to our analysis, indicating the value of using both reasonably large corpora and detailed discourse analysis techniques.

References

Alejo, Rafael. 2010. Where does the money go? An analysis of the container metaphor in economics: The market and the economy. *Journal of Pragmatics* 42. 1137–1150.
Anthony, Laurence. 2018. *AntConc* (Version 3.5.7) [Computer Software]. Tokyo, Japan: Waseda University. Available from http://www.laurenceanthony.net/software.
Arrese, Ángel & Alfonso Vara-Miguel, 2016. A comparative study of metaphors in press reporting of the Euro crisis. *Discourse and Society* 27 (2). 133–155.
Beattie, Alan. 2012. Global economy: Tricks of the trade law. *Financial Times*, October 28.
Berber-Sardinha, Tony. 2012. Metaphors of the Brazilian Economy from 1964 to 2010. In Honesto Herrera-Soler & Michael White (eds.), *Metaphor and Mills: Figurative Language in Business and Economics*, 103–126. Berlin & New York: De Gruyter Mouton.
Bickes, Hans, Tina Otten & Laura Chelsea Weymann. 2014. The financial crisis in the German and English press: Metaphorical structures in the media coverage on Greece, Spain and Italy. *Discourse and Society* 25 (4). 424–445.
Boyd, Richard. 1993 [1979]. Metaphor and theory change: What is 'metaphor' a metaphor for? In Andrew Ortony (ed.), *Metaphor and Thought*, 2nd edn. 481–532. Cambridge: Cambridge University Press.
Cameron, Lynne, Robert Maslen, Zazie Todd, John Maule, Peter Stratton & Neil Stanley. 2009. The Discourse Dynamics Approach to Metaphor and Metaphor-Led Discourse Analysis, *Metaphor and Symbol* 24 (2). 63–89.
Cai, Dongman. Forthcoming. *Corpus studies of the form and function of metaphor in public economic discourse.* Unpublished PhD thesis, University of Leeds.
Charteris-Black, Jonathan. 2004. *Corpus approaches to critical metaphor analysis*. Palgrave: Macmillan.
Charteris-Black, Jonathan. 2011. *Politicians and rhetoric: The persuasive power of metaphor*. Palgrave: Macmillan.
Charteris-Black, Jonathan & Timothy Ennis. 2001. A comparative study of metaphor in Spanish and English financial reporting. *English for Specific Purposes* 20 (3). 249–266.
Charteris-Black, Jonathan & Andreas Musolff. 2003. 'Battered hero' or 'Innocent victim'? A comparative study of metaphors for euro trading in British and German financial reporting. *English for Specific Purposes* 22 (2). 153–176.
Chow, Mei Yung Vanliza. 2014. The movements of the economy: Conceptualising the economy via bodily movement metaphors. *Metaphor and the Social World* 4 (1). 3–26.
Deignan, Alice, Jeannette Littlemore & Elena Semino. 2019. *Figurative language, genre and register*. Cambridge: Cambridge University Press.
Deignan, Alice, Elena Semino & Shirley-Anne Paul. 2017. Metaphors of climate change in three genres: Research articles, educational texts and secondary school student talk. *Applied Linguistics* 40(2). 379–403.
Fukuda, Kosei. 2009. A comparative study of metaphors representing the US and Japanese economies. *Journal of Pragmatics* 41 (9). 1693–1702.

Gabrielatos, Costas. 2007. Selecting Query Terms to Build a Specialised Corpus from a Restricted-access Database. *ICAME Journal* 31. 5–43.
Halliday, Michael & Ruqaiya Hasan. 1976. *Cohesion in English*. London: Longman.
Happer, Catherine & Greg Philo. 2013. Special thematic section on "societal change": The role of the media in the construction of public belief and social change. *Journal of Social and Political Psychology* 1 (1). 321–336.
Henderson, Wille. 1986. Metaphor in economics. In Malcolm Coulthard (ed.), *Talking about text*, 109–127. Birmingham, UK: University of Birmingham.
Herrera Soler, Honesto & Michael White (eds.). 2012. *Metaphor and Mills: Figurative Language in Business and Economics*. Berlin & New York: De Gruyter Mouton.
Hidalgo-Downing, Laura & Blanca Kraljevic-Mujic. 2017. Metaphor and persuasion in commercial advertising. In Semino, Elena and Demjén, Zsófia (eds.). *The Routledge handbook of metaphor and language*, 323–336. London & New York: Routledge.
Horner, Jennifer. 2011. Clogged systems and toxic assets: News metaphors, neoliberal ideology, and the United States "Wall Street bailout" of 2008. *Journal of Language and Politics* 10 (1). 29–49.
Kilgarriff, Adam, V. Baisa, J. Bŭsta, M. Jacubíček, V. Kovář, J. Michelfeit, P. Rychlý, & V. Suchomel. 2014. 'The Sketchengine, ten years on', *Lexicography* 1. 7–36. www.sketchengine.co.uk.
Kimmel, Michael. 2012. Optimising the analysis of metaphor in discourse: How to make the most of qualitative software and find a good research design. *Review of Cognitive Linguistics* 10 (1). 1–48.
Koller, Veronika. 2002. "A shotgun wedding": co-occurrence of war and marriage metaphors in mergers and acquisitions discourse. *Metaphor and Symbol* 13 (3). 179–203.
Koller, Veronika. 2005. Critical discourse analysis and social cognition: evidence from business media discourse. *Discourse and Society* 16 (2). 199–224.
Koller, Veronika, Andrew Hardie, Paul Rayson & Elena Semino. 2008. Using a semantic annotation tool for the analysis of metaphor in discourse. *Metaphorik.de* 15. 141–160.
Lakoff, George, & Mark Johnson. 1980. *Metaphors we live by*. Chicago: University of Chicago Press.
Liu, Ming. 2015. Scapegoat or manipulated victim? Metaphorical representations of the Sino-US currency dispute in Chinese and American financial news. *Text &Talk* 35 (3). 337–357.
McCloskey, Donald. 1983. The Rhetoric of economics. *Journal of Economic Literature* 21. 481–517.
McCloskey, Donald. 1995. Metaphors economists live by. *Social Research* 62 (2). 215– 237.
Musolff, Andreas. 2017. Metaphor and persuasion in politics. In Semino, Elena and Demjén, Zsófia (eds.), *The Routledge handbook of metaphor and language*, 309–322. London & New York: Routledge.
O'Mara-Shimek, Michael, Manuel Guillén Parra & Ana Ortega-Larrea. 2015. Stop the bleeding or weather the storm? Crisis solution marketing and the ideological use of metaphor in online financial reporting of the stock market crash of 2008 at the New York Stock Exchange. *Discourse and Communication* 9 (1). 103–123.
Pragglejaz Group. 2007. MIP: A method for identifying metaphorically used words in discourse, *Metaphor and Symbol* 22 (1). 1–39.
Rayson, Paul. 2008. From key words to key semantic domains. *International Journal of Corpus Linguistics* 13 (4). 519–549.
Resche, Catherine. 2012. Towards a better understanding of metaphorical networks in the language of economics: The importance of theory-constitutive metaphors. In Honesto Herrera-Soler, & Michael White, (eds.), *Metaphor and Mills: Figurative Language in Business and Economics*, 77–102. Berlin & New York: De Gruyter Mouton.

Rojo López, Ana María & María Ángeles Orts Llopis. 2010. Metaphorical pattern analysis in financial texts: Framing the crisis in positive or negative metaphorical terms. *Journal of Pragmatics* 42. 3300–3313.

Semino, Elena. 2002. A sturdy baby or a derailing train? Metaphorical representations of the Euro in British and Italian newspapers. *Text: An Interdisciplinary Journal for the Study of Discourse* 22 (1). 107–139.

Semino, Elena. 2008. *Metaphor in Discourse*. Cambridge: Cambridge University Press.

Semino, Elena, Zsófia Demjén & Jane Demmen. 2016. An integrated approach to metaphor framing in cognition, discourse and practice, with an application to metaphors for cancer. *Applied Linguistics* 39 (5). 625–645.

Skorczynska, Hanna & Alice Deignan. 2006. Readership and Purpose in the Choice of Economics Metaphors. *Metaphor and Symbol* 21 (2). 87–104.

White, Michael. 2003. Metaphor and economics: The case of growth. *English for Specific Purposes* 9. 131–151.

Xinhua. 2016. 15 years in WTO, China now standing as standard bearer of globalization. *China Daily (Europe).*

Xinhua. 2017 http://www.xinhuanet.com//english/2017-06/01/c_136331819.htm (dated 2017, accessed 2 Jan 2019).

Ekaterina Isaeva and Olga Burdina

Transdiscursive term transformation: The evidence from cognitive discursive research of the term 'virus'

Abstract: Current development of modern information oriented society requires special attention to the process of knowledge transfer and acquisition. This claim is particularly relevant for the sphere of professional communication, where "inadequate knowledge transfer and the ensuing ambiguity in knowledge acquisition result in problems on language and conceptual levels" (Bogatikova, Isaeva, Rukavishnikova 2014a). The evidence suggests that targeted language use underpins the deliberate conceptual frame creation, thus, provides a solid ground for adequate special knowledge transfer (Beger 2011; Bogatikova et al. 2014b, Cameron 2003; Steen 2011).

Another feature of modern society is the interplay of two opposite trends: intensification and specification of separate scientific fields, on the one hand, and reinforcement of interdisciplinary links, on the other hand. Hence, we believe, that the study of terminology that provides deep understanding and insight into the fundamental knowledge of a particular field of science as well as reasoning for interdisciplinary knowledge continuity is particularly topical.

Our research centered on the issue of term semantic transformation in different discourses provides evidence on both etymological and metaphorical consistency of the term *virus* in medical, pharmaceutical, and computer discourses. The invariability of conceptual frames of *virus* in the three discourses mentioned above has been proved via the implementation of the Five step method (Steen 2007).

Subsequently, we discuss the implication of our research for the special knowledge transfer enhancement, namely deliberate term usage for framing, coherent with both background and scientific knowledge of an addressee.

Keywords: metaphor in terminology, special knowledge transfer, computer discourse, medical discourse, pharmaceutical discourse

---

Ekaterina Isaeva, Department of English Professional Communication, Perm State University, Perm, Russia
Olga Burdina, Perm State Pharmaceutical Academy, Perm, Russia

https://doi.org/10.1515/9783110629460-005

1 The background of cognitive discursive studies of terminology

The current stage of society development can be described as information oriented. It is focused on finding effective ways of perceiving and transmitting various kinds of information including the broadcast of specialized knowledge. A distinctive feature of modern science is the interaction of two opposing trends: intensification and specification of separate scientific fields, on the one hand, and interdisciplinary links strengthening, on the other. This trend is particularly evident in the academic sphere with the growing number of interdisciplinary scientific journals (FACHSPRACHE, Interdisciplinary Sciences: Computational Life Sciences, Automatic Documentation and Mathematical Linguistics), dissertations (e.g., more than 15 PhD dissertations on linguistic research in different scientific areas, such as Medicine, Philosophy, Pedagogics, Computer security, Pharmacy, and others have been defended in Perm State University under the supervision of professor S.L. Mishlanova), research projects (e.g., the Russian foundation for basic research annually provides funding for projects of oriented fundamental research on interdisciplinary subjects of current interest), university courses (Applied mathematics and physics, Computational linguistics, Historical geography, Neurophysics, Neurobiology, and Geophysics) etc. The scope and implication of this tendency will be discussed further in the paper. These trends heightened great interest in the study of language for specific purposes, which captures specialized knowledge in language and represents this knowledge verbally in discourse.

It is a widely accepted notion, that the term in the system of science expresses a special concept (Golovin and Kobrin 1987; Grinev 1993; Superanskaya, Podolskaya, and Vasilyeva 2012), which changes in the process of functioning, hence the term appears as a dynamic phenomenon of language developing in a special discourse (Alekseeva 1998b; Burdina and Mishlanova 2017; Golovanova 2009; Karasik 1998; Leichik 2007; Manerko 2009; Shelov 1998).

In cognitive terminology, the variability of the term is one of the leading concepts, since the term is understood as a developing, dynamic phenomenon of language that "can reflect the existing structures of knowledge that organize the whole system of information representing a particular sphere of human activity"(Manerko 2009; Manerko, Baumann, and Kalverkämper 2014).

In the monograph by L. M. Alekseeva and S. L. Mishlanova the term is defined as "a component of the dynamic model of language, dialectically combining a stable sign system and its constant rethinking[1]" (Alekseeva and

1 Authors' translation

Mishlanova 2002: 15). The correlation of the term with the professional sphere is also indicated by E.I. Golovanova, defining the terms as "special nominative signs", created for "the designation of objects, phenomena, relations, communicatively and cognitively significant only in a special semiotic space – the space of one or another professional activity ... Only within some professional sphere terms are systematic, show their constitutive orientation properties, and perform many functions assigned to them. ... The term is a verbalized result of professional thinking, meaningful lingvocognitive means of orientation in professional communication. In the term, the mechanisms of cognition of a particular area of knowledge or activity are realized and the structures of special knowledge, which serve as the starting point in the comprehension of professional space and contribute to the optimal organization of the specialists' activity, are represented.[2]" (Golovanova 2008: 65–66). In this context term formation is seen as "the process of development of a terminological unit in the text, as a certain moment of verbal communication[3]" (Alekseeva 1998a: 7). The text in this case is understood as any speech construction containing a complete message about the results of the researcher' cognitive activity. The information enclosed in the term is information about a certain fragment of the world, about the mental form of reflection of this fragment, about the conditions for using such a sign and about its connection with other signs. The information is stored in the term in a structured form, as a complex of concepts, linked hierarchically and logically (Massalina and Novodranova 2009: 72). Many Russian cognitive terminologists, such as L.A. Manerko, V.F. Novodranova and others acknowledge the fact that concepts contain sensory, emotional, and evaluative components, which sometimes causes reduction of rational and growth of subjective components in the knowledge structure objectivized by the term.

This diversity and complexity of knowledge structure comprised by the term is reinforced with another topical problem of knowledge communication studies, namely adequacy of information perception by specialists working in related fields of knowledge. The problem is caused by intersection of terminologies of different scientific domains. A term borrowed from one field of knowledge to another one, acquires an additional semantic component and loses some part of its original content, enters into new system relations, and assimilates to the host science. Hence, the new semantics of the term is determined by both the place it

2 Authors' translation

3 Authors' translation

occupies in the term system of the scientific domain (Tabanakova and Koviazina 2007: 23) and its original semantic content.

As we have already discussed, knowledge in different sciences may be designated with the same term, however the semantics of the term actualized in different fields of science may differ to such an extent, that despite the etymological unity, the terms are perceived as homonyms.

These aspects of the term existence and evolution in different scientific areas are subject for cognitive discursive studies of potential term's metaphoricity as mapping of certain cognitive frames from one special knowledge domain to another one. This idea is comprehensively developed in the Perm school of metaphor initiated by L.M. Alekseeva and S.L. Mishlanova in Perm State University (Russia). The School works in the framework of anthropocentric paradigm of linguistics, which provides "new perspectives of metaphor studies, broadens the research context (the study of the language in man and for man), and thereby allows to consider the metaphor not only as a phenomenon of language, but also as a unique semiotic mechanism that determines the interaction of people in the process of their activity[4]" (Alekseeva, Mishlanova 2017: 9).

"It is noteworthy that the interrelation of cognitive and linguistic, derivational processes was put in the basis of the derivational theory of metaphor, having been developed in the studies of Perm linguists for four decades. ... The peculiarity of the Permian view on the metaphor was that the space of metaphor research was not limited to the word: the metaphor was understood as a phenomenon mediated by many factors, text, professional communication, and discourse" (Alekseeva, Mishlanova 2017: 9).

Following the tradition of the Perm School of metaphor we explore peculiarities of the term development in different fields of science. The aim of this study is to investigate the specificity of terminologisation of the word *virus* in three contemporary discourses, namely medical, pharmaceutical, and computer (computer security discourse).

To achieve this goal, we have analyzed the etymology of the lexical unit *virus*, considered the development of its polysemy and variability in different branches of knowledge, as well as the role of metaphorization featuring corresponding scientific discoveries.

4 Authors' translation

2 Etymology of the term *virus*

2.1 Etymological analysis of the words with the meaning "poison"

As known, vocabulary is the most flexible level of the language and the meaning of language units, including terms can change dramatically even over a short period of time.

The current meaning of the word *virus* in the Definition dictionary by S. I. Ozhegov, which is one of the most widely used dictionary in Russia, is defined as follows:

1) *Вирус, -а, м. Мельчайшая неклеточная частица, размножающаяся в живых клетках, возбудитель инфекционного заболевания. В. индивидуализма, стяжательства (перен.). * Компьютерный вирус (спец.) – специально созданная небольшая программа (в 6 знач.), способная присоединяться к другим программам ЭВМ, засорять оперативную память и выполнять другие нежелательные действия. || I прил. вирусный, -ая, -ое. В. грипп (Толковый словарь С.И. Ожегова, http://enc-dic.com/ozhegov/Virus-3399.html).*

   [Virus is the smallest noncellular particle, which propagates in living cells, pathogen agent of an infectious disease. e.g., the virus of individualism, the virus of acquisitiveness (indirect meaning). *Computer virus is a specially designed small program, capable of attaching itself to other computer programs, contaminating random access memory, and executing other unauthorized actions. adj. viral, e.g., viral influenza. *http://enc-dic.com/ozhegov/Virus-3399.html*]

As we can see, the main components of the mining of the word virus are small size and contamination. As presented above, the modern online edition of the dictionary by S. I. Ozhegov contains additional special meaning of a computer virus. The earlier hard copy of the dictionary, issued in 1994 did not contain any reference to a virus as a computer program:

> *Вирус, а, м. Мельчайший микроорганизм, возбудитель заразной болезни. В. Индивидуализма (перен.) || прил. вирусный, -ая, -ое. В. грипп. (Ожегов 1994: 72).*
>
> [Virus is the smallest microorganism, pathogen agent of an infectious disease. e.g., the virus of individualism (indirect meaning) adj. viral, e.g., viral influenza. (Ozhegov 1994: 72)]

Other modern dictionaries also record these basic meanings:

2) *Вирус -а; м. (мн. вирусы́, -ов). [от лат. virus – яд] 1. собир. Мельчайшие микроорганизмы, размножающиеся внутри живых клеток и вызывающие инфекционные заболевания у человека, животных, растений. Стойкий, нестойкий в. В. гриппа. 2. только ед. чего. О том, что является возбудителем каких-л. нежелательных социальных, психологических и т.п. явлений. В. индивидуализма. В. стяжательства. 3. Информ. Программа, способная самопроизвольно подсоединяться к другим программам компьютера и вызывать сбои в их работе. Компьютерный в. Проверить дискету на в. Ви́русный, -ая, -ое. В. грипп. В-ая инфекция. (Кузнецов 2010)*

[Viruses – 1) the smallest microorganisms, propagating inside living cells and infecting humans, animals, and plants. e.g., persistent, non-persistent virus, influenza virus; 2) something, which causes some unwanted social, psychological etc. phenomena. e.g., the virus of individualism, the virus of acquisitiveness. 3) in IT: a program that can automatically attach to other computer programs and cause malfunction. e.g., computer virus, scan the floppy for viruses, viral, viral influenza, viral infection (Kuznetsov 2010)].

3) *Ви́рус сущ., м., употр. сравн. часто.*
Морфология: (нет) чего? ви́руса, чему? ви́русу, (вижу) что? ви́рус, чем? ви́русом, о чём? о ви́русе; мн. что? ви́русы, (нет) чего? ви́русов, чему? ви́русам, (вижу) что? ви́русы, чем? ви́русами, о чём? о ви́русах.

1. Вирус – это мельчайший микроорганизм, который размножается в живых клетках и вызывает различные заболевания у человека, животных, растений. Вирус гриппа. | Трансформация вируса. | Люди, инфицированные вирусом СПИДа. | Вирус размножается. 2. Информационный, компьютерный вирус – это программа, цель которой в том, чтобы проникать в компьютерные сети, системы и причинять им вред. Вирусы часто пересылаются в виде приложений к электронной почте. Этот вирус разрушает системы распространения электронной почты, заставляя компьютер посылать в различные адреса огромное количество зараженных документов. • ви́русный прил. Вирусная инфекция. • вирусоло́гия сущ., ж. (Дмитриев: 2003 http://enc-dic.com/dmytriev/Virus-3432/).

[Virus, noun, relatively often used (morphology provided).

1. Virus is the smallest microorganism, which propagates in living cells and causes human, animals, and plants to have different illnesses. e.g., influenza virus, virus transformation, people infected with the AIDS virus, virus

proliferates. 2. Computer virus is a program, which aims at penetration into computer networks and computer systems and cause harm. e.g., Viruses are often sent as mail attachment. This virus destroys the systems of email delivery, making a computer send a huge number of infected documents to various email addresses. Viral – adjective. e.g., viral infection. Virology – noun. (Dmitriev 2003; http://enc-dic.com/dmytriev/Virus-3432/)]

Interestingly, not only the meaning 'a malicious computer program', but also 'small size' and 'infection' are not the original features of the word virus. This idea can be proved if we consider its etymology. By the etymological analysis of the term *virus* we have examined its origin (it came to the professional communication from the Latin language), semantics (it contains the meaning poison), and have defined its position in the range of other Latin words with the same meaning.

Initially the word virus meant 'poison'. Beside the word *virus*, the Latin meaning of poison is represented by the lexemes *toxicum* (in Greek *toxicon*) and *venenum*, which have a number of specific features. But just the lexeme virus had been widely used in special disciplines, such as Biology, Microbiology, and Medicine, and later was employed in a new developing terminology of Computer Security. The question why among these three synonymous lexemes the lexeme virus got more developed will be answered in the course of dictionaries data analysis. For this purpose, we have chosen the following dictionaries: the Latin-Russian dictionary edited by K.A. Tanaushenko (2002), which according to its annotation includes both vocabulary "from the classical period of development of the Latin language and the terms of anatomic, medical, pharmaceutical, chemical, and biological nomenclatures", and the Latin-Russian dictionary by I. Kh. Dvoretskii (2000) which is an expert scholarly edition among Latin – Russian and Russian – Latin dictionaries in Russia, the one which represents classic Latin.

Having examined the above-mentioned dictionaries we found out, that the most common, neutral meaning is delivered by *toxicum*. According to the Latin-Russian dictionary by K. A. Tanaushenko this word means as follows:

1) *toxicon* or *toxicum*, i *n* – poison for arrows, poison (in general).

The entry also contains the cognate adjective:

2) *toxĭcus, f, um* in medicine – toxic, poisonous.

The word is marked as specific usage in scientific area, i.e. medicine. The entry also includes cognate medical terms: *toxaemia, ae f* – presence of toxic substances in blood, *toxicologia, ae f* – science about toxic substances, *toxicosis, is f* – disease caused by toxic substanses.

The Latin-Russian dictionary by I. Kh. Dvoretskii records the same meanings:

1) *toxicum* and *toxicon*, i *n* (Greek) 1) poison for arrows; 2) poison (in general).

This dictionary has also got the meaning of the cognate to the word *toxicum* adjective:

2) *toxicatus, a, um* – (Greek) poisoned.

Thus, the word *toxicum*, adopted to Latin from Greek, has the general meaning 'poison' and is widely used in medicine as a derivational element (-tox-) in the term formation of clinical medicine, the feature typical of the words of the Greek origin.

The word *venenum* means a toxin produced by venomous animals and injected into victims by means of a bite, sting or other sharp body features. In the ancient Greek mythology *venenum* is a phytotoxin, liquid potion, prepared by Venus, who was a love goddess. This potion had a besotting effect on people, but it was not a deadly potion.

The specificity of the usage of the word *venenum* is also connected with its etymology. The word *venenum* is cognate with the name of Venus, the goddess of love. This contributes to the meaning of the word, which includes magic potion, magic drink, spell, charm, and poison (only the third meaning of the word). The word also contains the semes death, misery, paint, dye, remedy, and balm, which are inherent in love and the languor of love (extract from a medical plant); later it acquired a negative connotation, i.e. phytotoxin. The name of the goddess (*Vĕnus, ĕris f*, Venus, Jove and Dione's daughter or sea-born, according to another myth, Vulkan's wife, Cupid and Aeneas's mother; the ancestress of the Julian race (Tanaushenko 2002) is frequently used as a poetic symbol of love, both sublime and physical. Accordingly, this word appears in pharmaceutical and medical terminology as designation of phytotoxin (*venenum)* in the former and notation of sexually transmitted diseases (*morbus venerius* – veneral diseases caused by love, a derivative of *venereus, a, um* as fleshy, sexual) in the latter.

The dictionary by K. A. Tanaushenko comprises the definitions of the following cognate to the lexeme *venenum* words*:*

1) *venēnum, i n* (1) juice; (2) poisoned drink, venom, poison; (3) poison, death, misfortune; (4) magic drink, spell; 5) colouring matter, dye, purple paint, blusher.
2) *venefica, ae f* 1) the one who makes poison; (2) enchantress, sorceress (p. 899)

3) *veneficium, i n* (1) making poison; (2) poisoning; (3) poisonous drink; (4) preparing magic portion; (5) spellcraft.
4) *I veneficicus, a, um* (1) poisonous; (2) mesmerizing, magic.
5) *II veneficicus, i m* (1) the one who makes poison, poisoner; (2) wizard, magician.
6) *venenatus, a, um* (1) poisonous; (2) acrid, sharp; (3) dangerous, harmful; (4) mesmerizing, magic.
7) *venenĭfer, ĕra, ĕrum* poison bearing, venomous.
8) *venēno, āvi, ātum, āre* to poison (pp. 672–673).

As shown above the initial meaning of the word *venenum* is love portion made by Venus. Note that among the three words with the meaning 'poison' the preeminently *venenum* has the widest derivational field which contains Latin suffixes adding special shade of meaning to the words:
- suffix *-fic-* (derivative of the verb facio, denoting a dynamic action) is particularly productive in Latin word building; adds the meaning 'active', i.e. *veneficicus, a, um* (this type of word building is found in *portentifficus, a, um*. It means magic, portentous, which is the derivative of (1) *portentum, I n* meaning portent, omen, Prodigium, miracle; (2) *portendo, tendi, tentum, ere,* which stands for show, portend, herald. Compare with the standard adjectival suffix -os- in *portentosus, a, um* which means unusual, unnatural, supernatural)
- suffix *-fer-* with the meaning 'bring', derivative of the word *venenĭfer* standing for poison-bearing is also a productive suffix in Latin word building (e.g., the term *apis mellifera* is honey bee, from the Latin *Mel, mellis*, i.e., honey).
- suffix *–at* means 'containing', *venenatus* literally means 'containing poison', that is why it is used in the attribute of *planta venenata* (containing poison, poisonous plant). This is a productive suffix in pharmacy, namely in technologic terms: *charta paraffinata, charta cerata* (waxed paper as the type of special packing of medical products, paper covered with wax for preserving conditions for technologically correct storing of medical products); in the nomenclature of fixed combinations: *Linimentum ammoniatum* (ammonium liniment, i.e. liniment containing ammonia), *Unguenum camphoratum* (camphor ointment, i.e., salve which contains camphor).

It should be noted, that the adjectives *venenatus, a, um* and *venenosus, a, um* are frequently used as a specific signifier in the botanical, biological, and microbiological nomenclatures: *Rhus venenata* (poison sumac; archaic name of a plant *Toxicodéndron vérnix* laked decandiol), *Macrolepiota venenata* (poisonous lepiota), *Fusarium venenatum* (poisonous fusarium), *Toxicoscordion venenosum* (death camas) and others.

The third term *virus* stands for a slimy liquid, slime, a potent juice in its first meaning, and poison, especially of snakes, venom, poisonous secretion. Generalizing these meanings, we derive the meaning of *virus* as poison obtained from slime, secretion, and potent juice of animals. In addition, the word comprises a quality seme (toxicity, sarcasm, acrimony, bite), as well as olfactory and gustatory characteristics (disgusting smell, stench, pungent taste), namely, according to the dictionary by K.A. Tanaushenko (2002: 913):

1) *virus, i n* 1) juice, slime; 2) poison; 3) *in biology* virus.
2) *virosus, a, um* stinking, fetid;
according to the dictionary by I. Kh. Dvoretskii (2000):
3) *virus, i n* 1) slime (cochlearum *PM*); slimy juice (pastinaceae *PM*), animal seminal fluid V, PM; 2) poisonous exudation, poison (*serpentis V*): *ferro v. inest O* envenom arrow; 3) virulence, vitrol, acrimony, acidity (*acerbitatis C; linguae, mentis Sil*); 4) sharp disgusting smell, stench (*paludis Col; animae ursi pestilens v. PL*); 5) acrid taste, heat (*vini PM*); poignancy, bitterness (*sc. maris Lcr; ponti Man*).[5]
4) II *virosus, a, um* [virus] 1) covered with slime (*piscis CC*); 2) redolent (*castorea V*); 3) poisonous (spinae – *Ap*)[6]
5) *virulentia, ae f* [virulentus] stench (*hircorum Sid*)[7]
6) *virulentus, a, um* [virus] poisonous (serpens *AG*); *indirect* pernicious (pestis[8] *Eccl*).

So, we can state, that the lexeme *virus* acquired a stable meaning "animals' byproduct". Note that in pharmacy the term *virus* is used literally as zootoxin, poison, obtained from animals, which results in the appearance of the terms *virus apium* (apitoxin) and *virus viperarum* (snake venom), still used in medication orders.

It should be pointed out, that the academic dictionary does not contain the meaning 'small size', 'infection'. These meanings appeared later with the development of biological (precisely microbiological) terminology.

---

5 virus cochlearum – snail slime, virus pastinaceae – the slime of plants of the parsnip family; virus serpentis – snake venom; virus paludis – swamp smell; animae ursi pestilens – the smell of a sick (plague) animal, bear; virus vini – wine sharpness, virus maris, ponti – bitterness / sourness of the sea, sea depths (the shaft of sea waves). Here and after the notes are ours (by E. Isaeva and O. Burdina)

6 The first example is translated as 'fish slime', the second – 'castor', the third – cerebral (spinal) substance of the animal and fish chines.

7 virulentia hircorum – goat stench.

8 Pestis – pestilential.

As a result of the etymological analysis of the words with the meaning 'poison', used in in the terminologies and nomenclatures of such natural sciences as medicine, pharmacy, biology, microbiology, and botany we can draw the following conclusions:

- all three terms have their own specificity in their meaning, what enabled their integration into terminologies of different scientific areas;
- on the basis of the general seme poison the three words establish genus-species relationships; here the generic word is *toxicum*, while *virus* and *venenum* have a more partitive, specific, and clarifying meaning: zootoxin and phytotoxin respectively, which are lexicalized in educational and reference materials in the Latin language for students of medical and pharmaceutical universities (for example, in the textbook "*The Latin language and medical terminology basics*" by M. N. Cherniavsky).

2.2 Evolution of the term *virus*

As we mentioned earlier it took some time for the word virus to acquire its current meaning as a small particle capable of infecting other organisms. The dynamics of the word virus and the appearance of the new meaning are connected with the development of microbiology.

The modern meaning of the word virus appeared after 1892, when the Russian botanist D. I. Ivanovskii established filterability of the pathogen agent of the mosaic disease of a tobacco plant (tobacco mosaic). He showed, that when the cellular fluid of the plants infected with this disease is infiltrated through the filters constraining bacteria, preserve the ability to infect sound plants. Five years later another filterable agent, namely the causative agent of Aphtae episootica (foot and mouth disease of cattle) was discovered by the German bacteriologist F. Lefler. In 1898 the Dutch botanist M.W. Beijerinck has repeated these experiments in an extended form and managed to confirm D.I. Ivanovskii's findings. He named the filterable poisonous agent causing tobacco mosaic a "filterable virus" (Knowledge fund "Lomonosov", virus, http://www.lomonosov-fund.ru/enc/ru/encyclopedia:0130031).

The word virus appeared to be the most productive of the three Latin words with the seme poison, for the rest are used with a narrow (specialized) meaning and have fewer derivational capabilities.

This may be due to the seme of activity, only inherent to the lexeme *virus*, i.e. it is the subject of an action (animal, a living being that produces poison). In contrast to *virus, venenum* stands for a poison that is extracted, which means being an object of an action; likewise, *toxicum* is mainly a quality and a characteristic of an effect a substance or an object has on an organism.

Thus, the word virus underwent the stage of terminologisation and became the term for designation of a harmful biological agent of a cell.

2.3 Specialization of the term *virus*

The pace of science development has led to a widespread use of the term *virus* in various fields of knowledge. This entailed specialization (semantic discrepancy) of the term. In our study we consider specialized meanings of this term in the medical (including biological and microbiological), pharmaceutical, and computer discourses.

Current approach to terms interprets them as dynamic phenomena (Alekseeva 1998; Alekseeva and Mishlanova 2002), which undergo the process of terminologization. The latter is understood not only as the process of words transition from the language for general purposes to the language for special purposes but including the further development of the terms. This development, i.e., the appearance of new meanings, leads to the emergence of polysemy. Due to this, in the cognitive perspective terminologisation is described as a two-stage process. Herewith, the first stage of a lexical unit transition from a general vocabulary to a special one is traditionally distinguished by linguists as terminologisation itself, while the second stage is understood as a further development of a linguistic unit in a specialized sphere, which causes the development of intrabranch polysemy.

Indeed, in microbiology the term virus has undergone its development, i.e. there has appeared the whole class of viruses (*Viridae*) which are "any member of a unique class of infectious agents, which were originally distinguished by their smallness (hence, they were described as filtrable" because of their ability to pass through fine ceramic filters that blocked all cells, including bacteria) and their inability to replicate outside of and without assistance of a living host cell. Because these properties are shared by certain bacteria (rickettsiae, chlamydiae), viruses are now characterized by their simple organization and their unique mode of replication. A virus consists of genetic material, which may be either DNA or RNA, and is surrounded by a protein coat and, in some viruses, by a membranous envelope" (The Free Dictionary, https://medical-dictionary.thefreedictionary.com/). There have occurred derivatives, such as *virion*, as the infectious form of a virus as it exists outside the host cell, consisting of a nucleic acid core, a protein coat, and, in some species, an external envelope (http://www.dictionary.com/browse/virion); classifications of viruses. A characteristic feature of viruses is that a viron contains only one of the nucleic acids: either DNA or RNA. Other living organisms contain both DNA and RNA simultaneously. Depending on the type of nucleic acid, the viruses can be divided into two large groups: DNA-containing and RNA-containing. The virus nucleic acid can consist of one strand (single-stranded) or two strands (double-stranded). Almost all RNA-containing viruses have a single-stranded RNA in their genome. DNA-containing viruses often have double-stranded DNA and rarely single-stranded DNA.

The dynamics of a knowledge field also implies change in the language for special purposes of this science and, consequently, fixation of new concepts in term systems (Alekseeva, Isaeva, and Mishlanova 2013; Golovanova 2008; Isaeva and Mishlanova 2013). As far as "a term system is commonly understood as a symbolic model of a particular theory of a specialized knowledge field, elements of which are lexical units (words and word combinations) of a certain natural language, and in general its structure is isomorphic to the structure of concepts of the theory[9]"(Shidlovskaya 2001: 104), a term system of any science develops along with the development of scientific knowledge, and at various stages of its formation it is enriched with new terms.

Although the term *virus* got a new role and development in the new term system, it has preserved its particular features: the virus is understood as a living process, ability to transfer a product/condition/information (as previously noted, to produce fluid/ excretion/smell), bearing an unpleasant for the receiver content. This means, that to some extent the term has its "genetic memory".

It is worthwhile mentioning, that the same tendency is observed in a new borrowing of the term *virus* in a completely new term system of computer security. One would think that this is an essentially different type of science. Information technology seems to have nothing in common with physiological and biological processes reflected in a computer term *virus*. However, the metaphorical mapping of the term into the new knowledge domain exhibits the main viral features in through the prism of the new digital reality, namely the ability of malware programs to interfere into the computer "living" activities and damage its running programs. Thus, the "genetic memory" of *zootoxin* helped the term virus not only to assimilate in the new term system, but also map some collocations originated in the previous term systems: *virus infects*, *virus evolves*, *virus reproduces*, *virus propagates*, *asexual reproduction*, *dissemination of viruses*, etc.

It is also interesting to observe the return of the term into the terminology where it used to be in practice. Likewise the term *virus* is employed in pharmaceutical terminology to designate the use animals' emissions as form of medication, e.g., snake and bee venom (*virus viperarum, virus apium*). Notably that the word *virus* is not used in the invented name of the medicine based on this product, but there is a reference to the animal, produced this substance. Furthermore the names of drugs containing the snake or bee venom, have such term elements as *-ap-* (from

9 Authors' translation

apis, i.e. bee), e.g., *Apisarthronum* (ointment, preparation of bee venom), *-vip (er)* – (from *vipera* i.e. snake), e.g., *Vipraxinum, Viperalginum* (aqueous solution of a common viper venom), *Nigvisal* (ointment with viper venom), or even in combination with the term element *-tox-* (from *toxum*, i.e. poison), e.g., *Vipratox* (Driomova and Bereznikova 2002: 89). However the segment *-vir-* is encountered in the names of drug preparation, but it denotes not the source of the substance it is made of, but its pharmacological class, namely the medications, eliminating a virus as a harmful small in size object able to propagate in a living organism, which in fact is the component of that term virus, the notion of which has been developed in microbiology, e.g., the names of antiviral drugs, such as *Zovirax* and *Acyclovir* (Burdina 2012: 83–84). This means, that the *virus*, which occurs in the names of antiviral drags becomes the homonym to the *virus* in the names of the medicines *Virus viperarum* and *Virus apium*, for they do not contain a common seme (this seme has been destroyed in the process of terminologisation of the term *virus* in biology).

Thus, in the literal sense the term *virus* is used in pharmacy, where it means zootoxin, i.e. poison obtained from an animal, which is reflected in the nomenclature units *virus viperarum* 'snake venom' and *virus apium* 'bee venom'. In other professional discourses, the term evolves in a different way.

2.4 Metaphorization of the term *virus*

Particular interest in the lexeme *virus* is connected with the fact that on its basis as a result of metaphorization the terms of two distantly related fields of knowledge, namely medicine and information technology were created. By metaphorization we mean a universal cognitive mechanism of naive and scientific knowledge integration, based on the transfer of the system of concepts from the Source domain to the Target domain (Lakoff and Johnson 1980).

In the computer discourse the term *virus* was originally introduced by Jürgen Kraus in "Selbstreproduktion bei Programmen" (Kraus 1980). In particular J. Kraus notes that living cells are characterized by the ability of self-replication and mutation. These qualities set the analogy in the field of information technology, comparing a self-replicating computer program with a living cell. To continue the analogy, J. Kraus indicates that biological viruses are not full featured organisms, but they are matter particles, i.e. they only consist of DNA. Their vital processes, such as self-replication and mutation occur if there are cells producing building materials and energy. The same features are also typical of self-replicating programs, i.e. such a computer program is not recognized until it penetrates an operating system. Only inside a computer when software is started the program is capable of self-replication and mutation using the energy of the computer.

Here is an example of how the polysemy of the term *virus* is explicated in the computer discourse. In a specialized information and computer technology dictionary we identify the following components of the computer virus concept: a program penetrating into a computer system, a malicious code; a malicious action (Vaulina 2003). Each of the above-mentioned meaning components has been derived in the process of metaphorization by mapping signs of biological and medical phenomena onto an item belonging to a new field of knowledge.

On the grounds of invariant semes such as small size, the ability to penetrate into other objects, and the risk of infection in the meaning of the lexeme *virus*, both in the medical and the computer discourses, which is reflected in the relevant specialized dictionaries (Vaulina 2003), it must be assumed that these properties are metaphorical mapping of medical knowledge onto the knowledge in the field of computer technology. This is due to the invariance principle described by Lakoff and Turner (1989), which consists in preservation of the Target domain topological stability even when mapping the Source domain model upon it. To prove this assumption, the contextual analysis of collocations of the word *virus* found in the specialized journals PC World, Compute!, and Popular Mechanics was carried out. These journals are specialized for Information Technology experts and are available in the Corpus of Contemporary American English (COCA). The results of the analysis were used to compile a concordance of collocations of the lexeme *virus* in the computer technology discourse.

3 Conceptual analysis of the term *virus*

To determine the peculiarities of conceptual mappings and framing the concept VIRUS we carried out the conceptual analysis (Steen 2007: 197–226) of the tokens where the Source Domain of a metaphorical mapping is not obvious from the introspective approach. The Five Step Method developed by G. Steen is the way to reconstruct indirect mappings on the basis of pre-identified metaphor related words in the text.

This procedure consists of five steps: 1) identification of metaphorical focuses; 2) identification of metaphorical ideas; 3) identification of indirect comparisons; 4) identification of indirect analogies; 5) identification of indirect mappings. (A detailed description of the procedure is presented in *Finding metaphor in grammar and usage: A methodological analysis of theory and research* (Steen 2007: 197–226).

Let us consider an example illustrating the application of the Five Step Method for simulating indirect mappings in an except from the article Virucide! by Stan Miastkowski, stored in the Corpus of Contemporary American English (indexed as COCA:1999:MAG PCWorld). This is "the largest freely-available corpus of English, and the only large and balanced corpus of American English. ... The corpus contains more than 560 million words of text (20 million words each year 1990–2017) and it is equally divided among spoken, fiction, popular magazines, newspapers, and academic texts (https://corpus.byu.edu/coca/x1.asp accessed 07.12.2017).

Example 1
File viruses still afflict the unwary, though less often than they did a few years ago (Miastkowski, S. (1999) Virucide! PC World. Vol. 17, Iss. 2; pg. 123).

Step 1. Identification of metaphorical focuses

A metaphorical focus is an expression that activates a "concept which cannot be literally applied to the referents in the world evoked by the text" (Steen, 1999: 61). For this purpose, we have applied Metaphor identification procedure (Pragglejaz Group 2007). The procedure comprises: (a) identification of the contextual meaning of a word under analysis, i.e., "how it applies to an entity, relation, or attribute in the situation evoked by the text" (Pragglejaz Group 2007: 3); (b) identification of a more basic meaning of the word in other contexts than the one in the given context (i.e. the meaning which is more physical, "concrete, easier to imagine, see, hear, feel, smell, or taste"; "more precise (as opposed to vague)", actual, body related, or "historically older" (Pragglejaz Group 2007: 3); (c) comparison of the contextual and basic meaning; (d) evaluation of similarity and contrast of the meanings. If the word "has a more basic ... meaning in other contexts than the given context" and "the contextual meaning contrasts with the basic meaning but can be understood in comparison with it, ... mark the lexical unit as metaphorical" (Pragglejaz Group 2007: 3).

In this extract the metaphorical focus is designated by the lexemes: *virus, file*, and *afflict*, for their contextual and basic meanings are in contrast, but the former meaning can be comprehended from the latter, as illustrated bellow:

virus – the contextual meaning is "a program that enters your computer and damages or destroys information that you have stored" (https://www.macmillandictionary.com/dictionary/british/virus (accessed 07.12.2017), the basic meaning is "a simple living thing that is smaller than bacteria and that can enter your body and make you ill; a disease caused by a virus" (https://www.macmillandictionary.com/dictionary/british/virus (accessed 07.12.2017)),

afflict – the contextual meaning is "inflict damage" (https://www.thefreedictionary.com/afflict (accessed 07.12.2017)), affect a digital device with a malware code; the basic meaning is "if you are afflicted by an illness or serious problem, you suffer from it" (https://www.macmillandictionary.com/dictionary/british/afflict (accessed 07.12.2017));

afflict is generally used with living beings; inflict is generally used with inanimate objects inflict takes 'on,' afflict takes 'with' (http://thesaurus.com/browse/afflict?s=t (accessed 17.12.2017)

file – the contextual meaning is "a collection of data or program records stored as a unit with a single name" (http://ahdictionary.com (accessed 03.12.2016)), a more basic meaning is a box or container in which papers are kept together (https://www.macmillandictionary.com/dictionary/british/file_1 (accessed 03.12.2016)), or taking into account, that the word afflict is mostly used with living beings, another more basic and bodily related meaning is "a line of people walking or standing behind each other" (https://www.macmillandictionary.com/dictionary/british/file_1 (accessed 03.12.2016)).

Step 2. Identification of metaphorical ideas

The second step is devoted to the examination of conceptual structures elicited by the focuses of metaphor. To link the words in the utterance and the concepts we build "linearly and hierarchically ordered series of propositions" (Steen 1999: 90). According to G. Steen (1999), a proposition is described as a minimal distinguished idea unit, which is represented in a form of a predicate and one or more arguments (linear distribution). The hierarchy starts with the proposition determining the main piece of information, which is usually conveyed by the predicate and the subject of the sentence, which is followed by the propositions denoting some relations, mostly between the subjects, objects, predicates, and their modifiers. These propositions appear subsequently lower in the hierarchy.

P1: (AFFLICTs P2t UNWARY) (1)
P2: (MOD VIRUSt FILEt) (2)
P3: (MOD AFLICT STILL)
P4: (THOUGH P5)
P5: (MOD P1 P6)
P6: (MOD OFTEN LITTLE)
P6: (COMARE P5 P7)
P7: (MOD P1 P8)
P8: (MOD P9 FEW)
P9: (MOD YEAR AGO)

Step 3. Identification of indirect comparisons

The third step is aimed at an indirect comparison identification. This "involves transition from activated concepts to the referents they designate in the projected text world" (Steen 2011: 91). This is done by means of splitting propositions, which contain references to both Target and Source domains, into two parallel lines, representing either concepts of the Target or Source domains. Each concept has a variable referent in the parallel domain line. These referents are signified with variables F, x, y and G, a, b substituting predicates and two arguments in the Target or Source domain respectively.

(1)
P1: (AFLICTs P2t UNWARY)
SIM{[]F, []x
[F P2 UNWARY]t
[AFLICT x UNWARY]s

(2)
P2: (MOD VIRUSt FILEt)
SIM{[]a, []b
[MOD VIRUS FILE]t
[MOD a b]s

Step 4. Identification of indirect analogies
The fourth step is devoted to the reconstruction of indirect analogies. The aim of this step is to infer concepts, which arrows in ones thought from the background knowledge automatically, triggered by the concepts that are not inherent for the current knowledge domain. Technically the reconstruction of the analogy is achieved by means of filling in the empty slots, designated with variables in the third step. The concepts to be inserted instead of the variables are determined by the dictionary entries, which define correlating meanings in corresponding knowledge domains.

(1)
SIM{
[AFFECT VIRUS UNWARY]t
[AFFLICT ILLNESS UNWARY]s

(2)
SIM{
[MOD VIRUS FILE]t
[MOD ILLNESS GROUP-OF-PEOPLE]s

Step 5. Identification of indirect mappings
In the fifth step we take down all the correlating concepts in the Target and Source domains received in the fourth step to present them in the form of the Source

– Target Domain mappings. The mappings obtained in this step are represented in Table 5.1.

Table 5.1: Example 1: Indirect mappings

Target Domain	Source Domain
VIRUS	ILLNESS
FILE	GROUP-OF-PEOPLE
AFFECT	AFFLICT

In the above example the concept VIRUS in the computer technology representing a malicious computer program that damages computer files, corresponds to the concept VIRUS representing a disease. The disease is particularly dangerous to groups of people, who either stay in a closed room or simply in contact. The reference is made to an infectious disease, which can be transmitted by contact from one person to another in a closed room. Thus, the naive understanding of a viral disease can be extrapolated to the area of computer sciences under the mechanism of metaphorization. This mechanism works automatically, appealing to the addressee's background knowledge, who subconsciously uses conventional metaphors to understand that file viruses can damage all the data within one file, i.e. stored under one name, if the user does not take any preventative measures, like installation of an antivirus program. In this case the user leaves out all the technical information of about the malicious software, its code and the way it functions within a computer system, for this information is alien for him and is not likely to become an acquired knowledge. Here we can see, that in technical text intended for a non-expert readership metaphor helps to get rid of odd information without the loss of the content.

Example 2
One of the features of a computer virus that separates it from other kinds of computer programs is that it replicates itself so that it can spread (via floppies transported from computer to computer, or networks) to other computers (Minasi, M. 1991 Computer viruses from A to Z// Compute! Vol. 13 Issue 10, p44-49).

Example 2 demonstrates that the term *virus* has preserved the semes, typical of the term *virus* in microbiology, namely being alive, capable to replicate, transmitted via some objects.

Step 1. Identification of metaphorical focuses

feature n
Contextual meaning: an important part or aspect of something (https://www.macmillandictionary.com/dictionary/british/feature_1 (accessed 09.12.2017),
Basic meaning: a part of your face such as your eyes, nose, or mouth (https://www.macmillandictionary.com/dictionary/british/feature_1 (accessed 09.12.2017))

separate v
Contextual meaning: to be the quality or detail that makes someone or something different from others (https://www.macmillandictionary.com/dictionary/british/separate_2 (accessed 09.12.2017))
Basic meaning: to divide something, or become divided, into different parts (https://www.macmillandictionary.com/dictionary/british/separate_2 (accessed 09.12.2017))

replicate v
Contextual meaning: to duplicate, copy, reproduce, or repeat (https://www.ahdictionary.com/word/search.html?q=replicate&submit.x=41&submit.y=19 (accessed 09.12.2017))
Basic meaning: To reproduce or make an exact copy or copies of (genetic material, a cell, or an organism) (https://www.ahdictionary.com/word/search.html?q=replicate&submit.x=41&submit.y=19 (accessed 09.12.2017)); if a virus or a molecule replicates, or if it replicates itself, it divides and produces exact copies of itself: the ability of DNA to replicate itself (https://www.ldoceonline.com/dictionary/replicate (accessed 09.12.2017))

spread v
Contextual meaning: to affect a lot of devices[10]
Basic meaning: if a disease spreads, or if something spreads it, it affects more people as it is passed from one person to another (https://www.macmillandictionary.com/dictionary/british/spread_1 (accessed 09.12.2017))

transport v
Contextual meaning: "to copy" the data to another location (https://www.pcmag.com/encyclopedia/term/53128/transport (accessed 09.12.2017))

10 Defined by the authors

Basic meaning: to move people or things from one place to another, usually in a vehicle (https://www.macmillandictionary.com/dictionary/british/transport_2 (accessed 09.12.2017))

network n
Contextual meaning: a set of computers that are connected to each other so that each computer can send and receive information to and from the other computers (https://www.macmillandictionary.com/dictionary/british/network_1?q=network+ (accessed 09.12.2017))
Basic meaning: a group of people, organizations, or places that are connected or that work together (https://www.macmillandictionary.com/dictionary/british/network_1?q=network+ (accessed 09.12.2017))

Step 2. Identification of metaphorical ideas
The extract under analysis is subdivided into two discourse units: DU1 – *One of the features of a computer virus that separates it from other kinds of computer programs is that it replicates itself;* DU 2 – *so that it can spread (via floppies transported from computer to computer, or networks) to other computers*

DU1
P1: (BE P5 P9)
P2: (MOD FEATUREs VIRUSt)
P3: (MOD FEATURE ONE)
P4: (SEPATATE FEATUREs VIRUSt)
P5: (FROM P4 P6)
P6: (MOD P7 OTHER)
P7: (MOD KIND PROGRAM)
P8: (MOD PROGRAM COMPUTER)
P9: (REPLICATE VIRUS)

DU2
P10: (CAN VIRUS SPREAD)
P11: (SPREAD COMPUTER TO)
P12: (MOD COMPUTER OTHER)
P13: (TRANSPORT FLOPPY VIA)
P14: (MOD FLOPPY P15)
P15: (TRANSPORT COMPUTER FROM)
P16: (TRANSPORT COMPUTER TO)
P17: (TRANSPORT NETWORK TO)

Step 3. Identification of indirect comparissons

P2: (MOD FEATUREs VIRUSt)
SIM{[]x, []b
[MOD x VIRUS]t
[MOD FEATURE b]s

P4: (SEPATATE FEATUREs VIRUSt)
SIM{[]x, []y
[SEPATATE x VIRUS]t
[SEPATATE FEATURE y]s

P9: (REPLICATE VIRUS)
SIM{[]F, []b
[F VIRUS]t
[REPLICATE b]s

P10: (CAN VIRUS SPREAD)
SIM{[]F, []b
[CAN VIRUS SPREAD]t
[CAN a b]s

P11: (SPREAD COMPUTER TO)
SIM{[]G, []b
[SPREAD COMPUTER TO]t
[G b TO]s

P13: (TRANSPORT FLOPPY VIA)
SIM{[]F, []b
[F FLOPPY VIA]t
[TRANSPORT b VIA]s

P15: (TRANSPORT COMPUTER FROM)
SIM{[]F, []b
[F COMPUTER FROM]t
[TRANSPORT b FROM]s

P16: (TRANSPORT COMPUTER TO)
SIM{[]F, []b
[F COMPUTER TO]t
[TRANSPORT b TO]s

P17: (TRANSPORT NETWORK TO)
SIM{[]F, []b
[F NETWORK TO]t
[TRANSPORT b TO]s

Step 4. Identification of indirect analogy
SIM{
[MOD FEATURE VIRUS]t
[MOD CHARACTERISTIC BIOLOGICAL-VIRUS]s

SIM{
[SEPATATE FEATURE VIRUS]t
[SEPATATE CHARACTERISTIC BIOLOGICAL-VIRUS]s

SIM{
[MAKE-COPY VIRUS]t
[REPLICATE BIOLOGICAL-VIRUS]s

SIM{
[CAN VIRUS SPREAD]t
[CAN BIOLOGICAL-VIRUS AFFECT-MORE-PEOPLE]s

SIM{
[TO SPREAD COMPUTER]t
[TO AFFECT-MORE-PEOPLE PERSON]s

SIM{
[COPY-DATA FLOPPY VIA]t
[TRANSPORT OBJECT VIA]s

P15: (TRANSPORT COMPUTER FROM)
SIM{[]F, []b
[COPY-DATA COMPUTER FROM]t
[TRANSPORT PERSON FROM]s

P16: (TRANSPORT COMPUTER TO)
SIM{[]F, []b
[COPY-DATA COMPUTER TO]t
[TRANSPORT PERSON TO]s

P17: (TRANSPORT NETWORK TO)
SIM{[]F, []b
[COPY_DATA NETWORK TO]t
[TRANSPORT GROUP-OF-PEOPLE TO]s

Step 5

The mappings obtained in Step 5 are represented in Table 5.2.

Table 5.2: Indirect mappings: Example 2

Target Domain	Source Domain
VIRUS	BIOLOGICAL-VIRUS
MAKE-COPY	REPLICATE
SPREAD	AFFECT-MORE-PEOPLE
COMPUTER	PERSON
FLOPPY	OBJECT
COPY-DATA	TRANSPORT
NETWORK	GROUP-OF-PERSONS

From the data received in Step 5 of Example 2 we can infer that here a computer virus is presented as a biological virus. Like its biological prototype, which exists in the body of one person, replicates there, is capable to be transported to the body of another person via some object (personal things or even parts of the body, like hands) and, thus, affect more people, a computer virus is part of a computer software, which is capable of making the copies of its own code and transmitting them without the computer user's concern via a storage device.

In the following example we will omit the procedure of applying the Five step method and submit only the results obtained in the fifth step providing our further inferences.

Example 3.
Here's an example of a simple virus, the Lehigh virus. The infector portion of Lehigh replicates by attaching a copy of itself to COMMAND.COM (an important part of DOS), enlarging it by about 1000 bytes. (Minasi, M. 1991 Computer viruses from A to Z// Compute! Vol. 13 Issue 10, pp. 44–49)

Table 5.3 represents the indirect mappings obtained for Example 3.

Table 5.3: Indirect mappings: Example 3

Target Domain	Source Domain
LEHIGH (VIRUS)	NIDUS-OF-INFECTION
MALWARE-CODE	INFECTOR-PORTION
MAKE-COPIES	REPLICATE
ATTACH	EMBED-INTO-DNA
DOS	GENETIC-SYSTEM
COMMAND.COM	DNA

Example 3 illustrates that the semantics of the term virus in genetics and microbiology has been mapped onto the semantics of the term virus in computer virology. Similar to a biological virus, which can replicate and embed into the DNA code and affect the host's genetic system, Lehigh virus automatically makes copies of it-self and inserts a malicious part of program code into the command line of the disc operating system.

Example 4.
For a program infector, the virus becomes active when you run the infected program (Minasi, M. 1991 Computer viruses from A to Z// Compute! Vol. 13 Issue 10, pp. 44–49).

Table 5.4 represents the indirect mappings obtained for Example 4.

Table 5.4: Indirect mappings: Example 4

Target Domain	Source Domain
VIRUS	BIOLOGICAL VIRUS
PROGRAM	CELL
RUN/USE (PROGRAM)	PRODUCE-VIRUS-PROTEIN
ACTIVE	ALIVE
INFECTED	CONTAINING-VIRUS

Example 4 provides more evidence on the analogy between a computer and biological virus. Here we can notice that the semantics of the computer term virus includes the following semes, attached to the term virus in microbiology: infection, existence inside a cell, parasitism, and dependence on the host's cell, which produces medium for the virus viability.

The examples considered in the paper illustrate the semantic diversity of the term *virus*, which contains reference to its current meaning in computer security discourse (malware, programming code, operates in a computer or the networks, etc.), as well as to the meanings it developed in other fields of science, namely medicine, biology, and pharmacy (poison, being harmful, being alive, infection, replication, penetration into a living cell, embedding into the DNA, etc.). These correspondences occur as a result of cognitive mechanism of metaphorical thinking, which helps to incorporate new concepts into the existing conceptual system, fitting them into ready-made frames. Once acquired the new knowledge enters into complementary regulations with the old knowledge, which means that the lack of frame elements is reconstructed from the analogical frame.

3 Conclusion

In this paper we have discussed the principles of cognitive-discursive approach to terms studies, paying special attention to the derivation of terms and the role of metaphor in this process. We have shown that term development is a dynamic process of knowledge fixation, representation, and modification in some knowledge areas and within interdisciplinary context. The evolution of the term has been shown on an example of the development of the term *virus*.

Based on the etymological analyses above it has been stated that the term *virus* originated from the Latin language and initially was one of three synonymous words (*virus*, *toxicum*, *venenum*) denoting poison. We have determined that thanks to the seme of activity, which was a distinctive feature of the word *virus*, this lexeme had been widely used in special disciplines, such as biology, microbiology, and medicine, and computer security.

By the end of the XX century the lexeme *virus* has undergone a number of changes. As a result of the specialization of the general meaning of poison the lexeme *virus* occurred in the medical and the pharmaceutical discourses. Therewith, the dominant semes in the medical discourse are the small size, penetration into another object, and infection, while in the pharmaceutical discourse they are zootoxin and medicine. Hence, the split of the polysemy and the formation of homonymous terms in different professional discourses take place.

The seme of activity is inherent in the term *virus* in biology (microbiology), medicine, and computer terminologies. A virus is not only capable of causing harm (poisoning or killing) but behaving like a living being (can live in another body, infect, and reproduce).

In the process of conceptualization of a new developing area of computer sciences the medical (biological, microbiological) term *virus* was used in computer terminology with the main conceptual features and relations preserved. It demonstrates that in computer security texts the term virus exhibits the semes undesirability, harmfulness, illness, pathogenicity, infectiousness, parasitism, small size. These semes confirm metaphorical nature of the term virus in computer terminology.

As a result, we have proved the evidence that terms are multi-aspect phenomena which require to be examined in language, in thought, and in communication, both statically (as a hierarchy of concepts with their cross disciplinary relations) and dynamically (as the process of term development). Our contribution to the discussion of current approaches to metaphor analysis is introduction of cognitive-discursive methodology of Perm metaphor school and the development of complex of methods for the examination of conceptual structure of terms.

Acknowledgments: The reported study was funded by RFBR according to the research project № 18-012-00825 A.

References in English

Alekseeva, Larisa M., Isaeva, Ekaterina V. & Mishlanova, Svetlana L. 2013. Metaphor in computer virology discourse. *World Applied Sciences Journal* 27 (4). 533–537.

Beger, Anke. 2011. Deliberate metaphors? An exploration of the choice and functions of metaphors in US-American college lectures. *metaphorik.de* (20).

Bogatikova, Eugeniia, Isaeva, Ekaterina & Rukavishnikova, Nadezhda. 2014. *Knowledge transfer in the scope of transdiscursive professional communication*. SGEM2014 Conference on Psychology and Psychiatry, Sociology and Healthcare, Education, Vol. 3, No. SGEM2014 Conference Proceedings, ISBN 978-619-7105-24-7/ ISSN 2367-5659, September 1-9. Vol. 3, 483–490 pp. DOI: 10.5593/sgemsocial2014/B13/S3.065.

Cameron, Linne. 2003. *Metaphor in Educational Discourse*. London/New York: Continuum.

Kraus, Jurgen. 1980. *Selbstreproduktion bei Programmen*. http://vx.netlux.org (accessed 02.03. 2013)

Lakoff, George & Mark Johnson. 1980. *Metaphors we live by*. Chicago: University of Chicago Press.

Lakoff, George & Mark Turner. 1989. *More than cool reason. A Field Guide to Poetic Metaphor*. Chicago: University of Chicago Press.

Manerko, Larissa A., Klaus-Dieter Baumann, & Hartwig Kalverkämper 2014. *Terminology science in Russia today: from the past to the future*. Frank & Timme GmbH.

Pragglejaz Group 2007 MIP: A method for identifying metaphorically used words in discourse. *Metaphor and Symbol* 22 (1). 1–39.

Steen, Gerard J. 1999. *From linguistic to conceptual metaphor in five steps*. In Raymond W. Gibbs & Gerard J. Steen (eds.), *Metaphor in cognitive linguistics*, 57–78. Amsterdam/ Philadelphia: John Benjamins.
Steen, Gerard J. 2007. *Finding metaphor in grammar and usage: A methodological analysis of theory and research*. Amsterdam: John Benjamins.
Steen, Gerard J. 2011. From three dimensions to five steps: The value of deliberate metaphor. *metaphorik.de* 21. 83–110.

References in Russian

Алексеева Л.М., Мишланова С.Л. *Пермская школа метафоры: достижения и перспективы* // Методологические основы исследования когниции и коммуникации в современной лингвистике: сборник научных трудов в честь доктора наук, профессора Ларисы Александровны Манерко / Под ред. В.А. Богородицкой и А.А, Шарапковой. – Москва: МАКС Пресс, 2017. С.9–20 [Alekseeva, Larisa M. & Mishlanova, Svetlana L. 2017. *Perm school metaphor: achievements and perspectives. Methodological Perspectives of Cognition and Communication in Contemporary Linguistics*: Collection of research papers after Larisa Aleksandrovna Manerko. ed. Bogoroditskaya, V.A., Sharapkova, A.A. Moscow: MAKS Press: 9–20.]
Алексеева Л.М. *Проблемы термина и терминообразования*. Пермь: Изд-во Перм. ун-та, 1998a. 119 с. [Alekseeva, Larisa M. 1998a. *The problems of terms and term formation*. Perm: PSU. 119p]
Алексеева Л.М. *Термин и метафора*. Пермь: Изд-во Перм. ун-та, 1998b. 250 с. [Alekseeva, Larisa M. 1998b. *Term and Metaphor*. Perm: PSU. 250p]
Алексеева Л.М., Мишланова С.Л. *Медицинский дискурс: теоретические основы и принципы анализа*. Пермь: Изд-во Перм. ун-та, 2002. 200 с. [Alekseeva, Larisa M. & Mishlanova, Svetlana, L. 2002. *Medical discourse: Theoretical Issues and Analysis Principles*. Perm: PSU.]
Богатикова Е.П., Исаева Е.В., Бурдина О.Б., Мишланова С.Л. *Семантическая трансформация термина в полидискурсивном пространстве*// European Social Science Journal. 2014b. № 3-2 (42). С. 199–205. [Bogatikova, Eugenia P., Ekaterina V. Isaeva, Olga B. Burdina & Mishlanova, Svetlana. L. 2014. Semantic transformation of the term in the poly-discursive space. *European Social Science Journal* № 3–2 (42). 199–205.] http://dx.doi.org/10.5593/sgemsocial2014/B13/S3.065.
Бурдина О. Б. *Употребление терминоэлементов, обозначающих специальное медицинское знание, в названиях лекарств* // Лингвистические чтения – 2012. Цикл 8. Матер. междунар. науч.-практич. конф. Пермь, 2012. [Burdina, Olga B. 2012. The usage of term elements denoting special medical knowledge in the titles of drugs. Linguistic readings – 2012 (8). *Procedings of the international scientific conference*. Perm]
Бурдина О.Б., Мишланова С.Л. *Параметры моделирования фармацевтического термина* // Методологические основы исследования когниции и коммуникации в современной лингвистике: сборник научных трудов в честь доктора наук, профессора Ларисы Александровны Манерко / Под ред. В.А. Богородицкой и А.А, Шарапковой. – Москва:

МАКС Пресс, 2017. С. 71–81. [Burdina, Olga B. & Svetlana L. Mishlanova. 2017. The parameters of the pharm term modelling. Methodological Fundamentals of Cognition and Communication Studies in Contemporary Linguistics: The Collection of Scientific Articles in Honor of Larissa Alexandrovna Manerko. eds. Bogoroditskaya V.A., and A.A. Scharapkova. Moscow; MAKS Press. 71–81].

Голованова Е.И. *Введение в когнитивное терминоведение: учебное пособие*. Челябинск: Энциклопедия, 2008. 224 с. [Golovanava, Elena I. 2008b. *Introduction to cognitive term studies: study guide*. Chelyabincsk: Encyclopedia. 224p.]

Голованова Е.И. *Эвристический потенциал когнитивных терминов и развитие терминоведения* // Терминология и знание. Материалы I Международного симпозиума (Москва 23-24 мая 2008 г.). М.: Институт русского языка им. В.В. Виноградова РАН, 2009. С. 51–64. [Golovanova, Elena I. 2009. Heuristic potential of cognitive terms and the development of term studies. Terminology and knowledge. *Proceedings of the I international symposium* (Moscow July 23–24, 2008) The institute of the Russian language after V.V. Vinogradov RAS: 51–64.]

Головин Б.Н., Кобрин Р.Ю. *Лингвистические основы учения о терминах:* Учеб. пособие для филол. спец. вузов. М.: Высш. шк., 1987. 104 с. [Golovin, Boris N., Kobrin, R.Yu. 1987. Linguistic basis for term studies: Study guide for the university philological specialties. Higher school. 104 p.]

Гринёв С.В. *Введение в терминоведение*. М. 1993. 309с. [Grinev, Sergey V. 1993. *Introduction to term studies*. М.: 309]

Дрёмова Н. Б., Березникова Р. Е. *Номенклатура лекарственных средств: особенности формирования и фармацевтическая информация*. Курск. 2002. [Driomova, N. B., Bereznikova, R. E. 2002. *Drug nomenclature: formation peculiarities and pharmaceutical information*. Kursk]

Исаева Е.В., Мишланова С.Л. *Метафорическое моделирование разных типов знания в дискурсе компьютерной безопасности*. Пермь, 2014. [Isaeva, Ekaterina V. & Mishlanova, Svetlana L. 2013. *Metaphor modelling of different types of knowledge in the discourse of computer security*. Perm]

Карасик В.И. *О категориях дискурса* // Языковая личность: социолингвистические и эмотивные аспекты: Сб. науч. тр. / ВГПУ; СГУ. Волгоград: Перемена, 1998. С. 185–197. [Karasik, Vladimir I. 1998. About discourse categories. Language personality: sociolinguistic and emotional aspects. Collection of research papers. VSPU; SSU. 185–197. Volgograd: Peremena.]

Лейчик В.М. *Терминоведение: предмет, методы, структура*. Изд. 3-е. М.: Изд-во ЛКИ, 2007. 256 с.[Leichik, Vladimir M. 2007. *Term studies: subject, methods, structure*. Edn 3. M.: LKI: 256p.]

Манерко Л.А. *Исследование концептуализации и категоризации в современном терминоведении*// Когнитивные исследования языка. 2009. № 1. С. 123–131. [Manerko, Larisa A. 2009. Study of conceptualization and categorization in modern terminology. *Cognitive study of the language* (1). 123–131.]

Массалина И.П., Новодранова В.Ф. *Дискурсивные маркеры в английском языке военно-морского дела*. Калининград: Изд-во ФГОУ ВПО" КГТУ", 2009. 278 с. [Massalina, Inga P. & Valentina F. Novodranova. 2009. *Discursive markers in the English language of naval science*. Kaliningrad: 278p]

Суперанская А.В., Подольская Н.В., Васильева Н.В. *Общая терминология: вопросы теории*. М.: Книжный дом "ЛИБРОКОМ", 2012. 248 с. [Superanskaya, Aleksandra V.,

Natalya V. Podolskaya & Natalia V. Vasilyeva, 2012. *General terminology: questions of theory*. M.: 248]

Табанакова В. Д., Ковязина М. А. *Моделирование английской и русской экологических терминологий в учебных целях: Учебное пособие*. Тюмень, Изд-во Тюменск.ГУ, 2007. [Tabanakova, Vera D. & Marina F. Koviazina. 2007. *Modelling of the English and Russian ecology terminology in learning goals: study guide*. Tyumen. Tyumen State University.]

Чернявский М.Н. *Латинский язык и основы фармацевтической терминологии:* Редактор: Галахова Н. А.5-е издание. Издательство: ГЭОТАР-Медиа, 2015 г. 400 с. [Cherniavsky, Mikhail N. 2015. *The Latin language and the the fundamentals of pharmaceutical terminology*. Ed. Galakhova, N. A. Edn. 5. GOETAR-Media. 400p.]

Шелов С.Д. *Определение терминов и понятийная структура терминологии*. СПб.: Из-во С.-Петерб. ун-та, 1998. 236 с. [Shelov, Sergey D. 1998. *Definition of terms and conceptual structure of terminology*. SPb: 236p]

Шидловская О. В. *Синонимия и полисемия терминов латинского и древнегреческого происхождения в предметной области трансплантации сердца*// Журнал Гродненского государственного медицинского университета. №4. 2011 г. С. 104–106 [Shidlovskaya, Olga V. 2011. Synonymy and polysemy of Latin and Ancient Greek medical terminology in the subject field of cardiac transplantation. *Journal of the Grodno State Medical University* 4. 104–106.]

Dictionaries and Online resources

Dictionary.com http://www.dictionary.com/ (accessed 03.12.2017).

English and American Heritage Dictionary. http://ahdictionary.com (accessed 03.12.2016).

Longman Dictionary of Contemporary English Online https://www.ldoceonline.com/ (accessed 10.12.2017).

Macmillan Dictionary for Advanced Learners. http://www.macmillandictionary.com (accessed 03.12.2017).

Thesaurus.com "charge," in *Roget's 21st Century Thesaurus, Third Edition*. Source location: Philip Lief Group 2009. http://www.thesaurus.com/browse/charge. Available: http://www.thesaurus.com/ (accessed 16.12.2017).

The Corpus of Contemporary American English (COCA) https://corpus.byu.edu/coca/ (accessed 10.12.2017).

The Free Dictionary By Farlex. http://www.thefreedictionary.com (accessed 03.12.2016)

Enciclopedia PCMag.com, The Computer Language Company Inc. 1981–2017, https://www.pcmag.com/encyclopedia (accessed 16.12.2017).

Ваулина Е. У. *Мой компьютер. Толковый словарь*. Под ред. Е. Ю. Ваулина. М.: Эксмо, 2003. [Vaulina, E. U. (ed.) 2003. *My computer. Definition dictionary*. Moscow: Eksmo]

Дворецкий И. Х. *Латинско-русский словарь* / Под ред. И. Х. Дворецкого М.: Русский язык, 2000. [Dvoretskii, I., Kh. 2000. *Latin-Russian dictionary*. Moscow: the Russian Language]

Кузнецов С.А. *Большой толковый словарь русского языка*. СПб: "Норинт", 2010 [Kuznetsov, S. A. 2010 Large definition dictionary of the Russian language. St Peterburg: "Norint".]

Латинско-русский словарь. ред. Танаушенко К.М. М.: ООО “Издательство АКТ”; Мн.: Харвест, 2002. – 1040 с. [Latin-Russian dictionary (2002). Ed. K.A. Tanaushenko. Moscow: OOO “Izdatelstvo AKT”: Harvest. P: 1040]
Ожегов С.И. *Словарь русского языка*. Екатеринбург: “Урал-Советы, 1994. – С. 72 [Ozhegov, S.I. 1994 The Russian language dictionary. Ekaterinburg: 72p]
Ожегов С.И. *Толковый словарь* [Ozhegov, S.I. Definition dictionary] http://enc-dic.com/ozhegov/Virus-3399.html (accessed 10.12.2017).
Толковый словарь русского языка Дмитриева Д. В. Дмитриев. 2003 [Definition dictionary of the Russian language by Dmitriev. (2003) Ed. Dmitriev, D.V.] http://enc-dic.com/dmytriev/Virus-3432/ (accessed 10.12.2017).
Фонд знаний “Ломоносов”, Вирус, [Knowledge fund “Lomonosov”] http://www.lomonosov-fund.ru/enc/ru/encyclopedia:0130031] (accessed 03.12.2017).

Valentina Apresjan

Metaphor in grammar: Mapping across syntactic domains

Abstract: The paper focuses on syntactic metaphor, which is manifested in the metaphorical mapping across syntactic domains, or in the metaphor-driven polysemy of constructions. Syntactic metaphor underpins the diversity of morphosyntactic expression of the Stimulus argument in Russian psych verbs. While the Experiencer role in Russian emotion verbs is normally coded as nominative or dative, there is no uniform expression of Stimulus. Different emotion types require specialized Stimulus expression: dative for 'to rejoice', instrumental for 'to be proud', genitive for 'to fear' and 'to be ashamed of', prepositional constructions for different types of 'JOY', 'SADNESS' and 'ANGER'. The paper employs corpus methods to demonstrate that all of the constructions used to encode Stimulus in Russian psych verbs are predominantly used to express other semantic roles. We suggest that, in each case, the role of Stimulus is the result of a metaphoric mapping from the domain of another semantic role, the latter determined by the type of emotion and the event structure of the corresponding psych verb. Thus, Stimulus in *radovat'sja* 'to rejoice' is syntactically metaphorized as Addressee (dative), because it implies overt manifestation of positive feeling directed at the stimulus. Anger involves a violent reaction. Hence the Stimulus in *serdit'sja* 'to get angry' is syntactically expressed as Patient of aggressive physical actions with 'at' construction. Other metaphoric mappings between semantic roles include PRIDE IS ATTRACTING ATTENTION, SADNESS IS THINKING and others. The paper also shows that conventionalized syntactic metaphor can give rise to a novel metaphor which occurs spontaneously in discourse, such as SILENCE IS AGGRESSION.

Keywords: syntactic metaphor, semantics, syntax, polysemy of constructions, psych verbs, semantic role, experiencer, stimulus.

Note: This research was supported by the grant of the Russian Foundation for Basic Research 19-012-00291A, "The fourth issue of the Active Dictionary of Russian".

Valentina Apresjan, National Research University "Higher School of Economics"; Vinogradov, Russian Language Institute of the Russian Academy of Sciences

https://doi.org/10.1515/9783110629460-006

1 Introduction

The current paper presents a corpus study of Russian emotion concepts. The main research question concerns predictability of linguistic and more specifically, syntactic properties of lexical items on the basis of their semantics.

The main hypothesis is that in situations when syntactic properties of a lexical item are sufficiently diverse, its semantics influences yet not entirely determines its syntax. Rather, semantic properties of a word provide a spectrum of syntactic properties it may possess depending on other factors – grammatical, historical, pragmatic, and others.

Among the important factors influencing the syntactic properties of words are conceptual metaphors associated with the corresponding emotions, which can influence not only conventional lexical metaphors, but also conventional syntactic metaphors. By lexical metaphors we mean metaphoric shifts that occur in the meanings of lexical items, as, for example, in the metaphor SUDDEN INTERRUPTION OF MOVEMENT IS COLD: *Freeze, or I will shoot*; *He froze when he saw her.*

By syntactic metaphors we mean metaphoric shifts that occur in the meanings of grammatical items, such as grammatical markers or constructions. For example, the use of instrumental case to express the meaning of itinerary points to the syntactic metaphor WAY IS INSTRUMENT, as in the Russian example

(1) *On shel lesom*
He walked forest-INS
'He walked by the forest road'

A further issue addressed in the paper concerns the influence of the conventional syntactic metaphor, via the conceptual metaphor it reflects, on the occurrence of novel metaphors in discourse. By novel syntactic metaphors in discourse we mean non-conventional metaphorical use of constructions as it occurs in natural language.[1]

Traditionally emotion metaphor has been treated as a mostly lexical phenomenon manifested in the polysemy of words and expressions. The present paper expands emotion metaphor studies, and also the studies of novel metaphors, into the grammaticalization domain. It focuses on syntactic emotion metaphor, as manifested in the metaphorical mapping across syntactic domains, i.e. in metaphor-driven polysemy of *constructions* used to express arguments of emotion words, as illustrated below.

1 We derive the notion of novel syntactic metaphor in discourse from the combination of novel metaphor (Lakoff and Turner 1989), syntactic metaphor (Lakoff 1993; Sullivan 2013), and metaphor in discourse (Semino 2008).

Previously, metaphoric relations in constructions were studied in (Sullivan 2013), particularly concerning ditransitive and resultative constructions, and in a collective volume on metonymy and metaphor in grammar (Panther, Thornburg, and Barcelona 2009). Cf. non-metaphorical and metaphorical usages of the Way construction: *to crawl one's way to the top of the mountain* vs. *to bribe one's way to this position*. A similar phenomenon, metaphoric syntactic roles, is described in (Lakoff 1993): cf. the role of 'PATH' in its direct and metaphorical realizations: *to drive through the tunnel* vs. *to get a job through one's uncle*.

In the current paper, syntactic metaphor is hypothesized to underpin the diversity of morphosyntactic expression of the Stimulus argument[2] in Russian psych verbs. The Experiencer role in Russian psych verbs is typically coded as nominative or dative[3]:

(2) *On* *raduetsja*
He-NOM rejoices
'He is rejoicing'

(3) *Mne* *grustno*
I-DAT sad-PRED
'I am sad'

However, there is no uniform expression of Stimulus. Different emotion types require specialized Stimulus expression: dative for *radovat'sja* 'to rejoice', instrumental for *gordit'sja* 'to be proud', genitive for *bojat'sja* 'to fear' and *stydit'sja* 'to be ashamed of', various prepositional constructions for different types of JOY, SADNESS and ANGER. Consider the following possibilities:

(4) *On* *raduetsja* *pobede*
He rejoices victory-DAT
'He is happy about the victory'

2 In our work, we partly rely on Dowty's understanding of thematic roles and argument selection (Dowty 1991), with certain additions to the inventory of semantic roles suggested in (Apresjan 2010: 370–377). We understand Experiencer as the sentient or perceiving participant of the situation, Stimulus as the causer of emotional reaction, Instrument as the thing that the Agent uses to implement an event, Goal as the thing or place towards which the action is directed, Content as the essence of one's knowledge, thought, or utterance.

3 Linguistic examples in the paper, unless specified otherwise, are mine.

(5)	*On*	*gorditsja*	*pobedoj*
	He-NOM	prides	victory-INS
	'He is proud of the victory'		

(6)	*On*	*serditsja*	*na*	*syna*
	He-NOM	angers	at	son-ACC
	'He is angry at his son'			

(7)	*Ona*	*grustit*	*o*	*proshlom*
	She-NOM	is sad	about	past-LOC
	'She is sad about the past'			

The phenomenon of the diversity of Stimulus expression is not unheard of typologically (Belletti and Rizzi 1988) and there have been attempts to explain it by the principle of lexical economy, or inheritance of verbal construction patterns from non-psych meanings of the corresponding verbs (Klein and Kutscher 2002).

However, Russian psych verbs, for the most part, are not metaphorically derived from non-psych verbs. Therefore syntactic diversity requires a different explanation.

It is also noteworthy that Russian psych verbs do not possess their own, unique expression for their Stimulus role, but avail themselves of constructions that are primarily used to express other semantic roles in other semantic classes of verbs.[4] For example, the primary role of the Dative case is the Recipient in TRANSFER verbs or Addressee in speech verbs.

The primary role of the Instrumental case is Instrument in causation verbs, as 'to cut something with something'.

The primary role of the 'at' construction is Goal in caused motion verbs, as 'to put something on something'.

The primary role of prepositional constructions with 'about' is Content in speech and thought verbs, such as 'to speak/to think about something'.

Each psych verb selects its own construction. Thus, while there are certain more universal means of expressing Stimulus, such as by causal construction *ot* 'from', *iz-za* 'because of' or by *chto* 'that' sentence, the more specific means of Stimulus expression are not interchangeable among different psych verbs. Therefore, the following phrases would be impossible:

4 By semantic classes we understand, following (Apresjan 1967, 1995, 2000, 2002), groups of lexemes with similar semantics that share a range of linguistic properties, including morphosyntactic realization of arguments. We partly use semantic labels for classes introduced in (Levin 1993) for English verbs.

(8) **On raduetsja pobedoj*
He rejoices victory-INS

(9) **On serditsja o syne*
He angers about son-LOC

(10) **Ona grustit na proshloe*
She is sad at past-ACC

On the basis of a corpus study, the paper identifies semantic components and conceptual metaphors associated with Russian psych verbs which are deemed to be responsible for the conventional syntactic metaphor manifested in the expression of their Stimulus semantic role. For different emotion clusters[5] and different emotion concepts within clusters, the semantics of the Stimulus may become flavored by an additional semantic role, licensed by its metaphorical conceptualization. For example, for the Russian concept of *blazhenstvovat'* 'to feel bliss', Stimulus is conceptualized as Place, which results in its morphosyntactic expression by means of various locative constructions, whereas in *radovat'sja* 'to rejoice', Stimulus is conceptualized as an Interlocutor or Addressee, which results in its conventional expression by the dative.

The paper further explores how this conventional syntactic metaphor may affect discourse. If the hypothesis about the conceptual metaphor underlying the conventional grammatical metaphor in the domain of psych verbs is true, one would expect that the same conceptual metaphor can give rise to novel, non-conventional syntactic metaphors in actual discourse, which would be adequately interpretable by speakers. In the same way, it happens with novel lexical metaphors, based on an existing conceptual metaphor model. In terms of Construction Grammar, this phenomenon may be described as coercion, or re-interpretation of the original meaning of a lexical item when placed in a construction it does not normally occur in (Goldberg 2006). And that is indeed what occurs in discourse.

An example from the domain of psych verbs, which illustrates this interaction of syntax and semantics, syntactic metaphor and conceptual metaphor, may be provided by the Russian verbs of PRIDE and SHAME clusters, as represented by *gordit'sja* 'to be proud of', *kichit'sja* 'make a parade of' vs. *stydi'tsja* 'to be ashamed of', *stesnjat'sja* 'to be embarrassed by'.

5 Emotion clusters are defined in (V. Apresjan 2011 a) as "a variety of emotion terms reflecting a range of emotion subtypes – related but subtly different feelings" which share the same prototypical scenario of occurrence.

Semantically, PRIDE and SHAME are antonymic, which means that their semantic structures are very similar, yet in some respect opposite. In the case of PRIDE and SHAME, the similarity concerns the Stimulus of emotion – in both cases, the feeling is caused by an action of the Experiencer herself, i.e. the Stimulus is an inalienable attribute of the Experiencer. The contrast involves the assessment of the action and the resulting feeling: in PRIDE, both are positive, and in SHAME both are negative. Hence the accompanying wishes differ likewise: PRIDE implies a desire to attract the attention of a potential audience, and SHAME a desire to avoid it.

Potentially, based on their partly coinciding semantic properties, SHAME and PRIDE could have either the same or different metaphoric conceptualizations and, hence, syntactic expressions. As it is, the conceptual metaphor underlying PRIDE in Russian is PRIDE IS ATTRACTING ATTENTION. The Stimulus argument is syntactically conceptualized as an Inalienable Part of the Experiencer that is moved in order to attract attention; it is expressed by the instrumental case: *gordit'sja pobedoj*-INS 'to be proud of one's victory'.

The explanation for the use of the instrumental case is that one of its non-metaphorical usages in Russian is, among others, the meaning of "part", as in *On poshevelil pal'cem*-INS 'He moved his finger' and/or "object attracting attention", as in *On pomaxal ej flazhkom*-INS 'He waved a streamer at her'.

In theory, Stimulus in SHAME could also be expressed by instrumental because SHAME incorporates the meaning "part"; yet in the presence of a focal element "desire to avoid attention", the former is rendered insufficient to license the use of instrumental.

In Russian, the Stimulus of SHAME is expressed by genitive with a general causal meaning: *stydit'sja porazhenija*-GEN 'to be ashamed of one's defeat'. Yet this strategy which distinguishes between the two emotion clusters is obviously not the only one possible: e.g., in English, both adjectives *proud* and *ashamed* govern a prepositional phrase with *of* (*proud/ashamed of something*) which might mean that in English, conceptual similarities of PRIDE and SHAME are stronger than their differences.

Therefore, the influence of conceptual metaphor on the conventional syntactic metaphor in the domain of psych verbs is to be expected in the form of tendencies and correlations rather than absolute laws, and semantics in their case is postulated to have explanatory more than predictive power.

Analyzing the entire field of emotions rather than single emotion clusters or concepts enables one to draw systematic parallels between event structures of psych verbs and conceptual metaphors underlying the corresponding concepts, on the one hand, and the conventional syntactic metaphors reflected in the morphosyntactic expression of their Stimulus role, on the other. In this way, it becomes possible to notice tendencies that lie outside of one specific emotion cluster and are shared by different emotion clusters.

Consider, for example, the construction with *pered* 'in front of': it is used to express the role of Stimulus in emotive nouns belonging to several emotion clusters, which are all united by the underlying metaphor FEELING IS STANDING IN FRONT OF A BIGGER OBJECT. Therefore, nouns that denote emotions where the Experiencer feels in some way dwarfed, diminished or awed by the Stimulus are used in this construction. The prototypical emotion to incorporate this metaphor is *strax* 'fear', but it also occurs in *umilenie* 'feeling tenderly moved', *vostorg* 'delight', *styd* 'shame'; cf. the following examples from the Russian National Corpus: *strax pered Bogom* 'fear before God', *umilenie pered tainstvom prirody* 'feeling tenderly moved before the mystery of nature', *vostorg pered talantom* 'delight before the talent', *styd pered uchitelem* 'shame before the teacher'.

The novelty of the proposed approach and its relevance for the linguistic theory lies in extending the traditional boundaries of semantics-syntax interface research to the domain of hereto inexplicable properties of psych verbs, as well as in invoking the notion of syntactic metaphor (Lakoff 1993; Sullivan 2013) in reference to the expression of the Stimulus role in psych verbs. In this respect, our work shares the approach of Mendoza and Mairal (2011: 72–80), which suggests the impact of "high-level metaphor" on grammar, and specifically, on the syntactic expression of arguments. However, we apply this approach to different lexical and syntactic material.

We also analyze novel syntactic metaphor in discourse. In the spirit of Semino (2008: 1–10), we expect that naturally occurring novel metaphors involve "interaction between conventionality and creativity" and that they will demonstrate a certain degree of both. In other words, we expect to find novel syntactic metaphors that are both truly novel, i.e., do not display conventional morphosyntactic behavior, and at the same time easily comprehensible, as they are based on the existing conventional metaphors. However, they might still be processed differently, as argued in Lai, Curran, and Menn (2009), where different neural mechanisms are suggested to underlie the processing of conventional and novel metaphor.

2 Methods and materials

Our research relies on the data from two corpora: the Main Corpus of the Russian National Corpus (ruscorpora.ru) and the corpus of RuSkELL (ruskell.sketchengine.co.uk). The Main Corpus of the Russian National Corpus (MC, RNC) is a balanced corpus with over 283 million tokens; it consists primarily of original prose representing standard Russian (from the middle of the 18th century) but also small volumes of translated works and poetry, as well as texts, representing the non-standard forms of modern Russian, such as spoken language. The corpus contains various types of texts, including fiction and nonfiction, in proportion to their share in real-life usage (http://www.ruscorpora.ru/en/corpora-structure.html).

RuSkELL ("Russian + Sketch Engine for Language Learning") is an online resource intended for researchers and learners of Russian, which incorporates a specially pre-processed corpus and the interface which allows users to search for phrases in sentences, extract salient collocates and show similar words. The corpus is Web-based and contains texts downloaded from the Russian Internet in 2011, with a total size of 975 million tokens (Apresjan et al. 2016).

The procedure of our data collection is as follows: first, we use RuSkELL sketches of all psych verbs in question to obtain information regarding their preferred morphosyntactic and lexical argument expression. Sketches are lists of salient collocates of the query word, divided into groups according to their grammatical relations to the query word. For example, the sketch for the verb *radovat'sja* 'to rejoice' includes information about the most frequent nouns in the nominative and dative cases, which occur with it, as well as prepositional constructions used with this verb (*za* 'for', *pri* 'at', *o* 'about', *ot* 'from'). Nominative forms express the Experiencer role (*rebenok* 'child', *malysh* 'baby', *mama* 'Mom', *roditeli* 'parents', etc.), and dative forms express the Stimulus role (*uspex* 'success', *pobeda 'victory'*, *vstrecha* 'meeting', *prixod* 'coming', *solnce* 'sun', etc.). Prepositional constructions also introduce the Stimulus argument. Thus, a complete sketch provides both the syntactic and the semantic "portrait" of the verb: it contains information about the preferred types of morphosyntactic expression of arguments, as well as the typical lexical fillers of different semantic roles.

Afterwards, the data obtained from RuSkELL is checked in the Russian National Corpus, which is a balanced corpus, unlike RuSkELL. Namely, we check the frequency of each type of argument expression, as well as establish other, non-frequent, types of argument expression which are not reflected in RuSkELL. The Russian National Corpus is also used for obtaining literary examples that illustrate our claims.

Finally, both RuSkELL and Russian National Corpus are used for eliciting novel syntactic metaphors. We use direct phrase queries to search for metaphorical argument expression, e.g., *grustit' pro* 'to be sad about something', *molchat' na* 'to be silent at somebody', where either psych verbs are used in constructions typical for non-psych verbs, or non-psych verbs are used in constructions typical for psych verbs.

We use examples from both corpora, as well as our own phrases, which represent simplified versions of corpus examples, to illustrate our claims.

3 Emotion concepts and their corresponding conceptual and syntactic metaphors

The paper considers the following groups of emotions: emotions as reactions to events and circumstances (joy, sadness), emotions as reactions to someone's actions (gratitude, anger), and emotions as reactions to one's own actions (pride, shame).

3.1 Emotions as reactions to events

This group includes JOY and SADNESS clusters; several subtypes of each one of the feelings are considered.

3.1.1 Reactions to good events: JOY cluster

There are many semantic and metaphorical subtypes of JOY; we consider three of them – JOY IS A MEETING, JOY IS BEING IN A PLACE, JOY IS BEING LOCATED ABOVE THE OBJECT.

The conceptual metaphor JOY IS A MEETING underlies the type of JOY expressed by the Russian verb *radovat'sja* 'to rejoice, to cheer'. The Stimulus role is conceptualized as Interlocutor and Addressee. As RuSkELL collocation frequency data demonstrates, this type of joy is typically caused by events, such as *uspexi* 'success', *podarki* 'gifts', *vesna* 'spring', *pobeda* 'victory', *pervyj sneg* 'first snow', *rozhdenije rebenka* 'the birth of a child'. Permanent states of affairs do not usually cause *radovat'sja*: cf. the awkwardness of ?*radovat'sja svoej dvadcatiletnej interesnoj rabote v universitete* 'to rejoice over one's twenty-year long work at the university.'

The happy event is conceptualized as an Interlocutor that suddenly appears in the sight of the Experiencer.

Even if the Stimulus argument is filled with an NP denoting a person, it is interpreted as an event of meeting that person:

(11) *Ona emu ochen' obradovalas'*
She he-DAT much rejoiced
'She was very happy at meeting him'

The phrase in (11) would be impossible if there were no actual contact taking place; e.g., such a phrase can be used to describe one's emotional reaction to seeing somebody or hearing one on the phone, but it cannot be used to describe one's happy reaction at receiving a letter or getting the news of one's visit.

In Russian, events are generally conceptualized as meetings; cf. the use of the verb *vstrechat'* 'to meet' in reference to holidays and other events: *vstrechat' Novyj god* 'to meet the New Year', *vstrechat' Rozhdestvo* 'to meet Christmas', as well as

(12)	*On*	*spokojno*	*vstrechal*	*pobedy*	*i*	*porazhenija*
	He	calmly	met	victories-ACC	and	defeats-ACC
	'He met victories and defeats with equanimity'					

In JOY, this conceptualization is additionally reinforced by the fact that *radovat'sja* 'to rejoice' favors the open expression of the feeling directed at its Stimulus:

(13)	*Oni*	*shumno*	*radovalis'*	*drugu*
	They	noisily	rejoiced	friend-DAT
	'They were noisily cheering at their friend's arrival'			

However, the conventional metaphor reflecting the conceptual metaphor JOY IS A MEETING is expressed grammatically rather than lexically.

As the data from the Russian National Corpus show, the prevalent morpho-syntactic expression of the Stimulus role in *radovat'sja* is the dative case. One of its primary functions in Russian is to express the Addressee argument in speech verbs: *govorit drugu* 'to say friend-DAT', meaning 'to say something to a friend'. The dative case is used to express the Stimulus argument in the verb *radovat'sja* in about 30% of its occurrences in the Russian National Corpus, with other means of expression considerably lower: *chto* 'that' construction is used in 12 % of occurrences, causal constructions such as *iz-za, po povodu* 'because of' are used in less than 1 % of occurrences (in the majority of cases the Stimulus argument is not explicitly expressed).

The Russian verb *ulybat'sja* 'to smile', which denotes one of the main overt manifestations of 'JOY', also incorporates the idea of an Addressee which is expressed by the dative case:

(14)	*Ona*	*emu*	*ulybalas'*
	She	he-DAT	smiled
	'She smiled at him'		

Other emotions which employ the construction with dative, share the same underlying metaphor, namely, FEELING IS A MEETING. They belong to the SURPRISE and GRATITUDE clusters; cf. *udivljat'sja chemu-libo* 'be.surprised something-DAT', *izumljat'sja chemu-libo* 'be.astonished something-DAT', *porazhat'sja chemu-libo* 'marvel something-DAT', where the Stimulus is conceptualized as a suddenly encountered Interlocutor and *byt' blagodarnym komu-libo* 'be.grateful somebody-DAT', where the Stimulus is naturally conceptualized as Addressee.

There is also a novel syntactic metaphor which occurs in the discourse and is interpretable due to the existence of the conceptual metaphor JOY IS A MEETING and the conventional syntactic metaphor of the dative construction (Addressee–Stimulus). Consider, for example, the Russian verb *smejat'sja* 'to laugh', which normally entails a Theme or Patient (rather than an Addressee) argument and expresses not joy, but the feeling of being amused. Consequently, its frequent expression is with *nad* 'at' construction (12 % of the total occurrences of the verb):

(15) *Vse smejalis' nad bednym mal'chikom*
All laughed at poor-INS boy-INS
'Everybody laughed at the poor boy'

Yet, there are certain dative usages of *smejat'sja* where it refers either to benevolent laughter (*smejat'sja shutkam* 'to laugh jokes-DAT', 'to laugh at somebody's jokes') or else, as in phrases (16) or (17), to joy:

(16) *My radostno smeemsja tomu chto nikto*
We happily laugh that-DAT that nobody
ne zabyl drug druga <MC, RNC>
not forgot each other
'We are laughing happily that nobody forgot each other'

(17) *My smejalis' vsem vstrechnym, oni mne nravilis'* (MC, RNC)
We laughed all-DAT passers-by they I-DAT appealed
'We greeted all the passers-by with laughter, I liked them all'

Not all types of JOY share the same metaphor FEELING IS A MEETING and can be expressed by the dative; e.g., the verbs *blazhenstvovat'* 'to be in a state of bliss, to bask' and *zloradstvovat'* 'to gloat' have different underlying conceptual metaphors and, as a result, different morphosyntactic expression.

For *blazhenstvovat'*, the underlying metaphor is JOY IS BEING IN A PLACE; consequently, about 75% of the total occurrences of this verb with an overt

Stimulus argument employ locative constructions, such as *blazhenstvovat' na solnce* 'to bask in the sun; lit. to be blissful at the sun-LOC', *blazhenstvovat' v vanne* 'to luxuriate in the bathtub; lit. to be blissful in the bathtub-LOC'.

For *zloradstvovat'*, the underlying metaphor is JOY IS BEING LOCATED ABOVE THE OBJECT, which also underpins the conceptualization of the speech act of mocking. Therefore, this verb allows expression with *nad* 'over, at' construction, typical for the verbs of mocking in Russian, such as *izdevat'sja nad kem-libo* 'to jeer at somebody', *nasmexat'sja nad kem-libo* 'to sneer at somebody', *glumit'sja nad kem-libo* 'to scoff at somebody', as well as the aforementioned verb *smejat'sja nad kem-libo* 'to laugh at somebody':

(18)	*V*	*shkolah*	*zloradstvujut*	*nad*	*temi,*	*kto*	*slabee* (MC, RNC)
	In	schools	gloat	over	those-INS	who-NOM	weaker
	'At schools, they often mock weaker students'						

Unlike JOY IS A MEETING and JOY IS BEING IN A PLACE, this metaphor is also found in English, as the *at*-construction is used to express the Stimulus argument in verbs of mocking, and the *over* construction is used to express the Stimulus argument in the verb *to gloat*, the closest translation equivalent of the Russian Schadenfreude verb *zloradstvovat'*.

3.1.2 Reactions to bad events: SADNESS cluster

As is the case with JOY, there are many semantic and metaphorical subtypes of SADNESS; we consider three of them – SADNESS IS A MEETING, SADNESS IS A THOUGHT ABOUT AN UNATTAINABLE OBJECT, SADNESS IS BEING LOCATED ABOVE THE OBJECT.

The metaphorical subtype SADNESS IS A MEETING is represented by the verb *ogorchat'sja* 'to be upset'. This subtype of SADNESS is, as the joyous feeling of *radovat'sja* 'to rejoice', caused by events, and not by permanent states of affairs, thus (20), unlike (19), is infelicitous:

(19)	*On*	*ogorchilsja*	*iz-za*	*ee*	*zvonka*
	He	upset-SELF	because of	her	call
	'He got distressed over her phone call'				

(20)	**On*	*ogorchilsja*	*iz-za*	*ih*	*dvadcatiletnej*	*razluki*
	He	upset-SELF	because of	their	20-year-long	separation
	'He got distressed over their 20-year-long separation'					

Unlike *radovat'sja*, in *ogorchat'sja* the event is not very important for the Experiencer: it is possible *ogorchat'sja iz-za dvojki na ekzamene* 'to get upset because of an exam failure', but not **ogorchat'sja iz-za smerti samogo blizkogo cheloveka* 'to get upset because of the death of one's nearest and dearest'. But what is more important is that *ogorchat'sja* describes a negative feeling with limited overt manifestations, not directed at the object of the feeling: it is a pure state, whereas *radovat'sja* includes an indication of a corresponding behavior. Hence the impossibility of (21):

(21) **Oni* *shumno* *ogorchalis'*
They noisily upset-SELF
'They got noisily upset'

As a state, rather than an Addressee-directed behavior, *ogorchat'sja* 'to get upset' lacks the additional motivation for the FEELING IS A MEETING metaphor that *radovat'sja* 'to rejoice' possesses; therefore, the dative expression of Stimulus is possible for *ogorchat'sja* (*ogorchit'sja neudache* 'to get upset by one's failure; lit. to get upset failure-DAT'), but it is significantly rarer than in *radovat'sja*. For *ogorchat'sja* it constitutes about 10 % of its total usages in the Russian National Corpus (as compared to 30 % in *radovat'sja* in the same corpus), while the main expression of Stimulus is by use of causal constructions with *iz-za* 'because of' and *po povodu* 'on the account of'. The fact that the conceptual metaphor FEELING IS A MEETING is considerably weaker in the SADNESS cluster than in the JOY cluster explains why it does not give rise to novel discourse metaphors.

The metaphor SADNESS IS A THOUGHT ABOUT AN UNATTAINABLE OBJECT underlies the subtypes of SADNESS expressed by the verbs *toskovat'* 'to long, to miss, to yearn', *gorevat'* 'to grieve' and *skorbet'* 'to woe'. They express long-term feelings that can stretch over considerable periods of time, that are caused by separation from a loved person (or other loved object, as in the case of *toskovat'*, or other irretrievable loss, as in *gorevat', skorbet'*), which is due either to distance (*toskovat'*) or to death (*gorevat', skorbet'*). These feelings are not experienced on a non-stop basis, but can be revived by thinking about their Stimulus. Consequently, the morphosyntactic expression of their Stimulus argument largely coincides with the expression of the Theme argument in mental verbs, such as *dumat' o* 'to think about', *razmyshljat' o* 'to ponder about', namely, they employ *o* 'about' prepositional construction:

(22) *Ona* *toskovala* *o* *ljubimom*
She longed about beloved-LOC
'She longed for her beloved'

(23) *On goreval ob umershej zhene*
He grieved about departed-LOC wife-LOC
'He grieved for his departed wife'

(24) *On skorbel o svoej utrate*
He woed about self's-LOC loss-LOC
'He woed his loss'

The metaphor SADNESS IS A THOUGHT ABOUT AN UNATTAINABLE OBJECT is sufficiently strong to license the use of *o* 'about' construction in verbs that do not, as a rule, allow it, thereby creating a novel syntactic discourse metaphor. Consider the following phrases from RuSkELL:

(25) *On lezhal bez sna i ogorchalsja o svoej utrate*
He lay without sleep and upset-SELF about self's-LOC loss-LOC
(RuSkELL)
'He lay in bed and grieved over his loss'

When the verb 'to be upset' is coerced into the 'about' construction, it is interpreted as a more profound feeling caused by a more important Stimulus, and it "chooses" a corresponding type of noun to fill the Stimulus role, as illustrated by the example above.

The same metaphor underlies certain types of FEAR and SHAME, namely fear for someone (*bespokoit'sja, volnovat'sja, trevozhit'sja o kom-libo* 'to worry about someone') and regret (*zhalet', sozhalet', sokrushat'sja o chem.-libo* 'to regret something, lit. to regret about something'). All these psych verbs also occur in the *o* 'about' construction: what they all have in common, are

a. longevity (they last much longer than their Stimulus),
b. temporal or spatial separation from their object,
c. and inability of the Experiencer to influence the situation.

The conceptual metaphor type SADNESS IS BEING LOCATED ABOVE THE OBJECT is represented by such verbs as *gorevat'* 'to grieve' and *skorbet'* 'to woe': *gorevat' nad ubitymi* 'to grieve over the dead', *skorbet' nad padshimi* 'to woe over the fallen', *skorbet' nad utratoj* 'to woe over the loss'. The locative component in the metaphor is explained by the Stimulus in 'grief' and 'woe': the prototypical Stimulus in these emotions is someone's death, and the locative 'over, above' describes the position of the Experiencer over the supine body of the dead person. When a verb denoting a different type of SADNESS is coerced into the *nad* 'above' construction, as in the following example with the verb 'to be sad', a novel discourse metaphor occurs, where the verb 'to be sad' is interpreted as 'to grieve' and "chooses" an appropriate Stimulus – a dead object:

(26)	*Mozhno*	*krasivo*	*i*	*prilichno*	*grustit'*	*nad*	
	Possible	prettily	and	decently	be sad	over	
	mjortvoj	*ptichnkoj*	*ili*	*nad*	*slomannoj*	*liliej*	(MC, RNC)
	dead	bird	or	over	broken	lily	

'One could beautifully and decently be sad over a dead bird or a broken lily'

3.2 Emotions as reactions to actions

The main reaction to somebody's good actions is GRATITUDE, which was mentioned above. In this section, therefore, we consider psych verbs belonging to ANGER and INSULT clusters, which both describe reactions to somebody's evil or wrong actions and share the same morphosyntactic expression.

Unlike the more depersonified JOY and SADNESS which are mainly triggered by events, ANGER and INSULT are emotions prototypically directed at a particular person and triggered by their actions. Therefore, the Stimulus argument in the prototypical verbs of these clusters is split into two: Object (person) and Cause (person's actions).

We consider the expression of the Object argument in verbs *serdit'sja na kogo-libo* 'to be angry at somebody-ACC' and *obizhat'sja na kogo-libo* 'to be offended at somebody-ACC'. Both these feelings are conceptualized in the FEELING IS AN ATTACK metaphor, with the Object of the feeling interpreted as Patient. Both verbs overwhelmingly express their Object argument by means of *na* 'at' construction (over 80 % of their total occurrence in the Russian National Corpus).

The primary, non-metaphorical meaning of the 'at' construction with accusative is directional, and the noun preceded by 'at' expresses the semantic role of the Goal. Its first metaphorical extension involves verbs such as *nabrosit'sja na kogo-libo* 'to throw oneself at somebody-ACC', *prygnut' na kogo-libo* 'jump at somebody-ACC', which describe aggressive motion towards the patient. In the next stage of metaphorization, this construction is used to express the Object role of aggressive emotions, which are conceptualized as attacks. Consider its development in Table 6.1:

Serdit'sja and *obizhat'sja* are not the only verbs in the ANGER and OFFENCE clusters that manifest the conceptual metaphor FEELING IS AN ATTACK, conventionally expressed in the syntactic metaphor with *na* 'at' construction.

Table 6.1: Metaphorization stages of semantic roles.

Goal ⇒	**Patient of aggressive motion ⇒**	**Stimulus of ANGER or GRUDGE**
brosit' mjach ***na*** *pol*	*brosit'sja* ***na*** *protivnika*	*serdit'sja* <*obizhat'sja*> ***na*** *otca*
'to toss the ball **on/at** the floor'	'to charge **at** the enemy'	'to be angry **at** <to hold a grudge **against**> one's father'

The verbs *zlit'sja na kogo-libo* 'to be angry, to feel spite at somebody-ACC', *dut'sja na kogo-libo* 'to sulk at somebody-ACC' demonstrate the same underlying conceptual metaphor and the same conventional syntactic expression. In the ANGER cluster, the frequency of the 'at' expression of the Object argument correlates with the degree of aggression the feeling incorporates: the more aggressive kinds of ANGER are more frequently expressed with *na* than the less aggressive ones.

Thus, *razdrazhat'sja* 'to be irritated' can only occasionally be expressed with *na* 'at' (only 5 % of the total number of hits in the corpus) because the feeling is not particularly aggressive. *Razdrazhat'sja na kogo-libo* 'to be irritated at somebody-ACC' is possible, but more often the feeling is caused by a certain state of affairs, rather than a person, and involves one synthetic role of Stimulus rather than the roles of Object and Cause: *razdrazhat'sja iz-za postojannyx zaderzhek* 'to be irritated because of constant delays'.

The 'at' construction is fairly well represented in its metaphorical meaning outside the emotion domain, as well. Consider, for example, the verbs of yelling, such as *krichat' na kogo-libo* 'to shout at somebody-ACC', *orat' na kogo-libo* 'to yell at somebody-ACC', which develop meanings of aggressive speech acts directed at the Addressee by the angry Speaker. Likewise, this construction is productive in novel discourse metaphor. Thus, the verb *besit'sja* lit. 'to be rabid', 'to run amock, to romp', which in Russian expresses strong, but undirected anger (unlike its English translation equivalents *to be furious, to be enraged*, it lacks the Object argument), when coerced into this construction, receives the meaning of aggressive directed anger, and the added semantic role is interpreted as Patient:

(27) *Ona besilas' na muzha* (MC, RNC)
She raged at husband-ACC
'She was furious at her husband'

Even totally unlikely verbs, when coerced into 'at' construction, are re-interpreted as expressing aggression; cf. the following example from child speech (Iosif G., 10 years old):

(28) *Mama, chto ty na menja vzdyhaesh', iz-za dvojki?*
Mom what you at I-ACC sigh-2.SG because of F-grade
'Mommy, why are you sighing at me, is it because of my F grade?'

The non-directed, non-aggressive reflex action of sighing is reinterpreted in this metaphoric construction as a kind of communicatively aggressive behavior caused by the angry feelings of the subject.

Interestingly, even silence is interpreted as aggression when the verb *molchat'* 'to be silent' occurs in this construction as part of novel syntactic metaphor in discourse; cf. the following example from RuSkELL:

(29) *Ne molchite na menja*
NEG be-silent-IMP at I-ACC
'Don't be silent at me'

4 Conclusion

We have discovered the following correlations between semantics and conceptual metaphor, on the one hand, and conventional syntactic metaphor, on the other.

There is a correlation between the semantics of STIMULUS-ORIENTED AGGRESSION in the meaning of a psych verb and the syntactic expression of its Stimulus argument by the *na* 'at' prepositional construction (*serdit'sja na kogo-l.* 'to be angry at somebody'). The more aggressive the emotion, the more frequent is the 'at'-expression, with *serdit'sja, zlit'sja* 'to be angry, to be mad at somebody' forming the "aggressive" pole of anger, *negodovat', vozmushchat'sja* 'to be indignant' the "non-aggressive" pole, and emotions like *razdrazhat'sja* 'to get irritated' positioned in the middle of the scale. This is due to the fact that the more aggressive types of anger are conceptualized as attack-type reactions, with Stimulus metaphorically treated as Patient. On the level of conventional syntactic metaphor, that invokes the use of constructions whose primary, non-metaphoric function is to express the semantic role of Patient in verbs with the meaning of aggressive movement, such as *nabrasyvat'sja na kogo-libo* 'to throw oneself at someone'.

Novel syntactic metaphors patterned along the same conceptual model that occur in discourse, and are easily interpretable, include, for example, the semantic domain of SILENCE, as in *Ne molchi na menja* 'Don't be silent at me', where silence is interpreted as an expression of underlying anger.

There is also a correlation between the semantics of STIMULUS-ORIENTED NON-AGGRESSIVE EXPRESSION in combination with the semantics of STIMULUS IS

AN EVENT in the meaning of a psych verb and the syntactic expression of its Stimulus argument by dative. Certain verbs of the JOY cluster (*radovat'sja pobede*-DAT 'to rejoice over a victory') and verbs of the SURPRISE cluster *(udivljat'sja tomu, chto on prishel* 'to be surprised at his coming') display a strong preference for dative expression. The underlying conceptual metaphor in *radovat'sja* 'to rejoice' and *udivjat'sja* 'to be surprised' is FEELING IS A MEETING, with the Stimulus conceptualized as an Interlocutor or Addressee. This metaphor is part of a larger conceptual metaphor EVENT IS A MEETING, expressed in the following conventional lexical metaphors: *Segodnja my vstrechaem Novyj God* 'Today we are meeting the New Year'; *On vstretil eto sobytie spokojno* 'He met this event with equanimity'.

Examples of novel syntactic metaphors in discourse reflecting the underlying FEELING IS A MEETING structure include the verb *vosxishchat'sja* 'to be delighted with something', which fulfils the first requirement (STIMULUS-ORIENTED NON-AGGRESSIVE EXPRESSION) but not the second, as well as the verb *ogorchat'sja* 'to get upset by something', which fulfils the second requirement (STIMULUS IS AN EVENT) but not the first. Their regular syntactic expression of Stimulus is different – instrumental for *vosxishchat'sja*, prepositional constructions for *ogorchat'sja*, but both occasionally allow the dative; cf. examples from the Russian National Corpus *Ja vosxishchajus' ego mudrosti*-DAT 'I am delighted with his wisdom' and *Ja ogorchajus' takim veshcham*-DAT 'I get upset by such things'.

However, the types of JOY that are caused by states (*blazhenstvovat'* 'to experience bliss'), or that involve aggressive expression (*zloradstvovat'* 'to experience Schadenfreude') are based on different conceptual metaphors and require different syntactic expression.

Finally, there is a correlation between the semantics of duration and unreachability in the meaning of a psych verb and the syntactic expression of its Stimulus argument by an *o* 'about' prepositional construction. Morphosyntactic expression with *o* 'about' is expected of the more permanent types of FEAR, SADNESS and REGRET. All these emotions imply that the Stimulus of emotion is beyond the reach and control of the Experiencer, due either to

a) physical distance between the Experiencer and the Stimulus: e.g., *volnovat'sja o syne* 'to be worried about one's son' usually means the son is absent;
b) temporal distance: e.g., *sozhalet' o svoix postupkax* 'to regret one's deeds' means that the deeds are in the past and cannot be undone;
c) existential distance: e.g., *gorevat' o druge* 'to grieve over one's friend' means that the friend is dead.

They all share the same underlying conceptual metaphor FEELING IS THINKING, where the Stimulus is conceptualized as the topic of thoughts. This explains their conventional syntactic metaphor: the main non-metaphoric function of the *o*-construction is to express the semantic role of the Theme in mental verbs, such as *dumat'* 'to think', *razmyshljat'* 'to ponder', etc. The novel metaphor that is encountered in discourse involves such kinds of short-lived SADNESS as *rasstraivat'sja* and *ogorchat'sja* 'to get upset'. When used in the construction with *o* 'about', they are interpreted as denoting long-term SADNESS over irreparably lost objects, which is the meaning they only acquire in this construction; cf. examples from RuSkELL *Dolgo eshe lezhal bez sna i ogorchalsja o svoej utrate* 'I had been lying for a while and getting upset about my loss'; *Ja niskol'ko ne rasstraivajus' o proshlom* 'I don't for a moment get upset about the past'.

To sum up, the paper makes the following contributions to the field of metaphor and discourse: it expands the study of conventional metaphors into the domain of syntax, and explains morphosyntactic properties of psych verbs through the conceptual metaphor underlying their semantics; it also demonstrates that novel syntactic metaphors that spontaneously occur in discourse are not accidental but reflect the existing conventional metaphors, and are therefore interpretable by language speakers. The limitations of the study concern mainly the volume of our research material. We have studied, with different degree of minuteness, seven emotion clusters, namely JOY, SURPRISE, GRATITUDE, SADNESS, ANGER, GRUDGE, PRIDE, FEAR, REGRET. Certain important emotion clusters, such as JEALOUSY, SHAME, DISGUST have remained outside of our attention. Also, our metaphorical approach cannot explain every morphosyntactic property of every psych verb; in many cases, the metaphor is already dead and not perceived as such by language speakers. Thus, a full account of the morphosyntax of psych verbs would include an excursion into history. One more of the possible future research venues is a more thorough study of novel syntactic metaphors in discourse; we have considered this issue insofar as it was necessary to illustrate the conceptual metaphoric motivation that underlies the process of their formation. It would be interesting to explore this domain more thoroughly.

References

Apresjan, Juri. 1967. *Experimental'noe issledovanie semantiki russkogo glagola* [Experimental study of the semantics of Russian verbs]. Moscow: Nauka.

Apresjan, Juri. 1995. *Integral'noe opisanie iazyka i sistemnaia leksikographija* [An Integrated Description of Language and Systematic Lexicography]. Moscow: Jazyki russkoj kul'tury.

Apresjan, Juri. 2000. *Systematic lexicography*. Oxford: Oxford University Press.

Apresjan, Juri. 2002. Principles of systematic lexicography. In Marie-Heléne Corrèard (ed.), *Lexicography and Natural Language Processing*. A Festschrift in Honour of B. T. S. Atkins, 91–104. Grenoble: Euralex.

Apresjan, Jury. 2010. Novaja nomenklatura semanticheskih rolej [New inventory of semantic roles]. In Jury Apresjan, Igor Boguslavskij, Leonid Iomdin & Vladimir Sannikov (eds.), *Teoreticheskie problemy russkogo sintaksisa: vzaimodejstvie grammatiki i slovarja* [Theoretical issues of Russian syntax: the interrelation between grammar and vocabulary], 370–379. Moscow: Jazyki slavjanskih kul'tur.

Apresjan, Valentina. 2011. Opyt klasternogo analiza: russkie i anglijskie emocional'nye koncepty. Čast' 1 [An attempt at cluster analysis: Russian and English emotion concepts. Part 1]. *Voprosy jazykoznanija* [Issues in linguistics] 1. 19–51.

Apresjan, Valentina, Vit Baisa, Olga Buivolova, Olga Kultepina & Anna Maloletnjaja. RuSkELL language learning tool for Russian language. In Tinatin Margalitadze & George Meladze (eds.), *Proceedings of the XVII Euralex International Congress. Lexicography and Linguistic Diversity (6–10 September, 2016)*, 292–299.

Belletti, Adriana & Luigi Rizzi. 1988. Psych verbs and theta-theory. *Natural Language and Linguistic Theory*, 6 (3). 291–352.

Dowty, David. Thematic Proto-Roles and Argument Selection. 1991. *Language*, 67 (3). 547–619.

Goldberg, Adele. 2006. *Constructions at Work: The Nature of Generalization in Language.* Oxford: Oxford University Press.

Klein, Katarina & Silvia Kutscher. 2002. Psych-verbs and Lexical Economy. *Theorie des Lexikons*, 122 (Arbeiten des Sonderforschungsbereichs 282). http://linguistics.ruhr-uni-bochum.de/~klein/papers/sfb282_122.pdf (accessed 29 March 2012).

Kövecses, Zoltán. 2000. *Metaphor and Emotion: Language, Culture, and Body in Human Feeling*. Cambridge: Cambridge University Press.

Lai, Vicky Tzuyin, Tim Curran & Lise Menn. 2009. Comprehending conventional and novel metaphors: An ERP study. *Brain Research*, 1284. 145–155.

Lakoff, George & Mark Johnson. 1980. *Metaphors we live by*. Chicago: University of Chicago Press.

Lakoff, George & Mark Turner. 1989. *More Than Cool Reason: A Field Guide to Poetic Metaphor*. Chicago: University of Chicago Press.

Lakoff, George. 1993. The Syntax of Metaphoric Semantic Roles. In James Pustejovsky (ed.), *Semantics and the Lexicon*, 27–36. Dordrecht: Kluwer Academic Publishers.

Levin, Beth. 1993. *English Verb Classes and Alternations*. Chicago: University of Chicago Press.

Ruiz de Mendoza, Francisco J. & Ricardo Mairal. 2011. Constraints on syntactic alternation: lexical-constructional subsumption in the Lexical Constructional Model. In Pilar Guerrero (ed.), *Morphosyntactic alternations in English. Functional and cognitive perspectives*, 62–82. London, UK & Oakville, CT: Equinox.

Panther, Klaus-Uwe, Linda Thornburg & Antonio Barcelona (eds.). 2009. *Metonymy and metaphor in grammar*. Amsterdam & Philadelphia: Benjamins.

Semino, Elena. 2008. *Metaphor in Discourse*. Cambridge: Cambridge University Press.

Sullivan, Karen. *Frames and constructions in metaphoric language*. 2013. Amsterdam: John Benjamins.

Montserrat Esbrí-Blasco, Carolina Girón-García
and María Luisa Renau Renau

Metaphors in the digital world: The case of metaphorical frames in 'Facebook' and 'Amazon'

Abstract: The Internet is overwhelmingly present in our daily activities, such as communication through forums, e-mails, chats, and social networks. It has profoundly affected the Linguistics field, as digital reality has prompted researchers to explore users' interaction with online genres. Accordingly to this technological revolution, information is nowadays increasingly found in digital format (electronic texts) rather than in print. This phenomenon has brought about the introduction of new word usage. Much research devotes to analyzing language on the Internet, and recent work suggests that digital navigation patterns may result from external guiding.

Nevertheless, there is little work on the role of semantic frames and metaphors. The aim of this paper is twofold: (1) Analyzing the most common words and expressions in the social network 'Facebook' and in 'Amazon'; and (2) finding out the 'Facebook' and 'Amazon' semantic frames for metaphor identification following the MIP Procedure (Pragglejazz Group 2007). In this context, the procedure follows three stages: (A) selection, (B) identification and analysis of the configuration of the conceptual frames evoked by particular lexical units, and (C) description of the metaphorical mappings and inferences between the elements of the evoked digital frame (contextual frame) and the elements of the literal frame. The findings suggest that culturally shared semantic frames adapt to virtual environments to bring about configurations of virtual (metaphorical) semantic frames. Dissimilarities between literal and contextual semantic frames lead to consider the existence of 'Metaphorical Transference', which enhances the users' adequate understanding of the digital frame. To conclude, the results help to unravel the role of metaphorical frames as knowledge configurations that provide coherence to Cybergenres.

Keywords: Semantic frames, lexical units, literal and contextual meanings, metaphorical units

Montserrat Esbrí-Blasco, Carolina Girón-García, María Luisa Renau Renau Universitat Jaume I, Departament d'Estudis Anglesos. Spain.

https://doi.org/10.1515/9783110629460-007

1 Introduction

Since the 20th century, the Internet plays a central role in our daily activities. Technology has improved significantly, allowing for the creation of an enormous number of tools which offer internet users new horizons of interaction, and consequently, cause the appearance of new genres.

A lot of work has been devoted to analyzing language usage on the Internet, and recent findings suggest that metaphorical models in our conceptual system may guide digital navigation patterns (Navarro i Ferrando 2008; Navarro i Ferrando et al. 2008; Navarro i Ferrando and Silvestre 2009; Girón-García and Navarro i Ferrando 2014). As Porto (2007: 196) argues, "metaphors are a very useful tool to interpret reality. The modern world is in permanent change and we must cope with new information and experiences all the time". Furthermore, this work will address a hitherto neglected aspect of conceptual frames, namely its vital role in the description of non-literal language (Sullivan 2013).

In this line, the aim of this study is to provide a thorough description of the conceptual frames evoked by particular lexical units found in Facebook and Amazon as well as to examine the specific role of those frames in the process of identifying metaphorical expressions. By doing so, different cognitive models will be portrayed with the aim of interpreting webpages such as Facebook and Amazon on the grounds of metaphorical knowledge configurations (section 3).

2 Cybergenres

Firstly, we explore the notion of 'Cybergenre' since the aim of our study is to shed some light on the role of semantic frames and metaphors in the setting of coherent Cybergenres.

With the increasing use of new technologies, there was a need to study the emerging virtual genres that the Internet was generating. Yates and Orlikowski (1992: 299–326) pointed out that "genres evolve over time in response to institutional changes and social pressures" (in Shepherd and Watters 1998: 1). In some cases, the changes undergone by an existing genre are so extensive that they lead to the emergence of a new genre. The marriage of the computer with the Internet has been so decisive that it has resulted in the emergence of a new class of genre altogether, which has been termed Cybergenre.

Cybergenre comprehension and use seems to be a type of cognitive process where users give meaning to digital environments through the implementation of previously well-entrenched cognitive models. This paper does not intend to state whether social networks are Cybergenres or whether they can be classified as a specific genre type. Instead, this work seeks to provide some evidence that metaphorical models play a role in the comprehension and production of texts, particularly digital texts on the internet. Moreover, this research aims at characterizing the role of metaphorical models and expressions in the construction of digital genres as different from other types of genre, as far as content organization and structure are concerned (Girón-García and Navarro i Ferrando 2014). Nevertheless, in the case of 'Facebook' and 'Amazon' the role of metaphorical expressions, and the frames these evoke, acquire special relevance because they help users to conceptualize the new virtual environment coherently.

3 Knowledge configuration notions

It is convenient first to introduce the diverse types of conventionalized knowledge configuration (ICMs) that shape the conceptual system (Lakoff 1987) of a cultural community. This paper focuses on the notions of frame, domain, script, and ICM, which, since the emergence of Cognitive Semantics, have been used to refer to the organization of conceptual knowledge (Fillmore 1982; Lakoff and Johnson 1980; Langacker 1987). However, the definitions of these constructs "overlap significantly and are often considered isomorphic by researchers" (Mischler 2013). In this respect, this work provides a more specific view of these notions, which in turn will serve to describe the configuration of existing metaphors that structure the content of the websites analysed.

3.1 Conceptual frames

Regarding the notion of frame, the basic idea proposed by Fillmore (1982: 111) is that a frame can be referred to as: "any system of concepts related in such a way that to understand any of them you have to understand the whole structure in which it fits; when one of the things in such a structure is introduced into a text, or into a conversation, all of the others are automatically made available". Nevertheless, more recent accounts of the notion of frame present a more specific definition, considering a frame as "a script-like conceptual structure that describes a particular type of situation, object or event and the participants and props involved in it" (Ruppenhofer et al. 2010: 5).

In an attempt to provide a more operational definition, frame is conceived here as a schematic human knowledge configuration in the long-term memory that represents a prototypical situation type, object or single event, where concepts may be more or less central or peripheral and can be characterized either as participants or props. In this type of configuration, each participant concept has a semantic role, which allows for perspectivization. The meaning of a word cannot be understood – or known at all – without the comprehension of the whole semantic frame it evokes, so that the semantic frame is necessary to the meaning of the given lexical unit. In this same line, a lexical unit cannot be understood without evoking previous knowledge configurations that are integrated into the users' conceptual system.

3.2 Cognitive domains

In our view, frames are always part of larger cognitive constructs called domains (Langacker 1987). However, in the cognitive linguistics tradition, researchers have failed at offering a proper clear-cut definition of both frame and domain. Langacker (1987: 63) points out that "semantic units are characterized relative to cognitive domains, and any concept or knowledge system can function as a domain for this purpose". In this line, Kövecses (2010: 324) refers to cognitive domains as "our conceptual representation, or knowledge, of any coherent segment of experience. We often call such representations 'concepts', such as the concepts of building or motion. This knowledge involves both the knowledge of basic elements that constitute a domain and knowledge that is rich in detail".

The definitions above fail to offer a precise view of what a cognitive domain is. Here cognitive domains are understood as conceptual constructs or configurations that comprise (all) the concepts related to a particular area of human experience or human knowledge. That area may vary in its complexity, at any rate including the different prototypical situation types (frames) that humans share about that particular domain of experience. Thus, cognitive domains are not equated to frames, rather they consist of frames and their frame constituents, as well as frame sequences (i.e., scripts).

3.3 Scripts

The notion of 'script' is relevant in this study to the extent that it helps determine whether some structural patterns occur only in the literal meaning of the lexical unit analysed, or whether they also occur in the contextual meaning. Schank and Abelson (1977: 210) first defined a script as “a structure that describes appropriate sequences of events in a particular context. A script is made up of slots and requirements about what can fill those slots. The structure is an interrelated whole and what is in a slot affects what can be in another.” Along with this line, scripts are regarded here as sequences of frames that may occur in a particular context, rather than as a type of frame or domain.

4 Metaphor and cybergenres: the role of metaphorical models in websites

In this paper, the focus is on the role of metaphor and metaphorical models in the configuration of coherent Cybergenres. In Cognitive Linguistics, previous knowledge shared by a cultural community has been analysed in terms of Idealized Cognitive Models (ICMs). Their nature may influence users’ representations of various types of websites. “Prior knowledge” and “Shared knowledge” are two important concepts in metaphorical ICMs; the reason for this relies on the fact that if users share previous knowledge with others, the result is that shared knowledge becomes well-structured and built into conventional models, which at the same time are based on social and individual experience. Following from this, an ICM could be defined as a “cognitive structure” idealized with the aim of understanding and reasoning, and whose function is to represent reality from a certain perspective (Ruiz de Mendoza and Díez-Velasco 2002: 490; Navarro i Ferrando and Silvestre 2009).

The identification of metaphorical models and the description and classification of their mappings may reveal the conceptual configuration that helps in the conceptualization of new cybergenres. Given their contribution to hypertextual coherence and architecture, these mappings might characterize the types of reading strategies and modes (i.e. ‘user strategic mode’) that guide users along the interpretation of digital texts (Girón-García and Navarro i Ferrando 2015: 40).

In a digital context, the interaction between a human being and the Internet would not have a meaning unless metaphorical models (conceptual metaphors) provide a set of coherent structures for previously unknown realities. In other words, domains that do not allow for physical experience (virtual domains) need metaphor in order to be practically understood. In fact, interacting with websites, making decisions as screens are activated and using Internet materials and resources (Target Domain) would not be possible without cognitive domains adapted from previous experience (Source Domain) (Girón-García and Navarro i Ferrando 2015).

The present section characterizes source domains that map onto the target domain "website", a very recent domain in our conceptual system. Users do not seem to be aware of the systematic mappings between source and target domains. In fact, speakers' knowledge of such mappings is rather unconscious, and it is only for the purpose of the analysis herein that domain mappings are brought into awareness. As Kövecses (2010: 4) points out, the occurrence of metaphorical linguistic expressions discloses the existence of ways of thinking. In fact, it is rather difficult to speak about the domain of websites without turning to the usual linguistic expressions, which are the manifestation of the metaphorical models that constitute our object of study. Thus, to understand the mapping, it is necessary to build a sort of *literal-metalanguage* that serves to describe the domain as literally as possible. Thus, interacting with the Internet and the computer only in terms of representation of what wants to be activated and, consequently, read or visualized, would cause a rather weird and negative experience. For that reason, humans resort to metaphorical models – conceptual metaphors – that provide a coherent structure for unknown realities, domains that have not been previously experienced or do not allow for direct physical experience (abstract domains). The unknown, new or abstract domain is called a Target Domain, whereas the previously known, and well-understood one, is called a Source Domain because it is the conceptual source for understanding the Target Domain (Kövecses 2010; Lakoff 1993; Girón-García and Navarro i Ferrando 2014).

5 Method

The methodology employed in this study follows three stages:

1. The first step consists in selecting the most common lexical units in the target domain that fulfil a guiding function in the use or understanding of the virtual sites 'Facebook' and 'Amazon'. Once the lexical units are selected, their meanings are looked up in four well-known online dictionaries, Macmillan (http://www.macmillandictionary.com/), Cambridge (http://dictionary.cambridge.org/), Oxford (http://www.oxforddictionaries.com/), and Merriam-Webster (https://www.merriam-webster.com/). The shared meaning elements in the definitions of each lexical unit from all four dictionaries show the 'literal meaning'. Then, the 'contextual meaning' of each lexical unit is described in their virtual contexts in 'Facebook' and 'Amazon'.

2. The following step focuses on the identification and analysis of the configuration of the conceptual frames evoked by the lexical units under study.
3. The concluding stage is to examine the lexical units in both contexts (literal and contextual) by contrasting their frame elements. If there is contrast, and the contextual elements can be understood in terms of the elements of the literal frame, the lexical units can be considered metaphorical.

6 Results and discussion

Some of the most remarkable lexical units from the Web pages 'Facebook' and 'Amazon' are object of analysis here. Concerning 'Facebook', the lexical units *friend, friend request, message* and *event* are analysed. Regarding 'Amazon', the lexical units *car, gift card, departments, help, explore* and *pay* are analysed. Subsequently (1) their contextual and literal meanings in each individual frame (literal and contextual) are described, (2) their frame (literal and contextual), is outlined (3) a decision follows on whether the lexical units selected are considered metaphorical in the contextual virtual space, and finally (4) the analysis provides a description of the script each lexical unit evokes.

6.1 Facebook

6.1.1 Friend

The four dictionaries mentioned above show the literal meaning of *friend*. Regarding the literal meaning of the lexical unit 'friend', this concept refers to a mental space representing a person, someone one knows well and likes, with whom one has a bond of mutual affection but who is not a member of one's family, and with whom one does not have sexual relations. On the other hand, the contextual meaning shows a 'friend' as a person – usually, but not necessarily in all cases – who connects virtually with another person, institution, business in general through the social networking site. Usually, Facebook friends are website users who know each other before joining that site, or who know each other outside the website. They might be friends or acquaintances in the outside world, know each other through school, work or any other type of social institution, or might have a mutual acquaintance. The next step is to describe the contextual and literal meanings (see Table 7.1).

Table 7.1: Contextual and literal frame elements: 'friend'.

'FRIEND' FRAME: KNOWING PEOPLE	
CONTEXTUAL MEANING	LITERAL MEANING
Contextual Frame Elements	Literal Frame Elements
Person A	Person A
Person B	Person B
Virtually connected	Mutual affection
Social networking site	A and B know each other well
A and B may be relatives	No family relation
A and B may be close family members	No sexual relationship
A and B may be Institutions, groups, shops, etc.	
Shared experience is not necessary	Shared experience

Moreover, the literal meaning of the lexical unit 'friend' is understood or interpreted as a frame element in the 'friendship' frame, so that the background scene of this frame may be integrated in the context of friendship.

The word *friend* is specific concerning a background scene in which 'person A' knows 'person B'. Persons A and B can be considered as friends if they know each other well and like each other, if they have a bond of mutual affection not being members of the same family, and they do not maintain a sexual relationship. If they call each other friends, they necessarily share or have shared experiences.

On the other hand, in the contextual meaning, the lexical unit 'Friend' is specified concerning a virtual background scene in which person 'A' may or may not have met 'person B' physically. Friends in this prototypical scene are virtually connected. 'Friends' here are contacts on a social networking website who need or intend to stay connected. They can be considered as friends even if they do not know each other physically and even if they do not have a bond of mutual affection. In Facebook, friends can be members of the same family, maybe relatives, and they can even maintain sexual relationships. If they call each other friends, they do not necessarily share any (physical) experience. Either 'Person A' or 'Person B', or both, in this virtual scene, may not be a human being, but rather represent an institution, group, restaurant, association, shop, or any other type of social entity.

Therefore, the analysis shows that the contextual meaning contrasts with the literal meaning and can be understood by comparison with it. More precisely, there is a necessary bond of mutual affection in real life, but not in Facebook; a friend can be a member of one's family or a relative in Facebook, but not in real life. An institution, a shared interest group or even a shop or a restaurant is what we call a Facebook 'friend'. In conclusion, the lexical unit 'friend' is regarded as a metaphorical term in Facebook, since some of the literal frame elements contrast with the contextual frame elements and some other elements can be mapped.

6.1.2 Friend request

The literal meaning of the lexical unit 'friend request' can be comprehended as an act of asking for something politely or formally. Nevertheless, considering its contextual meaning, a 'Friend Request' is the most common type of request on Facebook.

When someone (person A) finds a person on Facebook and clicks on "add as friend", then someone else (person B) gets a request. At that point, person B chooses "Confirm" or "Ignore". Therefore, accepting a 'friend request' is a private affair, whereas sending a 'friend request' is a public affair.

Table 7.2: 'friend request' script.

1. Friend A searches Friend B on Facebook
2. Friend A finds B´s profile
3. Friend A sends a Friend Request to Friend B
4. Friend B gets the Friend Request
5. Friend B considers the option of confirming or ignoring this Friend Request
6. Friend B accepts the Friend Request
7. Friend A receives the acceptance of the Friend Request
8. Friend A and Friend B connect in the virtual network

Regarding the 'friend request' script on Facebook (see Table 7.2), the mapping with the literal meaning of 'friend' in the real world shows whether literal and contextual meanings share common frame elements. In this case, the Facebook script cannot be mapped onto a real life situation, and therefore, this script is only possible in the virtual world.

6.1.3 Message

The literal meaning of the word *message* is defined as "a verbal, written, or recorded communication sent or given to someone, especially when you cannot speak to them or be contacted directly". In contrast, in this virtual context, the noun "message", i.e., its contextual meaning, refers to an electronic piece of information that is sent/given to someone or received by someone and displayed on a screen (see Table 7.3).

Table 7.3: Contextual and literal frame elements: 'message'.

'MESSAGE' FRAME: (ELECTRONIC) PIECE OF INFORMATION	
CONTEXTUAL MEANING	LITERAL MEANING
Contextual Frame Elements	Literal Frame Elements
Person A	Person A
Person B	Person B
Virtually connected	Personal relationship
Social networking site	
May be relatives	
May have a business relationship	Business relationship
Institutions, groups, shops, etc.	
No shared experience is needed	

Table 7.4: 'send a message' script.

1. Friend A writes a personal message to Friend B on Facebook
2. Friend A sends the message
3. Friend B receives the message
4. Friend B answers the message to Friend A
5. Friend A and Friend B establish a virtual conversation

Table 7.4 shows the sequence of frames in the 'send a message' script. First, Friend A writes and sends a message to one of his/her Facebook friends, that is, Friend B. When Friend B receives and reads the message, the Facebook user decides to start an interaction with Friend A and answers back, then, establishing a virtual conversation.

6.1.4 Event

The lexical unit 'event' entails other related expressions such as 'create an event' and 'upcoming event'. The literal meaning of 'event' is defined as: "A planned or organized social occasion or activity that involves several people, and takes place during a social gathering (sports competition, birthday party...)"; secondly, the 'create an event' literal meaning as: "originate, to make something new or original, to invent" and finally, the 'upcoming event' literal meaning as: "happening (soon), appearing soon, about to happen, forthcoming" (cf. https://www.facebook.com/help/).

In the contextual meaning, a Facebook 'event' is understood as a feature that allows Facebook users or page operators to create a calendar-based invitation to an event. A Facebook event can be sent to other users and will include information about the event, the time and date of the event and even images related to it. A Facebook event provides a simple, hands-off way for Facebook users to send invitations to their friends. Because of the interactive nature of Facebook, a Facebook event can also help create commentaries about itself (cf. https://www.facebook.com/help/).

Furthermore, the 'create an event' contextual meaning implies that Facebook users or page operators can create a calendar-based invitation to an event, including time and date plus additional information about the event.

Finally, the 'upcoming event' contextual meaning incorporates the fact that Facebook users or page operators can view upcoming events. By default, events will appear in a chronological list view. In calendar view, events appear on the day of the month they occur. The frame elements evoked by 'event' are shown in Table 7.5, below.

Table 7.5: Contextual and literal frame elements: 'event'.

'EVENT' FRAME: HAPPENING OR ACTIVITY	
CONTEXTUAL MEANING	LITERAL MEANING
Contextual Frame Elements	Literal Frame Elements
Several participants (more than 2)	Several participants (more than 2)
Social occasion	Social and public occasion
Not all the participants necessarily know each other	Not all the participants necessarily know each other
A happening or activity	A happening or activity
Act that takes place	Act that takes place
There is an organizer	There is an organizer
It is not necessarily a setting	It is a setting
It is only for participants	It is not only for participants
It is not a routine	It is not a routine

On the one hand, the literal meaning of the lexical unit 'event' entails several participants (more than two people). It is a social and public occasion in which not all the participants know each other necessarily. An 'event' is a happening, activity, or act that takes place; and it involves an organizer, who might be one of the participants of the event. In this context, there is always a setting or place where the event takes place. Furthermore, it should be worth noting that this 'event' is not only for participants but also for the public in general, and it is not considered as a routine.

On the other hand, in the contextual meaning, the unit 'event' evokes a background virtual space in which more than two people participate. In this prototypical scene (see Table 7.6), an 'event' is a social occasion where not all the participants necessarily know each other. It is also a happening, activity, or an act that takes place, in which there is an organizer who is one of the participants at the event. This activity is not necessarily a setting or physical place where the event takes place, and it is not only organized for participants who virtually accept the invitation. Finally, a Facebook 'event' is not a routine, but rather a specific activity or function taking place at a given date, time and place.

Therefore, it seems that the contextual meaning contrasts with the literal meaning and can be understood by comparison with it. Nevertheless, only one element is different, i.e. the place where the event takes place. In Facebook, an 'event' may not be a physical place. Thus, the lexical unit 'event' is determined as a metaphorical term.

Table 7.6: 'event' script.

1. Friend A creates an event (meeting, party...) in the real world
2. Friend A sends an invitation to Friend B
3. Friend A sends an invitation to Friend B, C, and D
4. Friend B receives the virtual invitation to the event
5. Friend B considers the option of accepting this invitation or not
6. Friend B accepts/refuses the invitation
7. If Friend B accepts the invitation, Friend A and Friend B meet in the real world

6.2 Amazon

6.2.1 Cart

Concerning the contextual meaning of the lexical unit 'cart', a cart icon appears on the top right corner of the page that the user may click on, so that a new screen appears, showing a product or a list of products that the user intends to buy. In contrast, the literal meaning of 'cart' can be defined as "A wire basket on wheels that you push used in a supermarket for carrying the things that you want to buy" (Macmillan Dictionary).

Bearing in mind these definitions, the contextual and literal frames could be established in terms of 'adding products'. Along with this line, the following terms might be considered as contextual frame elements: Amazon, user, cart icon, clicking, opening a new screen, product(s) in a list. On the other hand, the following literal frame elements may be identified: supermarket, customer, cart, product(s), the action of putting products into the cart, pushing the cart.

The action of putting products into the cart implies that customers may add as many items as they wish by clicking the 'add to cart' box. Once the customer has added the products, one can continue looking for other products until the cart contains all the desired items. Then, by clicking the 'cart icon', one can see all the selected products. Furthermore, the fact of adding a product does not mean that it is going to be bought; since this action only takes place when clicking on the box 'add to order' followed by the box 'proceed to checkout', and the customer receives a confirmation email of the product(s) bought. One may also make modifications in the cart contents, modifying the number of products previously added and even eliminating them from the cart. Thus, because of this comparison, it may be confirmed that there is a metaphorical use because the contextual frame can be interpreted in contrast with the literal frame.

Therefore, to understand the main similarities and differences between both meanings described, it needs to be stressed that "users' minds need to import models from previous experience to process, structure and reason ..." (Navarro i Ferrando and Silvestre 2009: 284) about the contextual frame. Additionally, 'mapping' as a mental mechanism that allows that process is necessary when it comes to understanding the similarities and differences between the contextual and the literal meaning. However, not all contextual frame elements are mapped from their expected literal frame elements. By looking at the list of elements described in Table 7.7 (contextual and literal frame elements: 'cart') below, it can be observed that all the elements from the literal meaning map onto the elements in the contextual meaning. Some examples show that supermarket maps onto Amazon, the customer maps onto the user, and the action of looking at products (or the description of products) maps onto clicking and opening a new screen.

Table 7.7: Contextual and literal frame elements: 'cart'.

'CART' FRAME: ADDING PRODUCTS	
CONTEXTUAL MEANING	LITERAL MEANING
Contextual Frame Elements	Literal Frame Elements
Amazon	Supermarket
User	Customer
Cart icon	Cart
Clicking	The action of looking at products' description
Opening a new screen	The action of looking at products
Product(s) in a list	Product(s)
Adding products to the Amazon cart	The action of putting products into the cart
Browsing Amazon webpage	Pushing the cart

In the light of these observations (Table 7.7) and due to the similarities in both meanings, we suggest that there is a metaphorical relationship regarding the lexical unit 'cart'; and therefore, it might be considered as a metaphorical concept in its Amazon usage.

Table 7.8 (cart script) shows a structure that describes the prototypical sequence of events that occur in the context of adding products to a cart. Thus, as someone adds items in an Amazon cart: first, an Amazon account needs to be created; second, the user should be logged in to be able to select a product from a given department; third, an item which is already on Amazon can be selected; and finally, products can be added to the Amazon cart.

In this context, the description of this script is relevant because it demonstrates that this sequence of frames (i.e., script) is not only present in the literal meaning, but also in the contextual meaning.

Table 7.8: Cart script.

1. Create one's Amazon account
2. Sign in/log in
3. Select department
4. Select item(s)/product(s)
5. Add items to cart

6.2.2 Gift card

Regarding the Contextual meaning of the lexical unit 'gift card', this concept could be described as a link on top of the page that the user may click on, so that a new screen opens, laying out a set of actions that the user might consider to send a gift card to someone else. On the other hand, the literal meaning is defined as "a piece of plastic that can be exchanged in a store for goods of the value that is printed on it" (Cambridge Free English Dictionary and Thesaurus).

With regards to this definition, the contextual frame of 'gift card' is understood as 'sending an eGift card'. Moreover, the following elements constitute this frame: Amazon, user, gift card link, clicking, opening a new screen, clicking 'Gift cards', selecting sending method ('eGift', 'Print at Home', 'Mail'), and considering the amount of money to be spent. In contrast, the frame for the literal meaning is established as 'buying a gift card in a shop for someone else', whose frame constituents are: shop, person (customer), money (cash/credit card), cashier, cash desk, plastic card ('Gift card'), payment, method, payment options, ticket/bill/invoice.

Buying a 'gift card' implies exchanging money for millions of products. They are the ideal gift for any occasion by which one will fulfil family and friends' expectations since one allows the addressee to choose what they want or need. Nevertheless, they are mainly used to take advantage of offers and discounts, and to buy through the Internet from the comfort of one's home, allowing for purchases in any country to be realized.

Therefore, resulting from this comparison, a metaphorical use can be suggested, since the contextual frame contrasts with the literal frame.

Now, when observing the list of elements described in Table 7.9 (contextual and literal frame elements: 'Gift card'), it can be inferred that once again, not all the elements from the literal meaning map onto the elements in the contextual meaning, and vice versa. Some examples depict that 'shop' maps onto 'Amazon', and 'plastic card' ('Gift card') maps onto 'method' ('eGift', 'Print at Home', 'Mail'). Nevertheless, there is not a correspondence between the 'gift card' link, clicking 'Gift cards', and opening a new screen, and any elements in the literal frame.

According to Table 7.9 (Contextual and literal frame elements: 'Gift card'), 9 elements (3 from the contextual meaning and 6 from the literal meaning) do not map onto the contrasting frame. Nevertheless, in the light of these observations and due to a certain degree of similarity in both meanings, it may be considered that there is a metaphorical relationship for the lexical unit 'Gift card'; and thus, it may be considered as a metaphorical concept in its Amazon usage.

Table 7.9: Contextual and literal frame elements: 'Gift card'.

'GIFT CARD' FRAME	
SENDING AN 'eGIFT CARD (Contextual Frame)	BUYING A 'GIFT CARD' (Literal Frame)
CONTEXTUAL MEANING	LITERAL MEANING
Contextual Frame Elements	Literal Frame Elements
Amazon	Shop
User	Costumer
Gift card link	
Clicking 'Gift cards'	
Opening a new screen	
	Payment
	Method
Method ('eGift', 'Print at Home', 'Mail')	Plastic card ('Gift card')
	Payment options
	Ticket / bill / invoice
	Cashier
	Cash desk
Money (credit card)	Money (cash / credit card)

In Table 7.10 (eGift Card Script), the structure that describes the prototypical sequence of events corresponding to 'buying an eGift card' is outlined as follows: First, an Amazon account must be created by the user who must then log in onto the Amazon page. Then, when an Amazon gift card is added to the user's account, the funds will be stored in his/her account and is automatically applied to their next order. To add a gift card, users must go to their account and click on 'Gift cards', and subsequently select the sending method ('eGift', 'Print at Home', 'Mail'). In case 'Mail' is selected as the preferred sending method (the usual method, in fact), the user will be required to write their email address and password, and select the amount of money they desire to spend in purchasing a gift card. Finally, the user must log out from the Amazon webpage.

Table 7.10: eGift card script.

1. Create your Amazon account
2. Sign in/Log in
3. Click 'Gift cards'
4. Select sending method ('eGift', 'Print at Home', 'Mail')
5. Select the amount of money to be spent
6. Buy a gift card
7. Sign out/Log out

6.2.3 Departments

Regarding the contextual meaning of the lexical unit 'departments', it could be described as a link on the top left corner of the main page that the user may click on, so that a list of departments is displayed on the screen. As for its literal meaning, the Macmillan Dictionary defined it as 'areas in a large shop that sells a particular type of goods'. In both cases, the literal and the contextual meaning evoke the 'looking for a product' frame.

On the one hand, the contextual frame elements include the user, the 'departments' link, the act of clicking, selecting the department that the user needs, displaying products and selecting the products by clicking on them. On the other hand, the literal frame elements include the department store, the directory, the act of selecting a department from the directory, all the departments, the customer, watching the products, and finally, taking a product.

In the context of 'Amazon', the lexical unit 'departments' plays quite an essential role when users look for a specific product. First, the 'departments' link works as a directory which organizes all the products the website offers. In this way, it helps users to 'locate' more easily and quickly what they are looking for.

When comparing it with the literal frame evoked, there is also a customer who wants to buy a product, but first he/she goes to the directory. The directory has a guiding role for customers in that it leads them to the right section of the store.

Table 7.11 outlines a list of contextual and literal frame elements. Some of these elements can be mapped from the 'store frame' onto the 'Amazon frame'. These correspondences are the ones that provide coherence to the virtual space.

Table 7.11: Contextual and literal frame elements: 'Departments'.

'DEPARTMENTS' FRAME: LOOKING FOR A PRODUCT	
CONTEXTUAL MEANING	LITERAL MEANING
Contextual Frame Elements	Literal Frame Elements
Amazon	Supermarket
User	Customer
Departments link	Directory
Departments	Departments/sections
Clicking	
Selecting the department	Selecting the department from the directory
Displaying products	Watching the products on the shelves
Selecting a product	Taking a product

As shown in Table 7.11, only one element (clicking) is not motivated by the store model. The rest of the elements find a correlation with other literal frame elements and consequently it may be claimed that the lexical unit 'departments' is metaphorical (its contextual frame can be interpreted in contrast with the literal frame).

Hereunder, Table 7.12 depicts the script configured by the prototypical sequence of frames in this context:

Table 7.12: Script evoked by the lexical unit 'Departments'.

1. Create one's Amazon account
2. Sign in/log in
3. Click on 'Departments'
4. Select a department
5. Start shopping

Regarding the script that the lexical unit 'Departments' evokes, it can be said that first, the user needs to create an Amazon account (should the user still not have one); then, he/she must sign in and click on the link 'departments'. After that, the user can select the department they are looking for and start shopping.

6.2.4 Help

The fourth lexical unit analysed from Amazon is 'help'. When defining its contextual meaning, this refers to a link on the top of the page that the user may click on; in doing so, a new screen opens up and displays a set of 'help topics' that users might find useful at any stage of their shopping process. In contrast, the literal meaning of the lexical unit 'help' is 'to give someone support or information so that they can do something more easily' (Macmillan Dictionary). Therefore, the contextual and literal frames evoked by both meanings could be named the 'giving support' frame.

Regarding the frame elements pertaining to the frame evoked by the contextual meaning, these include the user, the user's doubt about the shopping process, the 'help' link, the act of clicking, the list of 'help topics' and the act of looking for the needed information.

On the other hand, the frame elements found in the frame evoked by the literal meaning include the customer, the customer's doubt, the department store, the assistant and the customer service department.

In the context of 'Amazon', the lexical unit 'help' provides users with a lot of useful information that they might need regarding different topics. When clicking 'help', information appears to be well organized so that the users themselves can look for and obtain the desired answer. In comparison with the literal frame evoked, there is also a customer who needs help on a particular matter. However, in the physical context customers must go to the 'customer service department', where some assistants can help them solve their doubts.

Table 7.13 shows the list of elements that belong to the literal and contextual frames evoked. The correspondences indicate that some elements from the store frame can be easily mapped onto elements in the Amazon frame.

Table 7.13: Contextual and literal frame elements: 'Help'.

'HELP' FRAME: GIVING SUPPORT	
CONTEXTUAL MEANING	LITERAL MEANING
Contextual Frame Elements	Literal Frame Elements
User	Customer
Amazon	Department store
Doubt	Doubt
Help link	Customer service department
Clicking	
List of help topics	
Looking for the needed information	Getting the answer from the assistants

According to Table 7.13, only two elements (clicking and list of help topics) are not motivated by the store model. However, the rest of the elements in the Amazon frame can be easily understood in terms of the department store elements, which may lead to regarding the lexical unit 'help' as metaphorical.

The following is an example of a script that could be evoked by the contextual meaning of 'departments' (see Table 7.14): First, users need to create an account and sign in. Once the user has logged in, they must click on the 'help' link to bring up the list of 'help topics'. When the user has selected the necessary topic, some information enables them to find a solution for their query.

Table 7.14: Script evoked by the contextual meaning of 'departments'.

1. Create one's Amazon account
2. Sign in/Log in
3. Click on 'help'
4. Select the 'help topic' needed
5. Find the solution/steps to follow

6.3 Discussion

In the light of the results expounded, it may be suggested that ICMs provide Cybergenre coherence because these have been previously entrenched in the users' long-term memory. Furthermore, ICMs help web users activate different mental models that make them navigate and interpret webpages, such as the ones analysed ('Facebook' and 'Amazon') in different ways. Hence, the extent to which users map previous knowledge configurations to the digital environment is related to the user's ability to project the conceptual content from literal to contextual frames.

The type of reading mode (or user reading strategy) has to do with the Cybergenre itself, its configuration, and the type of ICMs that are activated in the users' minds. The evokation of different cognitive models through the use of the digital environment demands the subsequent activation of different user reading strategies. In this process, the user activates a mental model that brings about a set of recurrent patterns or structures (i.e., a script) that facilitate web text/site interpretation. Thus, the conception of Cybergenres can be interpreted as a common ground where users' genre representations and ICMs meet in the Internet medium.

7 Conclusions

As the results indicate, the configuration and use of the digital environment is very much influenced by previous cultural knowledge (cognitive models). These models influence users' representations of websites. Therefore, semantic frames and metaphors are specially relevant for the analysis of the most remarkable lexical units that provide coherence to 'Facebook' and 'Amazon'. To show that metaphorical coherence this work has (a) described each lexical unit contextual and literal meanings in each individual frame (literal and contextual); (b) outlined their literal and contextual frames; (c) decided to what extent this choice of lexical units is considered metaphorical; and finally, (d) described the representation of the script evoked by each lexical unit.

Regarding the frames analysed, the results show that real life semantic frames adapt to virtual semantic frames. Furthermore, the differences between literal and contextual semantic frames suggest the existence of a 'Metaphorical Transference', i.e., the mapping of a real life frame onto a virtual one (in the users' conceptualization), which in turn enhances the coherence and understandability of the digital frame. Consequently, the identification, description and analysis of metaphorical lexical units, may help elucidate the connection between the digital environment and previous cultural representations.

Finally, further exploration and analysis is necessary to gauge to what extent lexical units in the virtual world are promoted through metaphorical competence, i.e., the users' ability to become consciously aware of ICMs and their mapping onto new domains of experience.

Acknowledgements: The work conducted in this chapter has been funded by the research project UJI-B2018-59 at Universitat Jaume I.

References

Fillmore, Charles J. 1977. Scenes-and-frames Semantics. In Antonio Zambolli (ed.), *Linguistic Structure Processing*, 55–82. Amsterdam: North-Holland Publishing Company.

Fillmore, Charles J. 1982. Frame semantics. In LSK (ed.), *Linguistics in the Morning Calm*, 111–137. Seoul, Hanshin Publishing Co.

Fillmore, Charles J. 1985. Frames and the semantics of understanding. *Quaderni di Semantica* 6 (2). 222–254.

Fillmore, Charles J. & Baker, Collin. 2009. A Frames Approach to Semantic Analysis. In Bernd Heine & Heiko Narrog (eds.), *The Oxford Handbook of Linguistic Analysis*, 313–340. Oxford: Oxford University Press.

Gawron, Jean M. 2008. *Circumstances and Perspective. The Logic of Argument Structure.* http://repositories.cdlib.org/ucsdling/sdlp3/1,October.

Girón García, Carolina & Ignasi, Navarro i Ferrando. 2014. Digital literacy and metaphorical models. *Multidisciplinary Journal for Education, Social and Technological Sciences* 1 (2). 160–180.

Girón García, Carolina & Ignasi, Navarro i Ferrando. 2015. Metaphorical models, cybergenres and strategic modes in virtual space. *Studia Universitatis Petru Maior. Series Philologia* 19. 32–43.

Kövecses, Zoltán. 2010. *Metaphor: A Practical Introduction*. (2nd Ed.) New York: Oxford University Press.

Lakoff, George. 1993. The contemporary theory of metaphor. In Andrew Ortony (ed.), *Metaphor and Thought*, 2nd edn. Cambridge: Cambridge University Press.

Lakoff, George & Mark Johnson. 1980. *Metaphors We Live By*. Chicago: University of Chicago Press.

Langacker, Ronald. W. 1987. *Foundations of Cognitive Grammar. Volume I: Theoretical Prerequisites*. Stanford, CA: Stanford University Press.

Mischler, James. 2013. *Metaphor across time and conceptual space*. Amsterdam: John Benjamins.

Navarro i Ferrando, Ignasi. 2008. Metaphorical ICMs in cybergenre representation, *Studia Universitatis Petru Maior. Series Philologia*, 7.

Navarro i Ferrando, Ignasi & Antonio J. Silvestre López. 2009. Cybergenre Representation and Metaphorical ICMs of Feature Websites in English. In Marta Navarro-Coy (ed.), *Practical Approaches to Foreign Language Teaching and Learning*, 269–292. Berlin & New York: Peter Lang.

Navarro i Ferrando, Ignasi, Villanueva Alfonso, M. Luisa, Girón García, Carolina & Silvestre López, Antonio-José. 2008. Cybergenres and Autonomous Language Learning: Pragmatic Strategies and Cognitive Models in the Production and Processing of Digital Genres. *INTED2008 Proceedings*. International Association for Technology, Education and Development, IATED. 1. 777–786.

Porto-Requejo, M. Dolores. 2007. The Construction of the concept Internet through metaphors. Cultura, lenguaje y representación 5. 195–207.

Pragglejazz Group 2007. MIP: A Method for Identifying Metaphorically Used Words in Discourse. *Metaphor and Symbol* 22 (1). 1–39.

Ruiz de Mendoza, Francisco J. & Olga Díez Velasco. 2002. Patterns of conceptual interaction. In R. Dirven & R. Pörings (eds.), *Metaphor and Metonymy in Comparison and Contrast*, 489–532. Berlin & New York: De Gruyter Mouton.

Schank, Roger C. & Robert Abelson. 1977. *Scripts, Plans, Goals, and Understanding*. Hillsdale, NJ: Lawrence Earlbaum Assoc.

Shepherd, Michael, & Carolyn R. Watters. 1998. The evolution of cybergenres. In Sprague, R.J. (ed.): *Proceedings of the Thirty-First Annual Hawaii International Conference on System Sciences (HICSS '98)*, vol. II 97–109. Hawaii: IEEE.

Steen, Gerard. 2007. *Finding Metaphor in Grammar and Usage*. Amsterdam: John Benjamins.

Steen, Gerard, Aletta G. Dorst, J. Berenike Herrmann, Anna A. Kaal, Tina Krennmayr, & Trijntje Pasma. 2010. *A Method for Linguistic Metaphor Identification*. Amsterdam: John Benjamins.

Sullivan, Karen. 2013. *Frames and Constructions in Metaphoric Language*. Amsterdam and Philadelphia, PA: John Benjamins.
Swales, John M. 1990. *Genre Analysis. English in Academic and Research Settings*. Cambridge: Cambridge University Press.
Yates, Joanne & Wanda J. Orlikowski. 1992. Genres of organizational communication: A structural approach to studying communication and media. *Academy of Management Review* 17 (2). 299–326.

Marianna Dilai and Tetyana Serafin

Metaphorical conceptualization in the Euromaidan discourse

Abstract: This study seeks to apply recent advances in the theory of conceptual metaphor to political discourse analysis. In particular, it focuses on the metaphorical framing of the Ukrainian Euromaidan discourse viewed as a communicative situation during a range of demonstrations and civil unrest in Ukraine (November 2013–February 2014) which ended up with a series of violent murders of protesters and change of political power.

The contemporary Conceptual Metaphor Theory, which originates from Lakoff and Johnson's (1980) *Metaphors We Live By*, provides valuable resources for revealing the essence and determining the significance of political discourse. Since metaphor is viewed as a matter of thought and reasoning rather than language, and as a cognitive device for the construction and interpretation of reality, the analysis of the Euromaidan discourse metaphors reveals how the social and political reality of those days was conceptualized in the minds of millions of Ukrainians. Moreover, by treating metaphor as an integral part of culture (see Kövecses 2005; Quinn 1991; Gibbs 1999), the study provides an insight into the understanding of the Ukrainian picture of the world and conceptualization system. In this respect, the objective of this study is to determine cognitive models underlying metaphorical expressions in the Euromaidan discourse, their target and source domains and explain mappings between them.

Keywords: conceptual metaphor, metaphorical mapping, political discourse, the Euromaidan discourse.

1 Introduction

Recent research on conceptual metaphor emphasizes that metaphor is not just a matter of language and thought, but also of communication, and therefore demands a social approach (Steen 2011: 27). This paper explores the metaphorical framing of the Euromaidan events in political discourse in Ukraine. The term *Euromaidan* refers to a range of demonstrations and civil unrest in Ukraine, which began on the night of November 21, 2013 with public protests in Kyiv and ended

Marianna Dilai and Tetyana Serafin, Lviv Polytechnic National University, Lviv, Ukraine

https://doi.org/10.1515/9783110629460-008

up at the end of February 2014 with a series of violent murders of protesters and change of political power in Ukraine. The second name of the Euromaidan – the Revolution of Dignity – reflects the historical, social and cultural significance of those events to the Ukrainian nation.

Carried out within the framework of contemporary Conceptual Metaphor Theory, this study aspires at providing a deeper insight into the Euromaidan events by showing how reality was conceptualized in the minds of millions of Ukrainians during those days. Since the cognitive approach to metaphor states that metaphor consists in direct reflections of deeper conceptual structures, we assume that metaphors used in the Euromaidan discourse will reflect the Ukrainian worldview. The aim of the paper is to present conceptual domain-to-domain mappings that reveal the way people thought of, reasoned and imagined the social and political situation during the Euromaidan events. In particular, the study shows how the abstract political concepts POWER, EUROMAIDAN, POLITICS, COUNTRY and NATION are structured and mentally represented in terms of metaphors in the Euromaidan discourse.

Furthermore, metaphors are viewed as "cognitive webs that extend beyond individual minds and are spread out into the cultural world" (Gibbs 1999: 146). The Euromaidan discourse as a communicative situation which emerged in Ukrainian society during the Euromaidan events is strongly embedded in the historical, social and cultural context of Ukraine. Due to this fact we assume that metaphorical framing of the Euromaidan discourse reflects a unique system of world conceptualization, reveals the cultural background and provides understanding of the Ukrainian mentality.

2 Theoretical background

Metaphors are generally recognized as an important aspect and distinguishing feature of particular types of discourse (Collins, Gentner and Quinn 1987). Recent discussions in linguistics, psychology and philosophy acknowledge the relevance of metaphor for social and political conceptualization. The founders of the Conceptual Metaphor Theory, George Lakoff and Mark Johnson, in their seminal work *Metaphors We Live By* (1980) provide ample evidence that "metaphors play a central role in the construction of social and political reality" (Lakoff and Johnson 1980: 159). The scholars reinforced the conceptual nature of metaphor even further stating that metaphoric language is a secondary reflection of "metaphorical thought, in the form of cross-domain mappings" (Lakoff and Johnson, 1993: 203). This claim put the study of political discourse on new footing and contributed to an array of research on political metaphors (Charteris-Black 2009; Chilton and Ilyin 1993; Chilton and Schäffner 2011; Chudinov 2013; Santa 1999).

According to Chilton and Schäffner (2011), political metaphor is "a crucial conceptual and semantic mechanism in the production of political meaning" (Chilton and Schäffner 2011: 320). Metaphor is viewed as a cognitive device for conceptualizing and communicating in some way problematic issues of reality. "The very systematicity that allows us to comprehend one aspect of a concept in terms of another [...] will necessarily hide other aspects of the concept" (Lakoff and Johnson 1980: 10), which means that a metaphor reveals only a certain facet of an issue. In this context, then "metaphor thus may be a guide for future action" (Lakoff and Johnson 1980: 156) and function as a powerful means of persuasion and propaganda in political discourse (Charteris-Black 2005; Chilton 2004; Musolff 2004, 2006, 2014, 2016ab, 2017). Authorities may intentionally choose a particular way of expressing ideas and presenting reality metaphorically in order to impose a certain ideology and paradigm of thought on the public.

Recent cross-cultural studies of conceptual metaphors discuss metaphor and culture models in formulating understanding, determine universal metaphors and their cultural variations. Metaphors are strongly argued to be culturally embedded (Kövecses 2005, 2010). Cognitive Metaphor Theory claims that metaphor is conceptual and constrains our understanding. Embedded conceptual metaphors can be detected from systematic observation of metaphorical expressions. These conceptual metaphors underlie and model our language, thought and culture through their pervasive power over people's conceptual system. This cognitive view has been challenged by cultural anthropologists (Quinn 1991). According to Quinn (1991), cultural models or schemas motivate the use of metaphors and metaphors do not produce new conceptual inferences, but just reflect existing understanding.

Current literature often presumes that while basic level conceptual metaphors, based on bodily experience, are universally shared, cultures differ in the interpretation of source domain entities and the linguistic means of their verbalization (Gibbs 1999; Kövecses 2005, 2010). This research supports the idea that metaphor is an inherent part of culture and metaphorical understanding of culture concerns intangible entities to which, among others, social and political institutions belong (Kövecses 2005: 2). Thus, when understood in a cultural context, metaphors offer a deeper insight into how a culture interprets certain salient abstract concepts such as, for instance, power or nation.

Based on the recent advances in the Conceptual Metaphor Theory, in this paper the Euromaidan metaphor is viewed as a cognitive device for the construction and interpretation of the Euromaidan events; it is culturally embedded and ideologically marked.

3 Methodology

The methodology applied to this research lies in the framework of the Conceptual Metaphor Theory which follows this direction: conceptual metaphors are established on the basis of metaphorical linguistic expressions and then analyzed and classified in accordance with the source and target domains. In order to identify metaphorical expression in discourse *bottom-up method of discourse analysis* will be employed.

From a methodological perspective this research integrates the Conceptual Metaphor Theory and critical metaphor analysis as an off-spring of the Critical Discourse Analysis. These are two theoretical traditions which are focused on metaphors as forms of organizing discourse conceptual structure. It has been suggested that valuable methodological tools for researching metaphors in political discourse can be gained by combining these two traditions (Charteris-Black, Musolff and Zinken 2009). In this respect, adopting the methodological apparatus of the Conceptual Metaphor Theory (i.e. source and target domains, conceptual mapping, etc.), while employing the reasoning of critical metaphor analysis in the sense of the significance given to metaphors in discourse and the role metaphors play in conceptualizing our social reality, can prove an effective way to reveal the essence of the Euromaidan discourse.

The research procedure consists of the following stages, namely (1) selecting relevant sources of data for research, (2) procedure of metaphor identification, (3) conceptual analysis and categorization of metaphorical models.

3.1 Selecting relevant data sources

To proceed with the investigation it is important to define the term Euromaidan metaphors. In this study Euromaidan metaphors refer to metaphorical expressions that occur in the Euromaidan discourse and reflect its conceptual structure.

From the perspective of discourse analysis, "texts are not containers of self-referential meaning, but the recorded traces of discourse activity which can never be completely reduced to text" (Angermüller 2001: 8). For many years, discourse analysis has emphasized the relevance of the study of social and cultural context for understanding many aspects of discourse. Text and context do not exist in isolation. In order to have a better understanding of the social and cultural context of the Euromaidan discourse some general information about the Euromaidan is to be provided. The Euromaidan is a range of demonstrations and civil unrest in Ukraine, which began in November 2013 with public protests on Maidan Nezalezhnosti, in Kyiv, demanding progress in European integration.

The scope of the protests expanded, with many calls for the resignation of President Viktor Yanukovych and his government. The protests ultimately led to the 2014 Ukrainian revolution. After a series of violent events towards protesters in Kyiv leaving 100 of them dead, President Yanukovych flees the country and gets impeached on February 22, 2014.

Understanding discourse as "a speech immersed in life" (Arutyunova 1990: 137) is linked with the notion of a communicative situation. In this study, the Euromaidan is seen as a communicative situation which emerged in Ukrainian society during the Euromaidan events. The two main participants of the Euromaidan communicative situation are political authorities and protesters. The channels of communication are demonstrations, public speeches on Maidan Nezalezhnosti and all kinds of addresses of President Yanukovych and other authorities to people. All that communication is reflected in mass media and has tendency to migrate from real world to the dimension of the Internet. As TV channels and the press were much censored by the authorities, the Internet turned into a reliable source of information during the Euromaidan. The role of social networks in the organization of protesters was crucial. That fact influenced the decision on selected material for the study. To perform this study, 180 texts (58,922 words) on the topic of the Euromaidan were searched in online archives of different mass media resources, including online newspapers, blogs, social networks pages, and YouTube channels. The texts were posted or published during the revolution (November 2013 – February 2014). They were selected randomly, regardless of the genre and the author, and served as the source data for the research, hereafter referred to as the Euromaidan discourse.

3.2 Procedure of metaphorical expressions identification

In order to single out Euromaidan metaphors in the selected texts we adopted the bottom-up approach to discourse analysis which is based on generalizations from collected examples of conventionalized linguistic metaphors found in the text. The procedure starts with identifying metaphorical focus (Steen 1999; 2002), that is, a linguistic expression used figuratively in the text that "stands out against the background of a literal frame" (Steen 2002: 394). A variety of specific metaphorical expressions are then classified into abstract conceptual metaphors. The network of conceptual metaphors represents an abstract whole which captures discourse features, while metaphorical expressions represent specific parts of the discourse.

However, not all metaphorical expressions were taken into consideration. The first criterion was relevance to the key concepts of the Euromaidan and its communicative situation (POWER, EUROMAIDAN, POLITICS, COUNTRY, NATION and POLICE). The second criterion was conventionalization of relevant metaphors which means that metaphors should appear at least a few times in the corpus. Relying on the researchers' intuition, 626 metaphorical expressions were identified. Any automated method of identifying metaphor will result in distortion of gained outcomes.

3.3 Conceptual analysis and categorization of metaphorical models

The concepts are analyzed by employing the method of conceptual analysis. Its essence can be defined as follows: based on the texts and dictionary definitions, it is observed how the word naming the phenomena of an abstract realm "behaves" in the text, what material objects it reminds of, and what kind of relation it bears with other synonymous means of expression (Teliya 1988).

According to Arutyunova (1999), the goal of conceptual analysis consists in concept modeling and establishing connections between concepts, which is implemented not only by describing their meanings, but also by defining the specific features of the whole conceptual field and logical relations between its components. The researcher identifies the semantic and pragmatic competence of native speakers, which serves for conceptual analysis. Understanding is granted by the knowledge of word meaning in sentences (semantic competence) and interpretation is possible due to the knowledge of mechanisms for language use (pragmatic competence).

To conduct conceptual analysis means to define the conceptual model that underlies a metaphorical expression (Arutyunova 1990: 137). Metaphorical models consist of a source domain, a target domain and a metaphorical mapping between them. Source domain is the conceptual domain from which we draw metaphorical expressions. Target domain is the conceptual domain that we try to understand. A mapping is the systematic set of correspondences that exist between constituent elements of the source and the target domain. To know a conceptual metaphor is to know the set of mappings that applies to a given source-target pairing.

While examining specific metaphorical models, some experts come to the conclusion that these models must be classified and systematized according to some concrete principle. For example, Chudinov (2013) claims that the process of systematization of metaphorical models is much more important than the result due to the fact that the possible ways of classification are very diverse and hardly any single classification will be accepted by all scholars working in the field of conceptual metaphor (Chudinov 2013: 32). We agree that the chances for elaboration of such unified and generally accepted classification of metaphorical models are slim. However, any attempts in this field are appreciated, since they enable to highlight the most frequent and productive models, as well as yield rich material for understanding the general laws of the metaphorical construal of reality.

In this paper, we adopted the classification suggested by Chudinov (2013) and classified metaphorical models by source domains into the following four categories: anthropomorphic, sociomorfic, naturemorphic and artifact (Chudinov 2013: 35–36). This classification was further extended by adding the spatial category of metaphorical models, initially introduced by Lakoff (1980).

4 Categories of the Euromaidan metaphorical models

The identified conceptual metaphors are categorized according to their source domains into anthropomorphic, sociomorphic, naturemorphic, artifact and spatial metaphorical models. In each category, the most common metaphorical models are identified and analyzed. These models certainly do not cover the entire spectrum of the real sources of metaphorical expansion, but form a comprehensive picture of the characteristic features of each category.

4.1 Anthropomorphic category of metaphorical models

The anthropomorphic model (personification) is the metaphorical attribution of human qualities to non-human phenomena (Chudinov 2013: 35). Anthropomorphic models belong to one of the most frequently used types of metaphor occurring in most languages and types of discourse. Within the Euromaidan discourse we have come across a number of metaphorical expressions which show that the concepts of a COUNTRY and EUROMAIDAN are perceived as human beings.

A COUNTRY IS A HUMAN BEING mapping forms a certain image of country with characteristics typical of human beings. State policy is viewed as actions of human beings and countries are reasoned about as humans; see (1).

(1) *Та чи може* ***Україна*** *досягти такого рівня добробуту,* ***не стаючи при цьому на коліна****?*

'Can **Ukraine** reach such a level of prosperity without **going down on its knees**?'

In this case (example 2), the metaphor A COUNTRY IS A HUMAN BEING shows that the heart of the country is Euromaidan. The implication is that the heart (the revolution) beats and gives life to the whole body (Ukraine).

(2) ***Серце*** *столиці –* ***Євромайдан*** *– б'ється ритмічно.*

'Euromaidan is the heart of the capital which beats rhythmically.'

POWER IS A DISEASE is another extension of the model A COUNTRY IS A HUMAN BEING. The political power – Yanukovich – is a disease for the nation. For example:

(3) *Та, можливо, тим, на Сході, на Заході і в Центрі, хто не хоче* ***культивувати спадкові політичні захворювання****, удасться виробити* ***загальний імунітет***

'So, perhaps, those in the East, the West and in the Centre who do not want to **cultivate political hereditary diseases** will **develop a general immunity**'

The source domain DISEASE is also revealed while referring to the Euromaidan. However, the Euromaidan is rather a virus than a disease, see (4). The conceptualization of the Euromaidan as a disease aims at emphasizing the speed of virus spreading rather than its damage to the health.

(4) *Відбувається психічне* ***зараження учасників*** *протестних акцій надією, оптимізмом, у тому числі й ворожістю до влади.*

'There is mental **contamination of protester** with hope, optimism and hostility to the government.'

EUROMAIDAN IS A HUMAN BEING is also conceptualized from the physical side in most of the cases, for example, by having face and voice and heart; see (5) and (6).

(5) *Сьогоднішня* ***революція має багато облич****. Ми не бачимо їх на трибуні, вони не пнуться в політики вищого ешелону. Це – наші з вами* ***обличчя****!*

'This **revolution has many faces**. We do not see them at the rostrum; they do not want to become senior politicians. These are our **faces**!'

(6) *Що нового про Україну вам* ***сказав Євромайдан****?*

'What new has **Euromaidan told** you about Ukraine?'

The concept of POWER includes President Viktor Yanukovych and his government. In times of the Euromaidan all political power was concentrated in hands of the President and his Cabinet of Ministers. In metaphorical expressions of POWER IS A HUMAN BEING only anatomical aspects of human beings are highlighted. This target domain is mainly expressed by the words *government* and *authorities*. Metaphorical focus is primarily pointed at hands; see (7) and (8). These hands have power and wealth.

(7) *Але, можливо,* ***влада*** *якимось дивом зміниться, [...]? Чи існує теоретична можливість* ***однією рукою*** *забезпечити незалежність бізнесу всередині країни, а* ***другою*** *– "заробляти" на зовнішньому ринку торгівлею суверенітетом?*

'But perhaps the **authorities**[1] will miraculously change [...]. Is it theoretically possible to ensure the independence of business in the country **with one hand**, and to "make profit" on trading sovereignty on the foreign market **with another hand**?'

(8) *Якщо наші силові структури в найближчі дні не розкриють злочин, – це означатиме, що* ***влада доклала до цього руку.***

'Unless our security forces investigate the crime in the nearest future, it will mean that the **government has put its hand to it**.'

POWER as a human being also has mouth and ears but it is mute and does not want to hear what happens; see (9) and (10). The use of this metaphor reflects a lack of communication between politicians and the Euromaidan, as well as deliberate ignorance of the Euromaidan demands by political authorities.

(9) *Розгублена, політично* ***німа влада*** *– найвиразніший стоп-кадр минулого тижня.*

'The confused and politically **dumb authorities** are a striking snapshot of the last week.'

(10) ***Вуху влади*** *миліше блеяння ягнят, які чекають Курбан-Байраму.*

'For the **government's ear** it is more pleasant to listen to the bleating of lambs at Eid al-Adha.'

1 The bold type shows the linguistic expressions that bear the metaphorical focus in the sentences.

Since countries are often conceptualized as humans, relationships between them are mainly presented as interpersonal. The most productive source domain used to illustrate relationships between countries is FAMILY. The European Union is conceptualized as a family which Ukraine wishes to become part of. This family is democratic and wealthy; see (11) and (12).

(11) *Незважаючи на те, що більшість громадян України прагне бути у вільній, демократичній та заможній* ***європейській сім'ї народів,*** *[...].*

'Despite the fact that most citizens of Ukraine want to be in the free, democratic and prosperous **European family of nations** [...].'

(12) *Ми повинні повернутися до* ***родини європейських країн.***

'We should return to the **family of European countries.**'

The metaphorical model INTERNATIONAL RELATIONS ARE FAMILY RELATIONS is an extension of A COUNTRY IS A HUMAN BEING, where members of a family (countries) are human beings. This model presents the European Union – Ukraine – Russia relationships as a love triangle; see (13) and (14). Ukraine is a woman who is about to get married and she is going to choose between Russia and the European Union. The EU-Ukraine Association Agreement is an engagement ceremony that was canceled last minute. While Ukraine is having difficulties in relationship with the European Union, Russia is firmly holding Ukraine in its arms.

(13) *У разі непідписання Асоціації у Вільнюсі Україна залишатиметься, як мінімум, кілька місяців, а то й років* ***"не зарученою"****[...]. Як ви оцінюєте ймовірність потрапляння України під час цієї паузи до Митного союзу?*

'If the Association Agreement with Ukraine is not **signed** in Vilnius, Ukraine will **"not be engaged"** at least for several months, or even years [...]. How do you assess the likelihood of Ukraine's joining the Customs Union during this pause?'

(14) *Тому,* ***обійми з Росією*** *не означають* ***заручини зі свободою.***

'So, **embracing** Russia does not mean **getting engaged to freedom**.'

The FAMILY domain is also used for describing the Ukrainian nation as a big family, for example:

(15) ***Брати і сестри українці!*** *Ми – європейці, ми – на своїй, Богом даній землі! І ніякий чужинець не продиктує нам свою волю.*

'Brothers and sisters, Ukrainians! We are European people; we are in our land given to us by God!'

In this case the family model is a source domain for the people of Ukraine as individuals who become a family. The president is father, citizens are brothers. President of Ukraine Viktor Yanukovych is called the father of the nation; see (16) and (17). However, he is a bad father who punishes his children for no reason.

(16) *[...] чому б* ***батькові націй не відвовтузити до напівсмерті непокірливих чад своїх, які вдома не ночують, а тусуються по майданах****?*

'[...] why doesn't **the father of the nation** beat to death his disobedient children who instead of sleeping at home hang out on the streets?'

(17) ***Не буває поганих дітей, бувають погані батьки. Із влади вийшла погана мати, а з Януковича – поганий батько.***

'There are no bad children, there are bad parents. **The power proved to be a bad mother, and Yanukovych proved to be a bad father.'**

Figure 8.1 illustrates distribution of metaphorical models across the anthropomorphic category. POWER IS A DISEASE is part of A COUNTRY IS A HUMAN BEING model, the country (a human being) suffers from this power (a disease). INTERNATIONAL RELATIONS ARE FAMILY RELATIONS is part of the COUNTRIES ARE HUMAN BEINGS model. A NATION IS A FAMILY includes POWER IS A HUMAN BEING and EUROMAIDAN IS A VIRUS as a virus that spreads in the family. The metaphorical model POWER IS A DISEASE takes a leading position that clearly shows a negative attitude

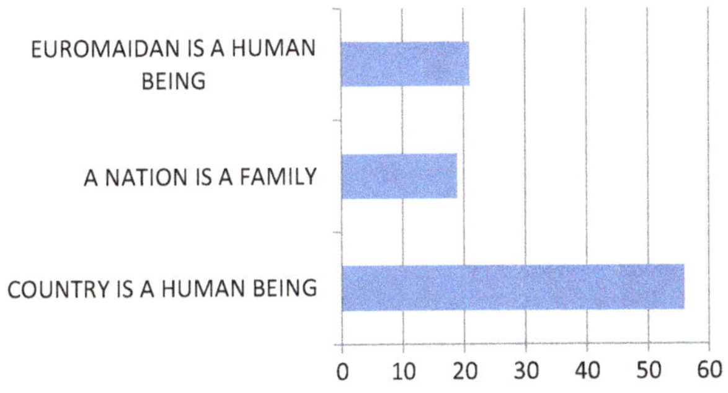

Figure 8.1: Anthropomorphic category of metaphorical models.

of Ukrainians to Ukraine's authorities (23 occurrences). The great number of linguistic expressions which verbalize conceptual metaphor INTERNATIONAL RELATIONS ARE FAMILY RELATIONS demonstrates that Ukrainians tend to reason about the abstract notion of international politics in terms of the everyday life notion of family relations.

4.2 Sociomorphic category of metaphorical models

Many aspects of political reality are often metaphorically modeled on the grounds of concepts taken from other social spheres of human activity. The sociomorphic category of the Euromaidan metaphors includes such source domains as CRIMINAL WORLD, WAR, THEATER and GAME.

The vast majority of the metaphorical expressions found in the corpus fall into the model EUROMAIDAN IS WAR. Linguistic data shows that from the very first day the Euromaidan has been conceptualized in terms of war, even before clashes between riot police and protesters. Ukrainians protested in favor of the EU-Ukraine Association Agreement, and also they were "fighting" for freedom, democracy, civil rights and dignity. The alternative name of the Euromaidan – The Revolution of Dignity – supports this fact, see (18) and (19).

(18) *......на холодних вулицях Києва чоловіків і жінок з прапорами ЄС,* ***що б'ються за цей європейський прапор****, – то це тому, що вони також* ***борються за Україну і за своє майбутнє****. Тому що вони знають [...]* ***Європа – це обіцянка надії і свободи.***

'...on cold Kyiv's streets men and women with the EU **flags are fighting for this flag** because they are fighting for Ukraine and their future [....] they know **Europe is the promise of hope and freedom.'**

(19) *Розгоном мирного зібрання у Києві вранці 30 листопада президент* ***оголосив війну власному народові.***

'By putting down a peaceful rally in Kyiv on November 30 the President **declared the war on his own people.**'

The fact that political life of Ukraine is highly influenced by Russia is metaphorically represented by a significant number of linguistic expressions in the analyzed texts. We have identified 52 cases in which Russia is conceptualized as ENSLAVER. For example:

(20) *Україна в небезпеці! Над нею нависла загроза реставрації* ***кремлівського колоніального ярма****. Ми не* ***безправний домініон****!*

'...Ukraine is in danger! We face the threat of resorting **Kremlin colonial burden**. We are not a **dominion deprived of rights.'**

Russia intrudes especially strongly in Ukraine's foreign affairs policy. Despite the fact that Russia did not participate in negotiations, its presence had been constantly felt since the beginning of the preparations for signing the EU-Ukraine Association Agreement. References to Ukraine's and Russia's common history are often noticed in metaphorical expressions.

Furthermore, Russia is conceptualized as an empire that dictates harsh policy towards Ukraine; see (21).

(21) *Український тріумф покладе* ***кінець ері Путіна****, і це станеться тут, на цій самій площі. У підручниках з історії скоро напишуть, що* ***Російська імперія припинила своє існування на Євромайдані****.*

'The Ukrainian triumph will put an end to **Putin's era**, and this will happen here on this square. It will be soon written in the history handbooks that the **Russian empire** stopped existing at the Euromaidan.'

Metaphors representing political activity as a criminal sphere are very typical of the Euromaidan discourse. In this case, politicians are represented as criminals with a particular "specialty" (thieves, crooks, gangsters, etc.), engaged in different criminal groups (gangs, "mafia family"). The diversity and pervasiveness of criminal metaphors suggests that Ukrainian politicians are mainly treated as criminals. This is not surprising since the level of corruption in Ukraine is ranked high and Ukrainians trust to politicians is critically low. The most popular slogans of the Euromaidan call Yanukovych a convict who is to be put back in prison: "*Зека геть! Януковича на нари!* Go away, con! Put Yanukovych back in prison!"

The decision of authorities to suspend preparations for signing the EU-Ukraine Association Agreement is conceptualized as an attempt of authorities to 'steal future' from Ukrainians; see (23).

(22) *Янукович і ПР* ***крадуть наше майбутнє****.*

'Yanukovych and Party of Regions are **stealing our future**.'

A great number of metaphorical expressions compare President's retinue to a family, which might make us think that these metaphorical expressions express a family frame. However, in this case the mafia frame is meant. Authorities are depicted as a type of organized crime syndicate. For instance:

(23) .... *сотні тисяч українців вийшли на Євромайдани в Україні та по всьому світові. Вийшли, щоб не дозволити* ***правлячій мафії*** *вбити наш європейський вибір, зламати наше життя.*

'...hundreds of thousands people are at the Euromaidans in Ukraine and all over the world in order to prevent the **ruling mafia (thugs)** from **murdering our European choice**'

In addition, the mafia authority is also often called the gang. One of the most popular revolution slogans calls Ukrainian authority the gang: *Банду геть!* 'Go away, gang!'

Despite the fact that the main function of police is to fight crime and put criminals behind the bars, outlaw actions of riot police during the Euromaidan resulted in strong association of police with the criminals; see (24).

(24) *Від волі президента зараз залежить покарання* ***злочинців у погонах,*** *які розганяли демонстрацію.*

'It is up to the President to punish the **criminals in uniform** who were putting down the rally.'

A wide range of political realities is conceptualized from the standpoint of profitable sale or purchase, profit or loss, thrift or prodigality, capital accumulation or bankruptcy; see (25).

(25) *Ви чули про те, як Віктор Янукович запропонував мені посаду прем'єр-міністра. Моя відповідь Януковичу наступна:* ***я не купуюсь за посади, пане президент. Купуйте своїх поплічників.***

'Have you heard that Viktor Yanukovych offered me the post of Prime Minister? My answer to Yanukovych is the following: You can't **buy me for posts**, Mr. President. **Buy your associates.**'

International politics is also perceived as trade where politicians, national interests and political agreements are objects of trade/articles of commerce, for example:

(26) *Що ж насправді зможе* ***виторгувати*** *Україна у Вільнюсі?*

'What can Ukraine actually **trade** in Vilnius?'

Ukraine very often is the object of international trade in various metaphorical expressions. This metaphor can be named A NATION IS A COMMODITY. Different participants are sellers, buyers, etc. There is a price for the commodity. For instance, President Yanukovych is the one who sells Ukraine, see (27). The two potential consumers are Russia and the European Union.

(27) *Коли ж потім у такий спосіб, як це було зроблено, він [Янукович] відмовляється від цих зобов'язань, **виставляє країну на тендер,** і починає якісь незрозумілі кроки.*

'Then in the same way as it was done, he [Yanukovych] abandons these obligations, **submits the country to the tender** and takes some strange steps.'

The Euromaidan as a notable political event is also conceptualized in terms of the THEATER. The upcoming events on the Euromaidan are often referred to as scenarios; see (28). The Euromaidan protesters, riot police and politicians are actors on the Euromaidan stage playing their prepared roles; see (29).

(28) *Що відбувається насправді, за якими **сценаріями можуть надалі розвиватися події** і, головне, що влада може не на словах, а на ділі протиставити існуючим викликам?*

'What is actually going on? Under which **scenarios can events develop?** And, most importantly, what actions can the government take to respond to the current challenges?'

(29) ***Ми – головні дійові особи в цій виставі.***

'We take the **leading roles in this play**.'

The conceptual metaphor POLITICS IS A GAME is quite pervasive in Euromaidan discourse. In most of the examples the concept of GAME is referred to in general, for example:

(30) *Студентський рух став заручником великих **політичних ігор.***

'The student movement is held hostage by big **political games.**'

In the rest of the cases metaphorical expressions mostly refer to card games and gambling games in general, which may point to risk and unpredictability of political action. Card games are often used to talk about international politics where countries are players. Russia is a devious player who always has best cards often due to cheating; see (31) and (32).

(31) ... *наш* ***північний сусід спробує тепер розіграти карту розколу України.***

'...our northern neighbor will try **to play the card of** Ukraine's splitting.'

(32) *Оскільки Брюссель продовжує діяти нерішуче, Росія продовжує* ***блефувати,*** *що вона у змозі переформатувати пострадянський простір згідно зі своїми уявленнями.*

'Since Brussels continues to act hesitantly, Russia continues to **bluff** that they are able to reformat the post-Soviet space according to their beliefs.'

In the following example the international relations between Ukraine and Russia are compared to boxing; see (33). The failure to sign the EU-Ukraine Association Agreement is just the first round of boxing won by Russia, but this is not the end of the game.

(33) *Проте* ***перший раунд Кремль вважає виграним – підписання асоціації поки що зірвали.***

'However, Kremlin believes that **they won the first round** because the signing of the Association was thwarted.'

Figure 8.2 shows distribution of metaphorical models across the sociomorphic category of metaphorical models in the Euromaidan discourse. The most numerous metaphorical model is EUROMAIDAN IS A WAR. Barely any article or public

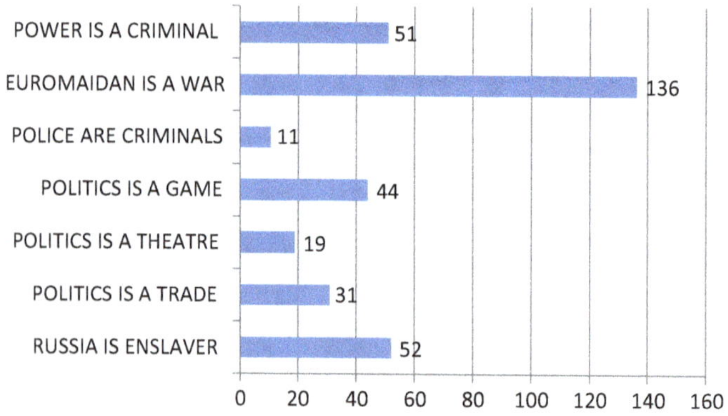

Figure 8.2: Sociomorphic category of metaphorical models.

speech on the Euromaidan stage goes without this conceptual metaphor. Such pervasiveness of this conceptual metaphor is an evidence of protesters' determination and power of will. The second place takes the metaphorical model RUSSIA IS AN ENSLAVER which reflects the perception of Ukraine-Russia relationships.

4.3 Naturemorphic category of metaphorical models

It is common knowledge that animate and inanimate nature serves as a model according to which the social and political reality is structured and conceptualized. In the analyzed texts, we have singled out the following metaphorical models falling into this category: POWER IS AN ANIMAL, EUROMAIDAN IS A PLANT, and EUROMAIDAN IS A NATURAL PHENOMENON.

Authorities are conceptualized as a special kind of animals, a parasite; see (34). This conceptual mapping explains that authorities are not serving their own country; quite on the contrary, they are constantly causing harm to Ukraine by taking away its vital power.

(34) *Та найголовніша цінність революції в тому, що вона справила ефект* ***потужного інсектициду****. Вона знищила* ***політичних паразитів.***

'But the main significance of the revolution is its powerful **insecticide** effect. It has eradicated political **parasites.**'

Predator metaphors are comparatively rare in the Euromaidan discourse and mostly used when talking about politicians and cruelty of the riot police; see (35):

(35) *[...]* ***"полюванням" міліції на поранених*** *після сутичок [...].*

'...**police preying on the wounded** after clashes [...].'

The rise of the Euromaidan is compared to a plant growing from a seed. For example:

(36) ***Зерно Євромайдану неминуче проросте*** *– просто тому, що такий об'єктивний історичний процес, подобається це комусь чи ні.*

'**The grain of the Euromaidan** will inevitably sprout, because it is an objective historical process, like it or not.'

The conceptual metaphor EUROMAIDAN IS A NATURAL PHENOMENON most frequently compares the Euromaidan to ocean, sea and waves. For instance:

(37) *Нову* ***хвилю Євромайдану*** *спровокував розгін мітингувальників в ніч проти суботи.*

'A **new wave of the Euromaidan** was provoked by the rally break up.'

(38) *Боляче. [...] Проте зрозуміли, що кожен із нас –* ***крапля в океані.***

'It hurts. [...] However, we have understood that each of us is a **drop in the ocean.**'

The conceptualization of the Euromaidan in terms of the whirl and fire indicates its fast spreading like a natural disaster that smashes all obstacles on its way; see (39) and (40).

(39) ***Тернопільський Євромайдан вирує.***

'Ternopil Euromaidan is in a **whirl.**'

(40) *Після того, як* ***вогонь революції перекинувся*** *на регіони і* ***став валити*** *президентську вертикаль, одеська влада організувала неабияку оборону своїх адміністративних будівель.*

'After the **fire of revolution** had spread to the regions and started **destroying** presidential hierarchy, Odessa's authorities organized a fair defence of their administrative buildings.'

Based on the analysis of linguistic examples, we may conclude that the riot police are associated with animals or even predators due to aggressiveness in its actions. The lifecycle of plants is used to metaphorically describe the rise of the Euromaidan. In addition, the Euromaidan is conceptualized as a natural phenomenon which reflects its massiveness and wide-spreading.

Figure 8.3 demonstrates distribution of metaphorical models across the naturemorphic category. The first place takes EUROMAIDAN IS A NATURAL PHENOMENON.

4.4 Artifact category of metaphorical models

This category includes two conceptual models: POWER IS A MACHINE and A COUNTRY IS A HOUSE.

The old-fashioned machine system, which dates from the industrial revolution, is a source domain which metaphorically interprets the Ukrainian political system. This mapping can be traced in the following example:

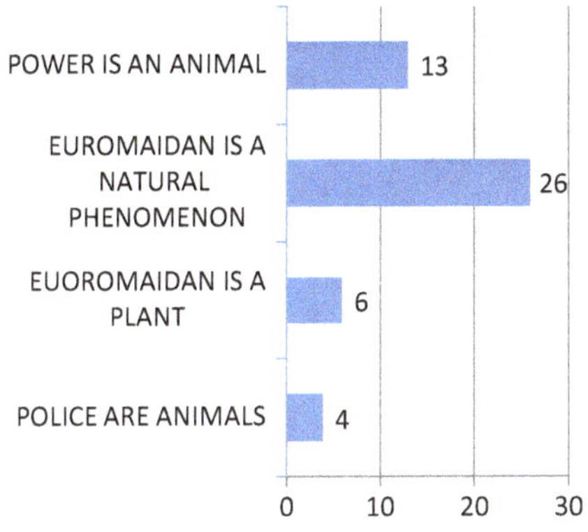

Figure 8.3: Naturemorphic category of metaphorical models.

(41) *Адже досі освітянські керівники, [...]* ***залишаючись здебільшого справними "гвинтиками" авторитарно-бюрократичної системи,*** *покірними виконавцями міністерських наказів і директив.*

'Still educational authorities being **operational "screws" of an authoritarian-bureaucratic system** remain obedient executors of ministerial orders and directives.'

The metaphorical mapping of the following example is based on assumption that political power in the country like a machine coldly applies forces and controls movement to perform an intended action. It is a tractor operated by the president that runs over people on its way, see (42):

(42) ***[...]*** *що влада* ***"їде по народу" як трактор.***

'[...] the government like a **tractor runs over people**.'

International politics as a global phenomenon is also considered a complex mechanism with different levers available to certain countries. For instance:

(43) *Я вважаю, що в руках ЄС і Німеччини, зокрема,* ***є важелі і механізми*** *для застосування санкцій.*

'I believe that the EU, in particular Germany, has **levers and mechanisms** for sanctions implementation.'

The metaphorical model A COUNTRY IS A HOUSE helps us to understand similarities between the abstract concept of country and the concrete one of a house. The similarities are as follows: each country is a house that is built by people. People want their houses to be big, bright and secure. The house has walls, windows, doors and foundation. These words are extended metaphorically to talk about the corresponding concepts in the target domain COUNTRY.

From life experience people know that buildings have to be designed and constructed by people, so one of the main appeals of protesters is to change current political power and start to build new country; see (44).

(44) *Давайте* ***будувати країну*** *мрій тут, в Україні.*

'Let's build a **dream country** here in Ukraine.'

The house is built from the foundation. The foundation is the most important part that provides support to the house. If the foundation is firm and solid, the house will stand steadily and secure for many years. Ukraine is believed to have the old foundation of the USSR that is weak and shaky. This prevents Ukraine from building a new, well-constructed and firm house; see (45).

(45) ***Фундамент країни*** *стоїть на СРСР, на кривавому дефективном радянському фундаменті.*

'**The foundation of the country** is the USSR, Soviet bloody defective foundation.'

The European Union is also perceived as a big house. The EU is believed to keep the door open for Ukraine; see (46). It means that the EU is still ready to sign the Association Agreement with Ukraine and continue further cooperation.

(46) *[...]* ***Європа*** *продовжує заявляти,* ***що її двері відкриті для України,*** *однак Київ уже повним ходом зближується з Росією.*

'[...] Europe continues to claim that the **doors are open** for Ukraine, but Kyiv is moving closer and closer to Russia.'

The author of the following metaphorical expression argues that opening the door to Europe does not result in closing the door to the East; see (47). Using this metaphor, the author is trying to say that cooperation with the EU does not result in breaking off relationships with Russia.

(47) ***Відчиняти двері на Захід не означає зачиняти двері на Схід****. Східне Партнерство є вигідним як для країн регіону, так і для її сусідів.*

'....to **open the door to the West** doesn't mean **shutting the door to the East.'**

The conceptual metaphor A COUNTRY IS A HOUSE highlights the construction of a well-structured and stable house as a creation of a strong political structure of the country.

Figure 8.4 illustrates the distribution of metaphorical models across the artifact category of metaphorical models. This category is represented by two specific metaphorical models. Both of them are quite common, yet A COUNTRY IS A HOUSE is more productive.

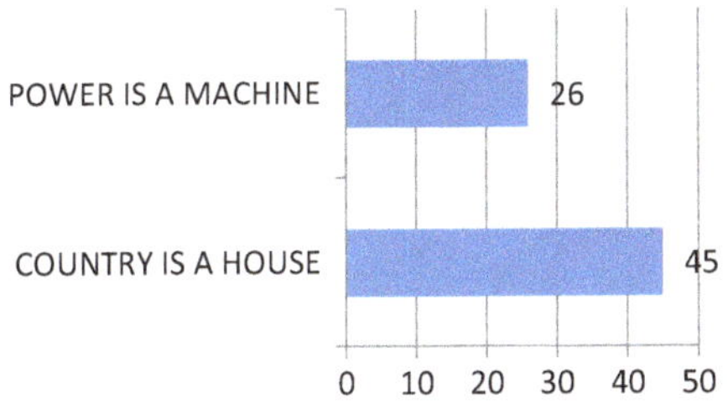

Figure 8.4: Artifact category of metaphorical models.

4.5 Spatial category of metaphorical models

The spatial metaphorical category in Euromaidan discourse is represented by the conceptual metaphor POLITICAL LIFE IS A JOURNEY. The analysis of this metaphorical model is based on Lakoff and Johnson's (1980) metaphorical mapping LIFE IS A JOURNEY. Its structure reveals correspondences between the source domain of JOURNEY and the target domain POLITICAL LIFE (see Table 8.1):

Table 8.1: POLITICAL LIFE IS A JOURNEY metaphorical mapping.

Journey	Political life
Traveler	Ukraine
Starting point	Russia
Destination	The EU
Route	State's Policy
Vehicle	The Association Agreement
Crossroads	Choices
Means for arriving at destination	The EU Integration
Changes of the route	Decisions about where to do

UKRAINE IS A TRAVELER

(48) *Україна отримає наступний шанс* ***стати на крок ближчою до Євросоюзу.***

'**Ukraine** will receive another chance to be **one step closer to the EU**.'

STARTING POINT IS RUSSIA

(49) ***Україна не може повертатися до Росії,*** *де порушують права людини, а потрібно* ***йти до Європейського союзу.***

'...**Ukraine cannot return to Russia**, where human rights are violated, we should **head for the EU.**'

DESTINATION IS THE EUROPEAN UNION

(50) *[...]* ***наш шлях у Європу,*** *можливо у* ***Януковича і його компанії маршрути інші.***

'[...] **Europe** is our destination, perhaps Yanukovych and his associates prefer other routes.'

MEANS FOR ARRIVING AT DESTINATION ARE ROUTES

(51) ***Шлях до ЄС – він тернистий.***

'The **path** to the EU is thorny.'

(52) *Янукович також порівняв шлях України до підписання асоціації з ЄС зі* ***сходженням на вершину,*** *нарікаючи на несприятливу погоду.*

'Yanukovych also compared signing the EU-Ukraine Association to **climbing to the top**, complaining about the bad weather.'

CHOICES ARE CROSSROADS

(53) *Україна знову стоїть на великому* ***перехресті історичного вибору.***

'Ukraine is again at the **historic crossroads**.'

DECISIONS ARE CHANGES OF THE ROUTE

(54) *Для України величезний виклик – куди* ***повернути****. Янукович ніколи* ***не поверне до Європи****. Він зробив усе, щоб* ***направити український напрямок у нікуди.***

'It is an enormous challenge for Ukraine to decide which **direction** to take. Yanukovych will never **turn** to Europe. He did his best to **direct** Ukrainian nowhere.'

THE VEHICLE IS EUROPEAN INTEGRATION POLICY

(55) ***Поїзд євроінтеграції рухається,*** *його жодними диспутами, дискусіями, війнами – не зупинити.*

'The **train of European integration** cannot be stopped ...'

Within the Euromaidan metaphorical model POLITICAL LIFE IS A JOURNEY Ukraine is viewed as a traveler. Russia is the starting point and the EU is the destination. The President of Ukraine, its leader, rejects to lead people to the desired destination and tries to change direction. As a result, Ukrainians consider Yanukovych a travelling companion who is free to go his own way rather than a guide. There are many routes to take but there is only one leading to the desired destination. This route is complicated and thorny. Yanukovych compares it to climbing a mountain in severe weather conditions. The failure to sign the Association Agreement is treated as a change of route or going backwards. The vehicle in conceptualization of POLITICAL LIFE IS A JOURNEY is a train. This might be due to the fact that train is considered to be the most save and cheap means of transport in Ukraine which is used mostly to travel long distances. In addition, trains follow a fixed track with no possible deviations. They are fast and their destination is determined. The period of time is fixed and short.

5 Discussion

In the course of research 17 metaphorical models in the Euromaidan discourse corpus have been identified and analyzed. Figure 8.5 illustrates frequency distribution of metaphorical models in the Euromaidan discourse corpus.

The findings show that the most productive metaphorical model is EUROMAIDAN IS A WAR (136 metaphorical expressions, i.e. 16%). Despite the fact that the massive rallies in the heart of the Ukrainian capital were completely peaceful from the very beginning, in the discourse offered by the media they were described as a

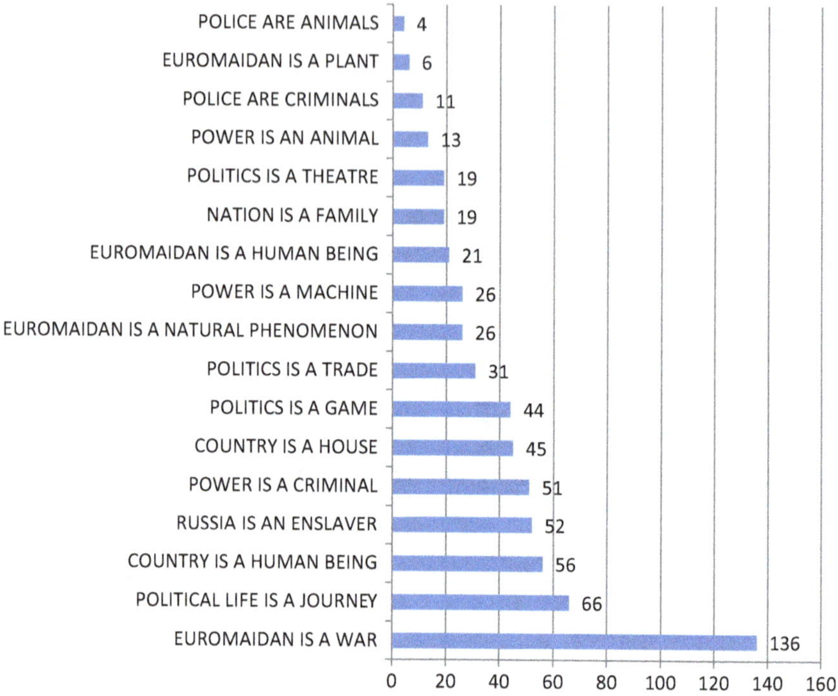

Figure 8.5: Metaphorical models in the Euromaidan discourse.

battle. Ukrainians did not only voice in favor of the EU-Ukraine Association Agreement, but they were also fighting for freedom, democracy, civil rights and dignity. The WAR metaphor also accentuates the risk and danger of the situation. EUROMAIDAN as a key concept of the Euromaidan discourse has been also associated with such concepts as HUMAN BEING, NATURAL PHENOMENON, PLANT and VIRUS.

The concept of POWER refers to President Viktor Yanukovych and his government. More than half of instances show POWER conceptualized as CRIMINAL. The diversity and pervasiveness of criminal metaphors suggests that Ukrainian politicians are mainly perceived as criminals. This is not surprising since the level of corruption in Ukraine is ranked high and Ukrainians' trust in politicians is critically low.

The concept of POLICE is linked to the source domains CRIMINAL and ANIMAL. This fact clearly points out the negative attitude to the police during the Euromaidan events. Despite the fact that the main function of police is to fight crime and put criminals behind the bars, outlaw actions of riot police during the Euromaidan resulted in the strong association of police with criminals. Within the domain ANIMAL police are mostly associated with predators which implies cruelty of riot police and people's feeling of fear and helplessness during the Euromaidan protests.

The target domain POLITICS is viewed in terms of GAME (unpredictable and risky), THEATER (fake and simulation), TRADE (gains and losses) and JOURNEY (goals, states and actions). The conceptual metaphor POLITICAL LIFE IS A JOURNEY takes a leading position. It reflects a pro-European orientation of Ukraine.

Unlike other countries, Russia got its distinctive conceptualization in the Euromaidan discourse. The metaphorical model RUSSIA IS AN ENSLAVER comprises 52 metaphorical expressions which is 6.2%. It reveals that political life of Ukraine was highly influenced by Russia at that time.

6 Conclusions

Contemporary Conceptual Metaphor Theory provides us with a solid theoretical foundation and methodological framework for revealing conceptual structure of political discourse, in particular revolutionary discourse. The system of conceptual metaphors presented within this study mirrors historical, social and cultural significance of the Euromaidan events to the Ukrainian nation. Based on empirical outcomes, we have arrived at the conclusion that metaphorical framing of the Euromaidan discourse is unique in the way it reflects the cultural background and provides an insight into Ukrainian mentality. According to the revealed mappings, the concept of EUROMAIDAN implies the fight of the Ukrainians for the implementation of European values. The major conceptual models are EUROMAIDAN IS A WAR, POLITICAL LIFE IS A JOURNEY, A COUNTRY IS A HUMAN BEING, RUSSIA IS AN ENSLAVER, POWER IS A CRIMINAL, A COUNTRY IS A HOUSE, POLITICS IS A GAME, POLITICS IS A TRADE, EUROMAIDAN IS A NATURAL PHENOMENON, POWER IS MACHINE, EUROMAIDAN IS A HUMAN BEING, A NATION IS A FAMILY, etc. The models suggest that the revolution is a natural reaction of Ukrainian people to the destructive policy of the current power, which is perceived as criminal, cruel, untrustworthy and strongly influenced by Russian. Further research on the metaphorical conceptualization of revolutionary discourse appears to be promising especially from the perspective of contrastive linguistic studies.

References

Angermuller, Johannes. 2001. Diskursanalyse: strömungen, tendenzen, perspektiven. Eine Einführung. [Discourse analysis: Strands, tendencies, perspectives. An Introduction]. In Johannes Angermuller, Katharina Bunzmann & Martin Nonhoff (eds.), *Diskursanalyse: Theorien, Methoden, Anwendungen*, 7–22. Hamburg: Argument.

Arutyunova, Nina, D. 1990. *Diskurs* [Discourse]. In N. V. Yartseva (ed.), *Linguistic encyclopedic dictionary*, 137–139. Moscow: Soviet Encyclopedia.
Arutyunova, Nina, D. 1999. *Yasyk i mir cheloveka* [Language and the human world]. Moscow: Yazyki russkoy kultury.
Charteris-Black, Jonathan. 2009. Metaphor and political communication. In A. Musolff & Jens Zinken (eds.), *Metaphor and discourse*, 97–115. Basingstoke New York: Palgrave Macmillan.
Charteris-Black, Jonathan. 2005. Politicians and rhetoric. The persuasive power of metaphor. Basingstoke: Palgrave-Macmillan.
Chilton, Paul & Christina Schäffner. 2011. Discourse and politics, In Teun A. van Dijk (ed.), *Discourse studies: A multidisciplinary introduction*, 303–330. London: Sage.
Chilton, Paul & Mikhail Ilyin. 1993. Metaphor in political discourse: The case of the "Common European house." *Discourse and society* 4 (1): 7–31.
Chilton, Paul. 2004. *Analysing political discourse. Theory and practice.* London and New York: Routledge.
Chudinov, Anatoly P. 2013. *Ocherki po sovremennoi politicheskoi metaforologii* [On contemporary metaphor studies]. Ekaterinburg: Ural.gos. ped. unt.
Collins, Allan & Dedre Gentner. 1987. How people construct mental models. In Dorothy Holland & Naomi Quinn (eds.), *Cultural models in language and thought*, 243–265. Cambridge: Cambridge University Press.
Gibbs, Raymond. W. 1999. Taking metaphor out of our heads and putting it into the cultural world. In Gibbs, Raymond W. & Gerard J. Steen (eds.), *Metaphor in cognitive linguistics.* Selected Papers from the 5th International Cognitive Linguistics Conference. Amsterdam, July 1997. 145–166. Amsterdam & Philadelphia: John Benjamins Publishing Company.
Kövecses, Zoltán. 2005. *Metaphor in culture: Universality and variation.* Cambridge: Cambridge University Press.
Kövecses, Zoltán. 2010. *Metaphor: A practical introduction*, 2nd edn. New York: Oxford University Press.
Lakoff, George & Mark Johnson. 1980. *Metaphors we live by.* Chicago: The University of Chicago Press.
Lakoff, George. 1993 [1979]. The contemporary theory of metaphor. In Andrew Ortony (ed.), *Metaphor and thought*, 2nd edn. 202–251. New York, NY: Cambridge University Press.
Musolff, Andreas. 2004. *Metaphor and political discourse.* New York: Palgrave Macmillan.
Musolff, Andreas. 2006. Metaphor scenarios in public discourse. *Metaphor and Symbol*, 2 (1), 23– 38.
Musolff, Andreas. 2014. The metaphor of the "body politic" across languages and cultures. In Frank Polzenhagen, Zoltán Kövecses, Stefanie Vogelbacher & Sonja Kleinke (eds.), *Cognitive explorations into metaphor and metonymy*, 87–99. Frankfurt: Peter Lang GmbH.
Musolff, Andreas. 2016a. Metaphor scenario analysis as part of cultural linguistics. *Tekst i Dyskurs – Text und Diskurs* 9. 47–69.
Musolff, Andreas. 2016b. *Political Metaphor Analysis. Discourse and Scenarios.* London: Bloomsbury.
Musolff, Andreas. 2017. How metaphors can shape political reality. The figurative scenarios at the heart of Brexit. *PiLaCS Papers in Language and Communication Studies* 1 (1). 2–16.
Quinn, Naomi. 1991. The cultural basis of metaphor. In James W. Fernandez (ed.), *Beyond metaphor: Theory of tropes in anthropology*, 56–93. Stanford: Stanford University Press.

Sandikcioglu, Esra. 2000. More metaphorical warfare in the Gulf: Orientalist frames in news coverage. In Antonio Barcelona (ed.), *Metaphor and metonymy at the crossroads: A Cognitive Perspective,* 299–320. Berlin & New York: De Gruyter Mouton.
Santa Ana, Otto. 1999. "Like an animal I was treated": anti-immigrant metaphor in US public discourse. *Discourse and society* 10 (2). 191–224.
Steen, Gerard J. 2011. The contemporary theory of metaphor – now new and improved! *Review of Cognitive Linguistics* 9 (1). 26–64.
Steen, Gerard, J. 1999. From linguistic to conceptual metaphor in five steps. In Gibbs, Raymond W. & Gerard J. Steen (eds.), *Metaphor in cognitive linguistics*. Selected Papers from the 5th International Cognitive Linguistics Conference. Amsterdam, July 1997. 57–77. Amsterdam & Philadelphia: John Benjamins Publishing Company.
Steen, Gerard, J. 2002. Metaphor Identification: A Cognitive Approach. *Style* 36 (3). 386–407.
Teliya, Veronika, N. 1988. *Metaforizatzyia i yeyo rol v sozdanii yazykovoi kartiny mira* [Metaphorization and its role in forming linguistic worldview]. In Rol chelovecheskogo factora v yasyke: Yazyk i kartina mira, 173–204. Moscow: Nauka.

Part II: **Consciousness in metaphor usage**

Valentina Cuccio and Gerard Steen

Deliberate metaphors and embodied simulation

Abstract: Recent studies of a behavioural kind (e.g., Glenberg and Kaschak 2002), neuroimaging kind (e.g., Kemmerer et al. 2008) and neurophysiological kind (e.g., Papeo et al. 2009) have shown that the sensorimotor system is involved in language understanding. Listening to the sentence "John grasps the glass" activates hand-related areas of the motor cortex even if we are not carrying out any hand-related action. This mechanism is known as Embodied Simulation (Gallese and Sinigaglia 2011) and has been shown to be a widespread mechanism in the brain, also characterizing the control of emotion and perception. The recruitment of Embodied Simulation has even been observed during metaphor comprehension (e.g., Boulenger et al. 2012; Desai et al. 2011). This has led Gibbs (e.g., 2015a, 2015b) to conclude that when processing bodily metaphors people recruit bodily knowledge as a function of cross-domain mapping. Yet the role of Embodied Simulation in the construction of figurative meaning is still controversial, with reports of contrasting empirical findings (e.g., Lai and Curran 2013). We will review this literature in the light of a novel definition of Embodied Simulation (Cuccio 2015a, 2015b, 2018) and its role at various stages of language processing, in interaction with the distinction between deliberate and non-deliberate metaphors (Steen 2008, 2015, 2017). We claim that this approach can explain the apparent incongruity of findings showing that the mechanism of simulation that has not always been found activated during the processing of action related figurative language. We claim that only deliberate metaphor use recruits the full mechanism of Embodied Simulation and its potential for affecting the resulting mental representation of a metaphor in working memory (Cuccio 2018; Steen 2018).

Keywords: Embodied Simulation; attention; deliberate metaphors; metaphor processing; bodily sensations.

Valentina Cuccio, Dept. of Medicine & Surgery Unit of Neuroscience, University of Parma.
Gerard Steen, University of Amsterdam – Department of Dutch Studies, Amsterdam.

https://doi.org/10.1515/9783110629460-009

1 Introduction

Many findings today show the involvement of Embodied Simulation in language and cognition. To define Embodied Simulation we first need to refer to the discovery of Mirror Neurons (di Pellegrino et al. 1992). Mirror Neurons are neurons in the premotor cortex that discharge both when we perform an action and when we just observe someone else performing that same action, mirroring her actions in our motor system. To give an example, the motor areas that in our brain control the action of grasping a fork will be activated not only when we effectively grasp a fork but also when we see someone else grasping a fork. Since then, it has been discovered that the mechanism of simulation is widespread in the brain. Embodied Simulation also characterizes brain areas involved in the processing of emotion and perception as well as cognitive tasks such as language comprehension or mental imagery. Thus, the motor areas that control the action of grasping a fork will be activated not only when we effectively grasp a fork and when we observe someone else grasping a fork but also when we see a fork, we read or listen to a proposition about someone grasping a fork or when we imagine ourselves or someone else grasping a fork (see Gallese and Sinigaglia 2011 for a discussion). This claim holds true even for the comprehension of bodily metaphors, namely metaphors based on our bodily experiences (e.g., Boulenger, Hauk, and Pulvermüller 2009; Boulenger, Shtyrov, and Pulvermüller 2012; Desai et al. 2011; Desai et al. 2013). Thus, the processing of a metaphorical expression such as "John grasps the idea" will determine the activation of hand-related areas of the motor cortex too. It has been suggested that, in this example, we comprehend the abstract concept of "understanding" (the target domain of the metaphor) resorting to the physical action of "grasping" (the source domain of the metaphor).

Yet divergent findings have been obtained in another set of studies (e.g., Aziz-Zadeh et al. 2006; Cacciari et al. 2011; Raposo et al. 2009). In these studies, the comprehension of figurative and abstract language did not always determine the activation of the mechanism of Embodied Simulation. For example, in a fMRI study, Raposo et al. (2008) asked participants to listen to arm- and leg-related verbs presented in isolation (e.g., "kick"), in literal sentences (as in "kick the ball") and idiomatic sentences (as in "kick the bucket"). A significant activation of the motor regions was observed in the first condition (verbs in isolation), a weaker activation was observed in the second condition (verbs in literal sentences) compared to the first, no activation of the motor and premotor cortices was observed in the third condition (verbs in idiomatic sentences). According to the authors' interpretation, these findings suggest that motor responses are context-dependent, rather than automatic and invariable.

As a consequence of these contrasting results, the role of Embodied Simulation in the construction of figurative meaning is still controversial (Cuccio et al. 2014; Gallese and Cuccio 2018). Further empirical research, together with theoretical work, is required if we want to understand how Embodied Simulation contributes to linguistic processing and, more specifically, to the construction of metaphorical meaning (cf. Cuccio 2017; Cuccio and Gallese 2018; Gallese and Cuccio 2018). In most research on this topic, Embodied Simulation is conceived as a mental representation encoded in bodily formats. We believe that this definition is highly controversial and this makes it even harder to understand what the real contribution is that Embodied Simulation provides to human cognition. Analytical and detailed discussions of the problematic aspects of a representational description of Embodied Simulation have already been presented in previous works (see Cuccio 2015a, 2015b, 2018). In these works, Cuccio suggested that we abandon every representational conception of the mechanism of simulation (Cuccio 2015a, 2015b, 2018) and provided for it an alternative definition: Embodied Simulation is more than a pattern of neural activation. It is a wider brain and bodily attitude.

In the present paper, in the light of this new interpretation of the mechanism of simulation, we will reframe the role Embodied Simulation has during the processing of bodily-related metaphors. Most importantly, the activation and role of this mechanism will be put in relation with the notion of deliberateness (Steen 2017). Differently from the main tenet of Conceptual Metaphor Theory, Deliberate Metaphor Theory predicts that only a few metaphors determine an online cross-domain mapping during linguistic processing (e.g., Steen 2018: 90). When this is the case, we pay attention to both the source and the target domain as two distinct referential domains. However, in the vast majority of cases, according to Steen (2015, 2017, 2018), metaphor processing does not determine anymore a cross-domain mapping that is needed to build the meaning of the utterance, with the consequence that we only pay attention to the target domain of the metaphors in our working memory. Metaphors that do determine cross-domain mapping during linguistic processing are identified as deliberate; those that do not are identified as non-deliberate.

Gibbs criticized the distinction between deliberate and non-deliberate metaphors and suggested that psycholinguistic and neuroscientific data contradict Deliberate Metaphor Theory. For example, Gibbs (2015b: 74) says that "[...] the psycholinguistic and cognitive neuroscience evidence directly contradicts Steen's assertions about so-called non-deliberate metaphors. Much empirical evidence, from a variety of experimental paradigms, clearly demonstrates that people infer embodied understandings of abstract words, such as the concrete action of filling when encountering 'a house filled with lights' (Gibbs 2011)". Gibbs concluded that the processing of bodily metaphors do entail cross-domain mapping and, hence, the recruitment of bodily knowledge, though he acknowledged that different degrees of conceptual metaphor activation might be observed, depending on individual, linguistic and conceptual factors (Gibbs 2015b: 75).

In Gibbs's view, however, although he admitted that conceptual metaphor processing might be context-dependent, leading to different degrees of activations of conceptual metaphors, it is difficult to explain why the data on the activation of Embodied Simulation have not consistently been replicated (e.g., Aziz-Zadeh et al. 2006; Cacciari et al. 2011; Raposo et al. 2009). In fact, Gibbs (2015: 75) continues:

> Different contexts may work to highlight or strengthen the impression that a cross-domain mapping is relevant to understanding what a verbal metaphor implies in context. Steen is correct to suggest that there may be different linguistic and contextual cues that add emphasis to the underlying metaphorical mappings implied by linguistic metaphors. He is dead wrong, though, when he continues to state that only a select few metaphors give rise to cross-domain mappings (i.e., deliberate metaphors), while most others do not (i.e., non-deliberate cases).

Thus, if conceptual metaphors always imply cross-domain mappings, as these lines seem to suggest, we cannot explain why only in some cases the processing of bodily metaphors elicits the activation of the mechanism of simulation.

Conversely, we maintain that Steen's (2008, 2015, 2017) distinction between deliberate and non-deliberate metaphors, in relation with the new definition of Embodied Simulation that will be discussed in the next section, allows us to make sense of the apparent incongruity of these findings and, hence, it allows us to better understand the role of the mechanism of simulation during the comprehension of metaphors (e.g., Aziz-Zadeh et al. 2006; Cacciari et al. 2011; Raposo et al. 2009).

2 An alternative account: Embodied Simulation as a brain and bodily attitude

Goldman and de Vignemont (2009; see also Goldman 2013) proposed an account of Embodied Cognition grounded in the notion of mental representation. They offered an analysis of four possible interpretations of embodiment and concluded that the most promising and plausible one is based on the notion of *mental representation in bodily format*. To better understand Goldman and de Vignemont's (2009) position in the current embodiment debate, consider the possible interactions between their hypothesis and the explanations of human cognition advanced in the framework of the Computational Theory of Mind (e.g., Fodor 1975), which is one main theoretical competitor for the Embodied Cognition paradigm. According to the Computational Theory of Mind all our cognitive processes are computations on *amodal symbols*. Amodal symbols can be defined as mental representations that have a format of representation such that it allows us to represent every type of content independently from the sensory modality that could have been involved in its perception. Mental representations are a crucial and unavoidable notion for the Computational Theory of Mind. By contrast, some of the scholars working in the embodiment tradition propose explanations of human cognition that do not resort to the notion of mental representation at all (for a discussion, Alsmith and de Vignemont 2012).

From this point of view, Goldman and de Vignemont's (2009) proposal seems to be a compromise solution. In fact, on the one hand, these authors still consider mental representations as a crucial element to explain human cognition; on the other, mental representations can also be encoded in a bodily format. This format can be: motoric, whenever the representation is about bodily movements carried out with different effectors; somatosensory, whenever the representation pertains to events occurring at the body's surface; affective or interoceptive, whenever the representation is about the physiological states of our body; and so on. Mental representations in bodily formats are patterns of neural activations elicited by actions, perceptual states and so on or by their simulation. To give an example, in Goldman and de Vignemont's (2009) view, the pattern of neural activation determined by the action of kicking a ball or by the observation of this same action carried out by someone else is considered to be a mental representation, encoded in a motoric format, of the action of kicking a ball. Any occurrence of Embodied Simulation is, thus, a mental representation in bodily format. In addition, as anticipated above, mental representations in bodily formats are not amodal. They are modality-specific, since the specific neural circuits in which the representations take place determine their format or modality of representation. Goldman and de Vignemont's (2009) proposal can, thus, be classified among moderate approaches to Embodied Cognition. The latter are usually contrasted with radical embodiment theories which propose non- representational explanations of human cognition.

Beyond the philosophically informed definition of the mechanism of simulation provided by Goldman and de Vignemont (2009), and in accordance with it, a representational account of this mechanism is currently widespread in the neuroscientific debate (e.g., Barsalou 1999, 2008; Clark 1997; Gallese and Lakoff 2005; Gallese and Sinigaglia 2011; Glenberg and Kaschak 2002; Glenberg, Witt, and Metcalfe 2013; Lakoff 2009; Meteyard et al. 2012; Pulvermueller 1999; Zwaan

2014). This representational account can be easily traced back to the influential work of Lawrence Barsalou (1999). His paper *Perceptual symbol systems* (Barsalou 1999), where he proposes a representational account of simulation routines, has been cited more than 7,000 times to date. In Barsalou's (1999) account, our bodily experiences are implemented in modality specific brain structures such as, for example, the visual cortex, the auditory cortex, the somatosensory cortex, the motor cortex or the olfactory cortex. Schematic representations of perceptual components of our bodily experiences can then be extracted and stored in memory. These representations, that are the building blocks of thought, are not abstract and amodal. They are encoded in modality specific neural circuits and can be reactivated by means of the mechanism of simulation. Hence, the activation of the mechanism of simulation is basically conceived of as the occurrence of a modality-specific representation.

Contrary to this dominant representational approach, we claim that Embodied Simulation is non-representational.[1] As an alternative we suggest that the only plausible way to describe the mechanism of Embodied Simulation is to resort to the notion of informationally sensitive responses to natural signs (Cuccio 2018; Hutto and Myin 2013: 78; Hutto and Myin 2017). Dynamic systems theory (Thelen and Smith 1994) is clearly the theoretical background for this notion. Physical systems are always embedded in their environment. Variables in the systems are considered to continuously change in response to environmental states and vice versa. In this framework, the behaviour of physical systems is explained in terms of dynamic laws without the need to resort to the notion of mental representation. We will not discuss in any more depth dynamic systems theory nor will we further scrutinize the critical hypothesis that all our behaviours, even very complex ones, can be explained according to dynamic laws. For the purposes of this paper it is enough to accept the less theoretically demanding hypothesis that at least basic forms of cognition can be described according to dynamic laws and that both basic cognitive processes and the neural activity that enables them do not imply any content (for a deeper discussion of this issue see Hutto and Myin 2017: xiv).

In the alternative view for the mechanism of simulation that is here proposed, we can only understand Embodied Simulation's contribution to cognition if we

---

1 It is worth noting that to advocate a non-representational account of Embodied Simulation is not necessarily equal to embracing a radical non- representational approach to Embodied Cognition. A non-representational account of Embodied Simulation is certainly fully compatible with explanations of human cognition that imply representations (see Alsmith and de Vignemont 2012; Chemero 2009; Clark 1997 for a discussion of radical and moderate approaches to Embodied Cognition).

free this mechanism from any representational load and contextualize its activation in a broader framework comprising both other brain activities and bodily, not merely neural, features. Embodied Simulation does not only determine the activation of some neural circuits. It also sets a more comprehensive bodily attitude and it sometimes, even, determines the arousal of bodily sensations. Bodily attitudes and sensations contribute to the implementation of cognitive tasks such as language comprehension and social cognition.

Neuroscientific data appear to support this account of the mechanism of simulation. In fact, it has been shown that, during simulation routines, areas of the brain that process bodily sensations are also elicited. For example, in a fMRI study, Costantini et al. (2005) studied the potential simulation triggered by both possible and biomechanically impossible movements of fingers. Both conditions activated the premotor areas, thus, leading to a simulation even of the biomechanically impossible movement. Interestingly, both the experimental conditions also determined the activation of the Posterior Parietal Cortex, an area of the brain that is involved in the processing of bodily sensations. But this area was significantly more activated in the biomechanically impossible movement condition where participants watched video-clips showing a hand undergoing an unnatural and potentially extremely painful movement. Thus, in both conditions, the simulation did not confine itself to the motor areas; it also involved areas related to the experience of bodily sensations. But, in the biomechanically impossible movement condition, this effect was amplified to the extent that participants of the studies reported to have felt "sensations" determined by the observation of the experimental stimuli.

These data suggests interesting considerations: bodily sensations may be elicited during Embodied Simulation and, most of all, these bodily sensations might be enhanced by some factors such as pain, as in Costantini et al.'s (2005; see also Abreu et al. 2012) study, but also emotion and, most importantly for the purposes of this paper, attention, as we will see in the next section (see Bach et al. 2007; Tipper et al. 2006; Vainio et al. 2007 on the interaction between attention and Embodied Simulation). In fact, this amplifying effect on the mechanism of simulation can also be observed when explicit attention is paid to the stimuli (linguistic or visual) being processed (Bach et al. 2007; Tipper et al. 2006; Vainio et al. 2007). This aspect will be particularly relevant when we will describe the interaction between the mechanism of simulation and the processing of deliberate metaphors, which depends on paying attention to concepts from the source domain as distinct referents in the discourse.

Summarizing, we propose that the cognitive contribution of Embodied Simulation can be better and fully understood only if we go beyond a neurocentric account to embrace a really embodied, and not merely embrained, description of this mechanism. Embodied Simulation, in this view, is not just the activation of a neural circuit but a more complex phenomenon that determines a bodily attitude and sometimes leads to the experience of bodily sensations.

With this new definition for the mechanism of simulation at our disposal and in the light of the distinction between deliberate and non-deliberate metaphor (Steen 2015, 2017, 2018), we can now advance a proposal on the processing of bodily-related deliberate metaphors. We claim that only deliberately processed bodily metaphors, compared to non-deliberate ones, recruit at full length the mechanism of simulation determining the activation of bodily sensations. This is possible because attention has a key role in deliberate metaphors processing. In fact, it is the attention we pay to the source domain of a metaphor that makes a metaphor a deliberately processed metaphor. Attention, as we will see, also has a key role in the modulation of the activation of Embodied Simulation. It follows that attention can also have a crucial role in relation to the activation of the mechanism of simulation when we deliberately process bodily metaphors. In fact, in this view, it is the attention we pay to the source domain of bodily-related metaphors that might determine a significant difference in the activation of the mechanism of simulation compared to the processing of non-deliberate bodily metaphors. Furthermore, we maintain that this new model for the processing of deliberate and non-deliberate metaphors can allow us to make sense of the inconsistency of findings on the activation of the mechanism of simulation during the processing of bodily metaphors.

3 A new model for metaphor processing

Based on Cuccio's new account of Embodied Simulation and Steen's notion of deliberateness, we can now briefly present a new model for the processing of bodily related metaphors (Cuccio 2018; Steen 2018). According to this model, the mechanism of Embodied Simulation, in its full length, is not always recruited by metaphor processing. Only deliberate metaphors do recruit this mechanism in all its complexity and likely trigger bodily dispositions and bodily sensations. This is so because they likely determine both an early and a late somatotopic activation. This means that, during the processing of action-related figurative words, cortical areas involved in motor control are automatically activated very early on, around 200 ms after the stimulus onset (Pulvermüller 2012: 443), as a function of early concept elicitation (early somatotopic activation). When bodily related metaphors are deliberately processed a late somatotopic activation, as a function of cross-domain mapping, is likely also observed. Indeed, attention paid to the source domain of the metaphor in the situation model[2] modulates the activation of the mechanism of simulation amplifying its effects. The simulation is, in this case, stronger and prolonged (Schuch et al. 2010). Only a stronger and prolonged activation of Embodied Simulation can determine the arousal of bodily sensations and dispositions (Costantini et al. 2005). The latter likely affect the communicative effectiveness of metaphors: when we deliberately process bodily-related metaphors, Embodied Simulation makes us able to feel in our own bodies the bodily experiences linguistically described and, importantly, it also makes us able to share these experiences with our interlocutors (Cuccio 2015b, 2018). Conversely, the processing of non-deliberate metaphors can only determine early somatotopic activation. There is no late somatotopic activation in this case. Hence, in this model, non deliberate bodily metaphors, compared to deliberate ones, are predicted to be less communicatively effective because they do not determine the involvement of phenomenological aspects of our bodily experiences during linguistic processing.

Attention has a crucial role in the deliberate processing of metaphors. In fact, deliberate metaphors are those metaphors that force us to pay attention to both the source and the target domain construing the referential meaning of a metaphor related utterance. It follows that to attend to the source domain of a metaphor in working memory (i.e., to deliberately process it as a separate domain of reference) drives the attention we pay to the sensory information activated by the mechanism of simulation. Hence, since deliberate metaphors force us to pay attention to the source domain of metaphors, for bodily metaphors, to deliberately pay attention to a bodily-related source domain is a way to amplify the activation of the mechanism of simulation that will then take place at full length.

One problem is that, so far, the interaction between deliberateness and Embodied Simulation has never been directly investigated. What we do have, however, is empirical findings on the interaction between attention and Embodied Simulation during action observation (Bach et al. 2007; Schuch et al. 2010; Tipper et al. 2006; Vainio et al. 2007). These can provide indirect support to the model here developed.

One example is Schuch et al. (2010), who carried out an electroencephalography study (EEG) to measure motor system activation and its potential interaction with attention during action observation. All the participants of the study watched videos displaying the action of grasping a cup. Two variables were manipulated: 1. the kind of grasp; 2. a color change in the cup. Motor system activation was,

2 In discourse analysis the notion of situation model refers to the representations of the world that speakers construct during language processing (van Dijk and Kintsch 1983, Steen in press).

thus, observed in two different experimental conditions. In the first condition participants were asked to explicitly pay attention to the kind of grasp, in the second condition they were required to pay attention to the color change. Schuch et al. (2010) found that both experimental conditions elicited the activation of the motor system (early somatotopic activation) while only the experimental condition where participants were asked to specifically attend to the grasping movement determined greater and prolonged activation of motor simulation (late somatotopic activation). To specifically pay attention to the action features in the videos amplified the simulation effect.

In line with these findings, we predict that only deliberately processed bodily metaphors imply the full process of simulation that goes from a very early somatotopic activation to a late activation that can then elicit the experience of bodily sensations. And the latter are specifically due to the amplifying effect determined by the attention we pay to the source domain of bodily metaphors. In the case of non-deliberately processed bodily metaphors, lexical disambiguation intervenes very early on to stop the automatic activation of the mechanism of simulation and, thus, preventing the process of simulation to unfold at full length. For these reasons, we maintain that early somatotopic activation observed during conventional metaphor comprehension can be considered a function of polysemous lexical access and early concept activation, irrespective of metaphor type, while late somatotopic activation during metaphor comprehension is a function of metaphor deliberateness and its role in utterance comprehension.

To illustrate how this model works we can now turn to the analysis of some linguistic examples. Steen (2018) discussed several experiments carried out in the framework of Conceptual Metaphor Theory (CMT) and showed that the linguistic stimuli used in these studies are often good examples of deliberate metaphor use. For example, he analyzed Pfaff, Gibbs and Johnson (1997) study which was aimed to show that people's metaphorical conceptualization of a topic influences the appropriateness rating and processing time of conventional and novel euphemisms and dysphemisms. According to the predictions advanced by the authors of this study, a metaphorically constructed paragraph, introducing a consistent novel metaphor, should prime the comprehension of that metaphor enhancing its processing time.

Paragraph primes SEXUAL DESIRE IS A HUNTING ANIMAL

Dirk is a real wolf. He prowls the singles bars looking for unsuspecting young women to proposition. One night, he saw a particularly tasty-looking morsel in a mini-skirt and said to his friend,

"I'm ready to pounce."

> *Paragraph primes* SEXUAL DESIRE IS AN ACTIVATED MACHINE
>
> Dirk is a real operator. He cruises the singles bars looking for young women to proposition. One night, he saw a particularly sleek-looking model with all the options and said to is friend,
>
> She's turning my crank."

Findings from this study confirmed the authors' predictions. Interestingly, according to Steen (2018), these results might depend on deliberate metaphor use displayed in the priming paragraphs. In fact,

> [...] they exhibit a combination of an A is B construction in the first sentence with a continuation in at least one striking and novel metaphor in the next sentences. Novel metaphors, including novel A is B metaphors, are deliberate because they require online cross-domain mapping to project an unknown target domain referent from a known source domain referent. Conventional A is B metaphors are potentially deliberate because they are ambiguous between two readings: one in which the source domain term is interpreted at target domain level, which would make the cross-domain mapping unnecessary and would lead to categorization, and one in which the source domain term is interpreted at source domain level, which would draw attention to the source domain in the situation model (Glucksberg, 2008). The latter reading would result in deliberate metaphor use. The positive findings of Pfaff et al. (1997) for CMT might hence be due to the fact that these linguistic realizations of the underlying conceptual metaphors are deliberate and require a separate representation of the source domain as a distinct referential domain in the situation model (Steen in press, 100–101).

Steen's (2018) reading of these data is clearly fully compatible with the account of Embodied Simulation here presented and with its role in metaphor processing. Although this is only a preliminary analysis, we predict that the comprehension of a novel metaphor such as "I'm ready to pounce", in the example here discussed, determines a stronger activation of the mechanism of simulation (both early and late somatotopic activation) to the extent that it triggers the experience of bodily feelings related to the action of pouncing. In a face to face conversation, by virtue of the activation of this mechanism, both hearer and speaker should, then, physically experience in their own bodies the bodily components of the metaphors and they should share this experience, thus, living similar bodily sensations. Both these conditions might determine a greater communicative effectiveness of deliberate bodily metaphors compared to non deliberate one.

4 Making sense of empirical data

In this section we will review some neuroscientific data on metaphor comprehension. This review is, however, far from being exhaustive. It can be considered a first preliminary attempt to apply our model to the analysis of empirical findings.

As we already know, neuroimaging studies have found a somatotopic activation of the pre-motor and motor cortical areas related to the literal meaning of action verbs during the comprehension of metaphors and idioms (Boulenger et al. 2009, 2012; Desai et al. 2011). However, these data have not been consistently replicated and, as a consequence, they appear to be still controversial. In fact divergent findings have been obtained in other neuroimaging or Transcranial Magnetic Stimulation (TMS) studies (Cacciari et al. 2011; Lai and Curran 2013; Raposo et al. 2009) where the activation of the motor system has not been always observed during the processing of figurative usages of action-related verbs.

These studies display crucial differences in linguistic stimuli, experimental procedures, and data analysis. Most importantly, they manipulate the conceptual structure of metaphors (conventional versus novel cross-domain mappings), their linguistic form (idiom, metaphor, simile), but not their communicative properties (deliberate versus non-deliberate use as metaphor). The latter are distinct from but can be related to the conceptual and linguistic properties, but in varying ways. The distinction between deliberate and non-deliberate metaphor use has not been employed in current neuroscientific studies. These could be the reasons why the activation of the mechanism of simulation during the processing of figurative language has not consistently been replicated in all these studies.

We propose that the apparently contradictory findings obtained so far are in fact not really contrasting. They may instead be explained with reference to a more sophisticated model relating their experimental differences to a more precise notion of Embodied Simulation, as previously defined, and the distinction between deliberate and non-deliberate metaphor use. What is important is that these studies differ in many respects, requiring a consistent and encompassing theoretical framework for directly comparing the data. Linguistic stimuli used in these studies are heterogeneous. In the neuroscientific studies carried out so far on the embodiment of body-related metaphors, deliberate and non-deliberate metaphors have both been used without sufficient control. Very different kinds of experimental tasks have also been carried out without taking into account the potentiality of some of these tasks to revitalize even very conventional metaphors. This heterogeneity of stimuli and methodologies has inevitably led to a great heterogeneity of results.

It could be possible that when Embodied Simulation has not been observed during metaphor processing, non-deliberate metaphors have been used as linguistic stimuli while, when the mechanism of simulation has been found activated, deliberate metaphors have been used. Furthermore, it might also be that particular experimental procedures can revitalize non-deliberate metaphors, thus, making them deliberate again. In this latter case, they also activate the mechanism of simulation. In the rest of this section we will analyze some examples to check whether this interpretation is correct.

In a Magnetoencephalography (MEG) study, Boulenger et al. (2012) found the activation of the mechanism of simulation during the processing of idioms containing action-related verbs (e.g., "Pablo grasps the idea", "John scraped the barrel", "John picks her brain", "Mary caught the sun", "Pablo kicked the bucket", "Anna walked a tightrope between the situations", "Pablo jumped on the bandwagon"). An analysis of the linguistic stimuli used in this study shows that metaphors and idioms selected by the authors were highly conventional and not deliberate. However, stimuli were presented word by word on a computer screen and the action verbs (e.g., "grasps") appeared on average 1.2 seconds before the critical word onset (e.g., "idea"). This procedure very likely revitalizes the metaphors because action verbs, processed before the onset of the disambiguating words, likely determined the activation of the concepts related to the source domain of the metaphors, that otherwise would have not been attended to. The experimental procedure adopted in the study determined their revitalization to the extent that linguistic processing triggered the somatotopic activation of the sensory-motor system.

In another fMRI study investigating the neural career of sensory-motor metaphors, Desai et al. (2011) found that, during the processing of action-related metaphors (e.g., "The jury grasped the concept", "The public grasped the idea"), the activation of primary motor and biological motion perception areas was inversely correlated with metaphor familiarity. In this study, the stimuli were presented on a computer screen. The sentences were presented in two parts, first the noun phrase (e.g., "The jury") and then the verb phrase (e.g., "grasped the concept"). In this way, action related verbs always appeared together with the disambiguating words (e.g., "grasped the concept").

Even though familiarity and deliberateness are partially different properties, pertaining to different dimensions of metaphors, in the Desai et al. (2011) study, familiarity can be considered as an index of deliberateness. In fact, unless a familiar metaphor is revitalized and used deliberately, it is commonly non deliberately processed. Since the Desai el al (2011) experimental procedure did not allow any revitalization of the figurative expressions, familiar metaphors were not deliberately processed as metaphors and hence did not determine the activation of the mechanism of simulation. The latter was, instead, found activated during the processing of non familiar metaphors.

In a fMRI study on the modulation of motor and premotor cortices by the processing of action related words, both literally and idiomatically interpreted, Raposo et al. (2009) found no involvement of the sensory-motor system when participants processed action related idioms. The linguistic items were presented in the vocal modality. Participants had to listen to literal or idiomatic sentences containing action related words while lying in the scan. Metaphors used in this study were highly conventional to the extent that they were explicitly considered as idioms (e.g., "The job offer was a great chance so Claire grabbed it"). Conventional metaphors[3] are usually not deliberately processed, unless they are presented in such a way to be revitalized. But the experimental procedure of this study, as in the previous one, did not allow any revitalization. Sentences were presented in the vocal modality without any interval between words. Authors of this study did not find any activation of the mechanism of simulation during metaphor processing while literal sentences did determine a somatotopic activation of the motor and premotor cortices.

As a last example, we will here discuss a study by Desai et al. (2013). In this fMRI study the authors investigated the modulation of the sensory-motor regions during the processing of literal, metaphorical and idiomatic sentences containing action related verbs (e.g., literal: "The instructor is grasping the steering wheel very tightly"; metaphor: "The congress is grasping the state of the affairs"; idiom: "The congress is grasping at straws in the crisis"). Results of this study indicated a gradual abstraction process whereby the reliance on sensory-motor systems is reduced as the abstractness of meaning as well as conventionalization is increased. This means that the activation of the sensory-motor system in this study decreased going from the literal, to the metaphorical to the idiomatic condition. No activation of the sensory-motor system was observed in the idiomatic condition. The sentences, displayed on a computer screen, appeared in two parts (first the noun phrase followed, after an interval, by the rest of the sentence: The congress is/ grasping the state of the affairs). This experimental procedure does not allow any revitalization of the figurative expressions because the metaphorically used verbs always appear together with the disambiguating words. The involvement of the sensory-motor system seems to be a function of the conventionalization of metaphors that, as previously discussed, can be here considered an index of deliberateness. The less conventional a metaphor is, the

3 The difference between conventional and familiar metaphors will be not discussed in this paper. We maintain that both conventional and familiar metaphors are usually not deliberately processed, unless they are revitalized.

more deliberately processed as a metaphor it can be considered. Results from this study confirmed this prediction.

This preliminary, and certainly not exhaustive, review seems to confirm the predictions we advanced on the basis of our model of metaphor processing. In fact, it seems that where Embodied Simulation is not elicited by the processing of action-related metaphors, this could be a function of metaphor type (deliberate vs non-deliberate) and of the experimental procedure of the studies (that could or could not revitalize metaphors). Only deliberate metaphors do trigger at full length the mechanism of simulation.

5 Conclusions

In this paper we presented a new account for the mechanism of Embodied Simulation. In a real embodied, and not merely embrained, description of this mechanism, Embodied Simulation was defined as a process that keeps together both the neural level and the level of bodily sensations. In this account, the mechanism of simulation goes from a very early somatotopic activation to a late activation that can also determine the involvement of bodily sensations and disposition, although these are often unconscious. These bodily sensations and dispositions are activated in particular circumstances, when factors such as emotion involvement and pain or pleasure (see section 2 of this paper; Abreu et al. 2012; Costantini et al. 2005) are at play. In these cases, the process of simulation takes place at full length and it is stronger and prolonged in time. The mechanism of simulation can also be modulated by attention. Attention is a key notion in defining deliberateness in metaphor processing, because it is the attention we pay to the source domain of a metaphor in working memory that makes a metaphor a deliberately processed metaphor. Starting from these premises, we hypothesize that deliberateness in metaphor processing can modulate the activation of the mechanism of simulation. Only deliberate bodily metaphors, in this hypothesis, imply the full process of simulation and, thus, only during the processing of deliberate bodily metaphors the mechanism of simulation goes from a very early somatotopic activation to a late activation that determines bodily sensations and dispositions, as a result of the attention we pay to the source domain of the metaphors. When bodily metaphors are non-deliberately processed lexical disambiguation intervenes to stop the first activation of the mechanism of simulation.

The new account of Embodied Simulation here discussed, considered in the light of the distinction between deliberate and non-deliberate metaphors, as this preliminary analysis seems to confirm, thus, allowed us to make sense of the apparent incongruent of results observed in the neuroscientific literature on metaphor processing.

Acknowledgements: This work was supported by the Nederlandse Organisatie voor Wetenschappelijk Onderzoek (NWO – Netherlands Organisation for Scientific Research) grant for high qualified senior researchers to Valentina Cuccio and Gerard Steen (grant number: 040.11.484).

Although both authors discussed and designed the article together, §§1, 2 and 4 were written by V.C., while §3 was written by G.S.

References

Abreu, Ana Maria, Emiliano Macaluso, Ruben T. Azevedo, Paola Cesari, Cosimo Urgesi, & Salvatore Maria Aglioti. 2012. Action anticipation beyond the action observation network: a functional magnetic resonance imaging study in expert basketball players. *European Journal of Neuroscience* 35. 1646–1654. DOI: 10.1111/j.1460-9568.2012.08104.

Alsmith, Adrian & Frederique de Vignemont, F. 2012: Embodying the mind and representing the body. *Review of Philosophy and Psychology* 3 (1).

Aziz-Zadeh, Lisa, Fumiko Maeda, Eran Zaidel, John Mazziotta & Marco Iacoboni. 2002. Lateralization in motor facilitation during action observation: a TMS study. *Experimental Brain Research* 144 (1). 127–131.

Bach, Patric, Nicholas Peatfield & Steven Tipper. 2007. Focusing on body sites: the role of spatial attention in action perception. *Experimental Brain Research* 178. 509–517.

Barsalou, Lawrence W. 1999. Perceptual symbol systems. *Behavioral and Brain Sciences* 22 (4). 577–609; discussion 610–560.

Barsalou, Lawrence W. 2008: Grounded cognition. *Annual Review of Psychology* 59. 617–645

Boulenger, Veronique, Olaf Hauk & Friedemann Pulvermüller. 2009. Grasping ideas with the motor system: semantic somatotopy in idiom comprehension. *Cerebral Cortex* 19 (8). 1905–1914. DOI: bhn217 [pii] 10.1093/cercor/bhn217.

Boulenger, Veronique, Yury Shtyrov & Friedemann Pulvermüller. 2012. When do you grasp the idea? MEG evidence for instantaneous idiom understanding. *Neuroimage* 59 (4). 3502–3513. DOI: S1053-8119(11)01291-2 [pii] 10.1016/j.neuroimage.2011.11.011.

Cacciari, Cristina, Nadia Bolognini, Irene Senna, Maria C. Pellicciari, Carlo Miniussi & Costanza Papagno. 2011. Literal, fictive and metaphorical motion sentences preserve the motion component of the verb: a TMS study. *Brain and Language* 119 (3). 149–157. DOI: S0093-934X(11)00104-0 [pii] 10.1016/j.bandl.2011.05.004.

Chemero, Anthony. 2009. *Radical embodied cognitive science*. Cambridge, Massachussetts & London: MIT Press.

Churchland, Patricia. 1986. *Neurophilosophy: Toward a Unified Science of the Mind-Brain*. Cambridge, Massachusetts: The MIT Press.

Clark, Andy. 1997. *Being there: putting brain, body, and world together again*. Cambridge, Massacchusetts & London: MIT Press.

Costantini, Marcello, Gaspare Galati, Antonio Ferretti, Massimo Caulo, Armando Tartaro, Gian Luca Romani, & Salvatore Maria Aglioti. 2005. Neural systems underlying observation of humanly impossible movements: an FMRI study. *Cerebral Cortex* 15. 1761–1767.
Cuccio, Valentina. 2015a. The notion of representation and the brain. *Phenomenology and Mind* 7. 247–258.
Cuccio, Valentina. 2015b. Embodied Simulation and metaphors. Towards a direct role of the body in language comprehension. *Epistemologia* 37. 97–112.
Cuccio, Valentina. 2017. Body-schema and body-image in metaphor processing. In Beate Hampe (ed.), *Metaphor: From Embodied Cognition to Discourse*, 82–98. Cambridge: Cambridge University Press.
Cuccio, Valentina. 2018. *Attention to Metaphor. From neurons to representations.* Amsterdam: John Benjamins Publishing Company.
Cuccio, Valentina & Vittorio Gallese. 2018. A Peircean account of concepts. Grounding abstraction in phylogeny through a comparative neuroscientific perspective. *Philosophical Transactions of the Royal Society B* 373. 20170128. http://dx.doi.org/10.1098/rstb.2017.0128.
Cuccio, Valentina, Marianna Ambrosecchia, Francesca Ferri, Marco Carapezza, Franco Lo Piparo, Leonardo Fogassi & Vittorio Gallese. 2014. How the context matters. Literal and figurative meaning in the embodied language paradigm. *Plos One* 9 (12). 1–24. https://doi.org/10.1371/journal.pone.0115381.
Desai, Rutvik H., Jeffrey R. Binder, Lisa L. Conant, Quintino R. Mano & Mark S. Seidenberg. 2011. The neural career of sensory-motor metaphors. *Journal of Cognitive Neuroscience* 23 (9). 2376–2386. DOI: 10.1162/jocn.2010.21596.
Desai, Rutvik H., Lisa L. Conant, Jeffrey R. Binder, Haeil Park & Mark S. Seidenberg. 2013. A piece of the action: modulation of sensory-motor regions by action idioms and metaphors. *Neuroimage* 83.862-869. DOI: 10.1016/j.neuroimage.2013.07.044.
Dijk, van Teun A. & Walter Kintsch. 1983. *Strategies of discourse comprehension*. New York: Academic Press.
di Pellegrino, Giuseppe (see Pellegrino).
Fodor, Jerry. 1975. *The language of thought*. New York, NY: Crowell.
Gallese, Vittorio & Cuccio, Valentina. 2018. The neural exploitation hypothesis and its implications for an embodied approach to language and cognition: Insights from the study of action verbs processing and motor disorders in Parkinson's Disease. *Cortex* 100. 215–225.
Gallese, Vittorio & George Lakoff. 2005. The Brain's concepts: the role of the Sensory-motor system in conceptual knowledge. *Cognitive Neuropsychology* 22 (3). 455–479.
Gallese, Vittorio & Corrado Sinigaglia. 2011. What is so special about embodied simulation? *Trends in Cognitive Sciences* 15 (11). 512–519.
Gibbs, Raymond W. Jr. 2006. Metaphor interpretation as embodied simulation. *Mind and Language* 21. 434–458.
Gibbs, Raymond W. 2015a. Do pragmatic signals affect conventional metaphor understanding? A failed test of deliberate metaphor theory. *Journal of Pragmatics* 90. 77–87.
Gibbs, Raymond W. 2011b. Evaluating conceptual metaphor theory. *Discourse Processes* 48. 529–562.
Gibbs, Raymond W. 2015b. Does deliberate metaphor theory have a future? *Journal of Pragmatics* 90. 73–76. DOI: 10.1016/j.pragma.2015.03.016.
Glenberg, Arthur M. & Michael P. Kaschak. 2002. Grounding language in action. *Psychonomic Bulletin and Review* 9 (3). 558–565.

Glenberg, Arthur M., Jessica K. Witt & Janet Metcalfe. 2013. From the Revolution to Embodiment: 25 Years of Cognitive Psychology. *Perspectives on Psychological Science* 8. 573–585.
Glucksberg, Sam. 2008. How metaphors create categories – quickly. In Raymond Gibbs (ed.), *The Cambridge handbook of metaphor and thought*, 67–83. Cambridge, MA: Cambridge University Press.
Goldman Alvin, Frederique de Vignemont. 2009). Is social cognition embodied? *Trends in Cognitive Sciences* 13 (4). 154–159.
Goldman, Alvin. 2013. The bodily formats approach to embodied cognition. In Uriah Kriegel (ed.), *Current controversies in philosophy of mind*, 91–108. London & New York: Routledge.
Holst, von Erik & Horst Mittelstaedt. 1950. Das reafferenz princip: Wedlselwirkungen zwischen Zentrainervensystem und Peripherie (The reafference principle: interaction between the central nervous system and the periphery). *Die Naturwissenschaften* 37. 464–476.
Hutto, Daniel & Erik Myin. 2013. *Radicalizing enactivism. Basic minds without content.* Cambridge, Mass.: MIT Press.
Hutto, Daniel & Erik Myin. 2017. *Evolving Enactivism. Basic Minds Meet Content.* Cambridge, Massachusetts: The MIT Press.
Kemmerer, David, Javier González Castillo, Thomas Talavage, Stefanie Patterson & Cinthia Wiley. 2008. Neuroanatomical distribution of five semantic components of verbs: evidence from fMRI. *Brain & Language* 107 (1). 16–43. DOI: S0093-934X(07)00261-1 [pii] 10.1016/j.bandl.2007.09.003.
Kilner, James M., Karl J. Friston & Chris D. Frith. 2007. Predictive coding: an account of the mirror neuron system. *Cogn Process* 8. 159–166. DOI: 10.1007/s10339-007-0170-2.
Lai, Vicky & Tim Curran. 2013. ERP evidence for conceptual mappings and comparison processes during the comprehension of conventional and novel metaphors. *Brain & Language* 127 (2). 484–496.
Lakoff, George. 2008.TheNeuralTheoryof Metaphor. In Raymond W. JrGibbs (ed.), *CambridgeHandbookofMetaphorand Thought*, 17–38.NewYork:Cambridge UniversityPress.
Meteyard, Lotte, Sara R. Cuadrado, Bahador Bahrami & Gabriella Vigliocco. 2012. Coming of age: a review of embodiment and the neuroscience of semantics. *Cortex* 48 (7). 788-804. DOI: 10.1016/j.cortex.2010.11.002.
Millikan, Ruth G. 1984. *Language, thought and other biological categories: new foundations for realism.* Cambridge, Massacchussets & London: MIT Press.
Miall, Christopher R. 2003. Connecting mirror neurons and forward models. *NeuroReport* 14 (16). 1–3.
Niziolek, Caroline A, Srikanta S. Nagarajan & John F. Houde. 2013. What does motor efference copy represent? Evidence from speech production. *Journal of Neuroscience* 33 (41). 16110-16116.
Papeo, Liuba, Antonio Vallesi, Alessio Isaja & Raffaella Ida Rumiati. 2009. Effects of TMS on different stages of motor and non-motor verb processing in the primary motor cortex. *PLoS One* 4 (2). e4508. DOI: 10.1371/journal.pone.0004508.
Pellegrino, di Giuseppe, Luciano Fadiga, Leonardo Fogassi, Vittorio Gallese & Giacomo Rizzolatti. 1992. Understanding motor events: a neurophysiological study. *Experimental Brain Research* 91 (1). 176–180.
Pfaff, Kerry, Raymond Gibbs & Mark Johnson. 1997. Metaphor in using and understanding euphemism and dysphemism *Applied Psycholinguistics* 18. 59–83. https://doi.org/10.1017/S0142716400009875.

Pulvermüller, Friedemann. 1999. Words in the brain's language. *Behav Brain Sci* 22 (2). 253–279; discussion 280–336.
Pulvermüller, Friedemann. 2012. Meaning and the brain: e neurosemantics of referential, in-teractive, and combinatorial knowledge *Journal of Neurolinguistics* 25 (5). 423–459. https://doi.org/10.1016/j.jneuroling.2011.03.004.
Pynn, Laura K. & Joseph F. DeSouza. 2013. The function of efference copy signals: implications for symptoms of schizophrenia. *Vision Research* 76. 124–133. DOI: 10.1016/j.visres.2012.10.019.
Raposo Ana, Helen E. Moss, Emmanuel A. Stamatakis & Lorraine K. Tyler. 2009. Modulation of motor and premotor cortices by actions, action words and action sentences. *Neuropsychologia* 47. 388–396.
Schuch, Stefanie E., Andrew P. Bayliss, Christof Klein, & Steven P. Tipper. 2010. Attention modulates motor system activation during action observation: Evidence for inhibitory rebound. *Experimental Brain Research* 205 (2). 235–249. https://doi.org/10.1007/s00221-010-2358-4.
Sperry, Roger Wolcott. 1950. Neural basis of the spontaneous optokinetic response produced by visual inversion. *Journal of Comparative and Physiological Psychology* 43 (6). 482–489.
Steen, Gerard J. 2008. The paradox of metaphor: Why we need a three-dimensional model for metaphor. *Metaphor & Symbol* 23 (4). 213–41.
Steen, Gerard J. 2011. The contemporary theory of metaphor—now new and improved! *Review of Cognitive Linguistics* 9 (1). 26–64.
Steen, Gerard J. 2015. Developing, testing and interpreting Deliberate Metaphor Theory. *Journal of Pragmatics* 90. 67–72. https://doi.org/10.1016/j.pragma.2015.03.013.
Steen, Gerard J. 2017. Deliberate Metaphor Theory: Basic assumptions, main tenets, urgent issues. *Intercultural Pragmatics* 14 (1). 1–24.
Steen, Gerard J. 2018. Attention and deliberateness in metaphor processing. In Valentina Cuccio, *Attention to Metaphor. From Neurons to Representations*, 89–109. Amsterdam: John Benjamins Publishing.
Thelen, Esther & Linda B. Smith. 1994: *A dynamic systems approach to the development of cognition and action*. Cambridge, Massacchussets & London: MIT Press.
Tipper Steven P.,Matthew A. Paul & Amy E. Hayes. 2006. Vision-for-action: the effects of object property discrimination and action state on affordance compatibility effects. *Psychonomic Bulletin Review* 13. 493–498.
Vainio, Lari, Rob Ellis, Mike Tucker. 2007. The role of visual attention in action priming. *Quarterly Journal of Experimental Psychology A* 60. 241–261.
van Dijk, Teun (see Dijk).
von Holst, Erik (see Holst).
Zwaan, Rolf. 2014. Embodiment and language comprehension: reframing the discussion. *Trends Cognitive Science* 18 (5). 229–34.

Antonio-José Silvestre-López

Deliberate metaphors in Buddhist teachings about meditation

Abstract: In recent decades, meditative practices have experienced a great expansion in many areas of our modern society. Meditators often use metaphors as an aid to help them shape their first-person subjective experiences in more conventional ways that they can share with others (Silvestre-López 2016a, 2016b). The use of metaphor becomes especially important in instructional settings, where the instructor needs to explain the basic procedures of meditation in simple and clear terms. Since metaphor is used in this context to fulfil particular communicative intentions and needs, its deliberate use (Steen 2010, 2014) may well be a key parameter in the discourse about meditation. This chapter surveys the use of deliberate metaphor in a selection of writings about meditation by two Tibetan Buddhist masters. Results reveal an array of deliberate metaphor uses based on explicit comparison devices (e.g., metaphorical similes, analogies and explicit metaphor formulae). These are associated chiefly with explanatory and reconceptualisation functions (Goatly 2011), together with the (re)creation of vivid scenarios that help the writer communicate the experience in more direct, vivid ways. The study concludes with a series of considerations about source domain genericity-specificity preferences in deliberate and non-deliberate uses, and addresses the ways deliberate metaphor may become a relevant tool in meditation-related instructional settings, these including Buddhist as well as other secular contexts stemming from the globalisation of meditation.

Keywords: Deliberate metaphor, metaphor functions, meditation, Buddhism, ATLAS.ti

1 Introduction

Over the last few decades, the benefits of contemplative practices rooted in eastern traditions, like mindfulness and meditation, have paved the way for their introduction in many areas of western society including personal development, leadership, medical care and even academic and educational contexts (Campos and Cebolla 2016). In traditions like Buddhism, meditation is envisaged as a means to develop

Antonio-José Silvestre-López, Universitat Jaume I, Avda Sos Baynat s/n, Castelló, Spain.

https://doi.org/10.1515/9783110629460-010

some of the qualities required for the individual to successfully walk the spiritual path and eventually reach enlightenment (e.g., a settled mind allowing for conscious awareness, wisdom and a clear understanding of reality to arise naturally). In the spheres of psychology and psychiatry, meditation is used as an effective technique to develop mindfulness abilities; and a range of meditative practices are used by western practitioners to promote mindful states of mind. The positive effects of this practice on mental health and general well-being have nowadays been attested over a wide range of scientific studies. Not only mindfulness-based but also loving kindness and compassion-based meditation protocols are nowadays part of fully acknowledged therapeutic programmes (cf. García-Campayo and Demarzo 2015). Although the spiritual origin of both mindfulness and compassion-based techniques is fully acknowledged (Gilbert and Choden 2013), meditation in this context is often addressed as a secular practice detached from religious connotations.

The bulk of research on meditation conducted to date has focused on the positive effects of the practice mainly in healthcare contexts or professional and educational settings, with cultural, communicative and linguistic aspects being generally overlooked. For example, the extent to which the range of social, cultural and linguistic models used to deal with the experience of meditation in eastern religious or spiritual traditions like Buddhism have been transferred to western contexts is an issue that still needs to be addressed by the scientific community. Due to the globalisation of meditation this seems no easy endeavour, but one possible initial step in this direction might involve identifying common topics raised to talk about the experience of meditation in a particular context or tradition, together with the linguistic resources used by speakers to model them.

Meditation involves becoming aware of both outer and inner phenomena, and meditators often take pains in putting subjective experiences related to feelings, emotions, and thoughts into words. In the process of linguistic encapsulation, meditators often use metaphors as a tool to help them shape their subjective experiences in more conventional ways that they can share with others (Silvestre-López 2016a, 2016b). While this holds true in most contexts, the use of metaphor becomes especially important in instructional settings, where the instructor or meditation master needs to explain the basic procedures of meditation in simple, clear and vivid ways. In this regard, studies like Silvestre-López (2016a, 2016b) have analysed the discourse of instructors and students in mindfulness courses in order to reveal conventional metaphors (at least in mindfulness instructional settings) used by speakers to communicate the experience and practice of mindfulness. Likewise, Silvestre-López and Navarro i Ferrando (2017) have also unravelled some of the metaphorical models used Buddhist meditation masters to explain the practice of meditation to the uninitiated audience. Since metaphor is used in this context as a pedagogical resource with specific communicative intentions (e.g., explaining a concept or practice), its deliberate use (Steen 2010, 2014) may well be a key parameter in the communication of the meditative experience. This paper analyses the use of deliberate metaphor in a selection of writings about mediation belonging to the Tibetan Buddhist tradition.

2 Theoretical considerations on conceptual metaphor

The notion of metaphor embraced here arises from Conceptual Metaphor Theory (Lakoff and Johnson 1980, 1999). One of its basic tenets holds that metaphor is not only a matter of *language* (e.g., a figure of speech or rhetorical device) but also – and primarily – a matter of *thought*. Metaphor is regarded as a cognitive mechanism that allows us to understand relatively complex, abstract or less familiar areas of experience in terms of other areas that are more concrete and/or experientially closer to us. This is achieved by projecting (or "mapping") a selection of the cognitive structure that captures one area of experience (the source domain) onto another (target) domain so that the latter is understood in terms of the highlighted structure of the former. For example, via conceptual metaphor, we are able to conceptualise time as a valuable resource, love as a journey or anger as a hot fluid (in a container). Such conceptual associations are assumed to motivate a variety of expressions: for example, we can use conventionalised terms like "save", "waste" or "spend" to talk about time as if it was money, we can suggest that our relationship "is taking us nowhere" or we can even "explode" with anger.

The way metaphors guide our understanding of such concepts is not random and the logic that allows particular linguistic manifestations of underlying conceptual associations has also been successfully parametrised by several scholars into a series of principles.[1] Although the cognitive and linguistic dimensions have been scrutinised in great depth since the early years of Conceptual

1 Metaphorical mappings are not random, but highly structured and principled cognitive operations that have been operationalised via principles like the Invariance Principle (Lakoff 1990; Turner 1990), the Extended Invariance Principle (Ruiz de Mendoza 1998) or the Correlation Principle (Ruiz de Mendoza and Santibáñez 2003) among others. See also Kövecses (2015b, 2017) and especially Ruiz de Mendoza and Galera (2014) for accounts on the hierarchical configuration of cognitive models in our conceptual system and how this affects the use of metaphor in language and culturally-situated communication.

Metaphor Theory, more recent developments (Cameron and Maslen 2010; Steen 2011) suggest that metaphor research must incorporate additional dimensions in order to allow for valid accounts of real metaphor use. Under this view, metaphor is still envisaged as a linguistic device and a cognitive mechanism, but it is also conceived of as a social and communicative tool used by speakers for explicit purposes in particular social domains. Steen (2011, 2014a), for example, proposed a three-dimensional model of metaphor (language, thought and communication) in which he has managed to systematise properties of metaphors like the linguistic *forms* in which they may appear in discourse, their degree of conventionality and novelty (as related to issues of processing by comparison or categorisation), consciousness in metaphor production and reception, and deliberate versus non-deliberate uses. This model has allowed him to establish clear limits across the set of disciplines, methodologies and theories by focusing on specific aspects of the properties mentioned above (cf. Steen 2011 for a review), ground his recently proposed Deliberate Metaphor Theory (Steen 2010, 2014b) in the communicative dimension, and draw (usually orthogonal) correspondences between the (non-) deliberate use of metaphor and other aspects of metaphor (especially linguistic manifestation, conventionality and consciousness) belonging to the dimensions of language or thought (Steen 2014b). As the study presented here focuses mainly on the linguistic and communicative dimensions, a series of theoretical considerations on discourse and communicative aspects of metaphors are addressed in the following sections.

2.1 Metaphor and discourse

In the analysis of metaphors in discourse, the metaphorical characterisation of discourse topics implies conceptually relating these topics (target domains) to other areas or domains of experience (source domains). These discourse topics can therefore be pictured or “framed” in different ways depending on the viewpoint, the communicative needs or the intentions of the speaker (Musolff 2016). Given that alternative source domains allow one or different sets of aspects of the target domain to be highlighted while downplaying others (Lakoff and Johnson 1980), an adequate selection of the source domain is of vital importance so as to emphasise the appropriate cognitive structure and pave the way for the desired interpretations and communicative effects. Source domain choice therefore has important implications at cognitive, discourse and applied practice levels (cf. Semino et al. 2016).

The notion of conceptual domain has traditionally been used in Conceptual Metaphor Theory to refer to broad areas of experience that are recruited as the cognitive structure to be projected in metaphorical mappings (Lakoff and Johnson 1980). Conceptual domains in the cognitive approach to metaphor analysis can be found to show different degrees of genericity, for they are used to embrace such diverse areas as MACHINES, WAR, THEORIES, LOVE, DIFFICULTIES, PURPOSES, etc. as the domains involved in different kinds of conceptually complex and primary (Grady 1997) metaphors. Identifying such general conceptual domains can not only help to account for a wide array of linguistic expressions, but is also especially useful in studies concerned with the analysis of cross-cultural and/or cross-linguistic patterns of metaphor use related to a particular area of experience, in general and specialised contexts (Kövecses 2005; Kövecses et al. 2015). However, in large-scale corpus studies, when dealing with the analysis of metaphorical examples related to a topic (target domain), one may find that the linguistic manifestations of the source domains with which it is metaphorically characterised do not reveal a single or homogeneous discourse pattern. That is to say, the variety of context-situated uses and communicative nuances of the linguistic expressions found to express a conceptual metaphor may not be coherently captured with the broad notion of domains at a conceptual level. Rather, they may be better described under the rationale provided by several complementary subdomains.

In connection with this, Musolff (2006, 2016) proposed the notion of *scenario* as a mediator between the generality of broad conceptual domains and the specificity of particular discursive realisations of conceptual metaphors (metaphorical expressions) in culturally and socially-situated discourse (cf. also Semino et al. 2016). Musolff (2016: 26–31) addresses the notion of scenario within the context of political and ideological discourse analysis. He illustrates, for example, how the two "father" models (STRICT FATHER VS. NURTURANT FATHER) of the famous NATION AS FAMILY metaphor proposed by Lakoff (1996) can be felicitously redescribed as two complementary scenarios exploited differently at discourse level.

Due to his analytical perspective, Musolff's conception of the construct incorporates notions like evaluative, social and emotional components. Scenarios capture relevant information about specific situations, the participants' properties and roles, as well as their immediate personal, social and communicative context. Thus, they help to organise the discourse manifestations of source concepts (and hence source domains) in terms of relevant discourse patterns that are sensitive to the nuances of language use in real communicative situations. Semino (2008: 10) uses the term metaphorical scenario "to refer to mental representations of particular situations, and the settings, entities, goals and actions that are associated with them (e.g., a BATTLE scenario as opposed to the broader conceptual domain of WAR)". The notion of scenario is conceived of here as the *discourse* equivalent of Ruiz de Mendoza and Galera's (2014) notions of low level and situational *cognitive* models.[2] These notions roughly correlate inasmuch as scenarios provide a rich situational structure that becomes readily available for the *inferential processes* needed to correctly apprehend any relevant aspect related to the participants involved, such as agency or power relationships (Semino et al. 2016: 13), mental or emotional state (Musolff 2006: 29) perceptions, as well as any potential evaluative aspects related to the situation in hand.

Kövecses's extensive work on metaphor and culture has allowed him to specify different levels of metaphor use across cultural-individual dimensions, namely, the supraindividual, individual, and subindividual levels (cf. Kövecses 2010). More recently he has also established a hierarchical distinction of the models involved in metaphor use which pivots on their degree of schematicity/specificity (Kövecses 2015b, 2017, 2019/this volume). These range from highly schematised and decontextualised (both culturally and linguistically) abstract structures to more contextually-bound, situational and usage-specific models, in this order: image schemas, domains, frames (Fillmore 1982; Sullivan 2013) and mental spaces (Fauconnier 1994). Kövecses (2017) places Musolff's scenarios, Fillmore's notion of conceptual scene (as a conceptual unit that can be associated with – and works below the level of – a conceptual frame) and Fauconnier's mental spaces at the lowest level of the hierarchy, thereby establishing a relative equivalence between them (all of them are proposed to work below the level of domains and frames while providing rich, contextualised information that can be used to handle particular communicative situations).

The notion of scenario, as employed in this study, refers to conceptually rich scenes or mental spaces which are used by speaker and hearer as a fully contextualised source of information allowing them to establish appropriate conceptual representations and to fulfil their communicative needs and/or intentions. Being fully-fledged informational structures, it is very likely that the use of scenarios in discourse metaphor – as opposed to the use of higher-level, more abstract or decontextualised domains – may also facilitate the realisation of particular discourse functions, such as explaining a concept, drawing the addressee's attention to a particular topic, or reframing (reconceptualising) it under a different perspective (among others). As such, they may well provide a more qualified breeding ground for the deliberate use of metaphor.

---

2 In general terms, these can be regarded as knowledge configurations that draw on our encyclopaedic knowledge and our understanding of conventionalised series of events to model relatively complex scenarios like "calling a taxi" or "going to a birthday party", while also including properties and relationships of the elements involved therein (cf. Ruiz de Mendoza and Galera 2014: 64–68, and the whole of Chapter 3 for a review).

2.2 Metaphor and communication: Deliberate metaphor

The standard view in Conceptual Metaphor Theory holds that metaphor works conventionally, automatically and unconsciously. However, despite its usage being largely unconscious in everyday language, speakers sometimes decide to use metaphor deliberately in communication. Moreover, whereas unconscious usage normally occurs as conventional forms and expressions, deliberate metaphor may manifest as novel language, as well as through conventional expressions (Steen 2011). It is with the purpose of characterising this variation in usage that Steen (2010, 2014a) proposed the three-dimensional model of metaphor mentioned earlier in this section. Steen (2014b: 180) defines deliberate metaphor as "an instruction for addressees to adopt an 'alien' perspective on a target referent so as to formulate specific thoughts about that target from the standpoint of the alien perspective. Typically this is achieved by some form of explicit, direct metaphor, such as a simile".

While the notion of "deliberate metaphor" works in the communicative dimension, in the linguistic dimension we call "direct metaphors" those that show deliberateness by means of certain linguistic form. In direct metaphors "there is some conceptual domain that functions as a source in a metaphorical mapping, and it is expressed directly as such by the language" (Steen 2010: 53–54). Thus, the "instruction for addressees" mentioned in Steen's definition often comes in the shape of a direct metaphor. Direct metaphors are "deliberate by definition" (Steen, 2014b: 185), and can be conceived of as reliable deliberate metaphor markers (Steen 2010: 56). An outstanding characteristic of deliberate metaphors is that they can be extended across clauses or sentences. When this happens, extendedness can also be interpreted as a signal of deliberateness (Steen 2016). Finally, deliberate metaphor may also be manifested in other less explicit – and much less frequent – elaborations, including indirect and implicit metaphor (cf. Steen 2014b: 185–187 and Steen et al. 2010: 39–40, 120–123 for a discussion on these features).

Ineluctably associated with deliberate usage and its different manifestations in discourse is the issue of discursive functions as fulfilled by means of metaphorical language. Landmark studies like Charteris-Black (2004), Semino (2008) or Goatly (2011) have surveyed some of the most outstanding functions of metaphor across different kinds of genres and discourse. These and other studies following their discourse-analytical perspective have shown that metaphors do fulfil cognitive (conceptual) functions but also others of a more interpersonal, emotional, and communicative kind. Goatly (2011: 155–177) provided a particularly complete account of major metaphor functions. Some of them have been used in the analysis of metaphors presented here and will be addressed in more detail in sections

4 to 6. Likewise, in its chapter 6, Goatly (2011) describes a wide range of textual markers that act as co-textual signals for potential metaphor use. Under the perspective of deliberate metaphor, such markers have been taken as signals of direct metaphor (Steen et al. 2010), hence working as discourse signals of potential deliberate metaphor use. Some of these signals have been used to trace deliberate metaphors in this study, and will also be discussed in the following sections.

3 Aims

The main aim of this chapter is to analyse the use of deliberate metaphor in the discourse of meditation within the Tibetan Buddhist tradition. With that purpose in mind, it draws on a corpus comprising a selection of texts by two well-known Tibetan Buddhist masters in which they talk about the meditation experience and explain some of its most basic procedures to the uninitiated audience (cf. section 4). The corpus was used as a source of data in a previous study (Silvestre-López and Navarro 2017) in order to uncover representative metaphors used by these masters when dealing with meditation verbally. Their analysis, however, illustrates general uses of metaphor without distinguishing between deliberate and non-deliberate uses or considering their particular forms and functions.

More specifically, this chapter addresses both linguistic and communicative aspects of these metaphors by analysing the use of deliberate metaphor in the corpus. This involves the identification of common formal realisations of deliberate metaphors as well as the main functions with which they are used in discourse. Finally, this analysis also seeks to detect possible convergence or divergence patterns in terms of deliberate and non-deliberate metaphor use in the corpus.

4 Method

The texts about meditation practice selected for analysis are Chapter 5 in the *Tibetan book of living and dying* (Sogyal Rinpoche 1993: 56–81) and Chapter 6 in *Cultivating a daily meditation* (Tenzin Gyatso 1996: 101–136), including its appendix on meditation for beginners. The corpus is deliberately small (22,928 words) in order to follow an inductive approach allowing the researcher to discover the range of categories involved in metaphorisation without prior preconceptions, while also providing for a wide spectrum of genericity-specificity of metaphorical targets and sources. This facilitates the inclusion of relatively generic domains as well as more fine-grained models represented in terms of scenarios, scenes, or particular entities involved in them (e.g., MEDITATION, MASS OF WATER, LANDSCAPE, OCEAN, SKY, WAVE, CLOUD, MEDITATOR, etc.). Encompassing this variety enables the possibility of unveiling potential patterns of genericity-specificity associated with the source domains involved in deliberate and non-deliberate metaphors.

The texts were coded and analysed with the qualitative analysis software ATLAS.ti following the methodological considerations proposed by Kimmel (2012). ATLAS.ti allows text fragments to be marked as *quotations* and one or various *codes* to be assigned to each quotation. The codes used in this study refer to particular kinds of target and source domains, but also to deliberate usage and formal traits and functions of metaphor in discourse. Coding target and source domains separately is a procedure known as "compositional coding" (Kimmel 2012: 13) which allows the researcher to cross-check any code at a later stage for qualitative analysis. The process often involves different steps which can be divided into two main stages: coding and data retrieval.

The coding stage was carried out collaboratively by two researchers and began with their reading the whole texts in order to get a global understanding of their contents (Kimmel 2012: 13–15). The identification of metaphorical expressions and the generation of quotations for them were carried out in subsequent readings. The Metaphor Identification Procedure Vrije Universiteit (MIPVU) (Steen et al. 2010) was applied for the identification of metaphorical expressions. Context was taken into account when coding text fragments to include metaphorical expressions. Thus, the quotation size for coded units ranges from word to various sentences (in the case of extended metaphors). This quotation size range was set to include the necessary linguistic structure to allow for the metaphorical expression to be processed in relation to the surrounding concepts without overlapping with other co-textual metaphors (each quotation was set to encompass only one target-source domain pairing).

The code list used to code all metaphoric phenomena was developed both inductively and deductively. The list of target and source domain codes was open and grew fully inductively as the coding process developed. Metaphorical signals were taken as indicators of potential deliberate metaphors. A "deliberate metaphor code list" was created by assigning one "deliberate metaphor code" to each metaphor signal (for example: *DELIBMET: B of A formula*). Likewise, a list of functions was created by assigning a "function code" per function (e.g., *FUNCTION: Explanatory*). The code list for deliberate metaphor signals is based on Goatly's metaphor signals (2011). The list of codes for metaphor functions draws on those identified in Semino (2008), Goatly (2011: 154–177) and Kimmel (2012: 8) and was devised to cover cognitive and interpersonal as well as textual functions. Both code lists were loaded into ATLAS.ti before the coding stage started.

However, during the coding process they were adapted to better reflect the nature of forms and functions of the metaphors found in the corpus. The final list of codes is provided in Appendix 1.

The data retrieval stage involved the reconstruction of conceptual metaphors out of the text fragments coded in the previous stage. Silvestre-López and Navarro (2017) identified five target domains as hot spots for metaphorisation in the corpus (MIND, THOUGHT, MEDITATION, EMOTION and MEDITATOR) and a range of source domains used to characterise them metaphorically. In this study, after the coding process, this was done by firstly running the ATLAS.ti code manager to gather the total number of quotations associated with each target domain. Once the main target domains had been identified, the Code Co-occurrence Table Tool was used to learn which source domains were more frequently associated (co-occur) with each target domain. Target-source domain co-occurrences were then used as a guide to run specific queries in the Query Tool (e.g., *TD_Mind & SD_Personification*) and retrieve the quotations underlying each co-occurrence. All quotations were manually reviewed to ascertain whether they contained genuine expressions fitting the conceptual metaphors in hand (e.g., real discourse realisations of the MIND IS A PERSON metaphor). Table 10.1 in section 5 provides an overview of major target and source domain pairings. The first column displays each target domain. The second column shows the range of source domains (the label corresponds to the code assigned in ATLAS.ti) as arranged in terms of the frequency with which they were found to correlate with the target domain to yield metaphorical expressions. The total number of expressions is expressed in square brackets and includes deliberate and non-deliberate realisations.

In order to retrieve the deliberate realisations of each metaphor, the target and source domain codes belonging to each metaphor formula were fused into ATLAS.ti higher-order code units called *supercodes*. For example, individual codes like "TD_Mind" and "SD_Personification" standing for the metaphor MIND IS A PERSON were joined into the unit "SUPERCODE: Mind is person". A supercode was created as well to gather all deliberate metaphor codes into a single code unit. Each "target & source" supercode was then run in the Query Tool in combination with the "deliberate metaphor" supercode so as to retrieve all deliberate metaphor realisations (in the form of quotations) of each target-source domain pairing The output of this process was extracted in the form of Query Reports (see below). Table 10.1 (section 5) displays the numbers of deliberate metaphor realisations related to each target-source domain pairing in the fourth column. Non-deliberate metaphor realisations are reflected in the third column.

In order to survey the global use of discourse functions and deliberate metaphor signals, the information retrieved in the above-mentioned Query Reports was used. A Query Report provides information concerning the whole set of codes associated with each quotation, hence providing a full picture of the targets and sources involved in each expression, as well as discourse functions and metaphor signal codes associated with each use. Each function and metaphor signal code was thus manually reviewed taking into account the surrounding contextual information of the metaphorical expression. The total number of "function" and "signal" codes was taken into account to calculate the percentages of use of each function/signal category. Figures 10.1 and 10.2 in section 5.6 show the result of this process.

5 Results and discussion

The results of this process are presented and discussed in this section as follows. Drawing on the information shown in Table 10.1, the main deliberate metaphors related to each target domain (first column in Table 10.1) are discussed and illustrated with examples from the corpus in sections 5.1 to 5.5. These sections also provide information on particular functions as linked to formal realisations of the examples commented therein. The global use of metaphor signals and discourse functions in the corpus is addressed in section 5.6.

Table 10.1: Main target and source domain pairings and their deliberate and non-deliberate realisations.

Target domain	Source domains			
	Source domain codes and total counts (all metaphors in the corpus)		Non-deliberate metaphors	Deliberate metaphors
Mind is...	SD_Personification	[20]	[19]	[1]
	SD_Space	[17]	[16]	[1]
	SD_Objectification (reification)	[16]	[15]	[1]
	SD_Animal	[12]	[11]	[1]
	SD_Landscape	[7]	[3]	[4]
	SD_Mass of water	[8]	[4]	[4]
A thought is...	SD_Objectification (reification)	[33]	[33]	[0]
	SD_Mass of water element	[6]	[0]	[6]
	SD_Landscape element	[4]	[1]	[3]
	SD_Personification	[3]	[3]	[0]

Table 10.1 (continued)

Target domain	Source domains			
	Source domain codes and total counts (all metaphors in the corpus)		**Non-deliberate metaphors**	**Deliberate metaphors**
Meditation is...	SD_Journey	[14]	[11]	[3]
	SD_ Place or Space	[11]	[11]	[0]
	SD_State: Mental States (General)	[9]	[9]	[0]
	SD_Heat	[2]	[2]	[0]
	SD_Light	[2]	[2]	[0]
Emotion is...	SD_Objectification (reification)	[9]	[9]	[0]
	SD_Journey: Obstacle	[4]	[2]	[2]
	SD_Prison: Prison cell	[3]	[1]	[2]
	SD_Live beings: Animal_Wild	[3]	[2]	[1]
	SD_Antidote	[2]	[2]	[0]
	SD_Mass of water element	[2]	[0]	[2]
	SD_Landscape element	[1]	[0]	[1]
Meditator is...	SD_Observer	[16]	[12]	[4]
	SD_Fragmented entity	[11]	[11]	[0]
	SD_R Landscape element	[4]	[0]	[4]
	SD_Ocean	[3]	[0]	[3]

5.1 Deliberate metaphors about mind

All metaphors found in the corpus model the target MIND as an entity or as a space. When MIND is reified as an entity, it is usually pictured as a person – for example someone we can "train" or "brainwash", as in example (1), as an animal (2) or an object; in this case it is worth noting that all non-deliberate instances of objectification of the mind (15 in total) simply refer to it as an object on which the meditator can focus their attention, but do not define its concrete properties. The only instance in which the object is defined (3) is used deliberately.

(1) ***"Training"*** *the mind does not in any way mean forcibly subjugating or brainwashing the mind* (Sogyal Rinpoche 1993: 58).

(2) *The eighth-century Buddhist master Shantideva said:*
If this ***elephant of mind*** *is bound on all sides by the cord of mindfulness,*
All fear disappears and complete happiness comes.
All enemies: all the tigers, lions, elephants, bears, serpents [of our emotions][2]
And all the keepers of hell, the demons and the horrors,
All of these are bound by the mastery of your mind,
And by ***the taming of that one mind****, all are subdued,*
Because from the mind are derived all fears and immeasurable sorrows.
[FOOTNOTE: 2.The ferocious wild animals that were a threat in ancient times have today been replaced by other dangers: our wild and uncontrolled emotions] (Sogyal Rinpoche 1993: 59).

(3) *At the moment,* ***mind is like a candle flame****: unstable, flickering, constantly changing, fanned by the violent winds of our thoughts and emotions. The flame will only burn steadily when we can calm the air around it; so we can only begin to glimpse and rest in the nature of mind when we have stilled the turbulence of our thoughts and emotions* (Sogyal Rinpoche 1993: 65).

Different metaphor signals render these examples as cases of direct metaphor.[3] The scare quotes in (1) indicate the author is somewhat conscious of the loose use of "training" to metaphorically refer to mind. In (2), "B of A metaphor formula" and extendedness hint as well at the deliberate use of MIND IS AN ANIMAL. In the case of (3), besides "like", deliberateness is marked in terms of extendedness in the paragraph narrative, with a scenario creating clear correspondences between the wind fanning the flame and the thoughts and emotions agitating the mind.

As far as functions are concerned, the three examples are clearly explanatory. Both (2) and (3) are also used to evoke vivid imagery, which helps to bring more perceptual-like properties to the abstract nature of the mind. In the case of (2), reframing the mind as a bounded elephant that needs taming recalls some sort of ancient cultural symbolism (set in eighth century Asia), which enhances the vivid imagery of the example. (2) and particularly (3) explicitly draw the reader's attention to the source domains of the metaphor (ANIMAL, FLAME) and invite them to consider the target domain from the perspective of the source domain, hence paving the way for the reconceptualization of mind in the terms set in each example.

Among the range of metaphorical expressions in the corpus that characterise the mind as some sort of space, most non-deliberate uses of MIND IS SPACE outline

3 Global details on deliberate metaphor marks and functions are provided in section 5.6. Due to space restrictions, only some of the main signals and functions will be commented on in sections 5.1 to 5.5 for illustrative purposes. Signals are marked in bold in the examples.

the notion of "spaciousness" of mind so that it is characterised as an undefined space where phenomena of mental perception (e.g., thoughts) arise. To highlight this, the generic domain of space (the second source domain related to mind in Table 10.1, with 16 non-deliberate occurrences) works as the source of the MIND IS SPACE metaphor. Less frequently, when this space is deployed in more detail, it is characterised either as a landscape or as a mass of water (cf. the last two domains related to mind in Table 10.1). In contrast, when the metaphorical characterisation of mind as space is deliberate, the source domain is *never* presented as a generic space but exclusively as finer-grained elaborations like a room (4) as well as in the form of a landscape (5) or some sort of mass of water (5).

(4) **Just as** *a room with many doors and windows allows the air to enter from many directions,* **in the same way,** *when your mind becomes open, it is natural that all kinds of experiences can come into it* (Sogyal Rinpoche 1993: 79).

(5) *The Buddha sat in serene and humble dignity on the ground, with the sky above him and around him, as if to show us that in meditation you sit with an open,* **sky-like** *attitude of mind, yet remain present, earthed, and grounded. The sky is our absolute nature, which has no barriers and is boundless, and the ground is our reality, our relative, ordinary condition. The posture we take when we meditate signifies that we are linking absolute and relative, sky and ground, heaven and earth, like two wings of a bird, integrating the sky-like, deathless nature of mind and the ground of our transient, mortal nature* (Sogyal Rinpoche 1993: 58).

(6) ***Just as*** *the ocean has waves or the sun has rays,* **so** *the mind's own radiance is its thoughts and emotions. The ocean has waves, yet the ocean is not particularly disturbed by them. The waves are the very nature of the ocean. Waves will rise, but where do they go? Back into the ocean. And where do the waves come from? The ocean.* ***In the same manner****, thoughts and emotions are the radiance and expression of the very nature of the mind. They rise from the mind, but where do they dissolve? Back into the mind* (Sogyal Rinpoche 1993: 77).

In examples like (4), the vague or undefined space highlighted in most non-deliberate metaphors turns into a more detailed representation of the mind as a room with several doors and windows through which air may come in and out or, following the analogy, as a space where all perceptual or experiential phenomena are "allowed" to go in and out. The analogy is especially appropriate in terms of explanatory purposes because it also brings to the fore desirable qualities of the meditator in the shape of entailments like non-reactivity and acceptance of "what is" (i.e. the experiences that come in and out). In example (5), the first sentence highlights the notion of spaciousness of mind (as in the generic space models), but the landscape imagery and symbolism makes it possible to set up a few more entailments related to the spiritual importance of meditation as a mediator between mind (the ethereal) and matter (the material). The grounds (Goatly 2011) of the metaphor are in fact made explicit in the remaining lines of the example. In (6), the mind is characterised as an ocean and thoughts and emotions as ocean waves. While deliberateness is signalled via analogies (e.g., *just as the ocean [...] so the mind*) and extendedness, the association between mind and ocean is afforded mainly by the syntactic parallelisms starting from the third sentence.

It is worth adding a final note here concerning the contrasts of source domain genericity found in the space-related metaphors of mind. One possible interpretation of this difference may point at deliberateness (this encompassing the producer's communicative purposes) as a factor influencing the degree of elaboration of the source domain SPACE when the metaphor is devised by the writer to fulfil particular discourse functions. For example, as the metaphors in examples (4), (5) and (6) have a clear explanatory function, the writer has more chances of being successful by explicitly using a metaphor that evokes familiar, well-defined areas of experience (as opposed to generic or abstract schematisations). Moreover, shifting the attention to a different topic seems more feasible (or at least easier) when the "alien" topic-domain is more down-to-earth (e.g., a room is more informative than undefined space).

5.2 Deliberate metaphors about thought

This interpretation is also consistent with the figures concerning deliberate and non-deliberate metaphors for the target domain THOUGHT. In this case, reifications are rendered exclusively through ontological non-deliberate metaphors. This is especially apparent in the case of THOUGHT IS AN OBJECT, with 33 instances of non-deliberate metaphors used to help characterise thought as a finite entity which the meditator can perceive, concentrate upon or simply place their attention on. In the case of the ontological characterisation of thought as an animated entity (personification), the only instances in the corpus (a total of 3) are also used non-deliberately.

In contrast to non-deliberate uses, deliberate metaphorical characterisations of thought seem to have a preference for more elaborated sources. This is so inasmuch as all metaphors referring to the mass of water source domain are deliberate, and characterise thought as agitated water in the form of waves (when the scenario for mind is the ocean, as in examples (6) above and the last sentence in (7)), waterfalls, rivers, etc. (see (7) below). Likewise, when thought is portrayed as a landscape element (4 instances in the corpus, 3 of them used deliberately), it takes the form of a cloud or wind itself, as in (8) and (9) below.

(7) *In the ancient meditation instructions, at the beginning thoughts will arrive one on top of another, uninterrupted,* ***like*** *a steep mountain waterfall. Gradually, as you perfect meditation, thoughts become* ***like*** *the water in a deep, narrow gorge, then a great river slowly winding its way down to the sea; finally the mind becomes like a still and placid ocean, ruffled by only the occasional ripple or wave* (Sogyal Rinpoche 1993: 77).

(8) *You will soon find that* ***thoughts are like the wind****; they come and go* (Sogyal Rinpoche 1993: 78).

(9) *When the* ***cloud-like*** *thoughts and emotions fade away, the* ***sky-like*** *nature of our true being is revealed, and, shining from it, our Buddha nature, like the sun* (Sogyal Rinpoche 1993: 76).

All these examples make use of explicit comparison devices to create vivid, quasi-perceptual representations of thought in order to foster comprehension of the basic message: as part of the mind, thoughts will always be present and also reflect its state (when the mind is agitated, thoughts will also work as perturbations of stillness). With meditation one may learn about the nature of thoughts while also calming the mind, hence contributing to a clearer view of reality. Deliberateness is marked with direct metaphor signals in all the examples, and with extendedness in narratives like (7).

5.3 Deliberate metaphors about meditation

The metaphorical characterisation of MEDITATION in the corpus is realised mostly in terms of non-deliberate metaphors configured around the PATH image schema so that meditation is seen mainly as a process (framed as a journey), as a place or as a space redescribed as a state (Silvestre-López and Navarro 2017). The only instances of deliberate metaphor found in the corpus follow the same logic, and develop the JOURNEY source domain in terms of a path (a road) leading to a destination (enlightenment) as in (10), or else as the metaphorical scenario "bringing the mind home" in (11).

(10) *The gift of learning to meditate is the greatest gift you can give yourself in this life. For it is only through meditation that you can undertake the journey to discover your true nature, and so find the stability and confidence you will need to live, and die, well.* ***Meditation is the road to enlightenment*** (Sogyal Rinpoche 1993: 58).

(11) *We are fragmented into so many different aspects. We don't know who we really are, or what aspects of ourselves we should identify with or believe in. So many contradictory voices, dictates, and feelings fight for control over our inner lives that we find ourselves scattered everywhere, in all directions, leaving nobody at home.* **Meditation, then, is bringing the mind home** (Sogyal Rinpoche 1993: 60).

In both examples, a short argumentation sets the ground before the metaphorical source (*a road to enlightenment* in (10) and *bringing the mind home* in (11)) is made explicit in the final sentence. This "A is B" metaphorical culmination becomes a powerful textual structuring device to compress information (including the set of inferences needed for the reconceptualisation of the target domain as the source) while also boosting the metaphor's explanatory potential. These functional effects are even more apparent in the case of (11), as "bringing the mind home" is the title of the chapter in which the example is found. "Bringing the mind home" activates a very familiar situational model grounded in our knowledge about home and family.[4] By reading the title, the scenario becomes available as a cognitive structure that may help to understand some parts of the chapter. Thanks to background knowledge on textual structure, the reader may have certain expectations about the usefulness of the title, but at that point it just works as a trigger for potentially useful cognitive content. It is only by reading the text fragment covered in (11) that previous expectations are sorted out and the title starts to make sense (due to its inclusion as the source domain of a metaphor about meditation).

5.4 Deliberate metaphors about emotion

The target EMOTION does not show high figures in terms of metaphorisation, but it does show similar patterns. For example, just like in MIND and THOUGHT, bare objectification metaphors of emotions (as undefined objects) are only realised

4 The syntactic formulation of "bringing the mind home" and our knowledge about the scenario allows the mind to be conceptualised as some kind of live entity (perhaps a child or an animal), but at this stage the scenario itself is not part of any other metaphorical projection.

through non-deliberate metaphors, while more well-defined scenarios seem better candidates for deliberate metaphor elaborations.

Just like thoughts, for example, emotions are pictured as waves and as elements of the sky like clouds. Examples (6) and (9) above instantiate these metaphors (i.e. EMOTIONS ARE WAVES and EMOTIONS ARE CLOUDS). In them, emotions are seen as part of the mind in accordance with its Buddhist conception; that is to say, the mind is understood as a combination of consciousness (*Citta* in Pali) and mental factors (*Cetasika*). Overall, mental factors include thought and our (western) conception of emotions. Examples (6) and (9) are used as an attempt to explain the relationship between mind, thoughts and emotions in a neutral way. Nevertheless, most metaphorical examples of emotions picture them as elements that disturb the mind (i.e. negative mental factors) or have a negative influence on the meditative practice.

Following this logic, in the path of meditation, emotions may be portrayed as obstacles in the way, that is, impediments to motion that prevent the meditator from making progress. Some of them are overtly labelled "obstacles", as in example (12). The five obstacles mentioned in it are addressed in the same way throughout the text and in all of them the reader is warned about them and advised on how to overcome them. Thus, besides helping the author in his explanation, the metaphor clearly functions as a cohesive device to structure the text. Some other times the impediment to motion is subtly portrayed as a prison, as in (13).

(12) *In the writings of Maitreya and Asanga, five main obstacles to the achievement of single-pointed concentration and eight opponent forces are mentioned.* ***The first of the five obstacles is laziness*** (Tenzin Gyatso 1996: 105).

(13) *To release means to release mind from its* ***prison of grasping****, since you recognize that all pain and fear and distress arise from the craving of the grasping mind* (Sogyal Rinpoche 1993: 63)

Finally, only one deliberate use of EMOTIONS ARE ANIMALS was found in the corpus, but the example is worth considering here because of its particular signals. It is in fact embedded in example (2) above. The text is reproduced again for the reader's convenience.

(14) *The eighth-century Buddhist master Shantideva said:*
If this elephant of mind is bound on all sides by the cord of mindfulness,
All fear disappears and complete happiness comes.
All enemies: all the tigers, lions, elephants, bears, serpents [of our emotions][2]
And all the keepers of hell, the demons and the horrors,
All of these are bound by the mastery of your mind,

And by the taming of that one mind, ***all are subdued,***
Because from the mind are derived all fears and immeasurable sorrows.

[FOOTNOTE: 2. *The ferocious wild animals that were a threat in ancient times have today been replaced by other dangers: our wild and uncontrolled emotions]* (Sogyal Rinpoche 1993: 59)

Deliberateness in EMOTIONS ARE ANIMALS is signalled here with the "B of A" formula (*serpents of our emotions*), its extendedness throughout the fragment, the square brackets and the footnote. Two different layers can be distinguished here. The first one refers to the original writing by Shantideva. The fact that *elephant* is connected with *mind* and *enemy* in the example may seem somewhat puzzling. While the "B of A" formula (*elephant of mind*) points at a deliberate use of MIND IS AN ANIMAL (ELEPHANT) in line two, it is questionable whether this metaphor (i.e. the connection between mind and elephant) remains active – at least in Shantideva's mind – in the next appearance of *elephant* (line four: *all enemies: all the tigers, lions, elephants* [...] *horrors*). Rather, in that line Shantideva seems to develop a different mapping to characterise wild animals – together with other creatures dwelling in hell – as enemies. The formal realisation of the metaphor (colon after *enemies*) suggests that it is more likely to work as a categorisation device than as a cross-domain comparison, in which case this is a clue to its non-deliberate use (Steen 2011: 38). Accordingly, this might be considered a case of mixed metaphor (in different sentences of the same narration) involving one deliberate and one non-deliberate metaphor (cf. Steen 2016). Had Shantideva used (or had he been consciously willing to use) both metaphors deliberately, he would have been more likely to exclude "elephant" in the enumeration of line four, hence avoiding possible misunderstandings. This connects us with the second of the layers mentioned above, which is related to the author of the chapter in which the example is found (Sogyal Rinpoche). This author explicitly connects emotions and dangerous animals by adding the footnote to the bracketed text "*[of our emotions]*", most probably in order to clarify potential misunderstandings derived from Shantideva's mixed metaphor. In terms of functions, this is one of the clearest cases of explanatory metaphor that can be found in the corpus.

5.5 Deliberate metaphors about the meditator

In general terms, the metaphors found in the corpus combine to portray the meditator as the consciousness that becomes aware of inner and outer phenomena without reacting. While this explanatory purpose pervades all deliberate metaphors, two main sets of metaphors can be distinguished according to the aspects that they are devised to highlight. The first set of metaphors characterise the MEDITATOR AS AN OBSERVER in order to emphasise the basic procedure of mindful contemplation. This is instantiated through the use of "watching" in examples like (15), which becomes a useful resource to compress a handy set of inferences to understand the practice. On the one hand, this metaphor creates a separation between the observer and the observed, which fosters the disidentification of the individual with thought (cf. Silvestre-López 2016b); on the other hand, it also brings up cultural models on general perception and cognition (including the metaphor KNOWING IS SEEING) through which inner mental phenomena like concepts or ideas are conventionally handled as if they were physical objects. In this way it is easy to understand how the meditator can "watch" their breath, but also how they can observe their thoughts without becoming involved. This is in fact the underlying message conveyed in (16), which combines OBSERVER, OCEAN and SKY as sources to model the experience.

(15) *I have found three meditation techniques that are particularly effective in the modem world and that anyone can practice and benefit from. They are using an object, reciting a mantra, and **"watching"** the breath* (Sogyal Rinpoche 1993: 69)

(16) *Neither follow thoughts nor invite them; **be like** the **ocean looking** at its own waves, or **the sky gazing down** on the clouds that pass through it* (Sogyal Rinpoche 1993: 78)

The second set of metaphors is devised to highlight the notions of acceptance and non-reactivity (allowing for all phenomena to arise and vanish without clinging on to them). Apart from (16), these notions are emphasised in metaphors picturing the meditator as some of the elements that compose a landscape, for example as the vastness of the sky in (17) or the stability of a mountain in (18).

(17) *When you meditate there should be no effort to control and no attempt to be peaceful. Don't be overly solemn or feel that you are taking part in some special ritual; let go even of the idea that you are meditating. Let your body remain as it is, and your breath as you find it. **Think of yourself as the sky,** holding the whole universe* (Sogyal Rinpoche 1993: 75)

(18) *In the Dzogchen teachings it is said that your View and your posture should be **like a mountain**. Your View is the summation of your whole understanding and insight into the nature of mind, which you bring to your meditation. So your View translates into and inspires your posture, expressing the core*

> *of your being in the way you sit. [...] Sit, then,* ***as if you were a mountain,*** *with all the unshakable, steadfast majesty of a mountain* (Sogyal Rinpoche 1993: 66)

In this study, the category "Deliberate perspective changer in the view of an author or school of thought" was adopted to mark mental space builders introducing a different perspective from that of the author, as in "*In the Dzogchen teachings it is said that...*" (18). These can be regarded as support signals for potential deliberate metaphor use, provided that the mental space builder is obviously followed by at least a metaphorical expression. This formal category is often associated with the expression of cultural/traditional symbolism and is hence useful in marking otherwise unlikely comparisons in general discourse. (18) exemplifies this use inasmuch as the association between meditator and mountain may be perceived as rather creative (novel) in contexts or traditions that are different from the one marked in the example (i.e. the teachings of Dzogchen).

5.6 Metaphor functions and formal characteristics

Among all metaphor instances found in the corpus, deliberate metaphor use accounts for 19.4% of the cases, covering the same target domains and nearly the same target-source domain pairings as non-deliberate uses. As mentioned earlier in this chapter, the main purpose of the texts analysed here is to explain basic notions of meditation mainly to the uninitiated or to meditators with scarce experience. The results concerning the functions of deliberate metaphor (Figure 10.1) seem to fit the pattern of this kind of pedagogical texts, with 33% of all deliberate metaphors used with explanatory intentions.

Moreover, four out of the five topics characterised metaphorically are not "material" (MIND, THOUGHT, MEDITATION, EMOTION). The fact that meditation is an utterly subjective experience might further explain why 28% of deliberate metaphors are also used to capture vivid perceptual imagery (as thoughts envisaged as clouds or waves or the mind as a wild animal that needs to be tamed by the meditator). In other words, using a metaphor that evokes basic outer-world imagery and hence dwells on more familiar areas of external experience (at least perceptually speaking) may facilitate "viewing" inner phenomena from alternative perspectives. This might in turn foster their reconceptualisation (a function that is present in 16% of deliberate metaphor instances) and potentially provide for better understanding. The rest of the functions that deliberate metaphors were found to fulfil in the corpus (those showing a percentage below 10%) are listed

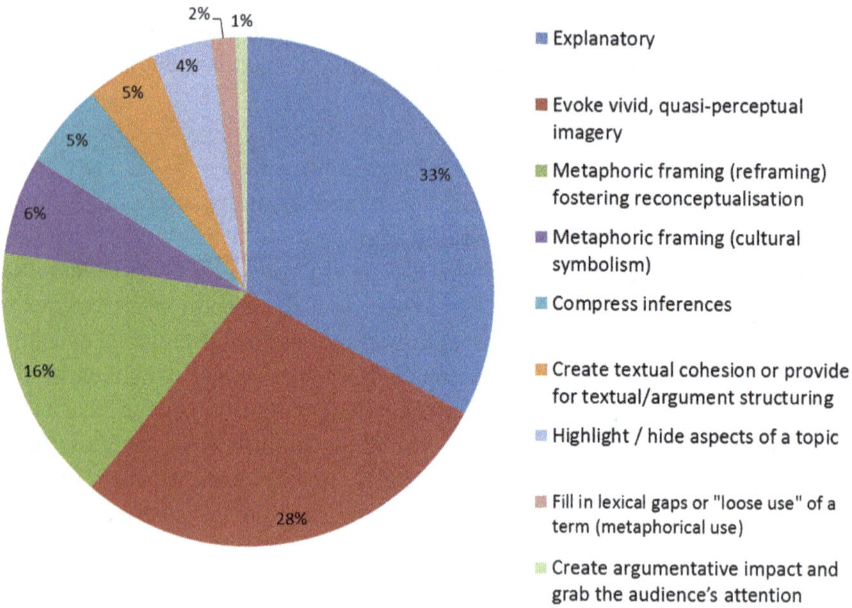

Figure 10.1: Deliberate metaphor functions in the corpus.

in Figure 10.1.[5] Just like the three most frequent functions, these also belong to the ideational or cognitive dimension (e.g., metaphorically framing a topic using cultural symbolism or compressing inferences to potentiate understanding), but to some extent they also permeate textual ones (apart from the explicit textual structuring function, for example, compressing inferences may also provide for textual coherence in some cases).

Figure 10.2 displays the list of major formal realisations of deliberate metaphors in terms of metaphor signals. While one metaphorical expression may fulfil various functions simultaneously, each expression is normally realised through one of the formal categories listed in Figure 10.2. The categories "metaphoric narrative" and "activated previously in discourse" are two exceptions, as they must necessarily appear[6] with one of the other formal categories (e.g., together with "B of A" metaphors). This is so because both categories are taken in this study as marks of metaphorical extendedness – the former dealing with metaphors

5 Those reflected in Appendix 1 but excluded from the list in Figure 1 were not found in the corpus. This also applies for metaphor signals in Figure 10.2 (see below).
6 Each category in Figure 10.2 is in fact an ATLAS.ti code, so that in this case two "metaphor signal codes" might be assigned to the same expression.

usually developed throughout uninterrupted fragments (paragraphs) and the latter with metaphors reappearing after an interruption.

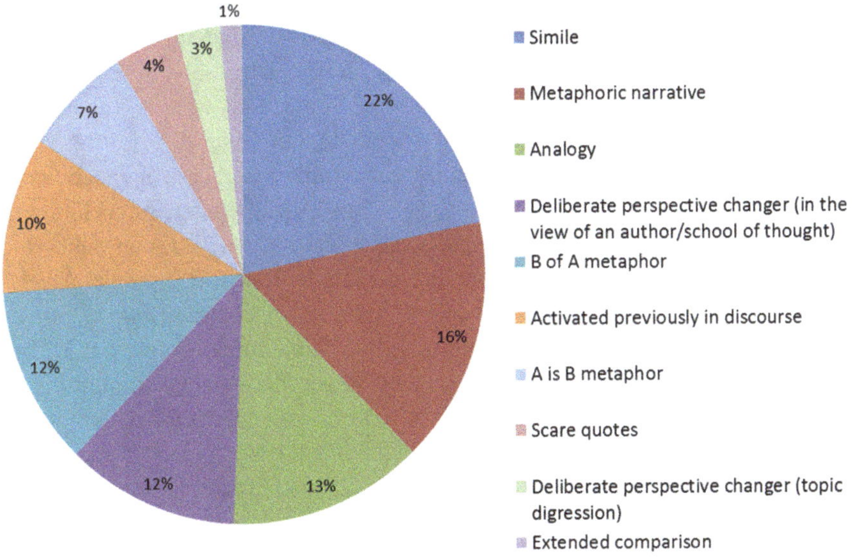

Figure 10.2: Deliberate metaphor signals in the corpus.

In connection with major discourse functions, the authors of the texts seem to have a preference for direct metaphor realised in terms of signals like simile (22%) or analogy (13%),[7] followed by "B of A" (12%) and "A is B" (7%) explicit metaphor formulae. This suggests that the authors regularly try to establish explicit cross-domain correspondences (a basic feature of deliberate metaphor) between different entities or areas of experience, which helps them to provide clearer explanations of the experience. Moreover, these formal marks co-occur with the deliberate metaphor signals "metaphoric narrative" (16%) and "activated previously in discourse" (10%), which in turn suggests that in at least 26% of the cases deliberate metaphor is developed at suprasentential levels (a sign of extendedness).

7 These percentages reflect similes or analogies in which the elements compared belong to different domains of experience (and hence instantiate proper metaphorical realisations).

6 Conclusions

The analysis of metaphors carried out by Silvestre-López and Navarro (2017) focused on a general (discursive) approach to metaphor use without a special focus on the communicative dimension of metaphor (that is, the distinction between non-deliberate and deliberate uses). The five target domains analysed in their study yield similar metaphorical projections (that is, the general target-source domain correspondences are similar, cf. Table 10.1). However, an important difference must be highlighted concerning the degree of genericity of the source domains triggered in non-deliberate and deliberate uses, as found in the study presented here. As far as can be gleaned from the data, non-deliberate uses of metaphor usually embrace more generic and abstract models. A clear example is the reification of the target domain as an object so that it can be addressed discursively as a finite entity. In the three domains where this kind or reification happens (MIND, THOUGHT, OBJECT) non-deliberate metaphors show some of the highest figures in the corpus. Additional support for the argument that deliberate metaphor could have a preference for more specific and elaborated models may be found in the kind of elaborations found in non-deliberate and deliberate realisations of the MASS OF WATER and LANDSCAPE source domains across the MIND, THOUGHT and MEDITATOR targets (the remaining target domains analysed failed to correlate with such source domains). In Silvestre-López and Navarro (2017), the terms "mass of water" and "landscape" were adopted, due to a methodological decision, as umbrella terms so as to allow researchers to cover a similar set of elements belonging to the same scenario under the same analytical category (e.g., piece of land, sky, agitated as opposed to calm water, etc.). When dealing with deliberate metaphors, the realisations of these models boil down to only three specific elaborations: SKY as a more specific development of the LANDSCAPE model, plus OCEAN and JAR (only one instance of the latter) as particular elaborations of the MASS OF WATER models.

All these considerations are consistent with the line of reasoning proposed above, that is, deliberate metaphor use requires a more detailed and contextualised elaboration of the source domains so as to better characterise the target domain and guide the addressee's interpretation in accordance with the addresser's communicative intentions and purposes. Although conscious elaboration of these metaphors is not necessary, the conscious use of metaphor (as metaphor) may be an added value here, for it might be found to effectively correlate with highly contextualised lower-level models and scenarios as source domains, and perhaps with more communicatively felicitous acts. Nonetheless, at this stage this is but a prediction which must be translated into testable hypotheses as the object of study of further lines of research. As parameters like processing and consciousness are involved in it, testing such hypotheses would require the collaboration with other areas like psycholinguistics or psychology.

All in all, this chapter has attempted to describe the general use of deliberate metaphor in a small selection of texts on meditation stemming from the Tibetan Buddhist tradition. In general terms, it has shown how communicative aspects of metaphor are worth considering in instructional texts like the ones analysed here, not only because of the relatively high percentage of deliberateness in the corpus, but also in connection with the way metaphors are used deliberately. More specifically, it has shown how the particular set of deliberate metaphors handled in this study (uses signalled in discourse like direct metaphor realisations, extended metaphor or metaphor-driven topic digressions) are used widely as an aid to foster understanding of the practice by reconceptualising utterly abstract phenomena (mental percepts) in terms of more basic entities like persons or animals, often recalling areas from the realm of nature. This suggests that deliberate metaphors in this context could be envisaged as a valuable pedagogical tool to foster more felicitous explanations, but perhaps also to help develop other cognitive and interpersonal functions. Diverse types of discourse and genres vary in terms of the functions that metaphors are commonly found to fulfil (Semino 2008). This issue is relevant for this study to the extent that the metaphors analysed in the context of a religious or spiritual tradition may help constitute a standard body of conceptual tools to be applied in meditation instruction in a different range of social settings. A crucial aspect of that transfer process would involve the mechanisms for adapting discursive functions to a new genre or type of discourse. While this falls way beyond the scope of this study, it opens the door to a new research area that must be addressed in the near future.

Finally, a note about corpus length must be added here. As pointed out in the method, the corpus used here is purposefully small to allow for the inductive discovery of the range domains used in major metaphorical mappings. While large-scale generalisations from the data analysed would be risky, this analysis has yielded a set of metaphorical correspondences that can be used as the departure point in more deductive approaches in larger corpora, for example, covering more authors and extensive texts belonging to the same Tibetan Buddhist tradition (cf. Charteris-Black 2004 or Semino 2008 for a discussion on how small and large corpora may combine in this hybrid approach to metaphor analysis).

Acknowledgements: Research for this chapter has been funded by the project UJI-B2018-59. I would like to thank the anonymous reviewers for their useful comments on earlier drafts of this chapter, and the institutional support provided by Universitat Jaume I and IULMA.

References

Campos, Daniel & Ausiàs Cebolla. 2016. Enseñar mindfulness: Contextos de instrucción y pedagogía. *Revista de Psicoterapia* 27 (103). 103–118.

Cameron, Lynne & Robert Maslen (eds). 2010. *Metaphor analysis: Research practice in applied linguistics, social sciences and the humanities*. London: Equinox.

Charteris-Black, Jonathan. 2004. *Corpus approaches to critical metaphor analysis*. New York: Palgrave Macmillan.

Fauconnier, Gilles. 1994 [1985]. *Mental Spaces. Aspects of meaning construction in natural language, 2nd edn*. Cambridge: Cambridge University Press.

Fillmore, Charles J. 1982. Frame semantics. In The Linguistic Society of Korea (ed.), *Linguistics in the morning calm*, 111–137. Seoul: Hanshin.

García-Campayo, Javier & Marcelo Demarzo. 2015. *Mindfulness y compasión: La nueva revolución*. Barcelona: Siglantana.

Gibert, Paul & Choden. 2013. *Mindful compassion: Using the power of mindfulness and compassion to transform our lives*. London: Robinson.

Goatly, Andrew. 2011 [1997]. *The language of metaphors*, 2nd edn. New York: Routledge.

Grady, Joseph. 1997. Theories are buildings revisited. *Cognitive Linguistics* 8 (3). 267–290. https://doi.org/10.1515/cogl.1997.8.4.267 (accessed 15 October 2016).

Kimmel, Michael. 2012. Optimizing the analysis of metaphor in discourse: how to make the most of qualitative software and find a good research design. *Review of Cognitive Linguistics* 10 (1). 1–48. https://doi.org/10.1075/rcl.10.1.01kim (accessed 15 October 2016).

Kövecses, Zoltán. 2005. *Metaphor in culture. Universality and variation*. Cambridge: Cambridge University Press.

Kövecses, Zoltán. 2010 [2002]. *Metaphor: A practical introduction*, 2nd edn. Oxford: Oxford University Press. https://doi.org/10.1017/S0047404503254051 (accessed 15 October 2016).

Kövecses, Zoltán. 2015a. *Where metaphors come from. Reconsidering context in metaphor*. New York: Oxford University Press. https://doi.org/10.1093/acprof:oso/9780190224868.001.0001 (accessed 15 October 2016).

Kövecses, Zoltán. 2015b. Distinguishing levels of metaphor use: some theoretical and methodological consequences. Paper presented at the 4th International Conference on Metaphor and Discourse: New Cognitive Domains in the 21st Century, Universitat Jaume I, 3–4 December.

Kövecses, Zoltán. 2017. Levels of metaphor. *Cognitive Linguistics* 28 (2). 321–347. https://doi.org/10.1515/cog-2016-0052 (accessed 15 August 2018).

Kövecses, Zoltán. 2019. Some consequences of a multi-level view of metaphor. In Ignasi Navarro i Ferrando (ed.), *Current approaches to metaphor analysis in* discourse, 1–13. Berlin & New York: De Gruyter Mouton.

Kövecses, Zoltán, Veronika Szelid, Eszter Nucz, Olga Blanco-Carrion, Elif Arica Akkök & Réka Szabó. 2015. Anger metaphors across languages: A cognitive linguistic perspective. In Roberto Heredia & Anna Cieslicka (eds.), *Bilingual figurative language processing*, 341–367. Cambridge and New York: Cambridge University Press. https://doi.org/10.1017/CBO9781139342100.001 (accessed 15 October 2016).

Lakoff, George & Mark Johnson. 1980. *Metaphors we live by*. Chicago: University of Chicago Press.

Lakoff, George & Mark Johnson. 1999. *Philosophy in the flesh. The embodied mind and its challenge to western thought*. New York: Basic Books.

Lakoff, George. 1990. The invariance hypothesis: Is abstract reason based on image-schemas? *Cognitive Linguistics* 1 (1). 39–74. https://doi.org/10.1515/cogl.1990.1.1.39 (accessed 15 October 2016).
Lakoff, George. 1993 [1979]. The contemporary theory of metaphor. In Andrew Ortony (ed.), *Metaphor and thought*, 2nd edn., 202–251. Cambridge: Cambridge University Press. https://doi.org/10.1017/CBO9781139173865.013 (accessed 15 October 2016).
Lakoff, George. 1996. *Moral politics: What conservatives know that liberals don't*. Chicago: University of Chicago Press.
Musolff, Andreas. 2006. Metaphor scenarios in public discourse. *Metaphor and Symbol* 21 (1). 23–38. https://doi.org/10.1207/s15327868ms2101_2 (accessed 15 October 2016).
Musolff, Andreas. 2016. *Political metaphor analysis. Discourse and scenarios*. London/New York: Bloomsbury. https://ueaeprints.uea.ac.uk/id/eprint/57189 (accessed 15 August 2018).
Nacey, Susan. 2013. *Metaphors in learner English*. Amsterdam: John Benjamins. https://doi.org/10.1075/milcc.2 (accessed 15 October 2016).
Ruiz de Mendoza, Francisco J. 1998. On the nature of blending as a cognitive phenomenon. *Journal of Pragmatics* 30 (3). 259–274. https://doi.org/10.1016/S0378-2166(98)00006-X (accessed 15 October 2016).
Ruiz de Mendoza, Francisco J. & Francisco Santibáñez. 2003. Content and formal cognitive operations in construing meaning. *Italian Journal of Linguistics* 15 (2). 293–320.
Ruiz de Mendoza, Francisco J. & Alicia Galera. 2014. *Cognitive models. A linguistic perspective*. Amsterdam: John Benjamins. https://doi.org/10.1075/hcp.45 (accessed 15 October 2016).
Semino, Elena. 2008. *Metaphor in discourse*. Cambridge: Cambridge University Press. https://doi.org/10.1080/10926480903310393 (accessed 15 October 2016).
Semino, Elena, Zsófia Demjén & Jane Demmen. 2016. An integrated approach to metaphor and framing in cognition, discourse, and practice, with an application to metaphors for cancer. *Applied Linguistics Advanced Access* amw028.1–22. http://applij.oxfordjournals.org/content/early/2016/09/21/applin.amw028.full (accessed 15 October 2016).
Silvestre-López, Antonio-José. 2016a.The discourse of mindfulness: What language reveals about the mindfulness experience. In Pilar Ordóñez-López & Nuria Edo-Marzà (eds.), *New insights into the analysis of medical discourse in professional, academic and popular settings*, 173–198. Bristol: Multilingual Matters.
Silvestre-López, Antonio-José. 2016b. Metáfora y metonimia en la construcción del espacio conceptual y lingüístico en la práctica de la atención plena. *Anuario de Letras* 4 (2). 335–398. http://dx.doi.org/10.19130/iifl.adel.4.2.2016.1400 (accessed 15 August 2018).
Silvestre-López, Antonio-José. & Ignasi Navarro i Ferrando. 2017. Metaphors in the conceptualization of meditative practices. *Metaphor and the Social World* 7 (1). 26–46. https://doi.org/10.1075/msw.7.1.03sil (accessed 15 August 2018).
Sogyal Rinpoche. 1993. *The Tibetan book of living and dying*. New York: HarperCollins.
Steen, Gerard J. 2010. When is metaphor deliberate? In Nils L. Johannesson, Christina Alm-Arvius & David C. Minugh (eds.), *Selected papers from the Stockholm 2008 Metaphor Festival*, 43–63. Stockholm: Acta Universitatis Stockholmiensis.
Steen, Gerard J. 2011. The contemporary theory of metaphor—now new and improved! *Review of Cognitive Linguistics* 9 (1). 24–64.
Steen, Gerard J. 2014a. The cognitive-linguistic revolution in metaphor studies. In Jeanette Littlemore & John R. Taylor (eds.), *The Bloomsbury companion to cognitive linguistics*, 117–142. London: Continuum.

Steen, Gerard J. 2014b. Deliberate metaphor affords conscious metaphorical cognition. *Cognitive Semiotics* 5 (1–2). 179–197. https://doi.org/10.1075/rcl.9.1.03ste (accessed 15 October 2016).
Steen, Gerard J. 2016. Mixed metaphor is a question of deliberateness. In Raymond. W. Gibbs Jr. (ed.), *Mixing metaphor*, 113–132. Amsterdam & Philadelphia: John Benjamins. https://doi.org/10.1075/milcc.6.06ste (accessed 15 August 2018).
Steen, Gerard J., Aletta G. Dorst, J. Berenike Herrmann, Anna A. Kaal, Tina Krennmayr, & Trijntje Pasma. 2010. *A method for linguistic metaphor identification. From MIP to MIPVU.* Amsterdam: John Benjamins. https://doi.org/10.1075/celcr.14 (accessed 15 October 2016).
Sullivan, Karen. 2013. *Frames and constructions in metaphoric language.* Amsterdam: John Benjamins. https://doi.org/10.1075/cal.14 (accessed 15 October 2016).
Tenzin Gyatso, the 14th Dalai Lama. 1996. [1991]. *Cultivating a daily meditation*, 3rd edn. Dharamsala: Library of Tibetan Works & Archives.
Turner, Mark. 1990. Aspects of the invariance hypothesis. *Cognitive Linguistics* 1 (2). 247–55.

Appendix 1 Final list of functions and deliberate metaphor signal codes

FUNCTIONS

Compress inferences
Create argumentative impact and grab the audience's attention
Create common ground in discourse (establishment of reference)
Create textual cohesion or provide for textual/argument structuring
Evoke vivid, quasi-perceptual imagery
Explanatory
Fill in lexical gaps / loose use of a term (via metaphor)
Highlight / hide aspects of a topic
Mark discourse boundaries
Metaphoric framing (cultural symbolism)
Metaphoric framing (reframing) fostering reconceptualisation

SIGNALS

A is B metaphor
Activated previously in discourse
Analogy
B of A metaphor

Deliberate perspective changer (in the view of author/school of thought, etc.)
Deliberate perspective changer (topic digression)
Extended comparison
Metaphoric narrative
Scare quotes
Simile

Rocío Cuberos, Elisa Rosado and Joan Perera

Using deliberate metaphor in discourse: Native vs. non-native text production

Abstract: This study explores the occurrence of developmental patterns in the use of metaphors by native and non-native speakers of Spanish in discourse. Underlying this analysis is the assumption that intentionally using figurative language – and thus engaging a cross-domain mapping from a source to a target domain – is a communicative choice on the part of the speaker-writer. Taking into account the universality, and creativity of metaphor, this study aims to determine the effect of age, L2 proficiency level, discourse genre and modality of production in the production of deliberate metaphorical expressions by non-native vs. native Spanish speakers. For this purpose, we analyze the oral and written expository and narrative texts produced by 30 native and 47 non-native speakers (L1= Arabic, Chinese) of Spanish of three different age groups (grade-school, junior-high, and university students). The results of the study provide a developmental framework of the production of deliberate metaphor in discourse. Even though the results of the study do not show a significant proficiency development framework for the production of metaphor in discourse, we offer valuable insights into how creativity and transfer have an impact on the use of metaphors in non-native discourse.

Keywords: deliberate metaphors, L1 & L2 discourse, later language development

1 Introduction

This study explores the occurrence of developmental patterns in the use of metaphors by native and non-native speakers of Spanish in discourse. Despite being the Conceptual Metaphor Theory (Lakoff and Johnson 1980) our initial starting point, and in line with Steen's three-dimensional model of metaphor (Steen 2007, 2008a, 2008b), we strictly refer here to deliberate metaphors (henceforth DMs).

Rocío Cuberos, Elisa Rosado and Joan Perera, Universitat de Barcelona, Passeig de la Vall d'Hebron, Barcelona

https://doi.org/10.1515/9783110629460-011

Underlying this analysis is the assumption that intentionally using figurative language – and thus engaging a cross-domain mapping from a target to a source domain – is a communicative choice on the part of the speaker-writer. Accordingly, we see deliberate metaphors as rhetorical devices that language users may employ with the purpose of activating metaphorical reasoning in the receivers' minds (Nacey 2013; Steen et al. 2010). Hence, the study of the appropriate use of deliberate metaphor as part of later language development must necessarily be conducted in the context of text production.

We know from previous L1 literature that the development of the linguistic repertoire involves gaining control and ability to use language in different discursive contexts attending to the constraints of genre, register, stance, and modality of production (Berman 2001, 2015). The development of the skills involved in text production, both oral and written, extends from childhood to adulthood (Ravid and Tolchinsky 2002; Tolchinsky et al. 2005). The complexity of this process increases for non-native speakers since they have to deal not only with a different linguistic system but with different rhetorical conventions too. Becoming a literate speaker-writer of a given language requires adapting linguistic expressions to different communicative settings (Berman and Nir 2010; Steen 1999) and level of language along with a continuum from informal to formal contexts (Biber 1995; Grimshaw 2003), as much as is needed to adjust one's verbal expression to the needs of both interlocutor and text (Berman, Ragnarsdóttir, and Strömqvist 2002; Du Bois 2007), and being consistent with the distinctiveness imposed by speech and writing (Berman 2015). In very broad terms, text production then consists in combining different structures and linguistic forms to produce messages that meet specific communicative functions. Particularly, when it comes to figurative language, the ability to differentiate what is said from what is meant is affected by genre (Lee, Torrance, and Olson 2001; Tolchinsky 2004) and, in fact, metaphor density depends on register too (Berber-Sardinha 2015; Steen et al. 2010). Therefore, a (discourse) context-specific framework seems to be necessary for the study of figurative language use. This study is set out to analyze the use of deliberate metaphorical expressions in discourse across two modalities of production (writing and spoken) and two genres (narrative and expository).

Crucial for communication, vocabulary is essential for the study of L1 and L2 development, and its analysis provides a necessary perspective on language acquisition and processing since is the base of linguistic and conceptual knowledge (Clark 1993; Ravid 2004). Lexical development plays a crucial role in later language development because lexicon is subject to unlimited growth through the lifespan (Lenneberg 1967; Nippold 2002). There is a constant reciprocal relationship between lexical development and literacy in which growth in word knowledge leads to better comprehension of texts, which in turn, sets the stage for further extension of the lexicon (Sternberg and Powell 1983). Likewise, a landmark in lexical development is mastery of figurative language (Tolchinsky 2004). Full native language acquisition implies development of figurative language (Levorato and Cacciari 2002; Peskin and Olson 2004). Findings suggest that metaphoric competence, as a cognitive skill, develops with age both in L1 (Tolchinsky 2004) and L2 (Billow 1975; Johnson 1989, 1991; Kogan 1983; Littlemore 2010). Nevertheless, figurative competence in L2 was observed to lag behind their L1 figurative competence and behind the figurative competence of native speakers (Danesi 1992; Howarth 1998; Kecskes 2000; Kecskes and Papp 2000; Kövecses and Szabo 1996). Metaphorical competence is, then, crucial for L2 lexical development since it is linked to the way in which language and/or culture organize the world (Danesi 1995), helping learners to develop their sociolinguistic, illocutionary, grammatical, discourse, and strategic competence (v. Littlemore and Low 2006). Knowledge and use of metaphorical expressions underlying the conceptual system of a language increase speech naturalness (Danesi 2004). In a study examining the contribution of different patterns of metaphorical language use to writing grades in the essays produced by non-native (L1= Vietnamese) undergraduate English speakers at four different year levels, Hoàng (2015) found that conventional and novel metaphors were positively associated with the scores assigned to narrative written texts.

Thus, the study of non-conventional meaning in discourse is especially interesting from a native and non-native language developmental point of view, and must be considered in order to achieve a thorough perspective of the linguistic competence of a given speaker. It is our aim to get insights into the development of metaphorical competence with age and/or L2 proficiency level.

Conceptual metaphors are largely or mostly universal, however metaphors vary along cross-cultural and within-cultural dimension, not only because the verbalization of the same conceptual metaphor may vary between different speech communities and across different languages, but also because certain metaphors appear to be unique to a given language or culture (Kövecses 2000, 2005, 2010; Yu 1995, 1998). Additionally, when it comes to L2 production, metaphorical creativity arises because L2 speakers, consciously or not, may create novel metaphors simply by reproducing standard images from their native language (Nacey 2013; Pitzl 2012; Seidlhofer 2009). Next idioms from Chinese with their equivalents in Arabic, Spanish, and English illustrate cultural variation and (not so) universal metaphors:

(1) 火上加油
huo shang jia you
'add oil to the fire'

يصب الزيت على النار
yasubb alzzayt ealaa alnnar
'pour oil into the fire'

Spa.: *echar leña al fuego*
'add firewood to the fire'
Eng.: add fuel to the fire

(2) 緣木求魚
yuan mu qiu yu
'climb trees to catch fish'

جلب لبن العصفور
jalab llaban aleasfur
'bring milk from a bird'

Spa.: *pedir peras al olmo*
'ask for pears to the elm tree'
Eng.: get blood from a stone

(3) 水火不容
shui huo bu rong
'incompatible as fire and water'

ناقر ونقير
naqir wanaqir
'percussionist and helium'

Spa.: *como el perro y el gato*
'like the cat and the dog'
Eng.: like cat and dog

(4) 羊入虎口
yang ru hu-kou
'the goat fell a prey to the tiger'

عرين الأسد
eryn al'asad
'lion's den'

Spa.: *meterse en la boca del lobo*
'get into the mouth of the wolf'
Eng.: go into the lion's den

In the case of L2 speakers, having access to (at least) two linguistic systems and the potential need of supplying language deficiencies may lead L2 users to produce non-native linguistic expressions by literally transferring metaphorical matter from the L1, resulting in incorrect collocations (Spa.: **hicimos la decisión la semana pasada*, from Eng.: 'we made the decision last week'; YEN, 25;5, male, L1=Chinese) or in acceptable and/or relatable idiomatic alternatives (Spa.: *no veía ni una gota de esperanza en la vida*; Eng.: 'he didn't see not even a drop of hope in life'; DIA; 24;7; female, L1=Chinese), in which it is typically hard to discriminate between errors and instances of creative innovation (Kachru 1985). In this sense, and considering that L2 creativity – at the very least – concerns awareness (Boden 2004), deliberateness might help discriminate between possible cases of metaphorical creativity and lexical errors. In order to get insights into this issue, our study analyzes whether or not non-conventional metaphorical linguistic expressions found in L2 discourse were result of 'mere' creativity or L2 transfer.

Whereas the distinction between conventional and creative metaphors refers to the linguistic dimension of metaphor, the deliberate and non-deliberate opposition applies to its rhetorical function (Nacey 2013; Steen et al. 2010). Since the appearance of a three-dimensional model of metaphor in discourse approach involving metaphor in language, thought, and communication (Steen 2007, 2008a, 2008b), discussions into this issue have arisen (Gibbs 2011, 2015; Steen 2011, 2015). However, there has been little research into the communicative feature of metaphorical deliberateness (e.g., Beger 2011; Nacey 2013; Ng and Koller 2013; Perrez and Reuchamps 2014), probably due to the lack of a systematic deliberate metaphor identification procedure.[1]

Research within the field of metaphor studies is primarily concerned with the investigation of metaphor use in native natural-occurring discourse (Berber-Sardinha 2008; Cameron 2003, 2008; Charteris-Black 2004; Deignan 1999; Deignan and Potter 2004; Marhula and Rosinski 2014; Steen at al. 2010a). Numerous studies have focused on the potential benefits of teaching metaphors to L2 learners explicitly to L2 learners (e.g., Boers 2013; Danesi 2008; Holme 2004). Yet, research into L2 metaphoric competence has mostly focused on the identification and quantification of linguistic metaphorical expressions in non-native discourse (Danesi 1995; MacArthur 2010; Nacey 2013), and on the development of metaphor production skills across proficiency levels (Littlemore et al. 2014; Teymouri and Dowlatabadi, 2014).

Littlemore et al. (2014) looked at the amount and distribution of metaphor used by L2 writers across Common European Framework of Reference for Languages (CEFR) levels in the essays produced by Greek- and German-speaking learners of English. They found that the overall density of metaphor increases from A2 to C2 levels. Likewise, when investigating the relationship between 60 Iranian EFL learners' metaphoric competence and their language proficiency, Teymouri and Dowlatabadi (2014) found a correlation between these two variables. These findings are incongruent with those of Littlemore (2001) who did not find a statistically significant relationship between metaphor production and communicative language abilities. Similarly, regarding metaphor interpretation, Johnson (1996), and Johnson and Rosano (1996) found that L2 proficiency is unrelated to L2 metaphor interpretation abilities.

These results suggest that different ways of conceptualizing and measuring metaphoric competence may lead to contradictory results (Hoàng 2015). In our study, metaphor is considered as both a communicative device and a rhetorical choice; hence, we focused on the use of deliberate metaphorical expressions.

1 Recently, Reijnierse, Burgers, Krennmayr & Steen (2018) developed such a procedure, a method for identifying potentially deliberate metaphor in discourse that will hopefully allow carrying out more thorough studies and it will help to build a detailed picture of deliberate metaphor use in different discourse environments.

Considering the universality, and creativity of metaphor, this study aims to determine the effect of age, L2 proficiency level, discourse genre and modality of production in the production of deliberate metaphorical expressions in native and non-native Spanish. For this purpose, we analyze the oral and written expository and narrative texts produced by native and non-native speakers (L1= Arabic and Chinese) of Spanish of three different age groups (grade-school, junior-high, and university students). Expository and narrative texts were selected because they represent two ends of a continuum: while the former analyzes a topic, the latter focuses on people who act in certain temporal and spatially defined circumstances (v. Berman and Verhoeven 2002).

2 Method

In this section, we describe the participants of our study, the tasks and materials used, the procedure followed in obtaining the data, including the elicitation procedure, and the procedure for data treatment, including the process of transcription and coding. Regarding the selection of the sample, the elicitation procedure of texts and the transcription criteria, methodology used in this study is inherited from previous research projects (v. Berman and Verhoeven 2002).

2.1 Participants

We analyze 308 texts produced by 47 nonnative (L1= Arabic and Chinese)[2] and 30 native speakers of Spanish (n=77), divided into three age/schooling experience groups: primary school (mean age=10;16; range=9–11;9); junior-high (mean age=13;78; range=12;3–15;8), and university (mean age=25;24; range=19;7–40;3). Non-native speakers were in turn also divided by L2 proficiency level (A1–A2=9; B1-B2-C1=33; C2=4). Information about the composition of the groups and participants' age and L2 proficiency level is provided next in Table 11.1.

All participants were administrated a questionnaire to gather information about their sociolinguistic background, literacy practices, and general cultural habits. All L1 Spanish participants were recruited in Córdoba (Andalusia, Spain),

2 We did not make a distinction between L1s because the goal of the study does not concern cultural variation. However, despite considering both groups together, we did control this variable to be able to detect potential different behavior by L1. No differences were observed when comparing patterns of L2 metaphor use between both groups.

and L2 Spanish participants were recruited in Madrid, Barcelona, and Murcia and they must have resided in Spain for at least four years to ensure minimum abilities to produce texts.

Table 11.1: Distribution of the sample by age and L2 proficiency level.

	L1 (control) Spanish & L2 Spanish			
L2 level	**9 yrs. (grade)**	**12–14 yrs. (junior-high)**	**Adults (university)**	**N**
A1–A2	4	4	1	9
B1–B2–C1	4	6	24	34
C2	0	0	4	4
Native	10	10	10	30
	18	20	39	77

2.2 Tasks and Procedure

In order to elicit the texts, participants were shown a five-minute video clip with no text, about conflict situations at school that acted as a target for unifying discourse content. After watching the video, participants were asked to tell and to write a personal experience narrative about a similar situation in which they had been involved (narrative genre), and to discuss, also orally and written, the kind of problems that were displayed in the video (expository genre). Participants produced the texts individually and tasks were counterbalanced for order of administration (Berman and Verhoeven 2002).[3]

All texts were orthographically transcribed, spelling mistakes were corrected, divided into clauses following Berman and Slobin's (1994) criteria, and coded following the conventions of CHAT format of CHILDES (MacWhinney 2000). Analyses were performed using CLAN programs (CHILDES).

The texts were analyzed following the Deliberate Metaphor Identification Procedure (DMIP) (Reijnierse et al. 2018) in search of potentially deliberate metaphors. This method takes a semiotic approach based on analyzing the

3 The data was gathered in the context of two research project: (1) "Developing Literacy in Different Contexts and Different Languages" (funded by the *Spencer Foundation*, Chicago; Ruth Berman, PI) for the L1 Spanish sample, and (2) "Lexical, morphosyntactic, and discursive markers in the development of text quality in L2 Spanish and Catalan" (funded by the Spanish Ministry of Economy and Finance; Joan Perera, PI) for the L2 Spanish sample. A full description of the data collection procedure can be found in Berman and Verhoeven (2002).

multidimensional meaning of metaphorical utterances in discourse. This kind of analysis doesn't make any claims about what happens in language users' mind, and, therefore, only cases of *potentially* deliberate metaphor can be identified (Nacey 2013; Steen et al. 2010). According to the DMIP, "a metaphor is potentially deliberate when the source domain plays a role in the representation of the referential meaning of the utterance" (Reijnierse et al. 2018: 134). Firstly, it is thus necessary to read the entire text to establish a general understanding of the content and identify metaphorical lexical units. As proposed by the DMIP, the texts were first analyzed following the Vrije Universiteit Metaphor Identification Procedure (MIPVU) (Steen et al. 2010) in search of metaphor related words (MRWs).

Following the MIPVU guidelines, the word is the unit of analysis, and multiword items are considered as a single lexical unit. However, specific demarcation of Spanish lexical units was needed in order to establish what counts as a lexical item. The criteria followed were though established by Argerich and Tolchinsky (2000): interposition, inflection and function.[4] Ambiguous cases were solved following Bosque (2006).

In broad terms, MIPVU consists in identifying (1) indirectly, (2) directly and (3) implicitly expressed linguistic metaphors, (4) signals of potential cross-domain mappings, (5) metaphor ambiguous cases, and (6) discarded for metaphor analysis cases. Starting by reading the entire text to establish a general understanding of the content, the analysis consists in identifying all the lexical units in the text, determining their meaning in context, and then deciding whether each one of them has a more basic contemporary meaning in other contexts. Basic meanings tend to be more concrete and precise, more related to bodily action and historically older. If a more basic meaning is identified, we decide whether its meaning in the text could be understood in comparison with this more basic meaning. If this was the case, then the lexical unit is marked as being indirectly used as metaphor. Likewise, similes, analogies and expressions of counterfactual reality were marked in order to also identify metaphor involving conceptual metaphor with directly used language. The MIPVU also recognizes metaphorical linguistic expressions expressed implicitly in the language. These implicit metaphors correspond to cohesive elements, such as third-person

---

4 (1) Interposition: multiword lexical items do not usually admit to an interposed determiner or quantifier, [*por cierto* (Eng. By the way)/**por muy cierto*.]

(2) Inflection: multiword items do not usually inflect for case, gender, number, etc. [*por ejemplo* (Eng. For example)/**por ejemplos]*.

(3) Function: it often changes when a word forms a lexical item with another word., *hasta vs. hasta que* "until"

pronouns, ellipses or demonstratives, which refer to a direct or indirect metaphor present in the discourse.

Likewise, DMIP involves identifying potentially deliberate metaphors in language use by following a top-down and bottom-up method. For this study, we only applied the bottom-up method in search for cues of deliberateness, domain constructions and clusters, considering all direct and explicit metaphors and the following linguistic constructions as potentially deliberate: all 'A is B comparisons' (see example 5), wordplays, similes (see example 6), extended comparisons and analogies (see example 7), s-quotes structures (see example 8) and creative metaphors (see example 9).

(5) *El aprendizaje es competición*
(the) learning is competition
'Learning is competition.'
[YEN, woman, ADU, Chinese, EW]

(6) *El docente debería ser más* ***como un dirigidor**** *de su crecimiento*
(the) teacher should be more **like a manager** of his growth
'The teacher should be more **like a manager** of (their students') growth.'
[MEN, woman, ADU, Chinese, NS]

(7) *La acción de* ***alejarse*** *no se ve tan obvia (...) no voy a demostrarle que a él no me gusta* ***acercar*** *(...) pero cuando habla conmigo voy a responderle (...) así poco a poco sería cada día más la* ***distancia*** *entre él y yo*

the action of **moving away** not see as obvious (...) (I)(am)not go to show(him) (I)don't like **getting close** (...) but when (he)speaks with me (I) (am)go to answer(him) (...) like (that), little by little (it)would be every day more the **distance** between he and me

'The action of **moving away** is not seen as obvious (...) I am not going to show him I don't like **getting close** (...) but when he speaks to me I am going to answer him (...) like that, every day **distance** between us would be more little by little.'
[WEH, woman, ADU, Chinese, NS]

(8) *Si copias, la nota no es* ***"real"***
if (you)copy, (the) grade not is **"real"**
'If you copy, your grade is not **"real"**'
[DIA, woman, ADU, Chinese, EW]

(9) *Necesitaba una* ***cartera de amigos*** *en el colegio*

(I)needed a **portfolio of friends** in the school

'I needed a friend protfolio at the school.'

[MAH, woman, ADU, Arabic, NS]

Guidelines of both procedures, MIPVU and DMIP were adapted to L2 production. Discrimination between novel and L1-based metaphors were performed by native speakers of Arabic and Chinese, and cases where the cross-domain mapping was impossible to follow were not marked as L1-based or creative metaphors but as errors, considering that communication was lost. Finally, we included three post-tags to the main categories (direct, indirect and implicit metaphors): (1) Spanish-based metaphors (see example 10), (2) L1-based metaphors (see example 11–12), and (3) creative metaphors (see example 13).

(10) *Los jóvenes que* ***hagan trampas*** *en los exámenes [YIA, woman, 25;7]*

(the) teenagers that **make tricks** in the exams

'Youngsters who **cheat** in the exams.'

[YIA, woman, ADU, Arabic, EW]

(11) *Hace falta aumentar la* ***fuerza de educar***

(it)makes need (to)increase the **strength of (to)educate**

'It is necessary to increase the **power of education.**'

[LEO, woman, ADU, Chinese, EW]

(12) *Esos niños no* ***van*** *bien conmigo*

those boys not **(they)go** well with me

'Those boys don't **get along** well with me.'

[OMA, boy, SEC, Arabic, NW]

(13) *Más bien pareces* ***un animal o una pared sin sentimientos***

rather (you)look **an animal or a wall without feelings**

'You look more like **an animal or a wall without feelings.**'

[ISM, boy, SEC, Arabic, NS]

3 Results and discussion

To gain a general perspective on the presence of metaphorical matter in our corpus, first, descriptive results of the total number and types of deliberate vs. non-deliberate metaphors identified in both L1 and L2 corpus are reported.

Next, results and distribution of deliberate metaphorical production data are analyzed for each group under study.

Due to the distribution and size of our sample, analyses were conducted with the total number of deliberate metaphors (DMs) and, depending on the type of data, a series of 2-tailed Mann-Whitney *U* or Kruskal-Wallis tests were conducted in all groups under study (native vs. non-native; age; L2 level; genre and modality of production). Because the participants produced texts of different length, all the analyses were performed on mean proportions over the total number of clauses in each text. Test are significant at the $p<.05$ level.

A total of 5,542 metaphors were found in the 308 analyzed texts, from which 243 were identified as deliberate metaphors. DMs represent therefore a 4.38% of the total metaphorical matter identified in the corpus, 0.48% of the 49,611 words examined and 2.40% of the 10,098 clauses. Information about total numbers of deliberate vs. non-deliberate metaphors by each category under analysis is provided in Table 11.2.

Table 11.2: Types and number of deliberate vs. non-deliberate metaphors.

		Deliberate vs. Non-deliberate metaphors	
Metaphors	5542	**deliberate metaphors**	243
indirect metaphors	5043	**indirect metaphors**	149
Spanish-based	4832	Spanish-based	118
L1-based	46	L1-based	0
Creative	160	Creative	32
direct metaphors	86	**direct metaphors**	86
Spanish-based	32	Spanish-based	32
L1-based	3	L1-based	3
Creative	33	Creative	33
Others	256	Others	8

As shown in Table 11.2, indirect DMs represented 61.31% of total deliberate DMs identified, while direct DMs represented 35.39%. A total of 150 DMs were Spanish-based, while only 3 DMs were L1-based metaphors. Considering deliberate and non-deliberate metaphors together, L1-based metaphors rose up to 49. These figures illustrate that non-native speakers showed no symptoms of 'figurative homoiophobia' (Kellerman 2000), that is, they did transfer metaphorical matter from their native language to the target language. Metaphorical transfer seems to work unconsciously, just as other types of transfer, since only 6.12% of L1-based metaphors were deliberately produced. At the same time, however, these low figures also illustrate metalinguistic reflection on the part of the speakers, because they seem to perceive idiosyncrasies by avoiding transferring a large amount of metaphorical matter and restraining from producing deliberately L1-based indirect metaphors.

In terms of creativity, our results are consistent with those found by Steen (2011) and Nacey (2013): when considering deliberate and non-deliberate metaphors together, creative metaphors represent only 3.48% of the total metaphorical production, therefore most of the MRWs have their metaphorical meaning described in the dictionaries. In addition, it is important to keep in mind that these figures are particularly high in L2 production, suggesting that the lack of linguistic resources occasionally results in a more creative use of language.

We examined the use of DMs in **native and non-native production** expecting that native would produce more DMs than non-native speakers. Native speakers produced a mean of 0.017 DMs (SD=.043), while non-native speakers produced 0.015 (SD=.044). As shown in Figure 11.1, in our sample there is a higher proportion of Spanish-based indirect DMs in native than in non-native production (M=.0103; SD=.0277 vs. M=.0054; SD=.0278). Most of DMs produced by native speakers are Spanish-based indirect DMs (M=.0103; SD=.0277), whereas non-native speakers' most of DMs production is distributed between Spanish-based indirect DMs (M=.0054; SD=.0278) and novel direct DMs (M=.0052; SD=.0198). Lack of confidence on the metaphorical load when producing L2 metaphorical matter, together with less availability of linguistic resources on the part of non-native speakers seems to convey them to make a creative use of language by producing novel metaphors. Conversely, the use of Spanish-based direct DMs is balanced in native and non-native production (M=.0020; SD=.0072 vs. M=.0017; SD=.0079). Both native and non-native speakers displayed a similar amount of novel indirect DM (M=.0021; SD= .0094 vs. M=.0023; SD=.0109). As shown, standard deviations are higher than means in both corpora, indicating a high degree of individual variability.

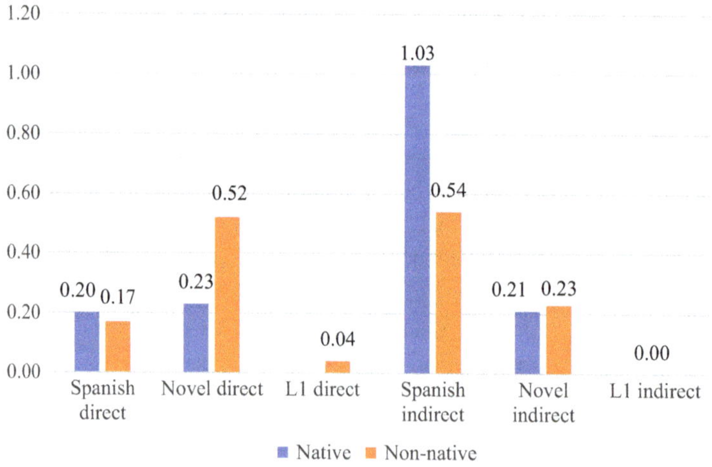

Figure 11.1: Mean percentage of types of DMs produced by native and non-native speakers

Even though no significant differences are found for any categories under analysis, when splitting non-native speakers by proficiency level, we do find differences between the beginner group, who do not produce any DMs, and native speakers (M=.0174, SD=.04398) for overall use of DMs (p=.001). It is apparent from the results that, as long as accessibility to the necessary linguistic resources permit it, the production of DMs is balanced between natives and non-natives. The use of DMs seems then to be equally essential in L1 and L2 discourse and metaphoric competence is assumed to imply not only linguistic skills but also cognitive operations. This premise is also supported by the use of DMs observed when examining the effect of age and L2 proficiency level.

Figure 11.2 displays the mean proportion of DMs produced in native and non-native discourse by age. When considering age together with L1, adult native speakers showed a more extensive use of deliberate metaphors than adult non-native speakers (p<.001). However, no significant differences were found between native and non-native speakers in the younger groups. This may be indicating that metaphors are certainly a rhetorical choice for expert native speakers who deliberately resort to them when needed; consequently, DM production seems to require mastery of 'more basic' linguistic resources. In our sample, native junior-high schoolers are overtaken by their non-native counterparts (M=.0026, SD=.0079 vs. M=.0133, SD=.0567), perhaps indicating a typically non-native use of DMs as communication strategy.

Our second goal was to determine the **effect of age** in the use of DMs. As expected, the same developmental pattern was observed in L1 and L2, and age

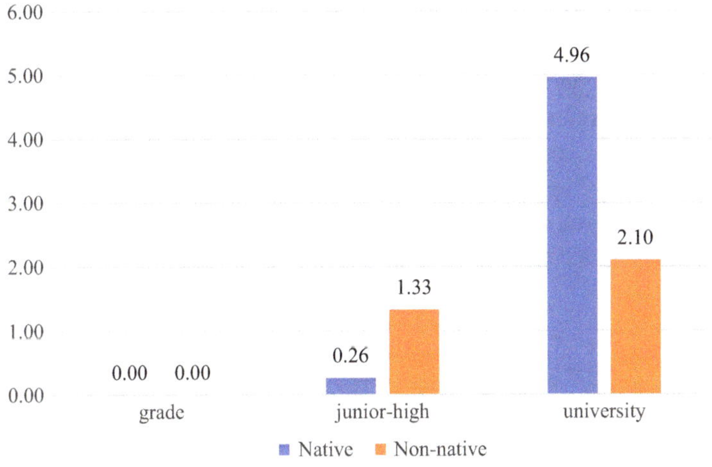

Figure 11.2: Mean percentage of DMs produced in native and non-native discourse by age

had a significant impact on the use of DMs in both samples (native: $p<.001$; non-native: $p=.001$). It was also apparent from the results that both L1 and L2 speakers made gains across different stages of development, since statistical differences were observed between all age groups considered (Native: grade vs. junior high: $p=.042$; grade vs. university: $p<.001$; junior-high vs. university: $p<.001$. Non-native: grade vs. junior high: $p=.040$; grade vs. university: $p=.001$; junior-high vs. university: $p=.038$). Absence of DMs in the youngest groups and the steadily increase across ages suggest that the use of DMs operates at a cognitive level.

Our third goal was to determine in what ways the use of DMs varies across three **different L2 proficiency levels**. We expected that DMs would be more frequent in advanced speakers than beginners. In order to confirm this prediction, three series of 2-tailed Mann-Withney *U* test was conducted for the overall use of DMs.

The production of DMs by L2 speakers was found to start off with none but increased gradually across the levels, with a statistically significant jump from the beginner to intermediate group (M=0.0188, SD=0.04819, $p=0.001$) and from beginner to advanced (M=.0257, SD=.04948, $p<.001$). However, statistically significant differences between intermediate and advanced were not found. Production of DMs seems then to stabilize once L2 speakers have at their disposal linguistic resources and although linguistic knowledge is obviously a prerequisite for the production of DMs, lack of linguistic knowledge does not hinder them from deliberately producing metaphors. Therefore, the use of DMs is not directly related to linguistic competence as might be expected.

Our last goal of this study was to determine how the use of DMs varies depending on **discourse genre and modality of production**. To do so, we ran two series of 2-tailed Mann-Withney *U* test for each category (genre and modality of production) for the overall use of DMs in L1 and L2 corpus together. From a discursive point of view, we assumed that expository texts would include more DMs than narrative texts. We also expected that written texts would contain a higher proportion of DMs than spoken ones. However, results indicated that the use of DMs was not affected by genre or modality of production, except when considering native and non-native speakers separately. In this case, expository texts produced by non-native speakers showed a higher proportion of DMs than narrative texts. The specific nature of these DMs might help to explain these two different behaviors.

4 Conclusions and suggestions for further research

This study is set out to determine the effect of age, genre discourse, modality of production, and L2 proficiency level in the production of deliberate metaphorical expressions in native and non-native Spanish, taking into account the universality and creativity of metaphorical use as well as the language-specific constrains operating in the production of metaphorical expressions.

Our results revealed that the use of DMs is essential in L1 and L2 production, despite being a rhetorical choice that shows high individual variability. In broad terms, results also suggest that the use of DMs operates not only at a linguistic but also at a cognitive level.

A main finding of our study is that the production of DMs in natural-occurring discourse affects approximately 5% of the total words examined and this is certain in L1 and L2 discourse. The production of direct and indirect DMs is, broadly speaking, quite balanced: most of DMs are conventional, i.e., Spanish-based, followed by creative and L1-based metaphors. In terms of metaphorical creativity, this appears to be a useful way to identify DMs in discourse, since largely creative metaphors are deliberately produced. However, when it comes to L2 production, lack of linguistic mastery may occasionally result in a more creative use of language, which may or may not be deliberate. Besides, although non-native speakers might avoid transferring or producing deliberately L1-based indirect metaphors, they do enrich their productions by unconsciously transferring metaphorical matter from their L1. The receiver might perceive these as creative metaphors, however, to track their origin seems essential to determine whether they are an outcome of transfer or rather the result of a (deliberate) process of metaphor-making. Future research should aim at tracking equivalent metaphorical patterns in L1 and L2 to determine whether analogy between languages helps (or hinders) producing deliberate metaphors.

Our findings also indicate that the need to deliberately produce metaphors prevails over the lack of linguistic mastery, since production of DMs is parallel in native and non-native speakers. Absence of DMs in the texts by the beginner group might stem from their inability to combine the cognitive effort required for the production of DMs with their struggle to produce texts with a limited set of linguistic means.

On the other hand, production of DMs differs between native and non-native speakers only when considering different age groups. The fact that native university speakers produce more DMs than their non-native counterparts might be indicating a more elaborate and sophisticated language use that can only be reached at native-like proficiency levels. A more thorough, detailed analysis of the nature of adult DMs in native vs. non-native DMs might shed light on this issue.

Our findings indicate that age is an essential factor in the study of DMs, and that the same developmental pattern is found in the deliberate production of metaphors for L1 and L2 discourse. This suggests that the cognitive demands imposed by production of DMs are not accessible before adolescence, and that metaphorical competence develops with age both in L1 and L2 discourse.

Additionally, deliberate production of metaphors is also subject to individual variability, and seems to involve personal rhetorical preferences not necessarily related to linguistic competence. It seems worth exploring whether these individual differences remain relatively stable across languages, and/or display similar tendencies in L1 and L2 (Littlemore 2010).

Once L2 speakers have the necessary linguistic tools to produce DMs, production remains across stages of linguistic development, though a developmental L2 proficiency pattern cannot be identified. An alternative way to get further insights into the use of DM in L2 discourse would imply a change of focus from the learner to the text, by examining the extent to which DMs contribute to explain variation when assessing text production. Future research should aim at analyzing whether the use of DMs in native and non-native discourse correlates with text quality evaluation (Cuberos in prep).

As for the effects of genre and modality of production in the use of DMs in our data, and against initial expectations, when considering L1 and L2 together DMs are equally present in expository and narrative texts, as well as in written and spoken texts. Nevertheless, DMs become more frequent in expository texts in the L2 corpus. A possible explanation for this revolves around the feasible use of direct DMs as a valuable communication strategy in absence of L2 vocabulary (Bialystok 1990). Future research should look further into the specific nature and context of the production of these DMs.

Certainly, the study of deliberate metaphors in non-native discourse would surely benefit from the analysis of a larger sample. Firstly, the distribution of our sample by L2 proficiency level constrains the scope for a generalization of our findings. Similarly, we believe that the relative infrequent use of DMs in (semi-)spontaneous discourse severely limits the generalization of the findings of our study too. Positively, valuable insights could be gained from the analysis of experimental data, by using a specially-designed task to elicit a more extensive use of metaphors (v. Lamartí 2011).

References

Argerich, Noemi & Liliana Tolchinsky. 2000. On a definition of lexical items in written and spoken texts. In Melina Aparici, Noemi Argerich, Joan Perera, Elisa Rosado & Liliana Tolchinsky (eds.), *Developing Literacy across Genres, Modalities, and Languages*, Vol. III, 197–204. Barcelona: Tel Aviv University Press.

Beger, Anke. 2011. Deliberate metaphors? An exploration of the choice and functions of metaphors in US-American college lectures. *Metaphorik.de* 20. 39–60.

Berber-Sardinha, Tony. 2008. Metaphor probabilities in corpora. In Mara Sophia Zanotto, Lynne Cameron & Marilda C. Cavalcanti (eds.), *Confronting Metaphor in Use: An applied linguistic approach*, 127–147. Amsterdam/Philadelphia: John Benjamins Publishing Company. DOI: 10.1075/pbns.173.09ber.

Berman, Ruth A. 2001. Setting the narrative scene: How children begin to tell a story. In Keith H. Nelson, Ayhan Aksu-Koç & Carolyn E. Johnson (eds.), *Children's language*, Vol. 10, 1–30. Hillsdale: Lawrence Erlbaum.

Berman, Ruth A. 2016. Linguistic literacy and later language development. In Joan Perera, Melina Aparici, Elisa Rosado & Naymé Salas (eds.), *Written and Spoken Language Development across the Lifespan*, Literacy Studies 11, 181–200. Barcelona: Springer International Publishing Switzerland. DOI: 10.1007/978-3-319-21136-7_12.

Berman, Ruth A. & Bracha Nir-Sagiv. 2010. The language of expository texts: Developmental perspectives. In Marilyn A. Nippold & Cheryl M. Scott (eds.), *Expository discoursein children, adolescents, and adults: Developmental disorders*, 101–123. New York: Taylor & Francis.

Berman, Ruth A., Hrafnhildur Ragnarsdóttir & Sven Strömqvist. 2002. Developing text production abilities in speech and writing: Aims and methodology. *Written Languages and Literacy* 5. 1–44.

Berman, Ruth A. & Ludo Verhoeven. 2002. Cross-linguistic perspectives on the development of text-production abilities: Speech and writing. *Written Language and Literacy* 5 (2). 1–172. DOI: 10.1075/wll.5.2.

Berman, Ruth A. & Ludo Verhoeven. 2002. Cross-linguistic perspectives on the *development of text-production abilities: Speech and writing. Written Language and Literacy* 5 (1). 1–135. DOI: 10.1075/wll.5.1.

Berton, Marco. 2014. *La riqueza léxica en la producción escrita de estudiantes suecos de ELE.* Stockholm: Stockholms universitet.

Bialystok, Ellen. 1990. *Communication Strategies: A Psychological Analysis of Second Language Use.* Oxford: Basil Blackwell.

Biber, Douglas. 1995. *Dimensions of register variation: A crosslinguistic comparison.* New York: Cambridge University Press.

Billow, Richard M. 1975. A cognitive developmental study of metaphor comprehension. *Developmental Psychology* 11. 415–423.

Boden, Margaret A. 2004. *The creative mind: Myths and mechanism.* London: Routledge.

Boers, Frank. 2013. Cognitive Linguistic approaches to teaching vocabulary: Assessment and integration. *Language Teaching* 46 (2). 208–224.

Bosque, Ignacio. 2006. *PRÁCTICO. Diccionario combinatorio práctico del español contemporáneo: las palabras en su contexto.* Madrid: Ediciones SM.

Cameron, Lynne. 2003. *Metaphor in Educational Discourse.* London: Continuum.

Cameron, Lynne. 2008. Metaphor and talk. In Raymond W. Gibbs Jr. (ed.), *The Cambridge Handbook of Metaphor and Thought*, 197–211. Cambridge: Cambridge University Press.

Charteris-Black, Jonathan. 2004. *Corpus Approaches to Critical Metaphor Analysis.* New York: Palgrave Macmillan.

Clark, Eve V. 1993. *The Lexicon in Acquisition.* Cambridge: Cambridge University Press.

Cuberos, Rocío. in preparation. *Indicadores léxicos de calidad textual en español nativo y no nativo.* Barcelona: Universitat de Barcelona.

Danesi, Marcel. 1992. Metaphorical competence in second language acquisition and second language teaching: The neglected dimension. In James E. Alatis (ed.), *Georgetown*

University Round Table on Languages and Linguistics, 489–500. Washington DC: Georgetown University Press.
Danesi, Marcel. 1995. Learning and teaching languages: The role of "conceptual fluency", *International Journal of Applied Linguistics* 5 (1). 3–20.
Danesi, Marcel. 2004. *Metáfora, pensamiento y lenguaje. Una perspectiva viquiana de teorización* . Sevilla: Kronos.
Danesi, Marcel. 2008. Conceptual errors in second language learning. In Sabine De Knopp & Teun De Rycker (eds.), *Cognitive approaches to pedagogical grammar*, 231–257. Berlin/ New York: De Gruyter Mouton.
Deignan, Alice. 1999. Corpus-based research into metaphor. In Lynne Cameron & Graham Low (eds.), Researching and Applying Metaphor, 177–199. Cambridge: Cambridge University Press.
Deignan, Alice & Lizz Potter. 2004. A corpus study of metaphors and metonyms in English and Italian. Journal of Pragmatics 36 (7). 1231–1252.
Du Bois, John W. 2007. The stance triangle. In Robert Englebretson (ed.), *Stancetaking in discourse: Subjectivity, evaluation, interaction*, 39-182. Amsterdam: John Benjamins Publishing Company.
Gibbs Jr., Raymond W. 2011. Are deliberate metaphors really deliberate? A question of human consciousness and action. *Metaphor and the Social World* 1 (1). 26–52.
Gibbs Jr., Raymond W. 2015. Do pragmatic signals affect conventional metaphor understanding? A failed test of deliberate metaphor theory. *Journal of Pragmatics* 90. 77–87.
Grimshaw, Allen D. 2003. Genres, registers, and contexts of discourse. In Arthur C. Graesser, Morton A. Gernsbacher & Susan R. Goldmand (eds.), *Handbook of discourse processes*, 25–82. Mahwah: Lawrence Erlbaum.
Hoàng, Thi Doan Ha. 2015. *Metaphorical language in second language learners' essays: products and processes*. Wellington: Victoria University of Wellington.
Holme, Randal. 2004. *Mind, metaphor and language teaching*. Basingstoke: Palgrave Macmillan.
Johnson, Janice. 1989. Factors related to cross-language transfer and metaphor interpretation in bilingual children. *Applied Psycholinguistics* 10. 157–177.
Johnson, Janice. 1991. Developmental versus language-based factors in metaphor interpretation. *Journal of Educational Psychology* 83 (4). 470–483.
Johnson, Janice. 1996. Metaphor interpretations by second language learners: Children and adults. *The Canadian modern language review* 53 (1). 219–241.
Johnson, Janice & Teresa Rosano. 1993. Relation of cognitive style to metaphor interpretation and second language proficiency. *Applied Psycholinguistics* 14. 159–159.
Kachru, Braj B. 1985. Standards, codification, and sociolinguistic realism: The English language in the outer circle. In Randolph Quirk & Henry G. Widdowson (eds.), *English in the World: Teaching and Learning the language and the literature*, 11–30. Cambridge: Cambridge University Press.
Kecskes, Istvan. 2000. Conceptual fluency and the use of situation-bound utterances in L2. *Links and letters* 7 (1). 145–161.
Kecskes, Istvan & Tunde Papp. 2000. Metaphorical competence in trilingual production. In Jasone Cenoz & Ulrike Jessner (eds.), *English in Europe: The acquisition of a third language*, 99–120. Clevedon: Multilingual matters Ltd.

Kogan, Nathan. 1983. Stylistic variation in childhood and adolescence: creativity, metaphor, and cognitive styles. In John H. Flavell & Ellen M. Markman (eds.), *A handbook of child psychology*, 695–706. New York: John Wiley and Sons.
Kövesces, Zoltán. 2000. *Metaphor and Emotion: Language, Culture, and Body in Human Feeling.* Cambridge: Cambridge University Press.
Kövesces, Zoltán. 2005. *Metaphor in Culture: Universality and Variation.* Cambridge: Cambridge University Press.
Kövesces, Zoltán. 2010. *Metaphor: A Practical Introduction*. New York: Oxford University Press.
Kövesces, Zoltán & Szabo, Peter. 1996. Idioms: A view from cognitive semantics. *Applied Linguistics* 1 (3). 326–355.
Lamartí, Rachid. 2011. *La conceptualización metafórica en aprendientes sinófonos de E/LE.* Barcelona: Universitat de Barcelona.
Lee, Elizabeth A., Nancy Torrance. & David R. Olson. 2001. Young children and the say/mean distinction: Verbatim and paraphrase recognition in narrative and nursery rhyme contexts. *Journal of Child Language* 28 (2). 531–543.
Lenneberg, Eric. H. 1967. *Biological foundations of language.* New York: John Wiley.
Levorato, M. Ciara & Cristina Cacciari. 2002. The creation of new figurative expressions: Psycholinguistic evidence in Italian children, adolescents and adults. *Journal of Child Language* 29 (1). 127–150.
Li, Ji & Norbert Schmitt. 2009. The acquisition of lexical phrases in academic writing: A longitudinal case study. *Journal of Second Language Writing* 18 (2). 85–102.
Littlemore, Jeannette. 2001. Metaphoric competence: A language learning strength of students with a holistic cognitive style? *TESOL Quarterly* 35 (3). 459–491.
Littlemore, Jeannette. 2010. Metaphoric competence in the first and second language: Similarities and differences. In Martin Pütz & Laura Sicola (eds.), *Cognitive processing in second language acquisition: Inside the learner's mind*, 293–316. Amsterdam/ Philadelphia: John Benjamins Publishing Company.
Littlemore, Jeannette & Graham Low. 2006. Metaphoric Competence, Second Language Learning, and Communicative Language Ability. *Applied Linguistics* 27 (2). 268–294.
Littlemore, Jeannette, Tina Krennmayr, James Turner & Sarah Turner. 2014. An investigation into metaphor use at different levels of second language writing. Applied Linguistics, 35 (2). 117–144.
MacArthur, Fiona. 2010. Metaphorical competence in EFL: Where are we and where should we be going? A view from the language classroom. *AILA Review* 23 (1). 155–173.
MacWhinney, Brian. 2000. *The CHILDES Project: tools for analyzing talk* (third ed.). Mahwah: Lawrence Erlbaum.
Marhula, Joanna & Maciej Rosinski. 2014. Identifying metaphor in spoken discourse: insights from applying MIPVU to radio talk data. *Zeszyty Naukowe Uniwesytetu Rzeszowskiego* 85 (11). 32–43.
Nacey, Susan. 2013. *Metaphors in Learner English.* Amsterdam/Philadelphia: John Benjamins Publishing Company. DOI: 10.1075/milcc.2.
Ng, Carl J. W. & Veronika Koller. 2013. Deliberate Conventional Metaphor in Images: The Case of Corporate Branding Discourse. *Metaphor and Symbol* 28 (3). 131–147.
Nippold, Marilyn A. 2002. Lexical learning in school-age children, adolescents, and adults: a process where language and literacy converge. *Journal of Child Language* 29. 449–488. DOI: 10.1017/S0305000902275340.

Perera, Joan, Melina Aparici, Elisa Rosado & Naymé Salas. EDU2012-34394. *El desarrollo de la calidad textual en castellano y catalán L2. Indicadores léxicos, morfosintácticos y discursivos.* Barcelona: Universitat de Barcelona.

Perrez, Julien & Min Reuchamps. 2014. Deliberate metaphors in political discourse: the case of citizen discourse. *Metaphorik.de* 25. 7–41.

Peskin, Joan & David R. Olson. 2004. On reading poetry: Implications for later language development . In Ruth A. Berman, *Language development across childhood and adolescence*, 55–81. Amsterdam: John Benjamins Publishing Company.

Pitzl, Marie-Luise. 2012. Creativity meets convention: Idiom variation and re-metaphorization in ELF. *Journal of English as a Lingua Franca* 1 (1). 27–55.

Ravid, Dorit. 2004. Derivational morphology revisited. Later lexical development in Hebrew. In Ruth A. Berman, *Language Development across Childhood and Adolescence*, 53-81. Amsterdam: John Benjamins Publishing Company.

Ravid, Dorit & Liliana Tolchinsky. 2002. Developing linguistic literacy: a comprehensive model. *Journal of Child Language* 29 (2). 417–447.

Reijnierse, Gudrun. 2013a. *Aristotle revisited: the rhetorical functions of (deliberate) metaphor.* [PowerPoint slides]. Retrieved from: https://www.academia.edu/4383847/Aristotle_revisited_the_rhetorical_functions_of_deliberate_metaphor.

Reijnierse, Gudrun. 2013b. *Deliberate metaphor as a means of transferring knowledge in written academic texts.* [PowerPoint slides]. Retrieved from: https://www.academia.edu/5246662/Deliberate_metaphor_as_a_means_of_transferring_knowledge_in_written_academic_texts.

Reijnierse, Gudrun. 2016. *DMIP: A method for identifying potentially deliberate metaphor in discourse.* Paper presented at the Metaphor Festival 2016, University of Amsterdam, 31 August – 3 September.

Reijnierse, Gudrun & Burgers, Christian & Krennmayr, Tina & Steen, Gerard. 2018. DMIP: A Method for Identifying Potentially Deliberate Metaphor in Language Use. Corpus Pragmatics. 2. 129–147.

Seidlhofer, Barbara. 2009. Common ground and different realities: World Englishes and English as a lingua franca. *World Englishes* 28 (2). 236–245.

Steen, Gerard J. 1999. Genres of discourse and the definition of literature. *Discourse Processes* 28. 109–120.

Steen, Gerard J. 2007. *Finding metaphor in grammar and usage: A methodological analysis of theory and research.* Amsterdam: John Benjamins Publishing Company.

Steen, Gerard J. 2008a. The paradox of metaphor: Why we need a three-dimensional model of metaphor. *Metaphor and Symbol* 23 (4). 213–242.

Steen, Gerard J. 2008b. When is metaphor deliberate? In Nils Lennart Johannesson, Christina Alm-Arvius & David C. Minugh (eds.), *Selected Papers from the Stockholm 2008 Metaphor Festival*, 43–64. Stockholm: Acta Universitatis Stockholmiensis.

Steen, Gerard J. 2011. From three dimensions to five steps: the value of deliberate metaphor. *Metaphoric.de* 21. 83–110.

Steen, Gerard J., Aletta G. Dorst, J. Berenike Herrmann, Anna A. Kaal & Tina Krennmayr. 2010. Metaphor in usage. *Cognitive Linguistics* 21 (4). 757–788.

Sternberg, Robert J. & Janet S. Powell. 1983. Comprehending verbal comprehension. *American Psychologist* 38. 878-893.

Teymouri, Maryam & Hamidreza Dowlatabadi. 2014. Metaphoric competence and language proficiency in the same boat. *Procedia - Social and Behavioral Sciences* 98. 1895–1904.

Tolchinsky, Liliana. 2004. The nature and scope of later language development. In Ruth A. Berman, *Language Development across Childhood and Adolescence*, 233–247. Amsterdam: John Benjamins Publishing Company.
Tolchinsky, Liliana, Elisa Rosado, Melina Aparici & Joan Perera. 2005. Becoming proficient educated users of language. In Dorti Ravid & Hava Baat-Zeev Shydkrot, *Perspectives on language and language development*, 375–389. Dordrecht, Holanda: Kluwer.
Yu, Ning. 1995. Metaphorical expressions of anger and hapiness in English and Chinese. *Metaphor and Symbolic Activity* 10. 59–92.
Yu, Ning. 1998. *The contemporary theory of metaphor in Chinese: A perspective from Chinese.* Amsterdam: John Benjamins Publishing Company.

Raquel Sánchez Ruiz

George Ridpath's use of metaphor, metonymy and *metaphtonymy* during the Peace Campaign (1710–1713) of the War of the Spanish Succession

Abstract: Figurative language is key in the political sphere as it allows speakers to present, mask, restructure, share or reject ideas, opinions, values and beliefs in a positive or negative way and so has an impact on society by persuading the reader and reproducing ideologies. Under these premises, the present chapter has two aims: first, to reveal the role of figurative language in the construction of an alternative reality for ideological persuasion in the political writings (*The Observator* and *The Flying Post; or, the Post-Master*) of George Ridpath during the Peace Campaign (1710–1713) of the War of the Spanish Succession. Second, to analyse the ideological implications of the persuasive devices identified in such context. The methods followed are Conceptual Metaphor Theory, Contemporary Theory of Metaphor, Critical Metaphor Analysis and MIPVU. The results will show how the author used figurative language to attack his opponents, discredit the opposition faction, shape the peace-war debate and support the Protestant succession; in short, to persuade the readership and reproduce ideologies.

Keywords: metaphor, metonymy, George Ridpath, *The Observator*, *The Flying Post; or, the Post-Master*

1 Introduction

Metaphors, metonymies and *conceptual complexes*[1] are essential in persuasive discourse as they influence the recipients' beliefs, attitudes and values by activating unconscious emotional associations and transferring the positive or negative

1 Conceptual complexes include *metaphorical amalgams* or single meaning-unit combinations of a metaphor with another metaphor, *metonymic amalgams* or combinations of a metonymy with another metonymy and *metaphtonymies* or combinations of a metaphor with a metonymy (Ruiz de Mendoza Ibáñez and Galera-Masegosa 2011: 1).

Raquel Sánchez Ruiz, University of Castilla-La Mancha, Departamento de Filología Moderna, Albacete, Spain.

https://doi.org/10.1515/9783110629460-012

correlations of the source to the target (Charteris-Black 2005: 13). By mediating between conscious and unconscious means of persuasion, a moral perspective on life (or ethos) occurs, which is "a central strategy for legitimisation in political speeches" (Charteris-Black 2005: 13). Hellín García (2009: 129) considers figurative language one of the most powerful linguistic devices employed by politicians of all nationalities, since it allows them "to develop persuasive arguments by applying what is familiar, and already experienced, to new topics to demonstrate that they are thinking rationally about political issues" (Charteris-Black 2011: 35). In fact, politicians' figurative, lexical choice and election of metaphors determines their leadership style, as it is a way to attract others to share a particular identity or reject ideas (Charteris-Black 2011: 312). Thus, figurative language, especially metaphors, contributes to the reproduction of ideologies as it may restructure concepts and opinions, and so build the social and political reality, as well as bring political changes (Kyratzis 2001: 64–65). Moreover, metaphorical conceptualisations do not only allow studying ideology, understood as "dominant discourse about a socially-culturally important subject matter that provides us with a particular perspective on that subject matter and also on other related subject matters" (Kövecses 2006: 151), but also reveal local culture, since they are determined by context, which is at the same time "characterized by physical, social, cultural, discourse, etc. aspects" (Kövecses 2010: 205).

Considering the above, this paper has two aims: to reveal the role figurative language plays in the construction of an alternative reality through which ideological persuasion occurs in the political writings of George Ridpath, particularly during the Peace Campaign (1710–1713) of the War of the Spanish Succession; and to analyse the social implications of the devices identified in terms of their influence on ideology and persuasion in such context. To assist in the interpretation of figurative language, I have relied on the frames of Conceptual Metaphor Theory first developed by Lakoff and Johnson (1980) and subsequently complemented by Kövecses (2010), the Contemporary Theory of Metaphor (Lakoff 1993, Steen 2011), Charteris-Black's Critical Metaphor Analysis (2004, 2011), Steen et al.'s (2010) MIPVU and polarisation (van Dijk 1998).

2 Theoretical framework

Conceptual Metaphor Theory propounds metaphors constitute a means to create, organise and understand reality and go beyond comparing two realities. Considering that human thought is based on metaphorical associations of concepts, speakers tend to relate those to their own experiences through figurative (metaphorical or metonymic) language to define them and, thus, conceptualise reality. This is essential in the analysis since the identification of potential "ideological intentions underlying metaphor choices through conceptual metaphor analysis" allows studying the influence of language use on persuasion (Charteris-Black 2011: 50).

From that viewpoint, Lakoff (1993: 203) understands metaphors as a set of conceptual and ontological correspondences between two domains: a *source domain*, belonging to a concrete reality, and a *target domain*, or the concept to be reified. According to the priority given to the values of the metaphorical construction, the reality presented might mask or reveal particular aspects through that conceptualisation (Crespo-Fernández 2008: 97). In the political sphere, this serves politicians' own interests and purposes because metaphorical expressions either help frame favourable arguments to the proposed case or put other issues into the background to conceal them (Charteris-Black 2011: 36). Therefore, figurative language connects with x-phemism insofar as euphemism has such power to veil or mask certain aspects and dysphemism assists in attacking the opponent either directly or indirectly through quasi-dysphemism.

Steen (2011: 59), following Lakoff's theory, redefines metaphor from a purely cognitive approach and offers a contemporary, three-dimensional model of metaphor: "metaphor may be theoretically defined as a matter of conceptual structure, but in empirical practice it works its wonders in language, communication and thought". This is also acknowledged by Charteris-Black (2005: 14), who attributes linguistic, pragmatic and cognitive characteristics to metaphors. The first characteristic refers to the semantic tension caused either by reification (use of concrete expressions for abstract concepts) or personification (giving animate qualities to inanimate concepts). Contrariwise, depersonification makes inanimate concepts seem animate (Charteris-Black 2004: 21). The second characteristic is essential in political argumentation as "it is motivated by the underlying purpose of persuading[,] [...] is often covert and reflects the speaker intentions within particular contexts of use" (Charteris-Black 2005: 15). Finally, the cognitive characteristic concerns the association between the source domain or original referent and the target domain, which is socially and culturally determined. "Therefore when these metaphors are used in politics they transfer a set of culturally based psychological associations and beliefs that we have about conflict on to political issues, thereby causing us to think about them in a new way" and so reproducing ideology (Charteris-Black 2005: 15). Kövecses (2010: 206) contributed to the contemporary understanding of metaphor by adding the notion of local context, by which one's selection of metaphors is linked to their own personality, experience, interests or vision of the world.

Metonymies are the association of two close entities inside the same conceptual domain. Ruiz de Mendoza Ibáñez (2000, cited in Ruiz de Mendoza Ibáñez and Galera Masegosa 2011: 5) categorises metonymies into: target-in-source, where a domain stands for one subdomain, and source-in-target, where "a subdomain stands for its corresponding matrix domain". Metonymies are particularly interesting in political speaking as they are ideologically more persuasive than metaphors for they tend to be more invisible (Charteris-Black 2011: 48). Due to their cognitive characteristics, the limits between metaphor and metonymy are sometimes fuzzy and so "metaphoric metonymies", which Goossens (1990: 323) called *metaphtonymies*, arise (Kövecses 2000: 38). Both devices have their origin in social and body experiences and resort to structures coming from the own body functions and perceptions (Lakoff 1987: 271–278).

Within this theory, different authors have classified metaphorical conceptualisations under different criteria. Considering that many conceptualisations are not based on everyday experience, Grady (1997) defined *primary* and *complex* metaphors. The latter are not directly motivated by correlations from experience but a combination of primary metaphors, indeed based on experience. Grady (1999) identified *correlation* and *resemblance metaphors* regarding the nature of the associations established in the metaphorical process. The former are based on the correlation between independent domains of experience which correlate in our minds easily (e.g., MORE IS UP). On the contrary, in resemblance metaphors, the source and target domains share some features which are non-literally perceived, as in PEOPLE ARE MACHINES (Lakoff and Johnson 1980: 132). Primary and correlation metaphors, as in THE BODY IS A CONTAINER, are the same, as the association between the two domains is based on experience.

There are other types of metaphors named and categorised differently. For example, Ruiz de Mendoza Ibáñez's (2000: 111–113) *multiple-correspondence metaphors* are Lakoff and Johnson's (1980) *structural metaphors*, where the source domain exports several correspondences to the target domain and, thus, are structured in a complex way (e.g., DEATH IS A JOURNEY). These same authors classified *ontological metaphors*, deriving from personal experience with physical objects, and *orientational metaphors*, organising a system of concepts in relation to one another and based on physical and cultural experience. Finally, *animal metaphor* is relevant in Ridpath's speech. This metaphor is included in *the Great Chain of Being* (Lakoff and Turner 1989: 166–181), a conceptual system under which all forms of life are organised from higher to lower: humans, animals, plants, complex objects and physical and natural things. Kövecses (2010: 201) states that "in the same way as animals can be metaphorically viewed as humans, humans can be viewed as animals". Even though this type of metaphors might seem ontological, because of the similarities between the two entities, animal metaphors are usually classified as *complex situational metaphors* (Ruiz de Mendoza Ibáñez and Pérez Hernández 2011: 166).

After having explained the types of metaphors found in the corpus, I move on to *Critical Metaphor Analysis*, which is a triphase process consisting in identifying metaphorical expressions and words used metaphorically, categorising them considering their linguistic content (source domain) and what they describe (target domain), and interpreting their meaning, ideologies and underlying messages (Charteris-Black 2011). In this study, this three-phase methodology is combined with the semantic-cognitive approach and complemented by a summary of the social context of the speeches and the verbal context of metaphors.

Finally, metaphor and metonymy are of paramount importance to *doublespeak* due to their ambiguity and expressive, persuasive power in political communication (Villagrá Terán 2011: 191–192). In fact, political metaphors, emotionally loaded owing to subjective association, are employed to positively or negatively represent a political party or opponent (polarisation or legitimation/delegitimation). *Legitimation* and *delegitimation* (Chilton 2004) correspond to van Dijk's *polarisation* (1998: 69), which is the construction of an ideological image of us/themselves and them/others for the positive self-presentation or legitimation of the ingroup and the negative other-presentation or delegitimation of the outgroup. These representations have social and cultural implications, since a value is given to the referent depending on such perceptions and so ideologies –"a self-serving schema for the representation of Us and Them as social groups"– are reproduced. Considering that ideology also "reflects Our fundamental social, economic, political or cultural interests" (van Dijk 1998: 69), figurative language can be used as a persuasive strategy to influence or even change others' behaviour and beliefs. However, metaphor and metonymy are a double-edged sword for they can be used against those who employ them, so intended legitimation might become delegitimation and vice versa (Charteris-Black 2011: 38).

3 Data and methods

The corpus consists of two periodicals (*The Observator* and *The Flying Post; or, the Post-Master*), 292 numbers and the four years of the Peace Campaign in the War of the Spanish Succession (1710–1713), when the press was an acknowledged organ of political influence (Crespo-Fernández and López Campillo 2011: 44). The choice of the author is not casual either, since despite his relevance, not much scholarly ink has been spilled over him. George Ridpath was a Scottish, anti-Catholic journalist, author of the abovementioned periodicals along with *The Medley*, who defended the Whig faction. Even though his political writings – such as his persuasive rhetoric (Crespo-Fernández and López Campillo 2011), his metaphors from 1709 to 1710 (Sánchez Ruiz and López Cirugeda 2015) or his use of evaluative adjectives and x-phemism from 1710 to 1713 (Sánchez Ruiz 2015, 2017) – have been studied, little attention has been paid to Ridpath's use of metaphor and metonymy during the Peace Campaign of the War of the Spanish Succession.

So as to analyse persuasion and underlying ideological intentions through figurative language, Charteris-Black's (2011) Critical Metaphor Analysis was employed. The three steps consist in identifying, interpreting and explaining figurative devices. The research methodology was also complemented by applying Steen et al.'s (2010: 25–26) bottom-up, systematic approach MIPVU (Metaphor identification procedure at VU University level), which means: finding metaphor-related words on a word-by-word basis and mark them as indirectly-metaphorically used, direct metaphor, implicit metaphor or metaphor flag. It must be also noted that when metaphors with the same source domain appeared in the same phrase, they were counted as a single metaphor. Likewise, when two or more source domains concurred in the same phrase, one was prioritised and counted as just one, particularly when the secondary use corresponded to another metaphor (Charteris-Black 2011: 60–61). A table per periodical was created to classify figurative devices employed in each year under the abovementioned criteria. In the analysis, examples are presented chronologically, per periodical, indicating the number in which they appear.

4 Historical and political background, George Ridpath and the periodicals

During the European conflict of the War of the Spanish Succession (1701–1713), political uncertainty reigned over both Great Britain and Spain. In Spain, the death of Charles II of Spain without an heir led to the struggle for power of the Austrian Habsburg and French Bourbon families. In Great Britain, such struggle was between Anne's – one of Charles II's nieces and his brother James's daughter, allegedly Catholic – and William and Mary's – a Dutch Protestant and another daughter of James – supporters. After their father had been deposed in the Glorious Revolution of 1698, William and Mary accessed the throne jointly. In 1702, when both had died and Britain was at war in the Grand Alliance, Anne became the queen of England, Scotland and Ireland.

In such scenario, Anne Stuart trusted the Tories in the first years of her government and distrusted the Whigs. Although the latter used their power to compel the queen to cease some Tory ministers from 1705 until 1708, she stood by the Tories' side eventually (López Campillo 2010: 79). By 1709, the population demanded the end of the War of the Spanish Succession, so the Tories defended the peace in Europe, even if it implied signing a treaty with France, to win the general election in 1710. The Tories' perspective was reflected in their slogan *Peace without Spain*. On the contrary, the Whigs thought that Great Britain could not sign a treaty with their French enemy, Louis XIV, to prevent Philip V from retaining the Spanish crown, so they advocated their slogan *No peace without Spain* (Losa Serrano and López Campillo 2007: 176). These negotiations towards achieving the mentioned peace, resulting in the Treaty of Utrecht in 1713, is known as the Peace Campaign (1710–1713). In a divided country, propaganda played a decisive role to manipulate public opinion towards each party's interests and vision of war.

In relation to the author, George Ridpath was an influential and controversial Scottish journalist and pamphleteer from the Whig faction. His anti-Catholic and Presbyterian actions, as well as his libels in *The Observator*, sentenced him to prison several times. *The Daily Post* of 7th February 1726 informed about Ridpath's death on the same day (5th February) as his old antagonist, Tory journalist Abel Roper. Both of them, along with Daniel Defoe and Charles Leslie wrote and published the most influential materials about the Anglo-Scottish issue during the reign of Anne Stuart (McLeod and McLeod 1979: ix). Moreover, Ridpath has proved to be relevant for the British public opinion since, while many supported either the Whigs or the Tories, some shifted sides due to the persuasion of the press. Nevertheless, swing voters usually preferred the Tories and only stood by the Whigs when a Catholic succession seemed in sight (Speck 1970: 114).

Ridpath started to write in *The Observator* after John Tutchin's death on 23rd September 1707. He also directed the Whig periodical *The Flying Post; or, the Post-Master* (onwards *The Flying Post*) and wrote for *The Medley* from 1712 (Wilson 1830: 253, 283). On the one hand, this first periodical, with its peculiar, dialogued structure, published two numbers a week and used to inform about the government's resolutions and accused them of their Jacobite and *Frenchfied* actions (López Campillo 2010: 155). In fact, it was the best opposition periodical (Swift 1711) and "the most important strictly political organ of the Whigs" (Trent 1952: 5). On the other hand, the triweekly *The Flying Post* was one of the best and most important periodicals, especially regarding news from Scotland (Dunton 1818: 428). While *The Flying Post* was more objective, providing with more data and information from abroad, *The Observator* was an opinion essay, so the language employed is close to literary articles and more persuasive devices can be found.[2]

2 For more information on the author or periodicals, see Sánchez Ruiz (2015: 112–114) and Sánchez Ruiz and López Cirugeda (2015: 399–400).

5 Results and discussion

5.1 *The Observator*, 1710–1712

The naval tradition of Great Britain originates resemblance metaphors. In 1710, the first source domain is ship. Ridpath uses PUBLIC CREDIBILITY IS A SHIP to affirm it is sinking due to the comments of publications such as *The Paris Gazetteer* against the nation (52, 54 and 56). In this same vein, in 1711, COMMERCE IS A SHIP the faction wants to sink for their own economic interests (34). In 1712, Ridpath employs the same metaphor to remark the French faction is doing their best to sink the national commerce (24).

In 1710 and 1711, resemblance metaphors also serve to point out Catholicism – represented as a burden or chains – intends to subjugate citizens through Popery and even slavery. In 1710, FRENCH POPERY AND SLAVERY ARE YOKES WREATHED AROUND BRITISH NECKS (IX97), a traditional image of slavery. Likewise, some victories of the nation have given them the opportunity to break the yoke the French king had prepared for the "neck of Europe" (61). Furthermore, one of the consequences of war is poverty and desolation in the country. In this sense, Ridpath concludes the POOR WILL BE A BURDEN *forever* because of the war (97). The use of hyperbole here contributes to reinforcing the persuasive sense of metaphor as it is intended to make an impression on readers through exaggeration. In this line, another resemblance metaphor: WAR IS A BURDEN, with a clear negative intention, is utilised to conceptualise this military conflict. Moreover, in 1711, slavery originated in religion appears again, since the sworn enemies of Liberty and true Christianity are using their joint endeavours to bring Europe under a yoke of bondage (33).

Within politics, metaphors take the human body as a source to create the *body politic* (Musolff 2010: 23). According to this author (2010: 25), this metaphorical conceptualisation implies the following: first, the body is complex and it can be separated into parts (e.g., dismembered, disembowel); second, the hierarchy of limbs, for instance, a toe nail does not have the same importance/centrality as the heart; and finally, the differentiation in health and sickness, as diagnosis, therapy, treatment or death follows. Metaphors and metonymies of this kind are fruitful, in fact the most common, in both periodicals.

In 1710, metonymy blends with metaphor to describe BLOOD IS A VALUABLE COMMODITY, where blood represents human life (59, 81). Thus, Ridpath employs this expression several times to remark the expensive cost of war for the country (IX99 and IX100). However, "theatre of blood and slaughter" is used to say providence is just with Spain and France (IX98). Likewise, THE HEAD IS A VALUABLE COMMODITY represents two human aspects: judgement and life. Other body parts, as in "the eyes of the nation are now so much opened" (62), are used to show they have knowledge of the French intentions. Metonymies where the part stands for the whole are included in source-in-target metaphors (Ruiz de Mendoza Ibáñez 2000: 122–123), which permit to cognitively expand the source domain allowing the access to the source domain from a particular perspective. Along with blood, in 1710, the most used body part is hands. For example, "having a hand in the transgressions" (8) criticises the faction's position towards Sacheverell. It is affirmed that "no man's eye or hand should foment a rebellion against the best of queens" (23), in which hands represent writers and sources of information through source-in-target metaphors.

There is a case of metonymic interaction where the cause stands for the effect in an already mentioned metaphor: COMMERCE IS A SHIP. Ridpath uses this conceptual combination to remark the faction's actions "break his heart" and they will lead to "the sinking of the bank-stock" (60). Catholicism is clearly rejected in examples like "his throat is not wide enough for swallowing Popery and slavery" (62). This body part also represents human lives, in expressions like "cut the throats" (4). The stomach forms other political images, such as "intestine divisions" (83) and "what a faction we have in our bowels" (IX99), but also "those who heard Dr. West's sermon had their stomachs so much turned" (8). In this same vein, "Spaniards' cruelties make their ears tingle and their hand stand on end" (IX98).

In 1711, publications and authors are usually represented by source-in-target metonymic projections related to the different body parts. For example, Ridpath criticises Abel Roper's way of informing by saying his "tongue is a great too big for his mouth" (83). Roper's mouth also trumpets falsehood through the nation (34) and the *Examiner*'s mouth is a source of notorious falsehood (100). Knowledge and judgement are metonymically represented through eyes. Thus, the observer prays God so that the nation "opens more their eyes to see the things that belong to their true peace" (99). He also asks "to set the *Examiner*'s head in its due posture, and remove the pins and webs out of his eyes" (30 and 34) and "to try to cure the blindness of the *Examiner*, Dr. Sacheverell and others of Abel's genuine sons of the church" (30). As Musolff (2010: 25) claimed, the heart symbolises the importance of something according to its hierarchy and centrality in the body, so the most relevant part of a place is "the heart of the capital" (61). In this year, blood symbolises ideologies, as in "Protestant blood" (103), or represents human lives, and so blood is a valuable commodity wasted at war (20, 32 and 102). Symbols of slavery, such as chains, are related to national political parties, as the Tories have enacted into a law to lock their chains around British necks (42). Finally, regarding this source domain, stomach and bowels equate with internal divisions because of war (100).

Ridpath uses the body politic (Musolff 2010: 23) in both periodicals to represent several concepts or groups. In 1711, despite each British citizen's individuality, Ridpath affirms "the body of the nation is universally against the Catholic pretender" (21). The unity of political parties is shown through expressions like "body of the Whigs" (49). Nevertheless, this metaphor is particularly fruitful inside the military world with "body of troops" (21).

In 1712, authors and sources are metonymically represented by different body parts. For instance, "Abel and his masters' foreheads are tipped with French metal" (14). The mouth usually represents the voice and beliefs of publishers, hence *The Observator*'s interest in stopping the mouths of the libellers (5). The heart is important to express emotions and true desires, as the French king has "war in his heart while he has peace in his mouth" (45) and "the *Examiner* and other libellers seem to have nothing so much at heart as to rail upon the confederates, and to create jealousies between them and the present ministry" (25). Eyes again represent human judgement, which is why the observer alludes to the necessity of opening the eyes of others who are resolved to wink hard or have a mist raised before them regarding the insolence of the Jacobite faction (50). Ridpath warns France's dexterity could dazzle the eyes of Her Britannic Majesty (6). Again, bowels are the image of the inner structure of the country, especially to point out the "intestine commotions at home" due to war (21). And the body politic is recurrent in this year as well through "body of troops" (47).

Fire is a common source domain symbolising hell for Christians. However, in 1710, fire does not represent hell, but exemplifies how "the moderation of Sacheverell's punishment does nothing at all lessen his crime, but on the contrary heaps coals of fire on the head of himself and his faction" (20). One of the physiological effects of being angry is increased body heat, hence the identification of fire with anger. This body reaction combined with the metonymic principle THE PHYSIOLOGICAL EFFECTS OF AN EMOTION STAND FOR THE EMOTION yields expressions like the abovementioned, based on the concurrence of two domains from experience which, though independent, correlate in our minds easily (Caballero 1999: 38). Contrariwise, in 1711, the real power of destruction of fire and its identification with hell – emphasised by the explicit allusion to God – originates expressions to desire "God in the course of his providence raises such a fire in the House of Bourbon, which has set all Europe in flames" (31). In line with this, in 1712, Ridpath hopes that an enquiry for Papists and other disaffected persons about town do not endanger the city by new flames (22).

Now I move on to the source domain of war, frequently used within political and persuasive debate to argue (Campos Vargas 2013: 50). In 1710, Ridpath states Sacheverell "breathed nothing but axes and halters against those who are not of arbitrary and tyrannical principles" (8). Warlike metaphors are essential for

Ridpath's persuasive intentions, since they help him represent the enemy/Tories/Catholics and the French King negatively through polarisation and so self-present the ingroup/Whigs/Protestants as a better option for the country.

Within the *Lakoffian* tradition, the notion of light is metaphorically used to convey positive messages (Crespo-Fernández 2013: 322). Whereas light represents knowledge, IDEAS ARE LIGHT SOURCES (Lakoff and Johnson 1999: 48), darkness symbolises ignorance and death. In 1710, LIGHT IS KNOWLEDGE when the observer admits a "matter seems to be set in a fair light by a letter in yesterday's *Flying Post*" (75). Contrariwise, the faction's works are said to be "those of the darkness" (34). Light-darkness is as related to van Dijk's polarisation (1998: 95) as peace-war, since the first term is used for positive self-presentation while the second is used for the negative representation of the opposition party. Lexical-semantic polarisations are an important strategy in political discourse as they clearly state whose group the receiver must choose or reject (Danler 2005: 52). In 1712, this precisely refers to the clear explanation the observer gives about the treaty of peace (15).

Planting is the image of negative intentions here. In 1711, DOCTRINES ARE SEEDS sown by those martyrs for High Church and cultivated by the Lesleys, Sacheverells, Higgins and Milburns (21). Seeds, thus, can be corrupted and so superstition and tyranny are harvested (23 and 57) and form the "root of despotic governments and arbitrary principles" (48).

Synesthesia is a neurological condition applicable to language to create cross-sensory metaphors or synesthetic metaphors, where discourse is voluntarily mixed with sensory or cognitive notions, especially colours and flavours. Ibarretxe-Antuñano (2011: 2) calls them *perception* or *sensory metaphors*, whose conceptual domain lies on perceptions: sight, hear, smell, touch and taste. In 1710, one of the most repeated images is associated to colours. These represent both religious and political beliefs: "faction in their proper colours" (15, 35), "flying colours" (20) and "if Sacheverell's speech be true, every man in England has lost the property of his native tongue [...], so that hence-forward we must call back white" (18). On the other hand, smell generally symbolises *dislikeable* feelings with a dysphemistic intention; concretely, bad smell or stink indicates bad character or repulsive features (Sweester 1990: 37, 43). In 1710, Ridpath affirms "while we have history in Great Britain, THE MEMORY OF PAPISTS WILL STINK and will be the execration of all [small caps mine]" (14) and SOME AUTHORS' RHYMES SMELL of the age of Sternhold and Hopkins (71). In this same line, in 1711, ABEL ROPER SMELLS SO RANK (34). Colours are also employed in this year, so "the Highflying Clergy acted so black a part in the tragedies of those times" (14), Sacheverell and the *Examiner* have their own colours (71) and they have to agree on "a better colour to enter upon it" (93) in the negotiation of peace with the French. In this year, taste is also used to talk about likes and dislikes (Ibarretxe-Antuñano 1999: 30) when Abel Roper's paper is presented as the salt which seasons the taste of the Jacobites (66). In 1712, synesthesia deals with sight – through colours –, taste and smell. First, A BAD ACTION/DECISION IS A BLACK STAIN (56). In fact, in other examples of the same year, black has the meaning Charteris-Black (2011: 71) attributes to darkness, as it is even explicitly associated to devil to talk about the *Examiner* (22 and 32). Moreover, colours do not only represent nations (14) but also the faction and their leaders who change colours and names as they please like a chameleon (22). Second, "French wine is sour and offends the stomach" (20). In this case two aspects merge: on the one hand, the wine is personified as it has the human capacity to offend and, on the other hand, a metonymy is used as a liquid standing for the nation that produces it and, by extension, its political and religious beliefs. Third and on this occasion, smell is used to stand positive aspects out, such as "gold smells never the worse" (38). Nevertheless, it is also employed to remark the French despicable behaviour, as "they stink in the nostrils of all men that wish well to liberty and religion" (21).

The last source domain analysed in this periodical is venom, which is linked to depersonification and the dysphemistic, ontological or resemblance metaphor: ENEMIES ARE ANIMALS, insofar as they sometimes constitute harmful plagues. Goatly (2006: 27) claims the derogatory metaphor HUMAN IS RODENT – HUMAN IS VERMIN here – portrays people as disgusting and harmful, in short, dangerous to society. In this sense, comparing people to despicable and dangerous animals leads to the necessity of eradicating them "for the safety of the community or even for humanity in general"; indeed, their elimination "is therefore not only justified, but also seen as a social and vital necessity" (Crespo-Fernández 2013: 318). Thus, in 1710, Ridpath affirms SACHEVERELL IS VENOM that spreads (13 and 30), which implies the necessity to eliminate it. Metonymies are also employed for this purpose: "Sacheverell's venomous tongue" (38). Not only is he the target of these metaphors, but also the "Jacobite fellows, who poison the country with their seditious speeches" (23) as well as the faction in general, "who diffuse their poison through the nation" (4, 8 and 13), and the usurpers, who poison the nation with their Evangelical principles (55) and try to poison the minds of the people with jealousies and prejudices against the House of Austria (IX99). In 1711, similar expressions are found for SOURCES AND AUTHORS ARE VENOM. For instance, the *Examiner* attacks the Duke of Marlborough "with all the venom he is capable to spit" (51). As this source is related to snakes, the dysphemistic purpose does not imply merely representing it as an animal, but as a reptile that slithers. This same periodical is not only considered a plague, but also a tumour that must be cut off from a country (22 and 49). Sacheverell and his false brethren have the capacity to pollute the nation (33), and the treasonable paper called *An Oath to an Invader* is considered "poison so industriously distributed" (70). In 1712, CATHOLICS ARE A PLAGUE to be eradicated (14) and the French are a disease that has infected the *Examiner*'s throat and lungs (20 and 32).

In 1710, dysphemistic metaphor blends with depersonification: TYRANTS ARE THE MEANEST INSECTS, which mainly refers to the French king, his power and his religion, Catholicism (77). In fact, THE FRENCH KING IS A TARANTULA AND A MAD DOG (61), and as it is a disgusting, dangerous animal, its elimination is justified. Other people, such as Sacheverell's supporters, are the target of this type of metaphor, and are considered "the same unhallowed sort of cattle" (24), which reinforces their lack of judgement represented by the behaviour of this kind of animals. What is more, SACHEVERELL'S FACTION ARE PAGAN BEASTS (24), so it justifies and legitimates the necessity of eliminating them for they are a danger to society. Likewise, Sacheverell is symbolised as a wolf in sheep's clothing, which remarks his falsehood and his evil intentions. In 1711, the term *plague* applies to the *Examiner* again. And in 1712, many depersonifications have the French king as their target. His arrogance and arbitrary power make him look like "a cock on his dunghill, raising his crest and clapping his wings" (14). Poultry is also used in relation to war: "the English hens have been too hard for our French cocks" (20). The image of a hen, usually linked to cowardice, is not casual, since it intensifies their victory as their conditions were worse in a principle. It also emphasises positive self-presentation by highlighting the victim's triumph and a superior rival's failure, either and in both cases if it is meant or if it is simply irony. Finally, the French and Jacobite faction are literally "a snake in the grass" (55); therefore, the animal metaphor is dysphemistically employed, especially considering it is a reptile that slithers.

In short, through the abovementioned figurative devices, Ridpath tries to persuade the British population to agree with his opinions and support the Whigs on the War of the Spanish Succession, especially regarding the Peace Campaign. For that, he remarks the opposite faction's negative characteristics and reinforces the sense of unity and community against what he considers a threat, that is, Tories, Catholics, the French, the Romans and all of those who support them, be them the mob, renowned people or publications.

5.2 *The Flying Post*, 1711–1713

In 1712, the first source domain to describe the situation in France due to war is ship: MONEY IS A SHIP, as in "the French funds are in a sinking condition" (3266). In 1713, the image of the sunken ship is also applied to the French, but this time to illustrate a mistaken military action in the Rhine (3405). Regarding the domain burden, all the examples used represent the same: WAR IS A BURDEN, not just *per se*, but also its consequences, like the increase on taxes (3405) and growing poverty (3402).

In this periodical, the most fruitful domain is body as well. In 1711, expressions related to military forces are especially prolific: body of hussars (3035), body of confederate troops (3040) and body of troops (3022 and 3058). Likewise, inside the body some parts stand out. For instance, the head describes authority, even inside the army (the head of his army, 3087). Another common aspect with the previous periodical is using metonymies to identify authors and sources. Thus, “letters from good hands” (3100) is employed to present reliable sources.

In 1712, the most frequent phrase refers to military forces: body of hussars (3229), body of troops (3242., 3243, 3261, 3266, 3280, 3284), body of Muscovites (3241), body of Savoyards (3258), body of the enemy (3226, 3256), body of men (3247), body of Spain (3307), body of the Earl of Albermale (3235) and body of German plenipotentiaries (3313). Within the persuasive message of the different authors, Sacheverell employs metonymy to compare his intentions and the French king’s, so while great Louis claims their bodies, Sacheverell their souls (3246). The heart also appears in this year, especially and traditionally linked to emotions and passions. Therefore, this image is used to remark the “hardness of heart of the French tyrant” (3210) and the “mischief in the enemies’ hearts” (3210). Furthermore, metonymic expressions stand for sources and authors again. By way of illustration, take the following examples: “perhaps in a free country it was neither right nor safe to restrain the tongues and pens of men” (3288) or “the following letter from Paris comes from a very good hand” (3240) and “there’s advice from good hands in the north” (3286). However, as it happened inside the military organisation, writers also symbolise the head of periodicals. The choice of this precise part is not casual, as its main function is to think. Thus, LEADERS ARE HEADS, in this case Abel Roper; although it also applies to religion, as in “to be at the head of the Protestant interest” (3270).

Finally in relation to this domain, in 1713, body also represents military forces (3332, 3338, 3355, 3366, 3380, 3382, 3386, 3391, 3396, 3400 and 3407). Likewise, a *metaphtonymy* employed in *The Observator* can be found here, as the term *blood* stands for humans and its loss remarks human lives wasted in the battlefield (3325 and 3369). Perception metaphors related to blindness are applied to groups such as the king of Prussia or Protestants, who can now open their eyes once they have listened to Ridpath’s explanations (3347, 3361 and 3392). Metonymies also apply to authors and sources here, when Roger asks the observer to stop Abel’s and the *Examiner*’s ungrateful mouths with his lines (3329). Hands can both refer to reliable sources (3328 and 3401) or wicked hands, that is, the *Examiner* and Abel Roper (3325).

The domain of light only appears in 1713, precisely the year that the peace was signed. Ridpath utilises the structural metaphor LIGHT IS KNOWLEDGE (Charteris-Black 2011: 71) to refer to his arguments in relation to his adversaries (3325). On the contrary, unknown situations or negative comments are bond to darkness, as happens with the peace with France (3385) or journeys in France (3335).

Another repeated domain in this periodical is planting. In 1712, there is just one example, which opposes to COMMERCE IS A [SUNKEN] SHIP to a certain extent, that is, COMMERCE IS A PLANT that flourishes (3262), which offers hope within the framework of a just ended war and the necessity for the nation to prosper. This same metaphor is found in 1713, when the peace was signed (3384). Therefore, together with light, these two domains are employed to convey a positive message regarding the end of the war. Furthermore, other images appear, such as FRIENDSHIP IS A PLANT, which must be grown and looked after daily, especially in times of social and political instability and war (3351). In these same terms, PEACE IS A PLANT that must be maintained with necessary and appropriate actions (3362).

The domain of position pertains to Lakoff and Johnson's (1980: 15) *orientational metaphors*. In 1712, PROTECTION IS DOWN indicates Ragoski's envoy is protected by France (3257), and in 1713 this same expression refers to protection of the Cossacks by Turkey (3398).

Along with the body, senses create synesthetic or perception metaphors, and both constitute the most fruitful domains in the two periodicals and six years analysed. Thus, the opposite faction's designs are black (3308), and so linked to evil forces associated to darkness (Charteris-Black 2011: 71). Colours also represent nations and political beliefs (3242). Additionally, as Sweester (1990: 37, 43) indicated, stinking represents bad character or repulsive features, as with the *Examiner*, whose stuff is considered nauseous (3285). In 1713, the adjectives *nauseous* and *stinking* apply to matters related to the French (3390). Likewise, black is associated to authors like Abel Roper, "who can easily turn black into white" and vice versa (3355). The Clergy and Sacheverell are accused of casting "black and odious colours upon his late Majesty King William" (3362). And black also symbolises the "calumnies of the enemies" (3348) and the "treasons prompted by the most dangerous seducers" (3363).

In 1713, "cruelty has cost the lives of so many poor innocents" (3328). Therefore, LIFE IS A VALUABLE COMMODITY, even enemies' lives (3406). This same conceptualisation merges with an already mentioned metonymy related to blood, which stands for human life: "the siege cost much blood" (3399) and "the neutrality cost our ancestors so much blood" (3405).

The last domain in this periodical is venom again, to vindicate the eradication of enemies as a social duty (Goatly 2006: 27). In 1711, the resemblance metaphor THE ENEMY IS A PLAGUE in the north (3040) is employed to justify its elimination. In 1712, Catholicism is spread as an infectious illness (3279). In 1713, DR. SACHEVERELL'S SERMONS ARE POISON to the nation (3362) and "the idolatry of Rome intoxicates" those who support it (3334). As Crespo-Fernandez (2013: 320) observed, emphasising the negative features of the referent being dealt with is a strategy so that the reader, through polarisation, chooses the group which is positively self-presented and rejects the one negatively presented (Danler 2005: 52), and to persuade the readership to agree with the author, reinforcing a sense of unity and community against a common threat. This is connected to Charteris-Black's (2011: 15) rhetoric devices, that is, those the speaker uses to engage emotionally with the audience through empathy and so persuade the recipient by heightening the emotional impact and sounding right in the right emotional climate. Finally, in this year, Ridpath employs a conceptualisation already used in *The Observator* to refer to Henry Sacheverell, that is, "to be dressed in animal skins" (3325). He also compares the Tories to "shock dogs" (3361), in both cases with a clear dysphemistic intention.

6 Concluding remarks

As Crespo-Fernández (2013: 328) found, political leaders know the language they use has "a tremendous potential for mass persuasion and a profound impact on how social and political phenomena are perceived". Therefore, language is a powerful tool for politicians not only to persuade the public opinion in favour of their interests (van Dijk's positive self-presentation or Chilton's legitimation), but also against their opponents (negative other-presentation or delegitimation).

Under these premises, and as Crespo-Fernández and López Campillo (2011: 60–61) demonstrated, Ridpath employs different devices, especially figurative language, and his characteristic "emotionally loaded language of patriotism" to attack his opponents, to denounce what he believes to be unfair within the political sphere and to persuade the reader to agree with his opinions and beliefs; thus, to reproduce ideologies.

Regarding the use of figurative language, the persuasive power of metaphor, metonymy or conceptual complexes is reinforced if the devices blend with hyperbole, as the latter leaves a mark on the reader through exaggeration. Moreover, metaphor and metonymy are frequently linked to dysphemistic purposes, as the analysis shows. The study also contributes to proving that metaphor, metonymy and *metaphtonymy* as well as personification/depersonification are essential within political communication since these devices allow legitimating the own group (positive self-presentation) or delegitimating the opponent (negative other-presentation). Consequently, it can be claimed that metaphorical language plays a relevant role in the creation of meaning, the understanding of reality and verbal attack, so typical and frequent in political discourse.

Concerning Ridpath's use of figurative language, in line with Sánchez Ruiz and López Cirugeda's 2015 work, I can conclude that the author's persuasive intentions are: (a) discrediting the opposition faction's or the enemy's sources and authors, mainly Abel Roper, Daniel Defoe, Henry Sacheverell, the *Examiner* and the *Review*, which would self-present Ridpath and his periodical in a positive way through polarisation; (b) shaping the peace-war debate along the historical conflict according to the Whig – who he is in favour of – or Tory ideologies and their political campaigns; and (c) supporting the Protestants in the succession issue against the Catholics.

Finally, this study has focused on the analysis of figurative devices employed by Ridpath during the Peace Campaign of the War of the Spanish Succession to persuade the readers to agree with his opinions, support a Protestant succession against the Catholics and the French and side with the Whigs. Due to the limited scope of this paper and the logical space limitations, I have not been able to analyse the influence of figurative language or metaphor mapping on people's mentality in the eighteenth century. Therefore, this could be the starting point of further research. It would also be interesting to analyse other persuasive devices employed by Ridpath and compare them with other authors and periodicals to have a complete view of the Peace Campaign and the public opinion of that time from diverse political perspectives.

References

Caballero, Rosario. 1999. What's in a title? The strategic use of metaphor and metonymy in *Some Like it Hot*. *Journal of English Studies* 1. 26–43.

Campos Vargas, Henry. 2013. El miedo en la argumentación: Una aproximación ética [Fear in argumentation: An ethical approach]. *Revista Ciencias Sociales* 141. 49–59.

Charteris-Black, Jonathan. 2004. *Corpus approaches to Critical Metaphor Analysis*. New York: Palgrave MacMillan.

Charteris-Black, Jonathan. 2005. *Politicians and rhetoric. The persuasive power of metaphor*. New York: Palgrave MacMillan.

Charteris-Black, Jonathan. 2011. *Politicians and rhetoric. The persuasive power of metaphor*. New York: Palgrave MacMillan.

Chilton, Paul. 2004. *Analysing political discourse. Theory and practice*. London: Routledge.

Crespo-Fernández, Eliecer. 2008. Sex-related euphemism and dysphemism: An analysis in terms of Conceptual Metaphor Theory. *Atlantis* 30 (2). 95–110.

Crespo-Fernández, Eliecer. 2013. Words as weapons for mass persuasion: Dysphemism in Churchill's wartime speeches. *Text & Talk* 33 (3). 311–330.

Crespo-Fernández, Eliecer & Rosa María López Campillo. 2011. Persuasive rhetoric in George Ridpath's political writings. *ES Revista de Filología Inglesa* 32. 43–67.
Danler, Paul. 2005. Morpho-syntactic and textual realizations as deliberate pragmatic argumentative textual tools? In Louis de Saussure & Peter Schultz (eds.), *Manipulation and ideologies in the twentieth century*, 45–60. Amsterdam: John Benjamins.
Dunton, John. 1818. *The life and errors of John Dunton, citizen of London with the lives and characteristics of more than a thousand contemporary divines, and other persons of literary eminence. Vol. II.* London: J. Nichols, son, and Bentley.
Goatly, Andrew. 2006. Humans, animals, and metaphors. *Society & Animals* 14 (1). 15–37.
Goossens, Louis. 1990. Metaphtonymy: The interaction of metaphor and metonymy in expressions for linguistic action. *Cognitive Linguistics* 3 (1). 323–340.
Grady, Joseph Edward. 1997. *Foundations of meaning: Primary metaphors and primary scenes.* Berkeley, CA: University of California dissertation.
Grady, Joseph Edward. 1999. A typology of motivation for conceptual metaphor: Correlation vs. resemblance. In Raymond W. Gibbs & Gerard Steen (eds.), *Metaphor in cognitive linguistics*, 79–100. Amsterdam: John Benjamins.
Hellín García, María José. 2009. Fight metaphors in Spain's Presidential speeches: J.L. Rodríguez Zapatero (2004–2007). *Revista Alicantina de Estudios Ingleses* 22. 127–153.
Ibarretxe-Antuñano, Iraide. 1999. Metaphorical mappings in the sense of smell. In Raymond W. Gibbs & Gerard J. Steen (eds.), *Metaphor in cognitive linguistics*, 29–45. Amsterdam: John Benjamins.
Ibarretxe-Antuñano, Iraide. 2011. Metáforas de la percepción: Una aproximación desde la lingüística cognitiva [Perception metaphors. An approach from cognitive linguistics]. In Cristián Santibáñez Yáñez & Jorge Osorio Baeza (eds.), *Recorridos de la metáfora: cuerpo, espacio y diálogo*, 1–18. Concepción: Cosmigonon Editorial.
Kövecses, Zoltán. 2000. *Metaphor and emotion.* Cambridge: Cambridge University Press.
Kövecses, Zoltán. 2006. Metaphor and ideology in slang: the case of WOMAN and MAN. *Revue d'Études Françaises* 11. 151–166.
Kövecses, Zoltán. 2010. Metaphor and culture. *Acta Universitatis Sapientiae, Philologica* 2 (2). 197–220.
Kyratzis, Sakis. 2001. Politicians on drugs: Functions of political metaphors across cultures. In Magda Stroinska (ed.), *Relative points of view. Linguistic representations of culture*, 61–80. New York: Berghahn Books.
Lakoff, George. 1987. *Women, fire and dangerous things: What categories reveal about the mind.* Chicago: The University of Chicago Press.
Lakoff, George. 1993. The Contemporary Theory of Metaphor. In Andrew Ortony (ed.), *Metaphor and thought*, 202–251. Cambridge: Cambridge University Press.
Lakoff, George & Mark Johnson. 1980. *Metaphors we live by.* Chicago: The University Chicago Press.
Lakoff, George & Mark Johnson. 1999. *Philosophy in the flesh: Embodied mind and its challenge to western thought.* New York: Basic Books.
Lakoff, George & Mark Turner. 1989. *More than cool reason: A field guide to poetic metaphor.* Chicago: The University of Chicago Press.
López Campillo, Rosa María. 2010. *Daniel Defoe y la Guerra de Sucesión Española* [Daniel Defoe and the War of the Spanish Succession]. Ann Arbor: ProQuest.
Losa Serrano, Pedro & Rosa María López Campillo. 2007. La Guerra de Sucesión Española: Swift, Defoe y la campaña para la paz [The War of the Spanish Succession: Swift, Defoe and the Peace Campaign]. *Revista Estudis* 33. 175–192.

McLeod, William R. & V. B. McLeod. 1979. *Anglo-Scottish tract, 1701–1714. A descriptive checklist compiled by W. R. and V.B. McLeod*. Lawrence, KS: University of Kansas Publications.
Musolff, Andreas. 2010. Political metaphor and *bodies politic*. In Urszula Okulska & Piotr Cap (eds.), *Perspectives in politics and discourse*, 23–41. Amsterdam: John Benjamins.
Ridpath, George. 1709–1710. *The Observator. Eighth Volume*. London: B. Bragge.
Ridpath, George. 1710. *The Observator. Ninth Volume*. London: B. Bragge/R. Janemay/ S. Popping.
Ridpath, George. 1711. *The Observator. Tenth Volume*. London: S. Popping.
Ridpath, George. 1711. *The Flying Post: or, the Post-master, 3032–3146*. London: William Hurt.
Ridpath, George. 1711–1712. *The Observator. Eleventh Volume*. London: S. Popping/ William Hurt.
Ridpath, George. 1712. *The Flying Post: or, the Post-master, 3186–3316*. London: William Hurt.
Ridpath, George. 1713–1714. *The Flying Post: or, the Post-master, 3319–3434*. London: William Hurt.
Ruiz de Mendoza Ibáñez, Francisco José. 2000. The role of mappings and domains in understanding metonymy. In Antonio Barcelona (ed.), *Metaphor and metonymy at the crossroads*, 109–132. Berlin & New York: De Gruyter Mouton.
Ruiz de Mendoza Ibáñez, Francisco José & Alicia Galera Masegosa. 2011. Going beyond metaphtonymy: Metaphoric and metonymic complexes in phrasal verb interpretation. *Language Value* 3 (1). 1–29.
Ruiz de Mendoza Ibáñez, Francisco José & Lorena Pérez Hernández. 2011. The Contemporary Theory of Metaphor: Myths, developments and challenges. *Metaphor and Symbol* 26. 161–185.
Sánchez Ruiz, Raquel. 2015. George Ridpath's use of evaluative adjectives as manipulative and persuasive strategies during the War of the Spanish Succession (1710–1713). *Journal of English Studies* 13. 109–134.
Sánchez Ruiz, Raquel. 2017. Euphemism and dysphemism during the War of the Spanish Succession (1710–1713): George Ridpath. *Cuadernos de Investigación Filológica* 43. 7–31.
Sánchez Ruiz, Raquel & Isabel López Cirugeda. 2015. Persuasion and manipulation through conceptual metaphors in George Ridpath's political writings (1707–1709). *US-China Foreign Language* 13 (6). 397–411.
Speck, William A. 1970. *Tory and Whig. The struggle in the constituencies 1701–1715*. London: MacMillan.
Steen, Gerard. 2011. The Contemporary Theory of Metaphor – now new and improved! *Review of Cognitive Linguistics* 9 (1). Special issue, Francisco Gonzálvez-García, María Sandra Peña Cervel & Lorena Pérez Hernández (eds.), *Metaphor and metonymy revisited beyond the Contemporary Theory of Metaphor*, 26–64. Amsterdam: John Benjamins.
Steen, Gerard J., Aletta G. Dorst, J. Berenike Herrmann, Anna A. Kaal, Tina Krennmayr & Trijntje Pasma. 2010. *A method for linguistic metaphor identification: From MIP to MIPVU*. Amsterdam: John Benjamins.
Sweester, Eve. 1990. *From etymology to pragmatics. Metaphorical and cultural aspects of semantic structure*. Cambridge: Cambridge University Press.
Swift, Jonathan. 1711. *Examiner*, 42 (17 May 1711).
Trent, W. P. 1952. Defoe. The newspaper and the novel. In Adolphus W. Ward & Alfred R. Waller (eds.), *The Cambridge history of English literature*, 1–25. Cambridge: Cambridge University Press.

van Dijk, Teun A. 1998. *Ideology. A multidisciplinary approach.* London: Sage Publications Ltd.
Villagrá Terán, María Monserrat. 2011. Análisis y didáctica del léxico perteneciente al lenguaje político [Analysis and teaching of the lexicon of political language]. Paper presented at VIII Encuentro práctico de ELE, Cervantes Institute of Naples, 29 October.
Wilson, Walter. 1830. *Memoirs or the life and times of Daniel De Foe: Containing a review of his writings and his opinions upon a variety of important matters, civil and ecclesiastical.* London: Hurst, Chance and Co.

Part III: **Metaphor analysis in multimodal discourse**

Elżbieta Górska

Spatialization of abstract concepts in cartoons. A case study of verbo-pictorial image-schematic metaphors

Abstract: In cognitive linguistics, spatialization of abstract concepts has been extensively studied in grammar and lexicon, forming one of the crucial assumptions on the spatial foundations of language (Heine 1997; Johnson 1987; Lakoff 1987; Langacker 1987). In Conceptual Metaphor Theory this issue has been commonly addressed on the basis of linguistic data alone (Kövecses 2000; Lakoff and Johnson 1980, 1999). In this paper, taking a multimodal approach to metaphor (Cienki and Müller 2008; Forceville and Urios-Aparisi 2009; Górska 2010, 2014a; Müller 2008a), I will focus on spatialization of abstract concepts (such as HAPPINESS, LOVE, WISDOM and STUPIDITY) in cartoons by means of metaphors that evoke an image schema or an image schema complex as their source domain and whose function is to highlight some aspect or aspects of these abstract concepts. The cartoons selected for this study are all by Janusz Kapusta (2014), a Polish artist. It is argued that they are a valuable source of insights into the relationship between space, cognition and language. The study provides supportive evidence for the claim that spatialization of abstract ideas in the visual medium may be independent from how such ideas are expressed verbally. This finding corroborates the results of gesture studies (Cienki and Müller 2008; Mittelberg 2010; Müller et al. 2013; Müller 2017), strengthening the view that metaphor, as a conceptual mechanism, has its manifestations not only in the verbal mode, but also in other modalities. Since the cartoons also rely on the verbal medium, they offer additional insights into multimodal representations of abstracts concepts, and the dynamic activation of metaphoricity.

Keywords: conceptual metaphor, multimodality, image schemas, spatialization of thought, cartoons, creativity

Elżbieta Górska, University of Warsaw, Institute of English Studies, Warszawa, ul. Hoża 69

https://doi.org/10.1515/9783110629460-013

1 Introduction

In cognitive linguistics, spatialization of abstract concepts has been extensively studied in grammar and lexicon, forming one of the crucial assumptions on the spatial foundations of language (see Correa-Beningfield et al. 2005; Evans and Chilton 2010; Heine 1997; Ibarretxe-Atuñano 2017; Johnson 1987; Lakoff 1987; Langacker 1987; Talmy 1983, 2003). In Conceptual Metaphor Theory spatial underpinnings of abstract target concepts have been commonly addressed on the basis of linguistic data alone (see, e.g., Kövecses 2000; Lakoff 1993; Lakoff and Johnson 1980, 1999). Building on this tradition, numerous studies of multimodal discourse have extended the research on spatialization of abstract concepts to include not only language, but also advertisements, gesture, comics, cartoons, music, film, and dance (see, e.g., Cienki 1998b; Forceville 1996, 2016, 2017; Forceville and Paling 2018; Górska 2010, 2014a, b, 2017a, b, 2018; Mittelberg 2010; Müller 2008a, b, 2017; Müller and Cienki 2009; Ortiz 2011, 2014; Zbikowski 2006, 2008; see also Forceville and Urios-Aparisi 2009a; Pinar Sanz 2013). Following this line of research, I will focus on the spatialization of abstract concepts (such as LOVE, PAIN, HAPPINESS, WISDOM, STUPIDITY, WORRIES) in cartoons by means of image-schematic metaphors, i.e. metaphors that evoke an image schema or an image schema complex as their source domain and whose function is to highlight some aspect or aspects of the target concept. Image schemas, let us also recall, are, in terms of their original conception (Johnson 1987; Lakoff 1987), prelinguistic patterns of sensory-motor experience which emerge from (or are grounded in) our bodily interactions with the environment, of which bodily movement through space, perceptual interactions, and manipulation of objects play a crucial role.[1] Experientially, image schemas often cluster together, hence the activation of image schemas clusters/complexes in metaphorical mappings is also common (Cienki 1997).

Given the cross-modal nature of image schemas (and their grounding in multisensory experience), their cross-modal activation in cartoons that dwell upon abstract ideas via verbal and pictorial means is by no means surprising. And, with respect to Lakoff's (1990) *Invariance Hypothesis*, it is only natural to expect that the inferencing about abstract concepts considered in this study will be a multimodal metaphorical version of spatial inferencing inherent in the image-schematic structuring of a particular source domain. It needs to be noted also that, following Forceville and Urios-Aparisi, I assume that a defining characteristic of a multimodal metaphor is that its "target and source are rendered exclusively or

1 For more on image schemas see Hampe (2005c) and Johnson (2007); subsequent additions to Johnson's (1987) original list of image schemas are reviewed by Hampe (2005a).

predominantly in two different modes/modalities" (Forceville and Urios-Aparisi 2009b: 4).[2] In this article, I will concentrate on the image-schematic structure of the cartoons, and other aspects of meaning construction (such as the creation of emergent concepts) will not be considered. For the present purpose, suffice it to clarify that I assume a multispace model of the Blending Theory (Brandt and Brandt 2005; Fauconnier and Turner 1998, 2002) and in these terms the discussed image schemas would capture the structure and organization of the verbal and/or the visual inputs, and define numerous correspondences between them.

The cartoons selected for this study are all by Janusz Kapusta, a Polish artist, whose works were originally published in a Polish weekly *Plus-Minus*, yet my data sample comes from a recently published book by Janusz Kapusta (2014) which marked the 10th anniversary of his weekly collaborations with this magazine. It comprises over 300 cartoons, out of about 500 published during this ten year period. Let me add that Janusz Kapusta has been living in New York since 1981, and since then his work has been also regularly published in, among others, *The New York Times*, *The Wall Street Journal*, and *The Washington Post*.

2 Verbo-pictorial image-schematic metaphors in Janusz Kapusta's cartoons

Let us first consider some aspects of the cartoons' structure, taking the cover of the book from which my data come as their exemplification.

© Janusz Kapusta

2 The terms mode and modality, as is common in the literature on the subject, are used here interchangeably (see Forceville and Urios-Aparisi 2009b: 4).

The cartoons always have a protagonist whose shape, as the cover indicates, reminds of a Buddha or a chess pawn who formulates a caption that is, as a rule, represented above the protagonist's head and linked to it by a short line segment (on the cover it points to the title *Plus-Minus*). As an enlightened sage (a Buddha) or an everyman (a pawn), the protagonist dwells upon a whole range of issues, including various aspects of human life and human condition, religion, politics and the world and universe at large. Functionally, the captions may be regarded as "speech balloons" or "thought bubbles", with the little line segment playing a role of a semiotic tool for interfacing the verbal and the pictorial. In accordance with the convention of the genre it is expected that the verbally and the pictorially expressed messages be interpreted in terms of each other so that each cartoon would constitute a single coherent communicative act.

Relying on the conception of two geometric shapes, the first cartoon provides an excellent example of how the affordances of the visual medium allow for a simultaneous activation of a number of image-schematic metaphorical source domains which may, but need not be activated verbally and, in effect, for enriching our understanding of the metaphorical target concepts that are evoked in the caption.

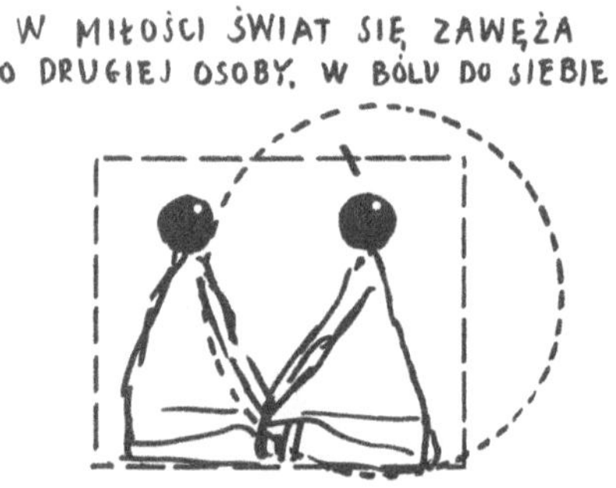

Example 1: *W miłości świat się zawęża do drugiej osoby, w bólu do siebie* 'In love the world narrows to another person, in pain to oneself' (Kapusta 2014: 27, transl. E.G.)[3]

The cartoon visualizes the contrast between the concepts of LOVE and PAIN by means of our knowledge about bounded spaces, known as the CONTAINER (Johnson 1987, 2007) or the BOUNDED SPACE (Lakoff and Turner 1989) image

3 All the cartoons are reprinted here with Janusz Kapusta's permission. I would like to express my thanks to the author for granting his permission to me.

schema: the emotional state of LOVE is depicted as the enclosure of two people within a rectangle, while the physical sensations of PAIN as the enclosure of a single person (the protagonist) within a circle. The metaphors which provide interpretation to this aspect of the cartoon are thus a multimodal creative reworking of the conventional metaphor: STATES ARE LOCATIONS (CONTAINERS/BOUNDED SPACES) (Lakoff 1993). In both cases the target concepts are expressed verbally, while the image-schematic source domain is evoked in the drawing by the two geometric shapes and in the caption by the preposition *w* 'in' which profiles a bounded space. For our purpose, the multimodal metaphors can be stated as: LOVE IS AN ENCLOSURE OF TWO PEOPLE WITHIN A RECTANGLE and PAIN IS AN ENCLOSURE OF AN INDIVIDUAL WITHIN A CIRCLE. Note also that the way the two geometric shapes are represented has an effect on how the two states are related to one another. From the spatial overlap of the circle and the rectangle in the drawing we can infer that being in love with someone can coincide with experiencing pain on our own. In turn, the shape of the circle itself may also serve to enrich the interpretation of the target concept of PAIN: since the circle evokes the simplest CYCLE schema (Johnson 1987: 119), the recurrence of this state may be expected. On the other hand, the fact that two figures depicting people in love are drawn as spatially very close and partly overlapping may serve to evoke a number of conventional metaphors of LOVE, namely: LOVE IS BOND, LOVE IS PROXIMITY, LOVE IS UNITY (Kövecses 2000: 26–28), whose source domains are also image-schematic in nature, and they reside in the activation of, respectively: the LINK, NEAR-FAR, and the PART-WHOLE image schema (Johnson 1987: 126). It may be argued further that the representation of the shapes of the rectangle and the circle by means of the broken line is also meaningful – in the respective target domains it may cue the temporariness of the two states.

Observe now that a different aspect of the target concepts is highlighted in the caption – by means of the causative verb *zawężać (do)* '(to cause to) narrow (to)' the verbal mode portrays these two states as causal forces which bring about the visually depicted "results", i.e. the two kinds of enclosures are the effect of the respective states causing the world (as it is experienced by an individual) to narrow down. Under this interpretation, the verbal mode evokes two conventional image-schematic metaphors: EMOTIONS/PHYSICAL SENSATIONS ARE FORCES and (EMOTIONAL) CAUSES ARE FORCES (Kövecses 2000: 83–85). In brief, the spatialization of the two abstract concepts in this cartoon rests on a complex interplay of image schemas that are evoked in the pictorial and verbal modes. The affordances of the visual mode allow for a straightforward realization of a number of image schemas, namely: the BOUNDED SPACE, CYCLE, LINK, NEAR-FAR, and the PART-WHOLE, while the image schema of FORCE (Talmy 1988), whose spatialization in the visual mode would be more difficult in this context,[4] is cued in the verbal mode only.

It needs to be observed at this point that, in terms of Müller's (2008a, b; 2017) dynamic approach to metaphor, co-expression of an aspect of meaning in different modalities functions as one of the "metaphoricity indicators",[5] whose amount is correlated with the metaphor's activation level. The latter assumption rests on the idea of iconic coding and the context of interaction. Specifically, it is assumed that the more cues direct the attention of the interlocutors to the metaphoric quality of an expression, the higher the degree of cognitive activation of metaphoricity in the producer and also potentially in the addressee. As Cienki and Müller put it: "clusters of attention-getting cues produce interactive foregrounding of metaphoricity and since what is interactively foregrounded is also interpersonally foregrounded, metaphoricity should in these cases be highly activated interpersonally" (2008: 495). Arguing along these lines we can expect that, in the case of the first cartoon, the BOUNDED SPACE schema has the highest degree of activation, since it is cued in the two modes (cf. visually – by the rectangle and the circle, and verbally – by the preposition *w* 'in') while the remaining schemas are cued monomodally and, therefore, their level of activation is much lower. This would imply also that the two creative multimodal metaphors which evoke the BOUNDED SPACE schema, namely, LOVE IS AN ENCLOSURE OF TWO PEOPLE WITHIN A RECTANGLE and PAIN IS AN ENCLOSURE OF AN INDIVIDUAL WITHIN A CIRCLE have the highest level of metaphoricity.

To see the relative contribution of each of the two modes to a multimodal characterization of HAPPINESS and UNHAPPINESS in example 2, let us first consider the caption, which reads: *Szczęście to linia rozpięta nad przepaścią, nieszczęście to przepaść rozpostarta pod liną*. 'Happiness is a line spread across/over a precipice, unhappiness is a precipice extending under/below a rope' (Kapusta 2014: 26, transl. E.G.). The prepositions *nad* 'across/over' and *pod* 'under/below' together with the noun *przepaść* 'precipice' cue the UP/DOWN (or, the VERTICALITY) schema. It is clear also that the verbal mode follows the basic logic of this schema: HAPPINESS is portrayed as UP while UNHAPPINESS as DOWN and, in effect, the evaluation of the two emotional states is motivated by the conventional

4 The term context is used here in a broad sense and, in particular, it may refer to both the verbal and the pictorial cuing of the source or target of a metaphor; for more on this topic see, e.g., Müller (2008a: 207, 2017).

5 According to Müller metaphoricity indicators include "verbal elaboration [of a metaphor, E.G.], specification, semantic opposition, syntactic integration, or coexpression of a metaphor in a co-occurring modality such as gesture or pictures" (2008a: 198). For more on this topic see Kolter et al. 2012; Górska 2014a, 2017b, 2018 .

metaphors: POSITIVE IS UP and NEGATIVE IS DOWN.[6] Note also that the caption introduces the notion of bounding: on the one hand, *przepaść* 'precipice' profiles a bounded area and, on the other hand, *linia* 'line' and *lina* 'rope', since they are portrayed as extending above it occupy a limited spatial expanse (cf. the expressions *linia rozpięta nad przepaścią* 'a line spread across/over the precipice' and *przepaść rozpostarta pod liną* 'precipice extending under/below a rope'). In brief, the verbal mode provides cues for the BOUNDED SPACE schema which may be evoked as the source domain for conceiving the two emotional states in terms of the conventional metaphor which has been already mentioned, namely STATES ARE LOCATIONS (BOUNDED SPACES/CONTAINERS).

Though highly schematic, the drawing contributes a lot of content to this multimodal communicative act.

Example 2: *Szczęście to linia rozpięta nad przepaścią, nieszczęście to przepaść rozpostarta pod liną*. 'Happiness is a line spread across/over a precipice, unhappiness is a precipice extending under/below a rope' (Kapusta 2014: 26, transl. E.G.)

Holding in his hands a line that represents HAPPINESS the protagonist is standing on a rope, as if trying to keep balance on it so that he does not fall down into the precipice of UNHAPPINESS. It may be argued that the spatialization of the two

6 Relying on a common association of the UP orientation with positive experiences and of the DOWN orientation – with negative, Krzeszowski (1987: 113) claimed that the UP/DOWN schema is axiologically charged with the PLUS-MINUS poles. A critical assessment of this view was given by Hampe (2005b: 107), who observed that "axiological dimensions have to remain default values because evaluation is never absolute" and argued that such default values are determined with respect to much broader and richer, contextualized cognitive models, of which image schema groupings form a part.

concepts in the drawing crucially relies on an image schema complex which comprises the two schemas that are evoked verbally – VERTICALITY and BOUNDED SPACE, and a number of schemas that are cued in the visual mode only: BALANCE, FORCE, SUPPORT, STRAIGHT (the activation of the STRAIGHT schema in the verbal mode alone is not evident), PATH and MOTION (the latter via the metonymy PATH FOR MOTION) as well as the GRASP schema (Chilton 2009). The creative multimodal metaphors that may contribute to a coherent interpretation of this cartoon can be rendered as: HAPPINESS IS HOLDING A LINE SPREAD ACROSS/OVER A PRECIPICE AND BALANCING ON A ROPE SPREAD ACROSS IT (A PRECIPICE). The spatialization of the two target concepts in the visual mode, since it evokes embodied concepts of GRASPING as well as of MOVEMENT, BALANCE and UP/DOWN orientation, may provide grounding for drawing a number of inferences about the concepts in question. On the one hand, the image of the protagonist grasping an abstract line may highlight the intangible nature of happiness. On the other hand, from his balancing on a rope that is spread across a precipice we can infer that happiness is very difficult to maintain and the effects of losing it – that is falling into a state of unhappiness – may be fatal.

In example 3, the spatialization of WISDOM and STUPIDITY is evident from the caption itself: the personified WISDOM is construed as capable of walking along the paths of STUPIDITY.[7]

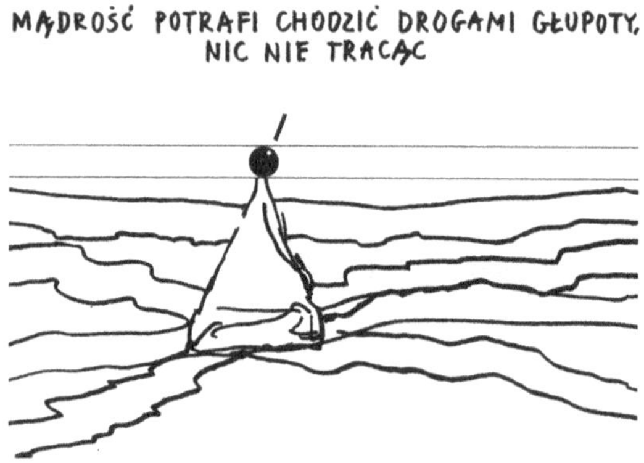

Example 3: *Mądrość potrafi chodzić drogami głupoty, nic nie tracąc* 'Wisdom can walk along the paths of stupidity, not losing anything' (Kapusta 2014: 158, transl. E.G.)

7 Analysis of this example is based on an excerpt from: Górska, Elżbieta. 2018. A multimodal portrait of WISDOM and STUPIDITY. A case study of image-schematic metaphors in cartoons. In Rafał Augustyn & Agnieszka Mierzwińska-Hajnos (eds.), *New insights into the language and cognition interface*, 98–117. Newcastle upon Tyne: Cambridge Scholars Publishing. The relevant parts are published with the permission from Cambridge Scholars Publishing.

In the drawing, the verbally personified WISDOM is pictorially represented as the protagonist[8] and the paths of stupidity are depicted as curved lines on which the protagonist is standing. The PATH schema is thus cued multimodally: verbally, it is evoked via the noun *drogami* 'paths, Instr.' and pictorially it is represented as the curved lines on which the protagonist is standing. On the other hand, the MOTION schema is explicitly cued only in the caption (cf. the verb *chodzić* 'walk'), however we can easily establish here a cohesive tie with the pictorial mode by a metonymic activation of MOTION from the paths depicted in the drawing.

Observe now that the curved shape of the lines which form a multimodal unit with the expression *drogami głupoty* '(along) the paths of stupidity' is in sharp contrast with two long straight parallel lines enclosing the protagonist's head. I would like to argue that the contrasting shape of these lines is by no means accidental here. The key to a coherent interpretation of this aspect of the cartoon lies in the STRAIGHT image schema (Cienki 1998a),[9] which provides metaphorical structuring to a whole range of abstract domains in Western culture, including DISCOURSE, MORALITY, EXPECTED SOCIAL BEHAVIOUR and, what is immediately relevant to our concern – the domain of THOUGHT. Crucially, as Cienki (following Sweetser 1987) and (Emanatian 1996) observes:

> A dominant model of serious thought in American society (but not exclusive to it) emphasizes its logical nature, and value is placed on the sequential development of each idea based on immediately preceding ones. Consistent with this model, logical thought is understood metaphorically as motion along a straight path, and illogical or insane thoughts or judgments, as well as those for whom such thought is characteristic, are *bent, warped, contorted*, etc. (Cienki 1998a: 121)

In short, image-schematic structuring of THOUGHT in terms of STRAIGHT/NON-STRAIGHT applies to both, its logical vs. illogical aspects and to sanity vs. insanity of an individual. Verbal manifestations of these oppositions, as Cienki (1998a: 121–122) shows, are cross-linguistically common. By way of illustration a few examples from Polish are listed in (1) and (2) below:

(1) (ORDERLY (LOGICAL) THOUGHT IS STRAIGHT and, by entailment)
UNORDERLY/ILLOGICAL THOUGHT IS NOT STRAIGHT
myśleć pokrętnie 'think twisted (Adv.) (think in an illogical manner)'

8 Note also that personification may be regarded as a specific realization of the OBJECT schema.
9 Johnson (2007: 21) refers to it as STRAIGHT-CURVED schema.

(2) AN INSANE MIND/INSANE THOUGHT IS NOT STRAIGHT
a. *Pokręciło go !* 'coll. he got twisted (he went mad/crazy)'
b. *Ale pokręcony*! 'coll. He is so twisted! (He is so crazy/stupid!)'

Seen in this context, the spatialization of WISDOM and STUPIDITY in example 3 can be interpreted by two creative metaphors: WISDOM IS MOTION ALONG A STRAIGHT PATH and STUPIDITY IS MOTION ALONG A NON-STRAIGHT PATH.

Note further that the embodied grounding of the STRAIGHT image schema provides, as Cienki (1998a) argues, experiential motivation for a typically positive evaluation of concepts metaphorically understood as STRAIGHT, and a negative evaluation of concepts which are conceived of as NON-STRAIGHT. Experientially,

> There is a significant relation between our bodies being straight, up, and in control; resisting the force of gravity, *standing up straight*, involves a specific kind of muscular tension. Contrast this with the relation between being bent, down, and a lack of control; when submitting to a force or influencing factor (e.g., fatigue), the body is bent over, slouched. The qualities of straightness, control, and being up, strong, and firm, therefore, commonly group together in our experience given how our bodies function, with a contrasting grouping being bent/curved, lack of control, down, weak, and soft. (Cienki 1998a: 111)

Moreover, it is part of our experience of bodily motion that "[i]t takes less time to get somewhere via a straight path rather than a curvy path given a set rate of movement" (Cienki 1998a: 112). Given the experiential motivation of the STRAIGHT schema and the earlier mentioned cultural model of thought, I would suggest that, in the presently considered cartoon, the pictorial cuing of WISDOM by means of two straight lines within which the protagonist's head is situated is likely to strengthen the positive evaluation of this concept. This would entail also that the representation of the "paths of stupidity" as curved contributes to the negative evaluation of its counterpart.[10]

In example 4, the visualization of a conceptual image of yet another intangible thing – real worries – relies on a grouping of the OBJECT, CONTAINER, BIG-SMALL, MOTION, FRONT-BACK and the FORCE image schemas.

---

10 A word of caution is in order, however. The fact that many STRAIGHT metaphors receive a salient positive evaluation in Western culture cannot be taken as universally valid. Rather, it should be seen as a result of a strong correlation of embodiment and particular cultural stereotypes. In Russian, for example, aside positive evaluation of LOGICAL THOUGHT which is STRAIGHT, there is also a salient association between STRAIGHT THOUGHT and lack of creative intelligence (see Cienki 1998a: 141). This conception reflects a different stereotype, namely of a person whose thinking is too straight and not flexible (see Cienki 1998a: 132). A parallel stereotype in Polish would also account for a negative evaluation of the Polish *prostak* '(pejor.) boor' and *prostacki* 'boorish, crude'.

Example 4: *Prawdziwe zmartwienia podróżują razem z nami* 'Real worries travel with us' (Kapusta 2014: 23, transl. E.G.)

The objectification of worries via the conventional metaphor IDEAS/EMOTIONS ARE OBJECTS is explicitly cued verbally – they are described as things that can travel with us. In the pictorial mode, their objectification can be inferred from the image of a huge suitcase containing the protagonist whose motion forward seems to be very difficult – he is depicted as dragging behind him a mooring anchor and bending under its burden. The suitcase seems to provide multiple cues for a coherent interpretation of this cartoon. On the one hand, it may function as a metonymic vehicle providing access to the concept of a JOURNEY, and thereby it may enhance the level of activation of the source domain for the LIFE IS A JOURNEY metaphor. On the other hand, its size, which has been given focal prominence in the drawing, may be considered as a pictorial cue for conceiving the intensity of the emotion in terms of the BIG-SMALL schema. Specifically, this interpretation could be regarded as an entailment of the STATES ARE CONTAINERS metaphor, which can be stated as: THE INTENSITY OF AN EMOTIONAL STATE IS THE SIZE OF THE CONTAINER. Moreover, the fact that the protagonist himself is depicted within the enclosure of the suitcase seems to open a possibility of constructing other aspect of the cartoon's meaning. Specifically, we may construe the protagonist as fully "contained" in his emotional state. It could be argued that this interpretation rests on a creative reworking of the conventional metaphor THE BODY IS THE CONTAINER FOR EMOTIONS (Kövecses 2000: 146) – via the figure-ground reversal of the CONTAINER-CONTENT relation real worries may be conceived as a CONTAINER for the BODY. A possible entailment of this metaphorical construal of real worries would be that the protagonist is unable to escape from them.

Observe now that the visualization of worries in the drawing also rests on well-entrenched conceptual metaphors in terms of which we conceive of emotional states which are difficult to cope with, namely DIFFICULTIES ARE BURDENS (or, EMOTIONAL DIFFICULTIES ARE BURDENS cf. Kövecses 2000: 45), SADNESS IS A

BURDEN and SAD IS DOWN (Barcelona 1986, qtd. in Kövecses 2000: 25). The source domains of these metaphors are evoked in the pictorial mode via an image of the protagonist who is dragging behind him a mooring anchor and bending down under its burden.

We have seen that in this cartoon the spatialization of the verbally evoked target concept of REAL WORRIES is to a large extent realized in the pictorial mode only. And, as in the case of cartoons discussed earlier, it is the creative visualization of conventional image-schematic metaphors that provides means for a coherent interpretation of the cartoon.

3 Conclusions

Spatialization of abstract meanings through their multimodal construction in the cartoons discussed in this study opens a window onto the relationship between space, cognition and language. On the one hand, it was argued that in a number of cartoons aspects of image-schematic source domains that are evoked for a metaphorical construal of abstract concepts are co-expressed in the two modes. In effect, in terms of the iconic principle of quantity, such overlapping aspects of meaning may be said to have more content and be more salient. Moreover, such increase in a number of metaphoricity indicators implies that there are more attention-getting cues available to the addressee which, according to Müller (2008a, 2017; Kolter et al. 2012), is likely to trigger a higher level of activation of a particular metaphor. However, multiplication of meaning via different semiotic modes allows not only for "awakening" of conventional conceptual metaphors (such as: STATES ARE LOCATIONS/ CONTAINERS/ BOUNDED SPACES; LOVE IS UNITY, LOVE IS BOND, POSITIVE IS UP, NEGATIVE IS DOWN, AN INSANE MIND IS NOT STRAIGHT, EMOTIONAL DIFFICULTIES ARE BURDENS), but also for their creative reworking, with the visual modality elaborating or extending the conventional mappings.

We have seen also that due to affordances of the pictorial mode image-schema clusters can be easily evoked in "one-shot". Suffice it to recall example 1, where the circle may cue both the bounded space schemas as well as the cycle schema; or the drawing of the protagonist balancing on a line in example 2, which evokes the cluster of the UP/DOWN, BALANCE, FORCE, PATH and MOTION image schemas; and the same goes for the huge suitcase in example 4, which may activate the CONTAINER, BIG/SMALL and metonymically – the MOTION schemas. Such co-activation of image schemas greatly enhances the condensation of the cartoon's meaning, which could not be achieved via the sequential mode of the verbal text alone. Likewise, it is the affordances of the pictorial mode that account for the fact that the drawings so easily provide iconic cues for construing the visualized aspects of abstract concepts (cf. e.g., the spatial overlap of the rectangle and the circle in example 1 may point to the temporal overlap of two states of love and pain; in example 2, the depiction of the protagonist as balancing on a line may point to difficulty in maintaining this position, from which we may infer the temporariness of happiness and the difficulty of maintaining it). In effect, the pictorial mode may be said to compensate for the low-iconicity of the verbal code (see Górska 2014a: 31).

Crucially, the frequent monomodal cuing of image-schematic source domains in the cartoons' drawings provides supportive evidence for the claim that spatialization of abstract ideas in the visual medium may be independent from how such ideas are expressed verbally (see also Górska 2017a,b, 2018). This finding corroborates the results of numerous gesture studies (see, e.g., Cienki 1998b; Cienki and Müller 2008; Müller 2008b, 2017; Müller and Cienki 2009; Müller et al. 2013), strengthening the view that metaphor, as a conceptual mechanism, has its manifestations not only in the verbal mode, but also in other modalities.

Finally, this study has shown also that spatialization of abstract meanings by means of different semiotic modes performs a number of rhetorical functions. In particular, it allows for a creative reworking of conventional conceptual metaphors, and thereby sheds a new light on well-established concepts and, in effect, renders the communicative act more memorable.

References

Barcelona, Antonio. 1986. On the concept of depression in American English: A cognitive approach. *Revista Canaria de Estudios Ingleses* 12. 7–33.

Brandt, Line & Per Aage Brandt. 2005. Making sense of a blend. A cognitive semiotic approach to metaphor. *Annual Review of Cognitive Linguistics* 3. 216–249.

Chilton, Paul. 2009. *Get* and the grasp schema. A new approach to conceptual modelling in image schema semantics. In Vyvyan Evans & Stéphanie Pourcel (eds.), *New directions in cognitive linguistics*, 331–370. Amsterdam & Philadelphia: John Benjamins.

Cienki, Alan. 1997. Some properties and groupings of image schemas. In Marjolijn Verspoor, Ken Dong Lee, & Eve Sweetser (eds.), *Lexical and syntactic constructions and the construction of meaning*, 3–15. Amsterdam & Philadelphia: John Benjamins.

Cienki, Alan. 1998a. STRAIGHT: an image schema and its metaphorical extensions. *Cognitive Linguistics* 9 (2). 107–149.

Cienki, Alan. 1998b. Metaphoric gestures and some of their relations to verbal metaphoric expressions. In Jean-Pierre Koenig (ed.), *Discourse and cognition*, 189–204. Stanford: Center for the Study of Language and Information.

Cienki, Alan & Cornelia Müller. 2008. Metaphor, gesture, and thought. In Raymond W. Gibbs. (ed.), *The Cambridge handbook of metaphor and thought*, 483–501. Cambridge: Cambridge University Press.

Correa-Beningfield, Margarita, Gitte Kristiansen, Ignasi Navarro-Ferrando & Claude Vandeloise. 2005. Image schemas and 'complex primitives' in cross-cultural spatial cognition. In Beate Hampe (ed.), 2005c, *From perception to meaning. Image schemas in cognitive linguistics*, 343–366. Berlin & New York: De Gruyter Mouton.

Emanatian, Michale. 1996. Intellectual and conversational paths. Paper presented at the Second Conference on Conceptual Structure, Discourse, and Language, State University of New York at Buffalo, April 12-14.

Evans, Vyvyan & Paul Chilton (eds.). 2010. *Language, cognition and space: The State of the art and new directions*. London & Oakville: Equinox.

Fauconnier, Gilles & Mark Turner. 1998. Conceptual integration networks. *Cognitive Science* 22. 133–187.

Fauconnier, Gilles & Mark Turner. 2002. *The way we think. Conceptual blending and the mind's hidden complexities*. New York: Basic Books.

Forceville, Charles. 1996. *Pictorial metaphor in advertising*. London & New York: Routledge.

Forceville, Charles. 2016. The FORCE and BALANCE schemas in JOURNEY metaphor animations. In Carla Fernandes (ed.), *Multimodality and performance*, 8–22. Newcastle-upon-Tyne: Cambridge Scholars.

Forceville, Charles. 2017. From image schema to metaphor in discourse: The FORCE schemas in animation films. In Beate Hampe (ed.), *Metaphor, embodied cognition, and discourse*, 239–256. Cambridge: Cambridge University Press.

Forceville, Charles & Sissy Paling. 2018. The metaphorical representation of DEPRESSION in short, wordless animation films. *Visual Communication* (published ahead of print 21-9-2018, at http://journals.sagepub.com/doi/10.1177/1470357218797994).

Forceville, Charles & Eduardo Urios-Aparisi (eds.). 2009a. *Multimodal metaphor*. Berlin & New York: De Gruyter Mouton.

Forceville, Charles & Eduardo Urios-Aparisi. 2009b. Introduction. In Charles Forceville & Eduardo Urios-Aparisi (eds.). 2009a, *Multimodal metaphor*, 3–17. Berlin & New York: De Gruyter Mouton.

Górska, Elżbieta. 2010. LIFE IS MUSIC: A case study of a novel metaphor and its use in discourse. *English Text Construction* 3 (2). 275–293. [Reprinted in Barbara Dancygier, José Sanders, & Lieven Vandelanotte (eds.). 2012. *Textual choices and discourse. A view from cognitive linguistics*, 137–155. Amsterdam & Philadelphia: John Benjamins].

Górska, Elżbieta. 2014a. Why are multimodal metaphors interesting? The perspective of verbo-visual and verbo-musical modalities. In Marek Kuźniak, Agnieszka Libura & Michał Szawerna (eds.), *From conceptual metaphor theory to cognitive ethnolinguistics. Patterns of imagery in language*, 17–36. Frankfurt am Main: Peter Lang.

Górska, Elżbieta. 2014b. The UP/DOWN orientation in language and music. In Matthias Brenzinger & Iwona Kraska-Szlenk (eds.), *The body in language. Comparative studies of linguistic embodiment*, 177–195. Leiden & Boston: Brill [Brill's Studies in language, cognition and culture 8].

Górska, Elżbieta. 2017a. Text-image relations in cartoons. A case study of image-schematic metaphors. *Studia Linguistica Universitatis Iagellonicae Cracoviensis* 134 (3). 219–228. DOI: 10.4467/20834624SL.17.015.7089.

Górska, Elżbieta. 2017b. The PATH schema in verbo-pictorial aphorisms on LIFE. In Przemysław Łozowski & Adam Głaz (eds.), *Route 66: From deep structures to surface meanings. A Festschrift for Henryk Kardela on his 66th birthday*, 219–235. Lublin: Maria Curie-Skłodowska University Press.

Górska, Elżbieta. 2018. A multimodal portrait of WISDOM and STUPIDITY. A case study of image-schematic metaphors in cartoons. In Rafał Augustyn & Agnieszka Mierzwińska-Hajnos (eds.), *New insights into the language and cognition interface*, 98–117. Newcastle upon Tyne: Cambridge Scholars Publishing.
Hampe, Beate. 2005a. Image schemas in cognitive linguistics: Introduction. In Beate Hampe (ed.), 2005c. *From perception to meaning. Image schemas in cognitive linguistics*, 1–2. Berlin & New York: De Gruyter Mouton.
Hampe, Beate. 2005b. When *down* is not bad and *up* is not good enough: A usage-based assessment of the plus-minus parameter in image-schema theory. *Cognitive Linguistics* 16 (1). 81–112.
Hampe, Beate (ed.). 2005c. *From perception to meaning. Image schemas in cognitive linguistics*. Berlin & New York: De Gruyter Mouton.
Heine, Bernd. 1997. *Cognitive foundations of grammar.* Oxford: Oxford University Press.
Ibarretxe-Atuñano, Iraide (ed.). 2017. *Motion and space across languages: Theory and application.* Amsterdam & Philadelphia: John Benjamins.
Johnson, Mark. 1987. *The body in the mind: The bodily basis of imagination, reason, and meaning.* Chicago & London: University of Chicago Press.
Johnson, Mark. 2007. *The meaning of the body. Aesthetics of human understanding.* Chicago & London: The University of Chicago Press.
Kolter, Astrid, Silva H. Ladewig, Michela Summa, Cornelia Müller, Sabine C. Koch, & Thomas Fuchs. 2012. Body memory and the emergence of metaphor in movement and speech. An interdisciplinary case study. In Sabine C. Koch, Thomas Fuchs, Michela Summa & Cornelia Müller (eds.), *Body memory, metaphor and movement*, 201–226. Amsterdam & Philadelphia: John Benjamins.
Kövecses, Zoltán. 2000. *Metaphor and emotion: Language, culture and body in human feeling.* Cambridge: Cambridge University Press.
Krzeszowski, Tomasz P. 1997. *Angels and devils in hell. Elements of axiological semantics.* Warszawa: Energeia.
Lakoff, George. 1990. The Invariance Hypothesis: Is abstract reason based on image-schemas. *Cognitive Linguistics* 1 (1). 39–74.
Lakoff, George. 1993. The contemporary theory of metaphor. In Andrew Ortony (ed.), *Metaphor and thought.* 2nd edn., 202–251. Cambridge: Cambridge University Press.
Lakoff, George. 1987. *Women, fire and dangerous things: What categories reveal about the mind.* Chicago & London: The University of Chicago Press.
Lakoff, George & Mark Johnson. 1980. *Metaphors we live by.* Chicago & London: University of Chicago Press.
Lakoff, George & Mark Johnson. 1999. *Philosophy in the flesh: The embodied mind and its challenge to western thought.* New York: Basic Books.
Lakoff, George & Mark Turner. 1989. *More than cool reason. A field guide to poetic metaphor.* Chicago & London: The University of Chicago Press.
Langacker, Ronald W. 1987. *Foundations of cognitive grammar.* Volume 1: *Theoretical prerequisites.* Stanford: Stanford University Press.
Mittelberg, Irene. 2010. Geometric and image-schematic patterns in gesture space. In Vyvyan Evans & Paul Chilton (eds.), *Language, cognition, and space: The state of the art and new directions*, 351–385. London & Oakville: Equinox.
Müller, Cornelia. 2008a. *Metaphors dead and alive, sleeping and waking. A dynamic view.* Chicago & London: Chicago University Press.

Müller, Cornelia. 2008b. What gestures reveal about the nature of metaphor. In Alan Cienki & Cornelia Müller (eds.), *Metaphor and thought*, 219–245. Amsterdam & Philadelphia: John Benjamins.
Müller, Cornelia. 2017. Waking metaphors: Embodied cognition in multimodal discourse. In Beate Hampe (ed.), *Metaphor, embodied cognition, and discourse*, 297–316. Cambridge: Cambridge University Press.
Müller, Cornelia & Alan Cienki. 2009. Words, gestures, and beyond: Forms of multimodal metaphor in the use of spoken language. In Charles Forceville & Eduardo Urios-Aparisi (eds.), 2009a, *Multimodal metaphor*, 297–328. Berlin & New York: De Gruyter Mouton.
Müller, Cornelia, Silva H. Ladewig & Jana Bressem. 2013. Gestures and speech from a linguistic perspective: A new field and its history. In Cornelia Müller, Alan Cienki, Ellen Fricke, Silva H. Ladewig, David McNeill & Jana Bressem (eds.), *Body – language – communication. An international handbook on multimodality in human interaction* , vol. 2, 55–81. Berlin & New York: De Gruyter Mouton.
Ortiz, María. J. 2011. Primary metaphors and monomodal visual metaphors. *Journal of Pragmatics* 43 (6). 1568–1580.
Ortiz, María J. 2014. Visual manifestations of primary metaphors through *mise-en-scène* techniques. *Image and Narrative* 15 (1). 5–16.
Pinar Sanz, María Jesús (ed.). 2013. *Multimodality and cognitive linguistics*. [Special issue]. *Review of Cognitive Linguistics* 11 (2).
Sweetser, Eve. 1987. Metaphorical models of thought and speech: A comparison of historical directions and metaphorical mappings in the two domains". In Jon Aske, Natasha Beery, Laura Michaelis & Hanna Filip (eds.), *Proceedings of the 13th Annual Meetings of the Berkeley Linguistic Society*, 446–459. Berkeley, CA.: Berkeley Linguistic Society.
Talmy, Leonard. 1983. How language structures space. In Pick Herbert & Linda Acredolo (eds.), *Spatial orientation: Theory, research, and application*, 225–282. New York: Plenum Press.
Talmy, Leonard. 1988. Force dynamics in language and cognition. *Cognitive Science* 12. 49–100.
Talmy, Leonard. 2003. The representation of spatial structure in spoken and signed language: A neural model. *Language and Linguistics* 4 (2). 207–250.
Zbikowski, Lawrence M. 2006. The cognitive tango. In Mark Turner (ed.), *The artful mind. Cognitive science and the riddle of human creativity*, 115–131. Oxford: Oxford University Press.
Zbikowski, Lawrence M. 2008. Metaphor and music. In Raymond W. Gibbs (ed.), *The Cambridge handbook of metaphor and thought*, 502–523. Cambridge: Cambridge University Press.

Data source

Kapusta, Janusz. 2014. *Plus-Minus. Podręcznik do Myślenia* [Plus-minus. A handbook for thinking]. Poznań: Zysk i S-ka.

Maarten Coëgnarts

Analyzing metaphor in film: Some conceptual challenges

Abstract: This chapter aims to discuss the notion of conceptual metaphor in relation to the visual manifestation level of films. The first part takes on the challenge of addressing a theoretical issue that is inherent to this level and that at first sight seems to impede a metaphorical analysis of film, namely the problem of iconicity. After having addressed this problem, the second part discusses how metaphor can be analyzed in film. Since conceptual metaphor can be conceived of as consisting of a relationship between image-schematic driven source domains and abstract target domains, this part is divided into three subparts. The first subpart shows how image schemas may be instantiated in visual images by means of the application of a variety of film stylistic means (e.g., camera movement, editing). The second subpart stresses the importance of metonymy in representing target domains in film. The third and last subpart makes their connection by illustrating, through a case-study taken from Francis Ford Coppola's *The Conversation* (1974), how stylistically motivated image schemas maybe be mapped onto the inferential logic of metonymically represented target domains.

Keywords: image schemas, film style, metaphor, metonymy

The most powerful conveyor of meaning is the immediate impact of perceptual form — Rudolf Arnheim

1 Introduction

Over the last years, research on conceptual metaphor has met with an increasing interest in manifestation modes other than the purely linguistic one, as predominantly analyzed in the field of cognitive linguistics (e.g., Coëgnarts and Kravanja 2012, 2015; El Refaie 2003; Fahlenbrach 2016; Forceville and Urios-Aparisi 2009; Kappelhoff and Müller 2011; Ortiz 2011). A reason for this widening of scope can be found in the nature of conceptual metaphor itself.

Maarten Coëgnarts, University of Antwerp, Department of Communication Sciences, Antwerp, Belgium

https://doi.org/10.1515/9783110629460-014

Since Lakoff and Johnson coined the term in the early 1980s, metaphor has been primarily regarded as a property of the *mind* rather than exclusively a property of *language*. Human thought is metaphorically structured and linguistic expressions are merely the outer and perceptible signs of this underlying cognitive mechanism. Given that conceptual metaphors are only in a derivative sense a matter of mode, it is plausible to assume that language is not the only way in which they may appeal to human senses. Addressing this assumption allows one to avoid an often raised critique against Conceptual Metaphor Theory (henceforth, CMT), namely, the fallacy that it attempts to demonstrate the conceptual nature of metaphor solely by considering linguistic concepts (see also Forceville 2009; Forceville and Jeulink 2011; Gibbs and Perlman 2006; Pecher, Boot, and Van Dantzig 2011). Critics might see this as a form of circular reasoning that would seriously compromise the central role of metaphor in cognition. For this reason support from other modes of expression is vital. Bringing conceptual metaphor outside the verbal realm, however, introduces a new complexity for CMT. Studying metaphor in a primarily non-verbal environment such as film requires that we take into consideration a question that, precisely because of the primacy of language, has been often overlooked, namely, the question of medium-specificity. How does film distinguish itself from language? Which unique features does the medium of film exploit in order to address the same conceptual metaphors as identified in language? Insofar as the emphasis was exclusively on one mode of expression (i.e., the verbal mode), it was not pivotal to address this question. With the increase of interest in the subject of multimodal metaphor (e.g., Forceville and Urios-Aparisi 2009), however, the question becomes particularly relevant. Notwithstanding previous structuralist attempts to systemize film *as* language (e.g., Metz 1974; Monaco 2000), both modes of expression are significantly dissimilar, having both a distinctive reality status. Language is characterized by an abstract and formal structure that bears no similarity with the state of affairs in the world that it denotes, whereas film has a nature that to an extent resembles the reality it represents. Precisely because of its ontological lack of analogy with language, film is encountered with a conceptual concern that at first sight seems to impede a metaphorical analysis of the medium. If metaphor involves a mapping between two different conceptual domains, and film, due to its "phenomenological richness of audiovisual information" (Grodal 2016: 101), does not consist of concepts, how is it possible then, that film, like language, can exhibit the property of expressing conceptual metaphors? Subsequently, one way for the cinematic medium to overcome this difficulty would be to contest its high degree of iconicity in favor of a more concentered and dense formal structure. The task, then, is to identify something that can impose such a structure. This chapter argues that this "something" can be specified by referring to the significance of film form. It is the central claim of this contribution, that this unity or "formal precision", as Arnheim (1957: 200) would call it, can be imposed onto the reality in front of the camera by the forced actions of filmmaking (e.g., mise-en-scène, framing, editing, etc.). The central argument underlying this hypothesis can be summarized in the following manner:

(1) Conceptual metaphors map the structure of concrete source domains onto abstract domains of experience.
(2) These source domains are driven by the inferential logic of image schemas (i.e., abstract patterns of human sensory-motor experience).
(3) In film, these image schemas are vividly triggered by the application of various cinematic devices. As a result, the filmed event obtains a formal unity that provides coherence: it acquires characteristics that, like language, can be analyzed.
(4) The articulation of these structural patterns in the filmed event, in turn, allows the possibility of metaphorical expansion, that is, the inferential spatial logic of image schemas, as elicited through one or more cinematic devices, may be mapped onto the inferential logic of abstract target domains (e.g., character subjectivity).
(5) These target domains are mainly elicited metonymically in film.

The chapter is structured in such a way as to mirror this problem-solving approach. The first part takes on the challenge of articulating and overcoming the problem of iconicity. The second part of this chapter takes on the task of clarifying the argument above, as it comprises the conceptual framework for analyzing metaphor in film. Since conceptual metaphor is conceived of as consisting of three basic components (the concrete image-schematic driven source domain (A), the abstract target domain (B), and the relation between A and B), this part is divided in three subsections. The first subsection investigates how image schemas can be identified in film. Central to this inquiry is the following question: How are cinematic means able to structure the reality in front of the camera in such a way as to instigate the ostensive appearance of image schemas? The second subsection discusses the significant role of metonymy in articulating target domains in film. Lastly, the third subsection considers their metaphorical connection: How can the inferential logic of image schemas, as elicited by their corresponding cinematic resources, be mapped onto the inferential logic of abstract target domains, as elicited metonymically in the filmed event? Answering and illustrating these questions will help us to better understand how metaphor can be analyzed in film.

2 Overcoming the problem of iconicity

The problematic nature of the relation between metaphor and film is best put in perspective by means of understanding the relation between metaphor and language. This inquiry implies finding an answer to a successive set of basic questions instigated by the three central concepts of this contribution (i.e., language, film and metaphor) and which can be listed as follows:

(1) What is the nature of language?
(2) What is the nature of film?
(3) What is the nature of conceptual metaphor?
(4) How does 1 relate to 3?
(5) How does 2 relate to 3 (in comparison to 4)?

A detailed discussion of each of these questions would be beyond the scope of this chapter. For current purposes, it is sufficient that we restrict ourselves to some of the essential points raised in the literature. One familiar theoretical framework that comes to mind in order to address the first two questions is Charles Peirce's well known triadic theory of signs (Chandler 2007: 36–37). This model refers to a distinction between three different ways that the form of the sign (the signifier) might relate to the object or event in the world to which it refers (the signified). Peirce distinguishes between three kinds of signs: the symbol, the icon, and the index. The icon refers to the way in which the signifier resembles or imitates the signified. The symbol refers to the way in which the signifier, due to its arbitrary and conventional form, does not resemble the signified. The index refers to the way in which the signifier is not arbitrary, but is directly connected in some way to the signified (e.g., a clock indicating the time of the day). In view of this typology, then, it is commonly accepted among scholars that the sign system of language is primarily symbolic in nature, whereas the audiovisual sign system of film, given its overall tendency to resemble the physical reality, is chiefly iconic and indexical. As Gaut (2010: 52, emphasis mine) observes, words "have a purely *conventional* relation to the things they denote", whereas "traditional film has a *causal* relation to what it denotes". We speak of a photograph of some object only if that object "caused a light pattern to be imprinted on the photographic emulsion". This causal relation, as Gaut points out, is not arbitrary, but "fixed by empirical facts". Grodal (2016: 103) considers film for this reason a "first-order" communication. It relies on a system that to some degree directly resembles the audiovisual salience of the events and objects in the world. Language, by contrast, is a "second-order" system of communication in that it only becomes meaningful insofar as the meaningless signifiers refer back to the first-order system, to the state of affairs in the world.

Let us now briefly consider the third question concerning the nature of conceptual metaphor. As implied in the name itself, the notion of conceptual metaphor refers to the understanding of one *conceptual* domain in terms of another (A is B) (Lakoff and Johnson 1980, 1999). The conceptual domain that is understood in metaphorical terms is called a "target domain" and is usually abstract in nature. It involves concepts such as time, emotions and mental functions such as knowing and understanding; concepts which are hard to understand without the assistance of metaphor. The conceptual domain that is used in order to structure the abstract target domain is called a "source domain" and is usually concrete in nature. For instance, we come to understand time in terms of space, understanding in terms of grasping and seeing, emotions in terms of containers, etc. In the literature this concreteness of the source domain is often further explicated in terms of the notion of "image schemas" (e.g., Johnson 1987; Lakoff 1987). Image schemas are recurring, highly schematic dynamic structures, which arise from, or are grounded in, human sensory-motor experience (Hampe 2005: 1). Examples include such concepts as FRONT-BACK, LEFT-RIGHT, TOP-DOWN, IN-OUT, etc. These concepts are directly meaningful in the sense that they do not require understanding through other concepts in order to become meaningful. For instance, the basic distinction between "in" and "out" arises directly from our bodily interaction with all sorts of bounded regions (rooms, vehicles, clothes, etc.) (Johnson 1987: 21). Likewise, the SOURCE-PATH-GOAL schema is grounded in our experience of physically moving from one location to another. Conceptual metaphor, then, is the cognitive mechanism that allows humans to connect the inferences true of these image schemas with the inferences true of abstract concepts. These correlations between elements of the source and target domains are technically called "mappings" (see also Evans and Green 2006: 167).

Consequently, when relating conceptual metaphor to language, as captured by the fourth question, one stumbles upon a terminological confusion, as both realities adhere to the level of "concepts". This poses the necessity of adding an additional adjective in order to preserve their difference: metaphors pertain to the notion of *mental* concepts whereas language pertains to the notion of *linguistic* concepts, to spoken or written words. Moreover, the confusion is heightened in that we are obliged to rely on linguistic concepts in order to communicate about conceptual metaphors. For this reason, metaphors are usually signaled in small capitals (e.g., the TIME IS SPACE metaphor) in order to denote their conceptual nature and to distinguish them from their linguistic manifestations (e.g., The deadline is *approaching*). Moreover, this distinction is further motivated by the central claim of CMT holding that it is mental concepts that are *embodied*, rather than the linguistic concepts *an sich*. Language is the form in which the embodied conceptual structure is manifested. Consider, for example, the two linguistic expressions below:

(1) *She trembled in fear.*

(2) *She comes in the visual field.*

Both sentences can be seen as examples in which the abstract target domains of emotion and perception are understood in terms of the inferential logic of the image schema of CONTAINMENT, here elicited linguistically by the spatial preposition *in*. Example (1) shows a linguistic manifestation of the conceptual metaphor EMOTION IS A CONTAINER (Kövecses 2000: 37) and (2) expresses a linguistic manifestation of the conceptual metaphor VISUAL FIELD IS A CONTAINER (Lakoff and Johnson 1980: 30). In both cases the abstract target domain is triggered verbally. The target domain of emotions is triggered by the linguistic concept of *fear*, the target domain of a visual field is elicited by the word *visual field*. It is precisely this analogy between the conceptual and verbal level that makes language such a popular medium for the study of metaphor. Because language, by virtue of its conceptual nature, is capable of labeling abstract target domains and image-schematic driven source domains directly and unambiguously, it is relatively easy for scholars to identify metaphorical mappings of the form A is B. More formally, this claim can be put as follows:

(1) The human mind structures the world of human perception and embodied existence into abstract patterns of sensory motor experience (i.e., image schemas), and uses their inferential logic, in turn, metaphorically in order to structure concepts that do not have sensory-motor features (i.e., abstract concepts).
(2) Language similarly structures the world by translating its objects into abstract linguistic concepts.
(3) Thus both language and mind share a conceptual structure ("the language of thought" hypothesis).
(4) Therefore the concepts of language are best fitted in order to verbalize the concepts of the mind (including the metaphorical mappings between concrete source domains and abstract target domains).[1]

It is exactly this shared process of abstraction that, Grodal (2016) further argues, motivates language to use metaphors. Abstraction leads to a loss of what he labels "qualia salience". "Qualia" or "raw feels' is the technical term that refers to

1 From this line of reasoning follows the often mistaken view that language is the only proper bearer of meaning and that all other arts can only have meaning if they are structured like language. Johnson (2013) calls this view the "propositional or linguistic view of meaning".

the "sensory qualities of mental states" (Kim 2006: 207). Think, for example, of our sense impression of the color red when we look at a ripe tomato. Language, Grodal argues, uses metaphor, then, to reactivate the qualia salience of these phenomenological experiences.

Film, by contrast, does not share the holistic and analytic nature of both language and mind. Consequently, the problem of iconicity, as implicitly inherent in the fifth and last question, becomes apparent once we retain proposition (1) from above, but change the subsequent propositions by speaking of film instead of language:

(2) The audiovisual medium of film, by its holistic and concrete nature, does not structure or translate the world into concepts. Rather than exhibiting a loss of qualia salience, film, to a large extent, exhibits a likeness with the audiovisual salience of the world that it represents.
(3) Thus film, in contrast to language, is not conceptual.
(4) Therefore, film is less adequate than language to express the concepts of the mind (including the metaphorical mappings between source domains and target domains).

Hence, Grodal (2016) points out, the need for film to reactivate the perceptual salience of the phenomenological world is less pervasive as compared to language, as the audiovisual medium already evokes this salience by its own nature.

If the medium of film wishes to facilitate the expression of metaphor it therefore has to meet an additional condition. This "necessity condition", as we might call it, directly challenges proposition (2) from above and can be articulated as follows:

(5) The capacity of film to express metaphor is heightened insofar as film, through its own medium-specific features, is able to impose a structure onto the reality it represents (i.e., to exhibit a capacity that resembles somehow the abstract-analytic ability of language).

The notion of "structure" is significant here, for it entails the concept by which images weaken their iconic nature and preserve their discrepancy with everyday perception. Subsequently, the question that arises from this assertion is: How can visual images, despite their concrete nature, elicit such general and abstract structures? A pioneering answer to this question has been provided by Rudolf Arnheim (1974, 1997). Arnheim systematically challenged the dualistic view of meaning according to which images of art (the domain of visual perception) cannot exhibit concepts (the domain of thought). According to this famous film theorist and perceptual psychologist, the visual arts offer more than merely illustrations of events or things. They are a homeground of what he calls "visual thinking" (Arnheim 1997: 254). To trace visual thinking in the images of art, Arnheim (1997: 255) argues, one must look for "well-structured shapes and relations", for it is through these "abstract patterns" that the "concepts or the central thought of the work" are spelled out. He illustrates his point by discussing numerous examples: from thinking in children's drawings to abstract patterns in visual art. One can find an illuminating example of the latter in his comparison of Camille Corot's figurative painting *Mother and Child on the Beach* and Henry Moore's non-figurative sculpture *Two Forms* (Arnheim 1997: 271–273) (see Figure 14.1).

Figure 14.1: Camille Corot's *Mother and Child on the Beach* (John G. Johnson Collection, Philadelphia) and Henry Moore's *Two Forms* (Collection, The Museum of Modern Art).

Both works convey a similar theme by their analogous structural skeleton and inherent patterns of forces. In both cases the themes of "protection" and "concern" are embodied in the way one figure (i.e., the mother, the larger of the two units) bends over and reaches to a second figure (i.e., the infant, the smaller of the two unites), thus "holding it down, protecting, encompassing, receiving it". As Arnheim (1997: 269) points out, this curving wave shape, as seen embedded in both works, is an "abstract pattern" of form. This abstractness displays a formal unity which allows the work to reach the conceptual essence of a kind of thing.[2] It is herein that, Arnheim believes, one may find art's ontological difference with everyday perception. Most of the objects of the world of perception were not made

2 The notion of "unity" is here used in the same sense as Arnheim (1997), that is, as a contrast to "the lack of unity" or "the lack of structure" which is commonly assumed to be characteristic of the everyday objects of perception (as opposed to works of art).

exclusively for being perceived. They carry visual shape in a manner that is unfiltered. As such, they rely heavily on the formative power of the spectator. Works of visual art, on the other hand, are made for the sole purpose of being perceived. As Arnheim (1997: 273) writes:

> Just as a chemist "isolates" a substance from contaminations that distort his view of its nature and effects, so the work of art purifies significant appearance. It presents abstract themes in their generality, but not reduced to diagrams. The variety of direct experiences is reflected in highly complex forms. The work of art is an interplay of vision and thought.

What Arnheim describes as "abstract patterns" are of course very close in content and meaning to what Lakoff and Johnson years later have labeled "image schemas". Likewise, one can see a resemblance between what Arnheim here calls "abstract themes" and what Lakoff and Johnson define as "target domains". Hence, there is an overlap of thought which might be put more densely as follows: Visual works of art are able to impose a structure onto reality because their formal properties activate abstract patterns (image schemas), and it is through the connection of these patterns to abstract themes (the metaphorical mapping of image schemas onto abstract target domains) that these works challenge the false distinction between perception and thinking. Consequently, if images are indeed able to structure the world and thus challenge the contingency of reality, and this unity is, as we have seen, conditional for initiating conceptual metaphors, then, we might assume that images are able to elicit conceptual metaphors as well.[3] In the next section, we will put this claim to the test by considering the question of how metaphor can be identified in film. In the first part, we show how film is able to structure reality through the notion of *film form*. More specifically, we demonstrate how the initiation of certain image schemas in the visual content of the filmic frame goes hand in hand with the application of certain cinematic devices. In the second part, we show how film is able to structure target domains metonymically. In the third and last part, we make their connection by illustrating, through a case-study taken from Francis Ford Coppola's *The Conversation* (1974), how stylistically motivated image schemas maybe be mapped onto the inferential logic of metonymically represented target domains.

3 On the difference between "structured movies" and "unstructured movies" and its effect on viewers' brain activity, see Hasson et al. 2008.

3 Analyzing conceptual metaphor in film

3.1 Image schemas and film form

To address the notion of structure in relation to film is to consider the significance of the concept of *film form*. David Bordwell and Kristin Thompson (2004: 49) broadly refer to film form as "the overall system of relations that we can perceive among the elements in the whole film". Consequently, because film is a unified set of related, interdependent elements, there must be some principles that help create the relationships among the parts. Bordwell and Thompson (2004: 175) further explicate these principles in terms of two general systems. Firstly, there are the principles of the *formal systems* of films. The formal system underlies, among others, an inquiry into the question of how films are organized by principles of narrative construction. Secondly, there are the principles of the *stylistic systems* of films. The stylistic system entails the question of how films are organized by the patterned and significant use of the features of the film medium. It involves an inquiry into the formal functions of such cinematic techniques as mise-en-scène, cinematography and editing. It is through the latter system that, we argue, film is able to elicit image schematic logic that, as we shall see later on, might be retracted for metaphorical purposes. The argument underlying this claim can be summarized more formally as follows:

(1) A system defines a relation between parts that depend on and affect one another.
(2) The techniques of filmmaking help to create such relationships among parts.
(3) Like systems, image schemas are internally structured, i.e., they are made up of very few related parts.
(4) Therefore, given the analogy between systems and image schemas, it is plausible to assume that the techniques of filmmaking also help to elicit image schemas in films.

What then are the techniques by virtue of which the medium film imposes image schematic structures onto the reality in front of the camera? Bordwell and Thompson (2004: 175) distinguish between four sets of cinematic techniques: two techniques of the shot (mise-en-scène and cinematography); the technique that relates shot to shot (editing), and the relation of sound to film. Unfortunately, space is too limited to discuss each technique in detail. For illustrative purposes, we will restrict ourselves to a discussion of some of the involving image schemas of what is commonly regarded as one of the most important aspects of the technique of cinematography, namely the *framing* of the shot. Broadly speaking, framing can be defined as the use of the edges of the film frame to select and to compose what will be visible on-screen. The frame actively defines what is visible for the viewer. For this reason, the frame is not a neutral border. As Bordwell and Thompson (2004: 252, 258) write, the frame "imposes a certain vantage point onto the material within the image. (...) From an implicitly continuous world, the frame selects a slice to show us, leaving the rest of the space off-screen". In this sense one can argue that film, through framing, imposes a first type of structure onto the world of human perception. As we have argued elsewhere (Coëgnarts and Kravanja 2016a: 115), this structure can be further described in terms of the CONTAINMENT schema. Through its edges the frame defines a bounded region with an interior (the space seen on the screen) and an exterior (the space blocked from being visible on the screen). Both parts do not exist independent of the schema. The concepts of off-screen and on-screen only make sense in relation to the container gestalt as a whole. If we cannot distinguish between an off-screen and an on-screen world, then the notion of frame does not longer hold. The conditions of the CONTAINER image schema have to be satisfied in order for us to speak of a "frame" at all.

The frame does not only impose a relationship between an inside and an outside world. In addition, there are other resources of framing that impose various image schematic structures onto the *inside* content of the frame (i.e., what the viewer sees on-screen). These resources include features of framing that apply to all sorts of pictures (angle, level, height and distance of framing) as well as resources that are specific to cinema (frame mobility). In what follows, we will show how each of these features, as discussed by Bordwell and Thompson (2004: 259–276), tends to elicit its own intrinsic and corresponding image schematic structure(s).

The *angle* of framing is the position that the frame takes in relation to the subject inside the frame. The camera can look down at the subject (a high-angle), be on the same level as the subject (a straight-on angle), or can look up at the subject (a low angle). Obviously, the image schema prompted by these angles, is that of VERTICALITY. A VERTICALITY schema is an image schema that involves "up" and "down" orientation. As Johnson (1987: xiv) points out, this schema is grounded in thousands of every day experiences, such as "perceiving a tree, our felt sense of standing upright, the activity of climbing stairs, forming a mental image of a flagpole, measuring our children's heights, and experiencing the level of water rising in the bathtub". The VERTICALITY schema is the abstract pattern of these experiences, images, and perceptions.

The *level* of framing pertains to the gravitational forces governing the filmed material and the frame. If the framing is level, the horizon inside the frame will be parallel to the horizontal edges of the frame and perpendicular to the vertical edges of the frame. If the horizon is a diagonal line, the frame is canted. The image schema that is intrinsically imposed onto the imagery by this resource is that of BALANCE. Likewise, we come to know the meaning of this structure, not by learning a set of rules or concepts, but by virtue of our bodily experiences. As Johnson (1987: 74–75) writes, these experiences include *acts* of balancing (e.g., juggling, standing up straight) as well as *experiences* of systematic processes and states within our bodies (e.g., the head is too hot, the hands are too cold, etc.).

The *height* of framing relates to the distance of the camera above the ground. The material inside the frame is filmed at low (high) height when the camera is positioned close to (far from) the ground. Note that the height of framing does not necessarily coincide with the angle of framing. For instance, the camera can be at low height while the angle is straight-on. Similarly, the underlying skeleton pattern is that of VERTICALITY.

The *distance* of framing, also known as *shot scale*, refers to the apparent distance between the camera and the mise-en-scène elements inside the container of the frame. Film scholars usually measure this distance in relation to the human body. The greater the distance, the smaller the human figure and the "emptier" the frame, and vice versa, the smaller the distance, the bigger the human figure and the "fuller" the frame. Consequently, one stumbles upon the structural logic of such image schemas as NEAR-FAR and FULL-EMPTY (e.g., Hampe 2005: 2). In film studies this difference is usually termed the range difference between an extreme long shot (far, empty) and an extreme close-up (near, full). In the first type of shot the interior element of the human body is depicted as barely visible. There is still enough space in the container to be filled in with the presence of the human body. In the second type of shot, by contrast, a detail of the face is isolated and magnified. In case of a stationary human figure, there are two ways of alternating between different shot scales (i.e., between near and far, between full and empty), that is, by the resource of the mobile frame (see below), or by cutting from one shot scale to another. Both techniques differ in their distribution of visual information. The mobile frame allows one to see all the various differences between the initial shot scale and the final shot scale, while editing allows one to see only a selection of shot scales.

All the resources of framing discussed so far are not specific to cinema. They are present in all sorts of images such as paintings, photographs, and comics. In comparison to other pictures, films are unique, as Bordwell and Thompson (2004: 266) point out, because of their ability to move with respect to the filmed material (e.g., the human body). For instance, the camera may rotate on a vertical axis scanning the space horizontally (panning), it may rotate on a horizontal axis scanning the space vertically (tilting) or it may travel in any direction (e.g., backward, forward) along the ground (tracking shot). In other words, the *mobile frame* is the resource that allows the frame to shift from one end of an oppositional schema (e.g., left, top, front) to another end (e.g., right, down, back). Underlying these various types of mobile framing is the generic image schema of SOURCE-PATH-GOAL with the source and goal being respectively coupled to the starting and ending point of the movement (e.g., Johnson 1987: 113–114).

In the third subsection below, we will show how some of the resources of framing and their underlying schematic structures can be elaborated metaphorically to connect up two different aspects of subjective meaning in narrative cinema, namely character perception and character emotions. To demonstrate this, however, we first have to answer a second question.

3.2 Target domains and metonymy

How can film images elicit target domains? We have already pointed towards film's discrepancy with language. Written or spoken signs are able to capture abstract target domains directly and unambiguously. The word "emotion" immediately evokes the concept of EMOTION. Film can also make use of verbal signs to provoke target domains directly (e.g., through the spoken language of characters), but herein lies neither the uniqueness nor the strength of cinema. The power of cinema lies in its ability to evoke abstract target domains *non-linguistically*. To achieve this goal, cinema has to rely on a cognitive tool that allows the viewer to infer the abstract target domains indirectly on the basis of the iconicity of the images. The fundamental cognitive resource that makes this possible is that of *metonymy*. In contrast to metaphors which involve mappings across two distinctive conceptual domains, metonymies involve mappings within one single conceptual domain. Metaphors map the inferential logic of a source domain onto the inferential logic of a target domain, while metonymies take one entity in a schema as standing for another entity in the same schema, or for the schema as a whole (Lakoff and Turner 1989: 103). The source entities that are attracted in metonymies usually refer to concrete objects seen in the physical world. Their concreteness implies that they can also be photographed. This makes metonymy particularly suitable for a visual medium such as film. The target entity to which the concrete object refers might be concrete (e.g., BODY PART FOR PERSON), or abstract (e.g., GRAVE FOR DEATH). It is through the visual representation of concrete objects, then, that film is able to communicate abstract concepts indirectly to the viewer. The number of concrete entities through which the camera can recall abstract concepts are of course numerous.

For illustrative purposes, we will restrict ourselves in this chapter to what is commonly considered as one of the most prominent entities of the big screen, namely the entity of the human body. Because narrative cinema is essentially human-centered, relying heavily on the actions of fictional characters, it can be assumed that meaning in film operates significantly through the bodily features and actions of the actors and actresses on-screen. In specifying the role of the human body in the construal of metonymies, cognitive linguists have repeatedly attributed significance to body parts and physiological and expressive responses. For instance, literature indicates that the features of the human head are particularly responsible for recalling two categories of abstractness, namely the category of *mental functions* (e.g., Yu 2003, 2004) and the category of *emotions* (e.g., Kövecses 2000). For instance, the head as a whole is commonly seen as standing for the cognitive faculty of thinking, while the perceptual organs of the head such as eyes and ears are generally seen as standing for the perceptual functions associated with them (seeing and hearing). Metonymies such as HEAD FOR MENTAL ABILITIES (Piquer Píriz 2008) or EYE FOR WATCHING (Hilpert 2006) can be considered subcategories of what scholars have labeled more generally the INSTRUMENT FOR ACTIVITY metonymy (Hilpert 2006) or THE BODY PART FOR ITS TYPICAL FUNCTIONS (Barcelona 2002). Likewise, people tend to metonymically relate particular facial cues with specific underlying cognitive functions and emotions. This gives rise to two metonymies, the FACIAL EXPRESSIONS FOR EMOTION metonymy (Kövecses 2000: 134) and the FACIAL EXPRESSIONS FOR MENTAL FUNCTION metonymy. Both metonymies are also supported empirically by several expert theories. Support for the former metonymy can be found in the work of the famous American psychologist Paul Ekman. Through a series of studies (e.g., Ekman, Friesen and Ancoli 1980; Ekman and Friesen 2003), he and his colleagues found a high degree of likeness among observers in their attribution of specific emotional labels to particular facial configurations. For instance, the raising of the mouth corners and the tightening of the eyelids were commonly associated with the emotion of joy, while the lowering of the mouth corners and the descending of the eyebrows to the inner corners and the drooping of the eyelids were usually interpreted as standing for sadness. Likewise, Klaus Scherer (1992) observed that facial expressions not only signal emotions, but also cognitive processes. For instance, frowning often occurs when we do some hard thinking, or when we encounter difficulties in problem-solving (Kaiser and Wehrle 2001: 287).

Many illustrations of facial cues can be found in cinema. Cognitive functions such as visual perception or thinking (e.g., of the past) and emotions such as joy are frequently triggered visually by images showing facial expressions of fictional characters. We have separated the facial expressions in Figure 14.2 for

Figure 14.2: FACIAL EXPRESSIONS FOR MENTAL FUNCTION/EMOTION in *Casablanca* (Michael Curtiz, 1942), *City Lights* (Charles Chaplin, 1931) and *Le jour se lève* (Marcel Carné, 1939).

illustrative purposes.[4] However, given that faces signal both emotions and cognitive processes, they often concur simultaneously. Furthermore, as pointed out elsewhere (Coëgnarts and Kravanja 2016b, 2016c), film often indicates a *causal* relation between the facial expression that cues the lower cognitive function of perception and the facial expression that cues the emotion or the higher cognitive function. It involves the percept that the viewer sees that the character's perception of an outer event as the cause of a higher mental faculty (Coëgnarts and Kravanja 2016b) or the cause of an emotional state in the character (Coëgnarts and Kravanja 2016c). Because viewers are so accustomed to these kinds of images, they often fall below any theoretical evaluation. In this sense, they are similar to the day-to-day linguistic expressions that are analyzed so rigorously by cognitive linguists. Nevertheless, such images form the backbone of meaning-making in narrative cinema. Regardless of how seemingly effortless these images look, they have to be carefully construed. In order for them to facilitate metonymical inferences between certain facial cues and specific cognitive functions and emotions, the viewer has to be able to "read" the facial cues. Filmic resources, such as those discussed earlier in this chapter, are pivotal to achieve this heightened sense of facial cues. This entails, among other aspects, that the distance of framing or shot scale is not too far, or that the lighting is not too dimmed, for otherwise the viewer would not be able to infer the metonymical link between the facial expression and the underlying emotion or cognitive function. Equally of importance is the art of acting. For instance, the idea of perception is often triggered visually by the way the actor or actress moves his face and eyes towards some object on-screen or off-screen. The actor or actress has to show to the viewer, through his or her craft of facial and gestural simulation, that he or she is looking at something, feeling something or thinking something. The clearer and the more unambiguous

4 All film stills in this contribution are treated as visual citations, in accordance with the established guideline for fair use of film stills from DVDs in scholarly writings.

the facial expression is cued to the viewer, the likelier the viewer will infer the underlying emotion or cognitive process.

3.3 Metaphor and film: A case-study

With the answers formulated above, we are now in a position to address the relation of metaphor to film: How can we map the logic of an image schema, as provoked cinematically by such resources of framing as shot scale and the mobile frame, onto the logic of an abstract target domain, as provoked metonymically by the visual content of the film? To illustrate this, let us analyze a brief, but significant film scene taken from Francis Ford Coppola's wiretap thriller *The Conversation* (1974). The film recalls the story of Harry Caul (Gene Hackman), a middle-class surveillance expert who is assigned by his wealthy client (Robert Duvall) to record a conversation between Ann, the client's wife, and her lover Marc (Frederic Forrest and Cindy Williams). In one scene Harry accidently stumbles upon Ann in the elevator of the client's office building. Harry has just refused to hand over the tapes of the conversation to the client's assistant, Martin (Harrison Ford). The intensity of the emotion increases as Harry now finds himself faced with the same woman whose voice he has recorded.

To structure the discussion somehow, we can think of the scene as an interesting illustration of what Kövecses (2000: 64) calls the "Western folk theory of emotions". According to the general notion of this theory (1) a cause leads to an emotion and (2) this emotion leads to some response. The scene, then, might be instantiated in this structure as follows: Harry's perception of Ann together with his perception of the tape recording in his hands leads to an intense emotional state which, in turn, leads to a response (i.e., bodily behavior). Or to put it more schematically (where the double-line arrow indicates "causes, leads to"): Harry's perception (Ann-tape) => Change of state in Harry [less intense emotional state; high intense emotional state] => Response of Harry [bodily behavior]. From this formulation we can identify two causes: perception and emotion. According to the general LOCATION EVENT-STRUCTURE metaphor of Lakoff and Johnson (1999: 184–186) CAUSES are typically conceptualized as FORCES. For instance, in English language, it is common to speak about causation by relying on verbs that denote forced movement such as *bringing*, *throwing*, *driving* and *pulling*. Consider, for example, such expression as *He drove her crazy* or *That experience pushed him over the edge*. As the authors point out, in their literal sense, these verbs point to instances of physical movement. Yet, in these expressions they are used metaphorically in order to designate abstract causation. Hence, given that the Western folk theory of emotion conceptualizes perception and emotion as causes, it follows that we might conceptualize them as forces as well: perception as the force that brings about an emotion (the cause of emotion) and emotion as the force that brings about a behavioral response (emotion as cause). In what follows, I will discuss both conceptualizations and consider their manifestations in the scene from *The Conversation*, as cited above.

3.3.1 The force of perception

In the case of perception, FORCE is instantiated in what is perhaps the best known and most studied metaphor for perception, namely PERCEPTION IS FORCE INTERACTION (OR CONTACT) BETWEEN PERCEIVER AND OBJECT PERCEIVED (Lakoff, 1995; Yamanashi, 2010; Yu, 2004). Perception is conceptualized as successful insofar both entities are spatially brought closer to each other. According to Lakoff (1995: 133–135) this general metaphor for perception comes in two metaphorical duals: PERCEPTION IS RECEPTION and PERCEPTION IS TOUCHING. The first metaphor has the object perceived moving through space until it is spatially linked to the perceiver. One way to conceive of this spatial linkage is by conceptualising it through, what Lakoff and Johnson (1980: 30) coin, the VISUAL FIELDS ARE CONTAINERS metaphor in which the object perceived, motivated by an internal or external force, enters a bounded region of spatial interaction that is mapped onto the perceiver's visual field. This embodied conceptual structure underlies such expressions as *The ship is coming into sight* or *He came into my visual field.* In this case the interaction is based on the inferential logic of the CONTAINMENT schema: the object perceived (or abbreviated, the OP) is spatially linked with the perceiver (or abbreviated, the PR) because the OP is *in* the visual field of the PR.

Similarly, one might argue that the same metaphor is manifested in *The Conversation* for the purpose of communicating Harry's perception of Ann. The point-of-view shot (henceforth, POV shot) provides the stylistic means to achieve this goal. The POV shot is a stylistic device that typically involves one objective shot showing the character in the act of looking, followed by another shot showing what the character is looking at. Figure 14.3a shows the first image, an objective shot of Harry's face in the act of looking. His eyes are directed toward the elevator door. The target domain of perception is elicited by the EYES STAND FOR SEEING metonymy. The subsequent image shows what Harry is seeing: the closed elevator door (see Figure 14.3b). The inside content of the frame (the container) is mapped onto Harry's visual field. Notice the importance of the prior shot for interpreting the subsequent shot. The viewer is only able to attribute a metaphorical (and hence subjective) quality to the second shot on behalf of the metonymy elicited in the first shot. In other words, without the connection of Harry's eyes to the visual content of the second shot, the viewer would not be able to activate the metaphor (HARRY'S) VISUAL FIELD IS A CONTAINER. The shot would have remained objective rather than subjective, meaning that the shot cannot be attributed to the perception of a character inside the narrative world. Something then occurs in the POV shot: the elevator door opens and Ann *enters* Harry's visual field (see Figure 14.3c). This is the moment when the spatial interaction between Harry and Ann takes place and by metaphorical definition Harry's perception of Ann. Harry sees Ann because Ann is now *inside* his visual field. It is interesting to see how this entrance is visualised in the POV shot. A common solution to this problem would be by letting the actor or actress enter the POV shot from the left or right side of the frame (the horizontal axis). However, when a character resides in the background of the frame, he or she is already inside of it. How, then, can the transition from inside to outside be visualised? For this problem to be solved, the character has to be introduced into the frame by a second container in the mise-en-scène such as a window or a door, or in this case, an elevator (i.e., a frame-within-frame configuration), that opens up to the character in the background. In this case, the inclusion inside the frame (the visual field) is not based on actual motion of the character (e.g., motion from the left or right side of the frame), but on what Dewell (2005: 375) labels "stative inclusion based on entry". Following the author this might be diagrammed conceptually by the dashed arrow in Figure 14.3 which is meant to represent pure conceptual motion with no corresponding motion by the subject (i.e., Ann).

The film, then, cuts to a closer medium shot of Harry (see Figure 14.4a) and back again to this visual field. In his visual field Ann now also enters the second container, the elevator (see Figure 14.4b). The camera follows her (and hence, Harry's visual field) as she comes to a halt inside the elevator (see Figure 14.4c). As a result, her appearance grows inside the container. She is now *in full view*. Underlying this action is the INCREASE OF VISIBILITY IS INCREASE OF SUBSTANCE IN A CONTAINER metaphor. The conceptual level that underlies the visual manifestation level might be diagrammed as in Figure 14.4 whereby the path arrows (the non-dashed ones) represent the actual objective motion of both subject and camera.

By contrast, the PERCEIVING IS TOUCHING metaphor has the perceiver moving his gaze in the direction of the object perceived until it makes contact with the object perceived. This metaphor underlies such expressions as *My eyes wander* or *My eyes make contact*. As Lakoff (1995: 133) argues, this metaphor conceptualizes the target domain of vision in terms of the source domain of limbs. The word *eyes* thereby designate the "visual limbs" that move, just as the word *gaze* can designate such visual limbs (e.g., *My gaze is out over the bay*).

Likewise, one might argue that a similar logic underlies Harry's perception of the tape recording of Ann's voice. However, in its attempt to express this metaphor

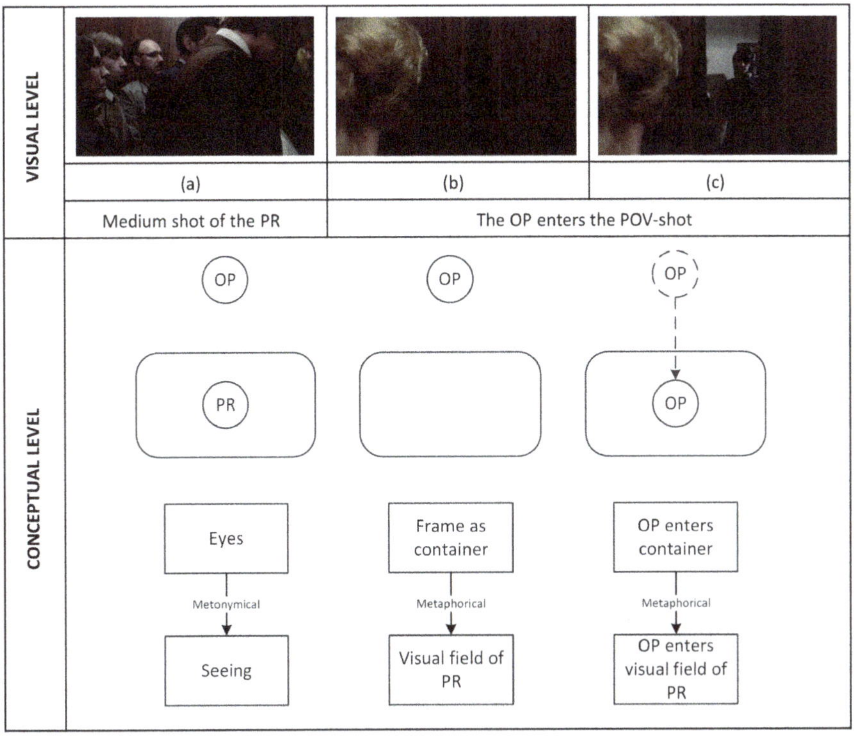

Figure 14.3: VISUAL FIELD IS A CONTAINER in *The Conversation* (Francis Ford Coppola, 1974).

visually, film finds itself confronted with an ontological problem, that is, its iconic nature prevents Harry's eyes from actually moving to the tapes. Therefore the film has to rely on other means to express this. This is where the role of camera movement comes in, as the camera might simulate this "eye movement" by moving from the PR's eyes to the OP. In the scene this simulation is initiated non-verbally by a facial cue of Gene Hackman (see Figure 14.5a). As he looks down, the camera slowly descends from his gaze (the source) towards the object of his gaze (the target) (i.e., the tape recording of Ann's voice) (see Figure 14.5b–c). Through camera movement and the underlying SOURCE-PATH-GOAL image schema, PR and OP are spatially linked to each other in one single shot. As with Figure 14.4, this spatial interaction is based on the logic of containment, albeit that now it is not the subject that *enters* the frame, but it is the frame itself, motivated by the PR's gaze, that now actively *encloses* the OP.[5] This might be diagrammed, as in

5 On the conceptual difference between ENTRY and ENCLOSURE, see Dewell (2005).

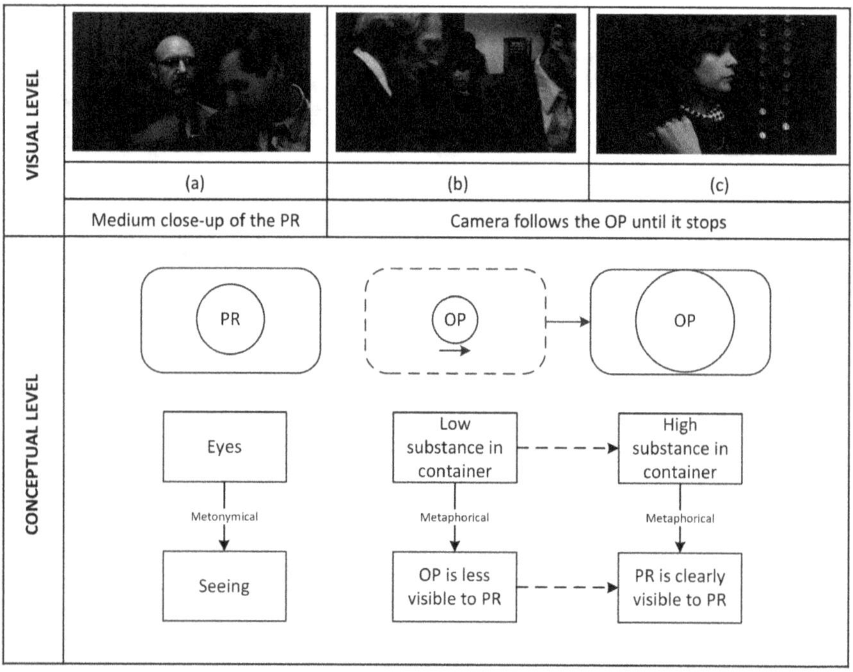

Figure 14.4: INCREASE OF VISIBILITY IS INCREASE OF SUBSTANCE IN A CONTAINER in *The Conversation* (Francis Ford Coppola, 1974).

Figure 14.5, by connecting the path arrow to the frame instead of the OP. Because the conceptual movement is accompanied by the actual movement of the camera, the arrow can be represented by a black line that is not dashed.

3.3.2 The force of emotion

When it comes to emotions, Kövecses (2000: 65–68) has argued that the generic-level metaphor EMOTION IS A FORCE might be instantiated by several specific-level metaphors. One of the best known and most studied metaphors in this regard is what the author labels the EMOTION IS INTERNAL PRESSURE INSIDE A CONTAINER metaphor. In this metaphor people are conceptualized as containers for emotions with the substance inside the container corresponding to the emotion. The substance exerts an internal pressure on the container. When there is very little substance in the container, the pressure is low and thus emotion is at low intensity. In that case, there is little motivation for the self to undertake action (i.e., to respond emotionally). By contrast, with an increase of the substance, the

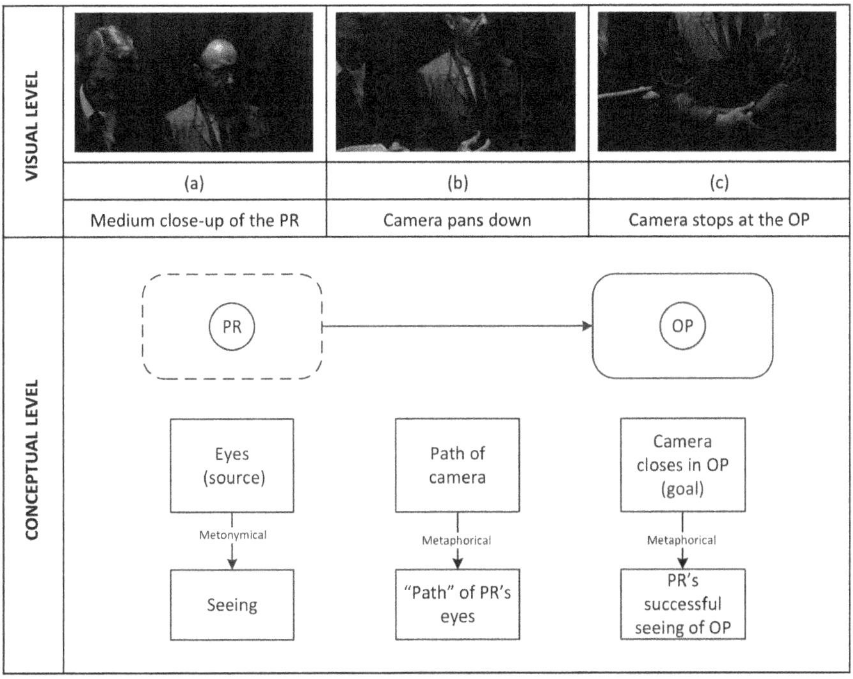

Figure 14.5: PERCEPTION IS ENCLOSING THE OP in *The Conversation* (Francis Ford Coppola, 1974).

pressure becomes higher, and thus also the intensity of the emotion. The higher the intensity of the internal pressure to bring about an effect, the higher also the intensity of the self's motivation to respond emotionally. If the intensity of internal pressure increases to the point that the substance goes out of the container, an external effect on the container takes place. In that case, the self performs an emotional response. This effect, however, might be prevented insofar as the container is able to keep the substance inside, that is, insofar as the self succeeds in controlling the emotional response.

Again, one might postulate that the same metaphor serves as a conceptual tool for expressing Harry's increase of emotional intensity after seeing Ann. On a formal level this metaphor is given form by gradually reducing the shot size with respect to Harry's face. As we already saw, at the beginning of the scene Harry is filmed in medium shot (see Figure 14.3a). Although the internal pressure on the container was high due to the presence of other people inside the frame, Harry's face (as the substance) did not occupy most of the total space inside the frame (i.e., the container). This, however, changes with the entrance of Ann in Harry's visual field (cfr. the analysis of the previous section). Figure 14.6a shows his response after seeing Ann. He does not appear in medium shot anymore, but in medium close-up. The internal pressure (and hence the intensity of the emotion) now increases as the camera reduces the distance between the sizes of the frame and Harry's face. As it was the case with perception, metonymy plays a conditional role in eliciting the target domain. It is through the acting of Gene Hackman that Harry's facial expression and hence the target domain of emotion is communicated to the viewer. In the absence of this metonymy, the viewer would not be able to map the change of shot size onto Harry's change of emotional state. The pressure increases even more at the end of the scene as the medium close-up now turns into an intense close-up of Harry (see Figure 14.6b). The scene reaches its emotional peak. Up until now Harry's face was still surrounded by a sufficient amount of empty space. The close-up, however, reduces this free space significantly thus causing the frame to be filled with Harry's face (i.e., the substance). Within the same shot, then, Harry attempts to control his emotion somehow by reducing the pressure again. He accomplishes this by taking a step backward, away from the camera, away from Ann, to a location more comfortable again. As a result, empty space takes over again and pressure (emotional intensity) decreases again (see Figure 14.6c).

4 Conclusion

The goal of this chapter was to provide the reader with a conceptual framework that enables him or her to analyze metaphor in film. Central to our argument was the claim that film, in order to activate metaphors, has to impose a structure onto the reality it represents. Only if film abstracts the perceptual richness somehow, it is able to create the necessary environment upon which metaphors can be built. This unity, we argued, can be reached by the application of cinematic resources such as framing. It is in the interaction of the techniques of film-making with the perceivable objects in the world that the patterns of image schemas (and by that the potential for conceptual metaphor) become manifested. However, the potential for metaphor becomes only actual once there are also target domains to which these image schemas may be appropriated. Herein, we argued, lies the importance of conceptual metonymy. Viewers are likely to map the inferential logic of image schemas onto the inferential logic of abstract target domains once the latter are also metonymically inferred on the basis of the concrete visual content of the film. We illustrated our argument by considering two abstract target domains of character subjectivity, namely character perception and character emotions. From the insights gained in the case-study, we can make an important and final

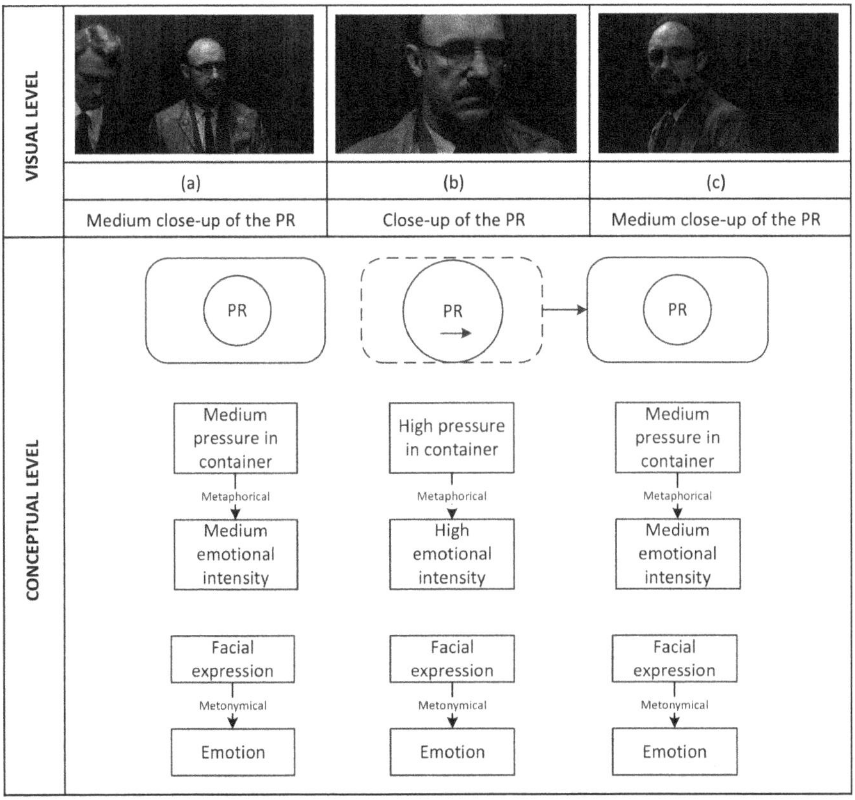

Figure 14.6: INCREASE IN EMOTIONAL INTENSITY IS INCREASE OF SUBSTANCE IN A CONTAINER in *The Conversation* (Francis Ford Coppola, 1974).

observation concerning the nature of metaphors in film. The majority of the examples of filmic metaphors discussed so far in literature have been mostly imaginative and highly visible. They are instances of what scholars have variously called "creative metaphors" (Forceville 2009), "image metaphors" (Lakoff and Turner 1989) or "resemblance metaphors" (Grady 1999). Despite these various labels they can be described as metaphors that map the concrete onto the concrete by virtue of a similar internal structure. Linguistic examples include such expressions as *Whose waist is an hourglass* in which both target and source are directly accessible to the senses. Likewise, as Forceville (1996, 2009: 388) pointed out, visual examples of this type can be found particularly in the field of advertising where the positive features of some other concrete object are projected onto the promoted target object (e.g., an elegant watch as a butterfly, beer as wine, etc.). A typical filmic example would be the scene from *Strike* (Sergei Eisenstein, 1925) in which the massacre of workers is intercut with the slaughter of a bull, thus evoking the metaphor WORKERS ARE SLAUGHTER-CATTLE (see also Grodal 2016: 108). These examples, however, stand in contrast to the filmic metaphors identified in this chapter, which lean more towards the conventional and structural metaphors as systemically discussed by CMT. They are more subtle, less visible and less idiosyncratic. They underlie trivial camera movements and sudden, unnoticeable changes in shot scale and framing. Nevertheless, it is through the "ordinary" level of film-making that, this chapter argues, Lakoff and Johnson's central tenet of "metaphors we live by" expresses itself. As such this contribution can be seen as supporting Mark Johnson's (2007: 208–209) broader theoretical hypothesis that meaning in the arts is built upon the same embodied processes of meaning that operate at the heart of our more prototypical meaning-making in language. This chapter, however, is not without its limitations. Given the space restrictions, we were only able to discuss a limited set of conventional metaphors in terms of one kind of cinematic resource (i.e., framing). Therefore it would be interesting to see how the same image-schematic driven conventional metaphors, as analyzed in this chapter, could be activated by other cinematic means such as sound and music, or how film activates some of the other well-known structural metaphors within CMT.

Bibliography

Arnheim, Rudolf. 1957. *Film as art*. Berkeley & Los Angeles: University of California Press.

Arnheim, Rudolf. 1974 [1954]. *Art and visual perception*. Berkeley & Los Angeles: University of California Press.

Arnheim, Rudolf. 1997 [1969]. *Visual thinking*. Berkeley & Los Angeles: University of California Press.

Barcelona, Antonio. 2002. Clarifying and applying the notions of metaphor and metonymy within cognitive linguistics: An update. In René Dirven & Ralf Pörings (eds.), *Metaphor and metonymy in comparison and contrast*, 207–278. Berlin & New York: De Gruyter Mouton.

Bordwell, David & Kristin Thompson. 2004 [1979]. *Film art: An introduction*, 7th edn. New York: McGraw-Hill.

Chandler, Daniel. 2007 [2002]. *Semiotics: The basics*, 2nd edn. London & New York: Routledge.

Coëgnarts, Maarten & Peter Kravanja. 2012. From thought to modality: A theoretical framework for analysing structural-conceptual metaphors and image metaphors in film. *Image [&] Narrative* 13 (1). 96–113.

Coëgnarts, Maarten & Peter Kravanja (eds.). 2015. *Embodied cognition and cinema*. Leuven: Leuven University Press.

Coëgnarts, Maarten & Peter Kravanja. 2016a. From language to film style: Reassessing the role of conceptual metaphor in cognitive film studies. In Lars C. Grabbe, Patrick Rupert-Kruse & Norbert M. Schmitz (eds.), *Yearbook of moving image studies 2016: Image embodiment: New perspectives of the sensory turn*, 108–134. Darmstadt, Germany: Büchner-Verlag eG.

Coëgnarts, Maarten & Peter Kravanja. 2016b. Perceiving causality in character perception: A metaphorical study of causation in film. *Metaphor and Symbol* 31 (2). 91–107.
Coëgnarts, Maarten & Peter Kravanja. 2016c. Perceiving emotional causality in film: A conceptual and formal analysis. *New Review of Film and Television Studies* 14 (1). 440–466.
Dewell, Robert. 2005. Dynamic patterns of CONTAINMENT. In Beate Hampe (ed.), *From perception to meaning: Image schemas in cognitive linguistics*, 369–394. Berlin & New York: De Gruyter Mouton.
Ekman, Paul & Wallace V. Friesen. 2003. *Unmasking the Face: A guide to recognizing emotions from facial clues*. Los Altos: Malor Books.
Ekman, Paul, Wallace V. Friesen & Sonia Ancoli. 1980. Facial signs of emotional experience. *Journal of Personality and Social Psychology* 39 (6). 1125–1134.
El Refaie, Elizabeth. 2003. Understanding visual metaphor: The example of newspaper cartoons. *Visual Communication* 2 (1). 75–95.
Evans, Vyvyan & Melanie Green (eds.). 2006. *Cognitive linguistics: An introduction*. Edinburgh: Edinburgh University Press.
Fahlenbrach, Kathrin (ed.). 2016. *Embodied metaphors in film, television, and video games: Cognitive approaches*. London & New York: Routledge.
Forceville, Charles. 1996. *Pictorial metaphor in advertising*. London & New York: Routledge.
Forceville, Charles. 2009. Non-verbal and multimodal metaphor in a cognitivist framework: Agendas for research. In Charles Forceville & Eduardo Urios-Aparisi (eds.), *Multimodal metaphor*, 19–42. Berlin & New York: De Gruyter Mouton.
Forceville, Charles & Eduardo Urios-Aparisi (eds.). 2009. *Multimodal metaphor*. Berlin & New York: De Gruyter Mouton.
Forceville, Charles & Marloes Jeulink. 2011. The flesh and blood of embodied understanding: The source-path-goal schema in animation film. *Pragmatics & Cognition* 19 (1). 37–59.
Gaut, Berys. 2010. *A philosophy of cinematic art*. Cambridge University Press.
Gibbs, Jr., Raymond W. & Marcus Perlman. 2006. The contested impact of cognitive linguistic research on psycholinguistic theories of metaphor understanding. In Gitte Kristiansen, Michel Achard, René Dirven & F. Ruiz de Mendoza Ibañez (eds.), *Cognitive linguistics: Current applications and future perspectives*, 211–228. Berlin & New York: De Gruyter Mouton.
Grady, Joseph. 1999. A typology of motivation for conceptual metaphor: Correlation vs. resemblance. In Raymond W. Gibbs & Gerard Steen (eds.), *Metaphor in cognitive linguistics*, 79–100. Amsterdam: John Benjamins.
Grodal, Torben. 2016. Film, metaphor, and qualia salience. In Kathrin Fahlenbrach (ed.), *Embodied metaphors in film, television, and video games: Cognitive approaches*, 101–114. London & New York: Routledge.
Hampe, Beate. 2005. Image schemas in cognitive linguistics: Introduction. In Beate Hampe (ed.), *From perception to meaning: Image schemas in cognitive linguistics*, 1–12. Berlin & New York: De Gruyter Mouton.
Hasson, Uri, Ohad Landesman, Barbara Knappmeyer, Ignacio Vallines, Nava Rubin & David J. Heeger. 2008. Neurocinematics: The neuroscience of film. *Projections: The Journal for Movies and Mind* 2 (1). 1–26.
Hilpert, Martin. 2006. Keeping an eye on the data: Metonymies and their patterns. In Anatol Stefanowitsch & Stefan Thomas Gries (eds.), *Corpus-based approaches to metaphor and metonymy*, 123–152. Berlin & New York: De Gruyter Mouton.

Johnson, Mark. 1987. *The body in the mind: The bodily basis of meaning, imagination, and reason.* Chicago: University of Chicago Press.
Johnson, Mark. 2007. *The meaning of the body: Aesthetics of human understanding.* Chicago: University of Chicago Press.
Johnson, Mark. 2013. Identity, bodily meaning, and art. In Tone Roald and Johannes Lang (eds.), *Art and identity: Essays on the aesthetic creation of mind*, 15–38. Amsterdam & New York: Rodopi.
Kaiser, Susanne & Thomas Wehrle. 2001. Facial expressions as indicator of appraisal processes. In Klaus R. Scherer, Angela Schorr & Tom Johnstone (eds.), *Appraisal processes in emotion*, 285–300. Oxford: Oxford University Press.
Kappelhoff, Herman & Cornelia Müller. 2011. Embodied meaning Construction: Multimodal metaphor and expressive movement in speech, gesture, and feature film. *Metaphor and the Social World* 1 (2). 121–153.
Kim, Jaegwon. 2006. *Philosophy of mind*, 2nd edn. Cambridge: Westview Press.
Kövecses, Zoltán. 2000. *Metaphor and emotion: Language, culture, and body in human feeling.* Cambridge: Cambridge University Press.
Lakoff, George & Mark Johnson. 1980. *Metaphors we live by.* Chicago: University of Chicago Press.
Lakoff, George & Mark Johnson. 1999. *Philosophy in the flesh.* New York: Basic Books.
Lakoff, George & Mark Turner. 1989. *More than cool reason: A field guide to poetic metaphor.* Chicago & London: The University of Chicago press.
Lakoff, George. 1987. *Women, fire and dangerous things: What our categories reveal about the mind.* Chicago: University of Chicago Press.
Lakoff, George. 1995. Reflections on metaphor and grammar. In Masayoshi Shibatani and Sandra A. Thompson (eds.), *Essays in semantics and pragmatics: In honor of Charles J. Fillmore*, 133–144. Amsterdam: John Benjamins.
Metz, Christian. 1974. *Film language: A semiotics of the cinema.* Chicago: University of Chicago Press.
Monaco, James. 2000. *How to read a film*, 3rd edn. New York: Oxford University Press.
Ortiz, María J. 2011. Primary metaphors and monomodal visual metaphors. *Journal of Pragmatics* 43 (6). 1568–1580.
Pecher, Diane, Inge Boot & Saskia Van Dantzig. 2011. Abstract concepts: Sensory-motor grounding, metaphors, and beyond. In Brian Ross (ed.), *The Psychology of learning and motivation*, 217–248. Burlington: Academic Press.
Piquer Píriz, Ana María. 2008. Reasoning figuratively in early EFL: Some implications for the development of vocabulary. In Frank Broers & Seth Lindstromberg (eds.), *Cognitive linguistic approaches to teaching vocabulary and phraseology*, 219–240. Berlin & New York: De Gruyter Mouton.
Scherer, Klaus R. 1992. What does facial expression express? In K. T. Strongman (ed.), *International review of studies on emotion*, 139–165. Chichester: Wiley.
Yamanashi, Masa-aki. 2010. Metaphorical modes of perception and scanning. In Armin Burkhardt and Brigitte Nerlich (eds.), *Tropical truth(s): The epistemology of metaphor and other tropes*, 157–175. Berlin & New York: Walter de Gruyter.
Yu, Ning. 2003. Chinese metaphors of thinking. *Cognitive Linguistics* 14 (2/3). 141–165.
Yu, Ning. 2004. The eyes for sight and mind. *Journal of Pragmatics* 36. 663–686.

M. Dolores Porto and Manuela Romano

Transmodality in metaphors: TIDES in Spanish social protest movements

Abstract: Multimodal discourse in general, and particularly multimodal and pictorial metaphors, have attracted a great deal of attention in the last decade. However, transmodality and its effects on discourse and on metaphors have only very recently started to be analysed. Transmodal metaphors are those which have migrated from one mode (verbal, visual or sonic) to another, often as a consequence of a change in the medium, which affects both the modes and the discursive practices involved. As a result, new mappings, meanings and functions are developed. This paper examines the effects of transmodality in the creation and development of *LAS MAREAS* (THE TIDES) metaphor in recent Spanish protest movements. Textual, pictorial and musical realizations of the metaphor in different media were collected from May 2011 to March 2016 and then analysed in specific socio-political, cultural and physical contexts in order to explain its different meanings as the metaphor migrated from one mode to another. The results show the evolution of the conventional metaphor A MASS OF PEOPLE IS A TIDE, first used to describe the demonstrations, to its consolidation as a conceptual metaphor for SOCIAL PROTESTS in general, as well as for new left-wing political parties (*En Marea, Mareas Gallegas*, etc.) and, more interestingly, how transmodality has contributed to the new semantic, pragmatic, rhetorical and affective values acquired by the metaphor throughout this evolution.

Keywords: multimodal discourse, transmodality, transmodal metaphors, protest movements, *Mareas* (Tides)

1 Introduction

This paper analyses the effects of transmodality in metaphors through a case study, the TIDES metaphor (*LAS MAREAS*) for protest movements in the Spanish

Note: This study has been carried out under the funding of research project FFI2016-77540-P, Spanish Ministry of Economy and Competitiveness.

M. Dolores Porto, Universidad de Alcalá, Dpto. Filología Moderna, C. Caracciolos, Spain
Manuela Romano, Universidad Autónoma de Madrid, Dpto. Filología Inglesa, F. Filosofía y Letras, Ciudad Universitaria Cantoblanco, Spain

https://doi.org/10.1515/9783110629460-015

media from 2011 until present. More specifically, we describe how the well-known, conventional metaphor A MASS OF PEOPLE IS A TIDE develops new, creative mappings and uses as it migrates from one mode to another, that is, from its verbal, written form to its pictorial and musical realizations. New semantic, pragmatic, rhetorical and affective values are incorporated to the metaphor as it is recontextualized from one protest group to another (teachers, physicians, unemployed, librarians, miners, etc.) and "translated" from one mode to another, distributed in different media and contexts, while creating novel and very powerful uses of the expression for new political parties and newspapers. The evolution of the metaphor, as we explain, cannot be separated from the socio-historical context of recent Spanish protest movements, nor from the new communication modes and media used to transmit their messages.

In this sense, this work has been carried out following the recent general agreement that communication is becoming increasingly multimodal. It is not only that more attention to modes other than verbal has been paid to within linguistic, semiotic and discourse research, it is also that the development of new technologies and new ways of communication has increased the range of affordances in communication (Kress 2011). For this reason, the study of discourse and interaction has been compelled to acknowledge the role of other modes of transmission beyond language (spoken or written) in order to analyse communicative events.

Accordingly, metaphor research has also started to consider pictorial and multimodal metaphors as an important part of the field (Forceville and Urios-Aparisi 2009). The increasing number of studies on the role of these metaphors in different kinds of discourses –advertisements, tv commercials, comics, political cartoons, protest slogans, architecture, etc. (Bounegru and Forceville 2011; Caballero 2014; El Refaie 2003; Forceville 1996; Hidalgo-Downing et al. 2016; Marín-Arrese 2008; Romano 2013; Tasić and Stamenković 2015), support the thesis that metaphors are not merely a linguistic phenomenon but an essential part of our reasoning, subsequently reflected in communicative interactions, whatever their mode. The study of multimodal metaphor must thus be addressed as a product of social and cultural practice, as new ways of communicating and new affordances are provided by technological advances. The close relationship between culture and metaphor is particularly manifest in multimodal discourse.

However, a new parameter influencing both the creation and spread of metaphors must be incorporated into its analysis, transmodality, that is, the way in which meaning is affected when "translated" to a different mode in a different medium (Murphy 2012). Transmodality in metaphors has only very recently started to be taken into account (Tomanić Trivundža 2015), but it is a promising field, particularly for metaphors with an openly persuasive intention, as is the case of *LAS MAREAS*.

In the following sections, we first explain the theoretical premises for the analysis of transmodality in metaphors (section 2), as well as the methodology for the case study of *LAS MAREAS* (section 3). Then, we introduce the socio-political context in which *Las Mareas* movement arises (section 4), as well as the evolution of the metaphor in its verbal mode (section 5). Next, in sections 6 and 7, the pictorial and musical metaphors are analyzed, and, finally, our preliminary conclusions are summarized in section 8.

2 From multimodal to transmodal metaphors: Theoretical and methodological tenets

Multimodality is an approach to the study of language and communication that accounts for the way in which different modes work together to produce meanings. This involves, not only a co-presence, but essentially also a co-dependence of different modes which results in a unified meaning that is "more" than what is conveyed by individual modes (Murphy 2012: 1967). Similarly, a multimodal metaphor is one in which target and source are presented in at least two different modes, to the extent that it becomes unidentifiable if one of them is deleted (Forceville 2007). Accordingly, in a multimodal metaphor, all the modes have to be present simultaneously, and the final emergent meaning of the metaphor goes far beyond the mere sum of its parts.

Multimodal metaphors have proved a fruitful field of study. They are common in a high number of everyday communicative interactions, particularly those with persuasive aims, such as advertisements and political slogans (Forceville 1996; Hidalgo-Downing et al. 2016; Romano 2013), as well as in artistic manifestations, from comics and posters to architecture or performances (Caballero 2014; Fabiszak 2016; Fernandes 2016; Gibbs and Cameron 2008; Tasić and Stamenković 2015). Besides, multimodal metaphors evidence the role of metaphors as central instruments in cognition, and not only as linguistic manifestations (Forceville 2007).

As already stated in the introduction, the aim of this paper is to analyse not multimodal, but transmodal metaphors, that is, those which have migrated from one mode (or more than one in multimodal metaphors) to another, e.g., verbal, visual or sonic. As Murphy (2012) states, in transmodality the focus is on the generation of semiotic chains that are discontinuous in time "rather than emphasizing the simultaneous layering of modes in single moments of interaction" (Murphy 2012: 1967). Transmodality, then, is presented as a "possible technique for expanding the analytic advantages of multimodality" (Murphy 2012: 1969).

Besides, the notions of modes and media are closely connected. Medium is "the substance in and through which meaning becomes available to others" (Bezemer and Kress 2008: 172) and it is partly characterized by the number and kind of modes that are possible in it (Forceville 2009b: 21). Therefore, dealing with transmodality also implies dealing with *transmediality*, as the changes in the way of distribution will affect both the resources available, i.e. the modes that can be used, and the discursive practices involved, in terms of production, interpretation and distribution (Kress and van Leeuwen 2001). Social networks, blogs, instant messaging, etc. involve not only new affordances, but most interestingly, new demands. The ideas, informative contents, opinions, etc. in them must be presented in a way that fits the new media, with the inescapable need to create new textual genres and subgenres. This, in turn, requires new literacies and skills that enable the community to produce and interpret this new kind of information exchanges, always constrained by the requirements of the different modes and media. The result is a bi-directional influence in which culture affects new ways of communication and these also affect culture (Chesebro and Bertelsen 1996, cited in Forceville 2007; Kress and van Leeuwen 2001).

Transmodality is not such a new phenomenon, apart from the fact that new technological media have become recently available.[1] First studied by Kress as *transduction* (Kress 1997; Kress and van Leeuwen 2001), it has always been present in human communication.

> Transduction is a part of human semiosis and has been as far back as there are records such as sculptures, paintings, carvings in caves, on rock faces, in sites of ancient habitation. But in the time scales of cultural histories of (Western) representation the present may be distinctive through the ubiquity, the "intensity," and the centrality of the process. The new media have made available new kinds of modal ensembles to very many users, offering possibilities of representation that had not existed before, or if so, then rarely (e.g., the opera). (Bezemer and Kress 2008: 176)

Transmodality brings with it some changes in meaning, as different modes have different meaning-affordances (Lemke 2002). The transformation of a verbal metaphor into a pictorial one, for example, produces new meanings in a very wide sense. Not only may the new modes amplify, reduce or contradict (Sindoni 2016: 29) the original meaning, but there can also be changes in terms of subjectivity, identity and affect (Newsfield 2014), as well as others related to social context, pragmatic functions, rhetorical intentions, etc. Therefore, in the migration of a metaphor from one mode or medium to another there will be "gains and losses"

1 See a full account of the development of the concept, including "transformation", "chains of semiosis" and the "transmodal moment" in Newsfield (2014).

(Bezemer and Kress 2008: 175), and for this reason, discourse context and shared socio-cultural knowledge play an essential role in their interpretation in order to determine, for example, metaphorical targets when these are not explicit. "In order for viewers to construe a metaphor in a picture, they must know something about who made it, and why" (Forceville 2007).

New social media are playing a leading role in recent social movements all around the world. Social protests expand faster and wider than ever before thanks to Twitter, Facebook and other similar social media, to the point that the terms "Twitter Revolutions" or "the Youtube War" have been coined to refer to those dissent movements that use these as their means to disseminate information and even to cross national borders and get the sympathies of foreign audiences, as was the case in the Iranian and Egyptian antigovernment protests in 2009 and 2011 (Burns and Eltham 2009; Christensen 2011; Lotan et al. 2011; Tomanić Trivundža 2015).

This transmodal approach to the creation and spread of the *MAREAS* metaphor is, in addition, grounded in and complemented by the latest socio-cognitive work in metaphor studies, namely metaphorical creativity and recontextualization in real discourse situations (Kövecses 2010, 2015; Porto 2012; Porto and Romano 2013; Semino et al. 2013), as well as applications of these models to the discourse of social protest movements (Martín-Rojo 2014; Montesano and Morales 2014; Pujante and Morales 2013; Romano 2013, 2015; Romano and Porto 2018).

The delimitation of possible modes in discourse is not a straightforward issue. Bezemer and Kress (2008: 171) define mode as "a socially and culturally shaped resource for making meaning" and more generally, in social semiotics, modes are equated to communication "channels", i.e. verbal, visual and aural. Forceville (2009b: 22–23) states that a distinction of modes in terms of signing systems interpretable by one of our five senses would be inaccurate, since writing and gestures, for example, would both be categorized as visual. Instead, this author suggests that a general account of modes should differentiate at least pictorial signs, written signs, spoken signs, gestures, sounds, music, smells, tastes and touch. However, for the purpose of our analysis, we will distinguish three different modes in which the *MAREAS* metaphor is represented in the Spanish media: written, pictorial and musical, as these are the modes in which it can be found and transmitted in newspapers, blogs, social networks and demonstrations.

3 Data and methodology

The metaphorical verbal, pictorial and musical expressions of the *MAREAS* metaphor in Spanish media were collected from May 2011 to December 2016 from several sources: photographs of slogans and banners at demonstration sites, newspaper headlines, both written and online, and different websites, blogs and social networks (Twitter and Facebook) of the protest movements. The written mode corresponds to the metaphorical expressions of the *MAREAS* metaphor in slogans and in newspaper headlines. The pictorial mode is represented by the visual and multimodal metaphors in posters, logos and cartoons. And the musical mode corresponds to the metaphors triggered by the songs by the *Solfónica*, a political choir that contributes to the spread of the movements by singing the contents of the protests with the melodies of popular songs during demonstrations.

The approach followed in this paper is mainly diachronic and qualitative, rather than quantitative, since our main aim, as stated in the introduction, is to understand how the migration of the metaphor from the verbal to the pictorial and musical modes affects its meanings, not only in terms of amplification, reduction or elaboration, but also regarding their pragmatic, rhetoric and affective values. So, for the identification and selection of the metaphorical expressions (either verbal, pictorial or musical), possible referents of the source domain were searched for and identified in the different multimodal texts mentioned above. Following this method, we selected verbal expressions from slogans and newspaper headlines where the words *marea* ['tide'], *olas* ['waves'], *tsunami*, etc. referred to the protest movements. Images in posters, banners, cartoons and websites, displaying associated elements like the sea, waves or tides, to represent the protests were also collected. Finally, we also considered those songs, created by the political choir *La Solfónica*, in which mappings could be established between the protests and tide-related domains evoked by the music.

Once identified, the metaphors were analysed in their context, taking into account factors such as specific socio-political situation, purpose of the text, political orientation of the source, discourse participants, etc. in order to determine their specific meaning in each mode, and more precisely their conceptual and pragmatic "gains or losses" (Kress 2005) in the different modes. More details on the types of metaphor, mode transfer, pragmatic functions, etc. are provided in section 5.

4 *Las Mareas*. The socio-political context of the protests

As a prototypical embodied, socially constructed metaphor, that is, a metaphor that has been situationally, discursively, conceptually and cognitively created (Kövecses 2010, 2015), the *MAREAS* metaphor is born within a specific social, cultural and historical setting, i.e. the socio-political and economic crisis suffered by Spanish society in the last 10 years. Within this context, *Las Mareas* represents one of the biggest social mobilizations experienced in Spain in the last decades against the Government's and Europe's austerity measures. Nevertheless, the drastic budget cuts in the state educational, health and welfare systems imposed by the regional government of Madrid since 2003 and by the national government since March 2008 alone –both in the hands of the conservative *Partido Popular*–, cannot explain the scale of the protests that welled up in 2011. As Grossi et al. (1998: 171, cited in Gil de Biedma 2013: 2) writes, "injustice in itself, is not sufficient to generate protests; there has to be an awareness of the situation and a social discourse, or an interpretation that relates injustice with specific policies exerted by power".[2] In this sense, the magnitude and outreach of the social protests called *Las Mareas* has to be understood within the specific context of the 15M Movement, and its alternative transforming discourses and forms of social protest (Martin Rojo 2014; Pujante and Morales 2013; Romano 2013, 2015; Romano and Porto 2018).

The 15M Movement is one of the first anti-austerity movements in Europe, called after the day, May 15th 2011, when a group of outraged citizens decided to meet and camp at the *Puerta del Sol* Square in Madrid until their demands to stop unemployment, welfare cuts, and, above all, political and financial corruption were heeded. In general terms, the protesters that gathered at the *Puerta del Sol* did not consider themselves to be represented by any of the traditional parties, neither right- or left-wing, nor the trade unions, and were outraged at politicians and bankers, whom they considered directly responsible for the current economic crisis or, in their own words "fraud". What is so interesting about the 15M Movement is that it was a spontaneous movement, self-organized by people, not trade unions, in which thousands of people from a wide variety of socio-cultural, political and economic backgrounds, as well as age groups, came together with the same general worries and demands. It was not another case of demonstrating within a specific labour sphere, but a horizontal, highly participative form of open democracy.

It is within this new social movement, with its new discourses and protest forms that the movement of *Las Mareas* emerges. Alternative forms of protesting and demonstrating that involved the whole community were created; in the case of state education: teachers, parents and students, and in the case of the health system, physicians, nurses, administrative staff, and, for the first time, patients. This highly horizontal and participative form of protest, characterized by a new discourse of optimism, festivity, creativity, etc., is enhanced by new

2 Authors' translation.

social networks – *Democracia Real Ya* ['Real Democracy Now'], *Juventud Sin Futuro* ['Youth with no Future'], etc., whose messages, slogans and summonings grew and spread at an enormous speed through Twitter, Telegram, Facebook, The Internet, etc., free from the more official and rigid forms and filters of the mass media and the traditional trade unions.

One of the first creations of the protestors encamped at the *Puerta del Sol* from May 15th to June 12th 2011, in addition to a great variety of commissions and offices such as communications, library, food supply, infrastructures, etc., was the *Solfónica*, the "choir of the outraged". The *Solfónica*, a blend created from *sol* ['sun'] + *sinfónica* ['symphonic'] is a prototypical example of the new festive protest forms and discourses born with the 15M. The *Solfónica* is in itself a symbol of the 15M Movement and its name derives from one of the most productive, creative multimodal metaphors of the 15M. *SOL* ['SUN'], a common source domain for conventional metaphors for HAPPINESS, HOPE, FUTURE etc. was soon recontextualized to the new socio-political situation through a metonymical interaction, as protesters had gathered at *Puerta del Sol* Square (Romano 2013, 2015). Since 2011 the *Solfónica* has become a stable popular choir that sings and plays at most political acts and demonstrations in Madrid, including the different *Mareas* or protests. Because of that, the choir and orchestra can be understood in terms of "reterritorialization", playing and singing in the streets and squares becomes another way of occupying and "reterritorializing" the common, public space (Martín Rojo 2014).

5 Origin and evolution of the TIDE metaphor: The verbal mode

Based on Romano and Porto (2018), this section summarizes how, within this socio-political and cultural scenario, the *MAREAS* metaphor develops and is recontextualized from a well-known image metaphor carrying neutral or negative connotations, A MASS OF PEOPLE IS A TIDE, to a new positive metaphor representing the different groups of protesters (teachers, physicians, unemployed, librarians, scientists, miners, among others), and from here, to its use for new grassroot political parties and a newspaper. The fact that the term *mareas* today is on its way towards grammaticalization, developing from a lexical word to a pragmatic expression, as we will see, proves that the metaphor is still active and highly entrenched in the community.

The metaphor A MASS OF PEOPLE IS WATER FLOWING is a well-known, conventional one, present in many European languages. The metaphor can be used with neutral connotations, as in example (1), where *marea rojiblanca* ['red & white tide'] metonymically represents the followers of the *Atlético de Madrid* football club wearing their team's red and white T-shirts, or with highly negative connotations as in (2), in which the words *thousands* and *inundate* trigger the concepts of CHAOS, DANGER, and RISK:

(1) *Una marea rojiblanca toma las calles de Munich.*
'A red and white tide takes the streets in Munich'.
(*Antena 3 TV*, 3/05/2016)

(2) *Human Tide of Refugees Diverted to Croatia: (...) thousands of refugees and migrants inundate the country.*
(*NBC News* 18/09/2015)

Linell (1998:144) defines recontextualization as the dynamic transfer-and-transformation of something from one discourse/text-in-context to another, which involves the extrication of some part or aspect from a text or discourse to another, and the fitting of this part or aspect into another context, into a new use and environment.[3] Following these ideas, the first recontextualization of *MAREA* into the new and more specific positive meaning, A MASS OF PEOPLE FIGHTING FOR THEIR RIGHTS IS A TIDE, can be traced back to September 2011. State education had been suffering severe cuts since 2003, and teachers had been demonstrating since then. But it is a month and a half after the 15M when the new more horizontal forms of protest emerge, and when the whole educational community – teachers, students, and parents, join the protests. As already explained in Romano and Porto (2018), protestors for state education decided to continue wearing the green T-shirt that teachers had been wearing since 2003 in all their periodically repeated demonstrations with the motto *escuela pública: de todos para todos* ['state school: of everyone and for everyone']. It is thus in September 2011 that the new metaphor STATE EDUCATION SUPPORTERS ARE A GREEN TIDE emerges, as can be seen in (3) and (4).

(3) *Una marea verde sale a las calles en defensa de la enseñanza pública.*
'A green tide comes out to the streets in defense of public education'.
(*ABC* 09/10/2011)

3 See Semino et al. (2013); Porto (2012); Porto and Romano (2013); Romano and Porto (2018) for recent socio-cognitive approaches of recontextualization to metaphor.

(4) *La marea verde pide al gobierno de Mariano Rajoy que acabe con los recortes.*
'The green tide requests Mariano Rajoy's government to stop the cuts'.
(*El País* 15/09/2012)

During the autumn of 2011, mobilizations welled up and spread throughout the whole country, since the austerity measures imposed by the national and regional governments affected almost all social and professional groups, from the health system, to researchers, unemployed, pensioners, miners, etc. Each group, recontextualizing THE GREEN TIDE and its positive evaluative connotations, chose among the colour palette the colour that best represented them metonymically or metaphorically. For instance, the movement supporting the national health system coined the term *marea blanca* ['white tide'], triggered by the white coats of health workers, for their demonstrations, and the miners, *marea negra* ['black tide'], black clearly standing metonymically for coal. The TIDE metaphor is thus recontextualized from one social group to another, using the whole palette of basic colours: red for unemployed and researchers, orange for social services, purple for Spanish emigrants, lilac for feminist movements, yellow for public libraries, etc. (see examples 5–7), until the whole colour spectrum is completed and demonstrators just use the term *marea* ['tide'] as a means of identifying with the ongoing global mobilizations, as is the case of *marea de tricornios* ['tide of civil guards'] or *marea de ortopedistas* ['tide of orthopaedists'].

(5) *La marea blanca contra la privatización y los recortes se extiende.*
'The white tide against privatization and cuts spreads'.
(*El País* 17/02/2013)

(6) *Nace la 'marea negra' en apoyo a los mineros y sus familias.*
'The "black tide" is born to support the miners and their families'.
(*El Periódico de Aragón* 02/10/2012)

(7) *Protestas de la marea granate por el 'voto robado' a los emigrados.*
'Protests of the purple tide because of the "stolen vote" of migrants'.
(*El País* 26/06/2016)

In short, as Romano and Porto (2018) explain, in this first recontextualization, the *MAREA* metaphor is readapted from one social/professional group to another because of the highly positive meanings it activates within the community, such as "strength", "union", "solidarity", "the possibility to change the present", etc. These connotations are so strong, that the metaphor is simplified and develops into

SOCIAL PROTEST IS A TIDE, and into its new coinage *Marea Ciudadana* ('Citizens' Tide'), when the first *Unión de Mareas* ['joint tide'] is organized on February 23, 2013.

THE *MAREAS* metaphor undergoes a second recontextualization when new meanings are created in different domains; that is, when TIDE is used as a source domain for a new target and context. First, a new newspaper called *La Marea* is created in 2012. Their editorial principles claim equality, laicity, defense of public services, sovereign power of people, fair economy, democratic regeneration, free culture, decent work and housing, and respect for the environment, etc.; principles which are very similar to those of the 15M Movement. And second, as the different local, regional, and national elections approached in 2015, new political parties stemming from the 15M and *LAS Mareas* movements emerged: *Mareas Ciudadanas, Mareas Gallegas, Marea Atlántica*, and *En Marea*. As Romano and Porto (2018) state, by using the same source domain, *MAREA*, the new newspaper and political parties make deliberate use of the already entrenched TIDE metaphor which activates mappings of CHANGE, SOLIDARITY, JOINT FIGHT, etc. In this sense, the name of one of the last coalitions, *En Marea* ('On the Tide'), clearly activates the dynamic connotations of water/people flowing/moving as a natural force, pushing things forward, washing out the past, etc.

Finally, we know the metaphor is consolidated and entrenched within the community because of the many elaborations it has developed, such as tsunami, waves, sediment, etc., as well as expressions that refer to the intensity of the tide's effects (examples 8 to 10).

(8) *Unir todas las mareas en un tsunami contra los recortes.*
'Unite all the tides in a tsunami against cuts'.
(Demonstration poster, 2013)

(9) *Dos meses de fuerte oleaje en la marea blanca.*
'Two months of rough waves in the white tide'.
(*Diagonal* 11/12/2012)

(10) *Mucho sedimento para ser una derrota.*
'Too much sediment for a defeat'.
(*Eldiario.es* 23/10/2013)

The TIDE metaphor is still active in speakers' minds and thus still being used (examples 11 and 12) and recontextualized into new meanings (13):

(11) *La marea blanca inunda cuatro capitales y cerca a Susana Díaz.*
'The white tide floods four capital cities and surrounds Susana Díaz'.
(*El Mundo* 15/01/2017)

(12) *Tercera dimisión en Salud por la presión de las 'mareas blancas' al Gobierno de Susana Díaz.*
'Third resignation in Health [Department] due to the pressure of the "white tides" on Susana Díaz's government'.
(*El Mundo* 02/02/2017)

(13) *Eva y la marea militante de los 73.940 'noes'.*
'Eva and the 7,940 "noes" of the tide of (socialist) militants".
(*El Mundo* 16/10/2016)

Its entrenchment within the community, as well as its emotional and persuasive power within social protest movements and grassroot political parties is also proved by the fact that it has undergone a process of grammaticalization, that is, the term *marea* has developed from a lexical word to a more grammatical element, in this case a pragmatic marker or expression used as one of the mottos for the new left-wing political party, *Unidos Podemos*, in the closing rally on June 24 2016. In this rally, their original motto *sí se puede* ['yes we can'], repeated after the most salient interventions in the rally, was suddenly changed into *hay marea* ['the tide is here'], clearly taking advantage of the highly positive connotations of *Las Mareas* movement within this segment of Spanish society, as well as of the fact that *Unidos Podemos* integrated other grassroot parties called *Mareas* for the 2016 elections.[4] In this last recontextualization, we see how the original mappings related to WATER have been completely lost, and only STRENGTH, HOPE, BETTER FUTURE, etc. remain.

6 The pictorial mode: Colour waves for the protest

For a protest movement like *Las Mareas*, expansion and diffusion are crucial. Their success is strongly linked to the number of protesters and sympathizers joining their movement. Therefore, posters calling to join demonstrations are among the first and most outstanding examples of the pictorial expression of the metaphor. Either pasted on the city walls, retweeted hundreds of times, or displayed on banners during the marches, the images of the *MAREAS* metaphor strive to catch people's attention and, essentially, to persuade them to join their protests.

4 *Mareas Gallegas* ['Galician Tides'], *Mareas Atlánticas* ['Atlantic Tides'], *En Marea* ['On the Tide'], etc.

In order to achieve these goals, the pictorial representations of the metaphor have to be readily identifiable in the first place and also appealing to the eyes through simple, colourful images as in Figure 15.1.

Figure 15.1: Poster summoning an assembly of the Green Tide.

As already explained in the section 5, colours are an essential part of the meaning of the metaphors as they facilitated identification and discrimination – green for protests in education, white for state health system, orange for social workers, etc. Ironically, these colours became even more significant when all the *Mareas* joined forces and finally converged into one, the *Marea Ciudadana* ('Citizens´ Tide'), and decided to march together. The summons to these joint demonstrations were performed through images displaying several wavy lines composed of different colours, as in Figure 15.2.

The images in the posters for these joint demonstrations evidence how the CITIZENS' TIDE metaphor amplifies its meaning in the pictorial mode by adding new associations to its previous domains. The merging of the specific interests of different protest groups into one global protest for citizens' rights, against budget cuts, corruption, etc., is represented by putting together the colours of the tides, which evokes the domains of UNITY, COLLABORATION, JOINT FORCES and particularly of INCREASE/ADDING, as the number of sympathizers mathematically grows when the different tides meet. These additional meanings can be seen in detail in Figure 15.3. The poster shows several

Figure 15.2: Posters for a joint demonstration of the Tides in a Citizens' Tide.

Figure 15.3: Poster for Citizens' Tide demonstration.

wavy lines with different colours "moving" together, as if following the same direction, displayed against a black and white crowd of demonstrators in the background.

A slightly different perspective can be seen in Figure 15.4, where more emphasis is placed on the domains of COLLABORATION and UNITY, by displaying two series of coloured hands holding together, and which clearly refer to the conventional metaphor COOPERATION IS JOINING HANDS. The source domain TIDE is only echoed in the wavy movement that can be seen in their posture, and the INCREASE mapping is just hinted in the way the image is cut at the bottom, suggesting a larger number of hands that cannot be seen in the poster.

Figure 15.4: Citizens' Tide poster.

The wavy lines and their associated colours are the elements that allow for an immediate identification of each of the protest movements, and this is why they are the only necessary components when images are schematized in the logos for the different tides (Figure 15.5). Once again, the Citizens' Tide is represented by the combination of the various colours.

More complex depictions of the TIDE metaphor can be seen in posters and cartoons that develop the meanings of the TIDE, often adding narrative senses. Among

Figure 15.5: Logos for the Orange Tide, the political party *En Marea* ('On the Tide'), and the Citizens' Tide.

these, a common elaboration, also present in many verbal manifestations, is that of the tides washing out corruption, cuts, traditional politics, etc., as in Figure 15.6, where big waves are about to swallow the President or the current ministers and their most recent legislative initiatives. Also the cartoon in Figure 15.7 shows the White Tide, in the form of big waves, carrying away the privatization of hospitals.

Once the metaphor is entrenched in ordinary discourse, critics and opponents to the movement also make use of it and develop their own elaborations, but, in this case, with a negative meaning.[5] Thus, the image created for the electoral campaign by *En Marea* (Figure 15.8), where the alliance of several parties is represented by combining their colours together (imitating the different colour tides in the Citizens' Tide) was contested in a local right-wing newspaper with the cartoon in Figure 15.9, where the different parties are swallowed into a whirlpool, presumably caused by the tide.

It is interesting to note that, as shown by the pictures above, the narrative meaning of the tides, i.e. that they rise and fall on a periodical basis, cannot be displayed in a static image. As a consequence, some associated meanings of the TIDE metaphor are lost in the transduction from the written to the pictorial mode, as it has to be represented in the form of waves. With this change in mode, more emphasis on the mapping MOVEMENT is provided and, instead of a uniform, increasing mass of water, recalling the image of crowds in demonstrations slowly advancing, a more direct action is suggested, especially when waves are depicted as if about to swallow politicians, decrees, etc.

As already pointed out by Kress (2005), whereas speech or writing show a temporal and sequential logic, in images, where all the entities are represented simultaneously, it is their salience which is significant, as well as their relations, even if expressed in spatial terms. Consequently, when compared with the *MAREAS* metaphor in its verbal mode, images show stronger links to domains

5 For another example on how a metaphor can be appropriated by adversaries and change their evaluative meanings see the ZOMBIE metaphor in Tomanić Trivundža (2015).

Figure 15.6: Cartoons used in posters representing the tides.

Figure 15.7: Cartoon by Atxe (*Huffington Post* 07/04/2013).

Figure 15.8: Image of *En Marea* for the 2016 electoral campaign.

Figure 15.9: Cartoon by Ed Cariosa (*La Voz de Galicia* 5/11/2015).

such as NATURAL FORCE, derived from the pictorial representations of waves, and JOINT FORCES, conveyed through the simultaneous representation of the different protest groups in the Citizens' Tide.

Besides, a more immediate identification has been found in the pictorial representation of the *MAREAS* metaphor by means of colours and simple lines, enabling a strong sense of identity for these movements, as well as a faster and easier transmission and dissemination in the media, which is crucial for social protest movements.

To sum up, the representation of the *MAREAS* metaphor in the pictorial mode brings with it necessary meaning changes, highlighting some aspects and overlooking others. This mode allows a gestaltic interpretation of the metaphor, that is, to establish immediate associations at first glance; associations which are often not fully conscious and that make the whole more persuasive than its parts. It is this persuasive power of images over words what makes them especially suitable for summoning demonstrations and mobilization.

7 The musical mode: "music is a weapon loaded with hope"

The third mode analyzed in this study of the *MAREAS* metaphor is the musical one, since songs, as already explained, are another of the strategies used by the movements in order to spread their protests and persuade people to join them.[6]

Music has always been closely connected with political and protest movements (Eyerman and Jamison 1988; Lyndon and McKerrell 2017; among others) and the concept of "musical activism" is not new. Particularly fruitful were the protest songs in the 1960s that gave way to others in the following decades: punk, rap, ska, etc. The most recent protest movements have often included music in their actions through political choirs (Gutiérrez-Rubí 2016), as is the case of *Occupy Musicians* that went along with the *Occupy Wall Street* movement, *30 days 40 songs* against Donald Trump's policies, *Lebenslaute* in Berlin or *Raised Voices* in London. The 15M Movement, and subsequently *Las Mareas*, soon understood the importance of music for their movements and that is how the *Solfónica* was born in June 2011 by singing a particular version of Beethoven's well-known Symphony no. 9.

Music in social protest contexts helps the construction of collective identities. An idea that the famous activist Abbie Hoffman already named "the mystic of movements": all those elements that allow people belonging to the same movement to recognize each other and communicate with others; words, slogans, gestures, music, etc., common affects rather than arguments, feelings rather than opinions (Garrido Arce 2013). Underlying this practice is the generally acknowledged claim that music is a strong persuasive tool, since it does not only activate our emotions (Aristotle's *pathos*) but also can influence our behaviour, an idea

6 The quote in the heading is the authors' translation of the *Solfónica's* motto.

that has recently been empirically proved (Salimpor et al. 2013; Zentner et al. 2008, among others).

> The arts have always played an important part in shaping the attitudes and ideas of any society, and even government policy. And within the arts, songs and music in general are intensely persuasive. (Kaufman 1981, cited in Bostrom et al. 2002)

Following this line of research, the *MAREAS* metaphor is also represented in the musical mode by recontextualizing well-known songs and melodies, writing new lyrics for them and so using music as a social persuasive tool, both as *pathos*, appealing to demonstrators' emotions, and as *logos*, providing the intended set of values, social attitudes and behaviour that the protest movements support.

According to Forceville (2009a), in multimodal metaphors, the musical mode can cue the source domain of the metaphor and also trigger the mappings of a source domain already signalled in a nonverbal mode. So, when a national anthem evokes the country or a rock song brings to the mind its title, these will act as sources for the metaphor, as long as the listeners can recognize there is a metaphorical intention. Besides, the discourse context will determine which one of a range of potential connotations is pertinent (Forceville 2007). Similarly, the musical metaphors analyzed in this section are readily identifiable because of the context, that is, because these songs are performed during specific protests and by a specific choir, *La Solfónica*.

One of the best-known songs by the *Solfónica* uses the melody of a popular Galician seafaring song, *Rianxeira*, whose chorus repeats *ondiñas veñen e van* ['waves come and go'] and the interpretation of the song is usually accompanied with a wavy movement of people when informally sung in celebrations. When the *Solfónica* sings this melody, with new lyrics that refer to budgets cuts, corruption, etc., the audience is provided with the necessary clues to construct the metaphor. Whereas the music activates the source domain, i.e. SEA, WAVES, TIDE, the lyrics refer to the target: FIGHTING CORRUPTION IS A TIDE. Not only that, it is a choral song commonly associated with happy moments, which also activates a number of positive emotions and domains of UNITY, HAPPINESS, CELEBRATION that are incorporated to the meaning of the metaphor.

This recontextualization device, i.e. writing new lyrics for well-known songs, is the main one used by the *Solfónica* for their creations.[7] On the one hand, they use the melodies of culturally entrenched songs, strongly associated by the community with the protests against Franco's dictatorship in the late 1960s – *Canto a la Libertad* ('Hymn to Freedom'), by Labordeta or *L'Estaca* ('The Stake') by Lluis

7 For other recontextualizations of songs with political intentions see Richardson (2017).

Llach. On the other, popular, well-known songs that evoke feelings and domains of HAPPINESS, OPTIMISM and HOPE, like Beethoven's 9th Symphony or *Do you hear the people sing* (*Les Misérables*), are also rewritten to convey the new messages of the protests. In this way, other metaphors, apart from the *MAREAS* metaphor, are created by the mappings triggered by the music, which both activates cognitive and cultural models of FIGHT, DEMOCRACY, FREEDOM, and arouses emotions and domains like HOPE and JOY (*pathos*) that make their lyrics more persuasive.

> With music we can all be doing one same thing, and feel there is union, a link, a connection. Different people, with different opinions, arguments coming together and sharing common affects and feelings. (Sánchez Castrillo 2015)[8]

8 Conclusions

The *MAREAS* metaphor started as a novel figurative expression for the people that marched for specific protests in education, health, civil rights, etc., and ended as the name of grassroot political parties, *Las Mareas*, that won local elections and are now in the government bodies in some of the most important cities in the country. This evolution and the fact that the metaphor is still active and productive demonstrate its success in the dissemination of the message. For social protest movements like *Las Mareas*, spreading their ideas is the key to success, and in order to reach large audiences, the *MAREAS* metaphor was distributed by all possible means – demonstrations, assemblies, social networks, posters, banners, songs, etc. Along this process, the metaphor has undergone several transformations in order to adapt both to the different affordances of the *modes* chosen for the representation and the different facilities of the *media* used for the distribution.

From the analysis of the different occurrences of the metaphor in each mode, we have seen how some mappings of the metaphor are highlighted in certain modes and ignored in others. Thus, for instance, the mental image of the tide is turned into waves in the pictorial metaphor, which emphasizes the concepts of MOVEMENT, ACTION and FORCE, whereas those of CYCLIC REPETITION and SPREAD, present in the verbal mode to refer to the demonstrations, are less evident. Similarly, choral singing of popular songs, as well as the joining of all the tide colours in the same image, reinforce the links to concepts like UNION and INCREASE that are not so explicit in the verbal mode.

8 Authors' translation.

Moreover, we have seen that the semantic changes affect not only the core meaning, but essentially the affective values and pragmatic intentions. Images and songs seem to be more persuasive than textual occurrences of the metaphor. As already pointed out, words necessarily follow a temporal sequence whereas in static images all the elements are present simultaneously, a fact that may have a role in the higher persuasive force of images. As for the musical metaphor, its persuasion is enhanced by establishing strong connections to positive emotions, both through the qualities of the sounds (pitch, tone, tempo, etc.) and through the associations that some songs can create with historical and cultural models shared by the community.

In short, as an embodied, socially constructed metaphor, the adaptation of the *MAREAS* metaphor to the different modes in order to facilitate its dissemination through different media has triggered specific changes in its meanings, mostly in terms of amplification, elaboration, positive evaluation and persuasive power that were transmitted by the movement itself, *Las Mareas*, and so contributed to its spread and success.

Finally, the migration of the *MAREAS* metaphor from one mode to another, as studied in this paper, can be considered a prototypical case of transmodality, ideal for a detailed exploration of the potential "gains and losses" of its meaning in each one of the modes in which it has been represented. Beyond this case study, however, far more work needs to be done to fully understand the effects of transmodality in discourse. Transmodal metaphors have proved to be a revealing starting point as well as a fascinating new research field.

References

Bezemer, Jeff & Gunther Kress. 2008. Writing in multimodal texts: A social semiotic account of designs for learning. *Written Communication* 25 (2). 166–195.

Bounegru, Liliana & Charles Forceville. 2011. Metaphors in editorial cartoons representing the global financial crisis. *Visual Communication* 10 (2). 209–229.

Bostrom, Robert N., Derek R. Lane & Nancy G. Harrington. 2002. Music as persuasion: Creative mechanisms for enacting academe. *American Communication Journal* 6 (1). http://ac-journal.org/journal/vol6/iss1/special/bostrom.pdf (accessed 4 August 2018).

Burns, Alex & Ben Eltham. 2009. Twitter free Iran: An evaluation of twitter's role in public diplomacy and information operations in Iran's 2009 election crisis. *Communications Policy & Research Forum*. 19th–20th November 2009, University of Technology, Sydney.

Caballero, Rosario. 2014. Thinking, drawing and writing architecture through metaphor *Ibérica 28*. 155–179.

Chesebro, James W. & Dale A. Berltelsen. 1996. *Analyzing media: Communication technologies as symbolic and cognitive systems*. New York & London: Guilford Press.

Christensen, Christian. 2011. Twitter revolutions? Addressing social media and dissent. *The Communication Review* 14 (3). 155–157.
El Refaie, Elisabeth. 2003. Understanding visual metaphors: The example of newspaper cartoons. *Visual Communication* 2 (1). 75–95.
Eyerman, Ron & Andrew Jamison. 1998. *Music and social movements: Mobilizing tradition in the twentieth century*. Cambridge: Cambridge University Press.
Fabiszak, Malgorzata. 2016. Multimodal discourses of collective memory. In Manuela Romano & M. Dolores Porto (eds.), *Exploring discourse strategies in social and cognitive interaction: Multimodal and cross-linguistic perspectives*, 159–186. Amsterdam & Philadelphia: John Benjamins.
Fernandes, Carla. (ed.). 2016. *Multimodality and performance*. Newcastle: Cambridge Scholars Publishing.
Forceville, Charles. 1996. *Pictorial metaphor in advertising*. London & New York: Routledge.
Forceville, Charles. 2007. *A course in pictorial and multimodal metaphor*. Semiotics Institute http://semioticon.com/sio/courses/pictorial-multimodal-metaphor/ (accessed 4 August 2018).
Forceville, Charles. 2009a. The role of non-verbal sound and music in multimodal metaphor. In Charles Forceville & Eduardo Urios-Aparisi (eds.), *Multimodal metaphor*, 383–400. Berlin: De Gruyter Mouton.
Forceville, Charles. 2009b. Non-verbal and multimodal metaphor in a cognitivist framework: Agendas for research. In Charles Forceville & Eduardo Urios-Aparisi (eds.), *Multimodal metaphor*, 19–42. Berlin: De Gruyter Mouton.
Forceville Charles & Eduardo Urios-Aparisi (eds.). 2009. *Multimodal metaphor*. Berlin & New York: De Gruyter Mouton.
Garrido Arce, Estrella. 2013. En la Solfónica no todos pensamos lo mismo, pero cantamos juntos. *Eldiario.es* (29/09/2013). https://www.eldiario.es/interferencias/Solfonica-pensamos-mismo-cantamos-juntos_6_201989803.html (accessed 4 August 2018).
Gibbs, Raymond W. & Lynne Cameron. 2008. The social-cognitive dynamics of metaphor performance. *Cognitive Systems Research* 9 (1). 64–75.
Gil de Biedma, Carla. 2013. El movimiento social de las Mareas: La reapropiación ciudadana de lo público. Cuando sube la marea. *Betiko*. http://fundacionbetiko.org/wp-content/uploads/2014/02/El-movimiento-social-de-las-Mareas.pdf (accessed 4 August 2018).
Grossi, Javier, Concepción Fernández & J. Manuel Sabucedo. 1998. Los movimientos sociales y la creación de un sentido común alternativo. In Pedro Ibarra & Benjamín Tejerina (eds.), *Los movimientos sociales. Transformaciones políticas y cambio cultural*, 165–181. Madrid: Trotta.
Gutiérrez-Rubí, Aantoni. 2012. Coros políticos. Blog Micropolítica. *El País* (26/6/2012). http://blogs.elpais.com/micropolitica/2012/06/coros-politicos.html (accessed 4 August 2018).
Hidalgo-Downing, Laura, M. Angeles Martínez & Blanca Kraljevic. 2016. Multimodal metaphor, narrativity and creativity in TV cosmetics ads. In Manuela Romano & M. Dolores Porto (eds.), *Exploring discourse strategies in social and cognitive interaction: Multimodal and cross-linguistic perspectives*, 137–158. Amsterdam & Philadelphia: John Benjamins.
Kaufman, Charles. 1981. Poetic as argument. *Quarterly Journal of Speech* 67. 407–415.
Kövecses, Zoltán. 2010. A new look at metaphorical creativity in cognitive linguistics. *Cognitive Linguistics* 21 (4). 663–697.
Kövecses, Zoltán. 2015. *Where metaphors come from: Reconsidering context in metaphor*. Oxford, UK: Oxford University Press.

Kress, Gunther. 1997. *Before writing. Rethinking the paths to literacy.* London: Routledge.
Kress, Gunther. 2005. Gains and losses: New forms of texts, knowledge, and learning. *Computers and Composition* 22. 5–22.
Kress Gunther. 2010. *Multimodality. A social semiotic approach to contemporary communication*. London: Routledge.
Kress Gunther. 2011. Multimodal discourse analysis. In James P. Gee & Michael Handford (eds.), *The Routledge handbook of discourse analysis*, 35–50. London & New York: Routledge.
Kress, Gunther & Theo van Leeuwen. 2001. *Multimodal discourse: The modes and media of contemporary communication*. London: Edward Arnold.
Lemke, Jay L. 2002. Travels in hypermodality. *Visual Communication* 1 (3). 299–325.
Linell, Per. 1998. Discourse across boundaries: On recontextualization and the blending of voices in professional discourse. *Text* 18 (2). 143–158.
Lotan, Gilad, Erhardt Graeff, Mike Ananny, Devin Gaffney, Ian Pearce & Danah Boyd. 2011. The revolutions were tweeted: Information flows during the 2011 Tunisian and Egyptian revolutions. *International Journal of Communications* 5. 1375–1405.
Lyndon C. S. Way & Simon McKerrell (eds.). 2017. *Music as multimodal discourse: Semiotics, power and protest.* London & New York: Bloomsbury.
Marín-Arrese, Juana. 2008. Cognition and culture in political cartoons. *Intercultural Pragmatics* 5 (1). 1–18.
Martín Rojo, Luisa. 2014. Taking over the square: The role of linguistic practices in contesting urban spaces. *Journal of Language and Politics* 13 (4). 623–652.
Montesano Montessori, Nicolina & Esperanza Morales López. 2014. Multimodal narrative as an instrument for social change: Reinventing democracy in Spain – the case of 15M. *Critical Approaches to Discourse Analysis Across Disciplines (CADAAD)* 7 (2). 200–219.
Murphy, Keith M. 2012. Transmodality and temporality in design interactions. *Journal of Pragmatics* 44. 1966–1981.
Newfield, Denise. 2014. Transduction, Transformation and the Transmodal Moment. In Carey Jewitt (ed.), *The Routledge handbook of multimodal analysis*, 100–114. London & New York: Routledge.
Porto, M. Dolores & Manuela Romano. (2013). Newspaper metaphors: Reusing metaphors across media genres. *Metaphor & Symbol* 28 (1). 60–73.
Pujante, David & Esperanza Morales López. 2013. Discurso (discurso político), constructivismo y retórica: los eslóganes del 15-M. *Language, Discourse, & Society* 2 (2). 32–59.
Richardson, John E. 2017. Recontextualization and fascist music. In C. S. Way Lyndon & Simon MacKerrell (eds.), *Music as multimodal discourse: Semiotics, power and protest*, 71–94. London & New York: Bloomsbury.
Romano, Manuela. 2013. Situated-instant metaphors: Creativity in 15M slogans. *Metaphor and the Social World* 3 (2). 241–260.
Romano, Manuela. 2015. La protesta social como 'laboratorio' de creatividad metafórica. *Discurso & Sociedad* 9 (1). 41–65.
Romano, Manuela & M. Dolores Porto. 2018. 'The tide, change, nobody can stop it': Metaphor for social action. *Discourse & Society* 29 (6). 655–673.
Salimpoor, Valorie N., Iris van den Bosch, Natasa Kovacevic, Anthony Randal McIntosh, Alain Dagher & Robert J. Zatorre. 2013. Interactions between the nucleus accumbens and auditory cortices predict music reward value. *Science* 340 (6129). 216–219.
Sánchez Castrillo, Álvaro. 2015. Solfónica 15M: La música es el acto de protesta más directo. *Infolibre.es* (04/04/2015).

https://www.infolibre.es/noticias/cultura/2015/03/21/solfonica_quot_verano_ensayamos_retiro_invierno_atocha_quot_30187_1026.html (accessed 4 August 2018).
Semino, Elena. 2008. *Metaphor in discourse*. Cambridge: Cambridge University Press.
Semino, Elena, Alice Deignan & Jeannette Littlemore. 2013. Metaphor, genre, and recontextualization. *Metaphor and Symbol* 28. 41–59.
Sindoni M. Grazia. 2016. The semantics of migration. Translation as transduction: Remaking meanings across modes. *Hermes – Journal of Language and Communication in Business* 55. 27–44.
Tasić, Miloš and Dušan Stamenković. 2015. The interplay of words and images in expressing multimodal metaphors in comics *Procedia. Social and Behavioral Sciences* 212. 117–122.
Tomanić Trivundža, Ilija. 2015. And the word was made flesh, and dwelt among us: On zombies, political protests and the transmodality of political metaphors *Družboslovne Razprave* XXXI (80). 29–46.
Zentner, Marcel, Didier Grandjean & Klaus Scherer. (2008). Emotions evoked by the sound of music: Characterization, classification, and measurement. *Emotion* 8 (4). 494–521.

María Muelas-Gil

Visual metaphors in economic discourse. An analysis of the interaction of conventional and novel visual metaphors in *The Economist*

Abstract: The present chapter introduces the results of a study that observes multimodal metaphor in printed media discourse. Starting from the basis of Multimodal Theory (Forceville 1992, 2002, 2006) and Multimodal Metaphor Annotation (Bolognesi et al. 2017; Šorm and Steen 2018), the study analyses a corpus of 28 covers of *The Economist* in order to observe metaphor frequency in the multimodal elements complemented by the headlines. Moreover, the communicative objective of the covers is also studied through personal interviews held with a sample of students during which they were asked to interpret the covers and comment on how the different elements of the cover (text and image) had contributed to their interpretation, which is in line with recent approaches such as the 'response-elicitation approach' (Robins and Mayer, 2000; Sopory, 2008). The outcomes of this pilot study reveal that the communicative objective of the covers is achieved in general terms and that, while visual metaphors tend to convey comprehension of the message on their own, it is the combination of image and text (i.e. multimodal metaphors) that achieve the most accurate understanding of the message that is being depicted. The study, then, contributes to the field of the communicative theory of metaphor (Steen 2011) as well as multimodal metaphor research.

Keywords: multimodal metaphors, printed media, economic discourse, response-elicitation approach, three-dimensional model.

1 Introduction: Visual and multimodal metaphors in the economic press

In the discourse of economics, metaphors play a vital role as they are pervasively used to explain the abstract processes and specific notions of the field (Mouton 2012; White 2003). The ubiquity of metaphor in this discourse has been largely studied

María Muelas-Gil, Universidad de Castilla-La Mancha

https://doi.org/10.1515/9783110629460-016

in the last decades (Charteris-Black 2000; Alejo González 2011; Herrera-Soler and White 2012; Koller 2004; Negro 2011; Richardt 2003; White 2003), and one of the common groundings is best summarized in McCloskey's words (1983), who firstly referred to the discourse of economics as "heavily metaphorical" and claimed that economists use metaphors to violate the rules of reality, presenting, instead, their own models and hypotheses.

In more recent years, Soares da Silva has been working on the use of metaphors in the discourse of economics. In one of his studies, he claims that economic discourse is full of metaphors of competition, conflict and hostility, factors that are characteristic of free market (Eubanks 2000; Herrera-Soler and White 2012; Koller 2004; Rojo López and Orts Llopis 2010) and he also justifies that the years of economic recession and finance bailout are naturally prone to create metaphorical thought, communication and action (Soares da Silva 2013a). His claims are relevant to this study since the data under analysis is entirely related to the economic recession in Europe.

Furthermore, metaphor in economics is not only found in its written form but also in visuals. Visual and multimodal metaphors have also been extensively analysed; Forceville (1996, 2002) is one of the pioneers on studies of multimodal metaphor and there has been a growing interest towards this modality (Caballero 2014; El Rafaie 2009; Gkiouzepas and Hogg 2011; Koller 2009; Phillips and McQuarrie 2004). One of the projects that analyses multimodal metaphors is the VisMet Baby corpus, developed by the Metaphor Lab in Amsterdam (firstly introduced in 2014, see Bolognesi et al. 2017), which contains an accessible repertoire of annotated visual metaphors, including images from advertising, artwork and political cartoons. In spite of its usefulness, this project does not cover the field of economics and finance. Some studies have been carried out lately on economics (Negro 2011, 2013), but this discipline needs further thorough research if compared to others such as advertising or politics (Bounegru and Forceville 2011; Forceville 1996; Negro 2015; Perez-Sobrino 2016; among many others).

The main motivation behind this study lies in two factors: (i) the pervasiveness of metaphor in the discourse of economics and (ii) the need for further studies concerning visuals in the field. Moreover, it aims at observing the communicative power of this discourse device when it is used in the printed media, following Herrera-Soler and White's question: "is metaphor use in economics ancillary to communication or is it systemic to economics discourse itself?" (Herrera-Soler and White 2012: 3). Finally, it is also founded on the groundings of Steen's three-dimensional model of metaphor (Steen 2011), according to which there are three levels of meaning: conceptualization, expression and communication.

Thus, the objective of the study is twofold. Its first part consists in a quantitative analysis which aims at observing the potential ubiquity of visual metaphors in the English news magazine *The Economist*.[1] This newspaper has previously and openly claimed to be heavily metaphorical (see references to find the links to the articles); however, it has made no reference to visuals. A total of 28 covers were collected from November 2014 to August 2015 and VisMIP procedure (Šorm and Steen 2018) was applied in order to address metaphor frequency in the data and observe whether the McCloskey's claim (1983) could be used to refer to visuals as well.

The second part consists in a quantitative and qualitative study. Out of the total number of covers that contained metaphor and/or metonymy, three of them (referring to the same financial or economic event in Europe) were selected and shown to 17 students in their early 20s, following recent approaches to metaphor understanding like the 'response-elicitation approach' (Robins and Mayer 2000; Sopory 2008), according to which the subjects are directly asked to interpret the discourse in which metaphor is involved. They were asked three questions so as to analyse whether they could correctly interpret the cover or, in other words, whether they understood (at least in general terms) the news that each cover referred to. In case they understood this part, the subsequent step was to observe whether metaphors were involved and to what extent.

Before introducing the data, the next subsection is devoted to reviewing previous research on written and multimodal metaphors in the press. Section 2 of the paper refers to the data used in the study, as well as the procedure followed in both parts; Section 3 contains the main research questions and hypotheses of this project; the results from both parts are individually explained in Section 4; finally, section 5 includes the discussion and comments that can be drawn from the results, alongside the conclusions and future paths of research.

1.1 Metaphor in the press

If metaphor is part of all types of discourse, it is necessary to specify its role in the type of discourse that concerns this study: the printed media. Journalists are trained to use all types of discourse devices to make the message seem one thing or another, to decorate it, magnify or even belittle it (Koller 2004/2008; White

1 Although *The Economist* is a magazine-shaped publication, it calls itself a newspaper (for more information, visit http://www.economist.com/blogs/economist-explains/2013/09/economist-explains-itself).

1997). In other words, the news that we read have been meticulously thought and elaborated and they are not just words on paper. Besides, I believe that the journalist does not only use a given discourse to convey one idea or another (Goatly 2007; Koller 2006; Wolf and Polzenhagen 2003), but also to facilitate the text comprehension by all readers, regardless of their beliefs (Koller 2004; White 1996). In line with this, Prince and Ferrari (1996) claimed that metaphors in printed media emphasize the explanatory power of a given piece of news, and therefore journalists make use of such advantage.

The idiom "A picture is worth a thousand words" is known by all in many languages and it represents one of the motivations behind our study. The first contact with any newspaper or magazine is made through the cover, as it captures the reader's attention. Same as newspapers use appealing and large headlines, a cover needs an image that is not only an attractive way of keeping their audience attentive but also an informative tool. Since metaphor is used to explain abstract and complicated notions by using familiar domains (Kövecses 2010; Lakoff and Johnson 1980), it can be expected to find many of them in newspapers or magazines covers.

Having reviewed the most relevant bibliography of this study and explained the motivations behind it, the forthcoming section provides the relevant information concerning the data and the methodology applied in the analysis, including an account of the aforementioned method, VisMIP project.

2 Data and methodology

2.1 Quantitative study: VisMIP applied

For the purpose of the study, 28 covers of the British news magazine *The Economist* were gathered from November 2014 to August 2015. For the following step in the procedure, VisMIP method was applied to observe metaphor frequency. This visual metaphor identification procedure, introduced by Šorm and Steen (2018), is a tool to determine whether a given picture contains metaphorical/metonymic elements or if, on the contrary, there is no figurative language involved. This method follows similar steps to those of MIP (see Pragglejaz Group 2007: 3 to consult the steps) and MIPVU (see Steen et al. 2010: 25–26) methods, which had the same objective and also followed established steps so as to confirm potential metaphoricity of a given word or expression in written discourse. Following this method, the researcher does not simply rely on introspection and suspicion, as even the most expert on visual metaphors could be misled. The steps to apply to a visual that is potentially metaphorical or that may contain metaphors are (see Šorm and Steen 2018)[2]:

1 – Establish general understanding
  1a. Describe denotative representational meaning
  1b. Search cues to symbolic, connotative meaning (abstract concepts/ features)
  1c. Describe argumentation (standpoint) and general topic
2 – Structure conceptual/semantic roles of the units
3 – Find incongruous visual units
  Distinguish topic incongruous from property incongruous
4 – Test whether the incongruities are integrated in the topic by comparison with something else
  Is there a unit or a property that would be literal (congruous with the topic)?
5 – Test if comparison is cross-domain (to exclude metonymy)
6 – Test if comparison is indirect discourse
7 – If 4-5-6 are true, then mark visual metaphor

The covers of the corpus were analysed individually and classified according to the following criteria: (1) it contains metaphor(s), (2) it contains metonymy, (3) it contains both metaphor and metonymy, and (4) it does not contain any rhetorical device. Once the classification process had been performed, three of them were selected: one containing metaphor, one containing metonymy and one containing both. These three covers (see Section 4) were subsequently showed to the interviewees during the second part of the analysis.

2.2 Qualitative study: Interviews

The aim of the second part of the analysis was to observe whether the interviewees could understand the news behind the cover. For such purpose, I designed a set of simple and straight questions following the three dimensions of meanings in line with Steen's (2011) model of metaphor: conceptualization, expression and communication. To start with, according to Steen's (2011) model, the communication dimension differentiates between deliberate and non-deliberate.

2 The steps were extracted from the lectures during the Metaphor Lab Summer School, held at the University of Amsterdam in June 2015

Whether the designers of the covers with metaphor are conscious or not of its communicative and appealing load, they do know that they are distorting a visual element by using devices as metaphor and metonymy. After all, as discussed above, metaphors are frequently used in the press because of their explanatory, appealing and ideological load. However, this dimension is discarded in the present study, which focuses on is the other two, namely conceptualization and expression.

The interviews consisted in a "think aloud" method inspired by Šorm and Steen's (2013) study, in which the subjects were presented with the three covers. However, it differed from the aforementioned study in that the subjects of this study were partially guided by a set of questions previously designed. It has to be noted, though, that no specific reference to metaphor or metonymy was made during the interviews so that their answers were not influenced by the deliberate use of metaphor (Steen 2011):

a. *What do you see? Describe the cover, being as precise as you can (expression dimension).*
b. *What do you understand? (conceptualization dimension)*
c. *What do you think might be the content in the news behind this cover?*
d. *How did you reach that conclusion?*
e. *Is there any specific hint that has helped you to think that?*
f. *Is there any particular element in the cover that has helped you to think that?*

The group of students were all in their early twenties (the youngest was 19 and the oldest, 23) and they were all students of a Degree in Primary School Education at the University of Castilla-La Mancha. The original purpose was to interview 20 subjects but, in the end, three of them could not contribute, resulting in a total of 17 interviewees. Although they were all students of English as a foreign language and most had an intermediate level, the interviews were held in Spanish and the texts accompanying the image were translated if necessary. Their native language was used to avoid facing any limitations or language barriers that would impede them from saying everything they thought of the covers. Equally, the interviewer did not stop or interrupt them at any moment and, on the contrary, encouraged them to say as much as possible. The interviews were held individually, and they were recorded and transcribed for study purposes. Finally, once the subjects had described what they could see (without interpreting it or giving their opinion), they had to explain their interpretation of the cover using their own words and being as precise as they could. This would help the researcher observe whether they had understood the piece of news entirely, partially or if, on the contrary, they had completely misunderstood it.

Before continuing with the results, the reasons for the selection of the three covers need to be clarified. First, I decided to separate them according to the rhetorical device they contained (metaphor, metonymy or both) and leave out those which did not contain any of these figures since the main goal was to see whether the use of metaphors had significance in terms of understanding a cover (we shall remember the interviewees were not experts on economics, finance or even the English press whatsoever). Then, I selected three covers that were related to the same topic: the European financial breakdown and, more concretely, the financial crisis that devastated Greece in recent years. This situation was familiar to the subjects as this country had been often compared to what simultaneously occurred in Spain. Therefore, although the piece of news they transmitted was complicated for a non-expert reader, the topic was not completely alien to them. Moreover, this topic was selected so that, even if the subjects had no previous knowledge or background on economy, they would at least observe a familiar problem to that of their country and their previous knowledge would also help interpret the news more easily.

The results from the interviews were annotated and each cover was individually analysed and compared to the other two with the purpose of observing the potential communicative role of the metaphor/metonymy in case the subject had understood the message.

Finally, as stated in the Introduction, this part of the study was mainly qualitative but also quantitative, as it compared numerically how many students understood each cover and in how many of these comprehension processes metaphor or metonymy were involved.

3 Research questions and hypotheses

3.1 Research questions

There are four main research questions that this study pursues. The first one can be answered in the first part of the analysis, while the remaining three are centred on the interviews.

a. How metaphorical are the covers of *The Economist?* In other words: out of 28, how many of them will contain metaphors?
b. Do they achieve their communicative purpose?
c. Does the viewer grasp the general meaning of the cover containing metaphors?
d. If so, is/are the metaphor(s) involved in the understanding of the news? To what extent?

3.2 Hypotheses

Concerning the hypotheses of the study, they were as follows:

- Manipulative devices in shape of metaphors/metonymies were to be largely found. This was expected mainly because of their communicative and attention-catching power; journalists know how to manipulate discourse, being this written or visual, and figurative devices are perfect tools for such purpose.
- General understanding of all three covers was also expected to occur, albeit at a different degree (for reasons of explicitness and for the potential effect of the headline).
- In those cases of understanding, which were largely expected as mentioned above, I assumed metaphors would play an important role in the interviewee's understanding of the news or message communicated in the cover, due to their explanatory load.
- Even if the focus of our study were visual metaphors and therefore the image containing them in the cover, the headlines and the rest of the text appearing alongside the image would probably prove to be important, to one extent or another, in the comprehension process.

4 Results of the study

4.1 Results of the quantitative analysis

Before discussing the results, we shall show several examples from our corpus of multimodal data. As explained in Section 2, all the covers were analysed individually and, in case of doubt, an expert on the method was consulted and their advice was followed. For example, the covers referred to below (see links[3]) depict covers that are examples of metaphorical uses in the discourse of the economic press.

Cover 1: https://www.economist.com/printedition/2015-05-09 (*The Economist*, May 2nd 2015)

Cover 2: https://www.economist.com/printedition/2015-05-02 (*The Economist*, May 9th 2015)

In the first cover we can observe the back of a human head with a USB plug in it. This cover was annotated as metaphorical since there are incongruities (human

3 A depiction of the covers has not been included due to copyright reasons, but the may be consulted freely online.

heads do not have USB plugs) and the comparison being made is cross-domain (humans and machines). Therefore, this cover contains the metaphor HUMANS ARE MACHINES. On the other hand, the second cover is an example of the opposite: there are no incongruities apart from the colours, which just symbolize, as they have done historically, the political stance of each of the politicians representing the left and the right parties.

The results of the first part of the analysis are specified in turn. It needs to be pointed out that representation is open to debate, even after applying an identification method whose aim is, precisely, to reduce ambiguous cases. As depicted in Figure 16.1, the results were as follows:
- 15 of the covers contained metaphor(s), as shown in the example of cover 1.
- Two covers contained metonymy, as will be shown in the next subsection.
- Three covers contained symbols, as in the example shown in cover 2 above, since the colours can be considered as symbols of an ideology (red standing for the left-wing and blue for the right-wing parties).
- Finally, eight covers did not contain any rhetorical device.

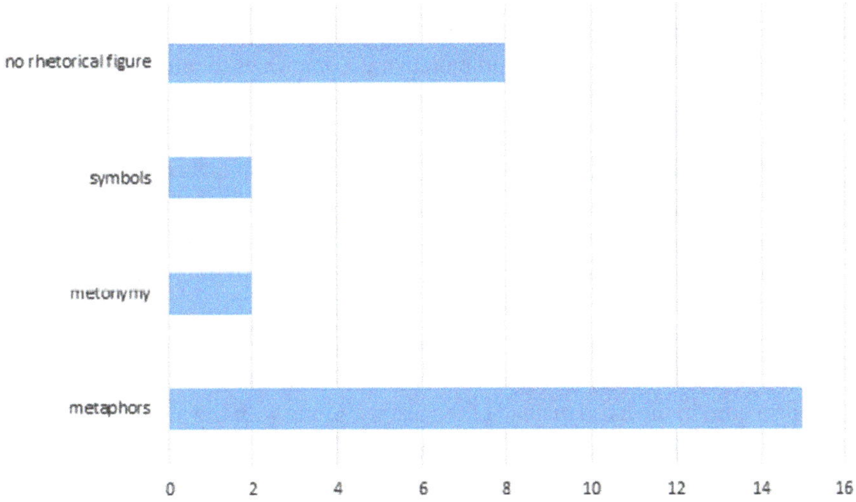

Figure 16.1: Distribution of rhetorical figures found

4.2 Results of the interviews

As stated in the previous section, the three covers selected for the second part of the analysis were all related to the bailout in Greece. At the time of the analysis, no cover was devoted to the situation in Spain specifically (the economic recession that was affecting the country); therefore, the most familiar situation (the economic crisis in Greece) was preferred.

To start with, Cover 3 (see link below) depicts a proud warrior walking away from a dragon that he has presumably killed, with a banner on it which reads "The financial crisis"; however, he is not looking at where he is going to get in, which is a much more dangerous and scary beast, with much bigger jaws than the previous one. This cover was annotated as metaphorical as there are several incongruities; the comparisons are all cross-domain, giving place to these two conceptual metaphors: THE FINANCIAL CRISIS IS A DANGEROUS BEAST and COUNTRIES ARE WARRIORS.

Cover 3: https://www.economist.com/printedition/2015-06-13 *(The Economist,* June 13th 2015)

On its part, Cover 4 (see link below), which reads "The way ahead", shows Alexis Tsipras, the president of Greece at the time of the study, rowing a small boat against the tide that is pulling him into a whirlpool, menacing to sink the boat, which has the flag of Greece in it (i.e., there is a symbol). Meanwhile, there is a big rock observing the situation and it has the shape of Germany's Chancellor Angela Merkel. This picture contains both metaphor and metonymy. Some ways to phrase the conceptual metaphor are THE BAILOUT IS A WHIRLPOOL and THE BAILOUT IS A DANGEROUS NATURAL FORCE (natural forces are frequent metaphors in the discourse of economics). Also, we find the flag of Greece, which constitutes a metonymy, and the shape of the Chancellor, who represents Germany (the metonymies can be understood as THE FLAG FOR THE COUNTRY and THE PRESIDENT FOR THE COUNTRY).

Cover 4: https://www.economist.com/printedition/2015-07-11 (*The Economist,* July 11th 2015)

Finally, in Cover 5 (see link below) we see the Discobolus of Myron, but it is holding a euro in the hand instead of the discus. Along with the picture, the headline reads "Europe's future in Greece's hands". This cover was selected as a representative one of those containing metonymy. The Discobolus represents Greece (it could be phrased as THE MONUMENT FOR THE COUNTRY) and the euro for the whole continent (THE CURRENCY FOR THE CONTINENT – EURO FOR EUROPE). This relation is clearly reinforced by the heading.

Cover 5: https://www.economist.com/printedition/2015-07-04 *(The Economist,* July 4th 2015)

Having commented on the three covers selected for the interview, the results obtained from it are gathered in Table 16.1 and depicted in Figure 16.2 below. 'Yes' and 'No' refer to whether the subject understood the piece of news behind the

Table 16.1: Results of the interviews.

	Cover 1			Cover 2			Cover 3		
Understands?	Yes	No	50%	Yes	No	50%	Yes	No	50%
	13	3	1	10	1	6	8	3	6
Image	5			14			3		
Headline	8			0			9		
Both	4			3			5		

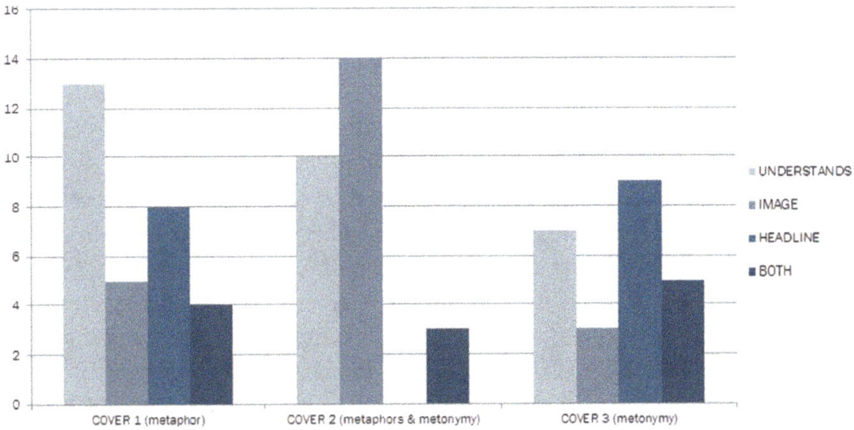

Figure 16.2: Results of the interviews

cover or not, and '50%' was assigned to those who partially understood it. It is divided into three options: 'image' if they deduced the meaning thanks to the image (regardless of whether it was the correct meaning or not), 'headline' if they did so but mainly thanks to the text, and 'both' if they declared that it was a combination of the picture and the text that had helped them reach their conclusion.

5 Discussion and conclusions

5.1 *The Economist* is a metaphor container

For practical reasons, we shall comment on the results separately. By applying VisMIP procedure to all the covers, we have observed that 15 out of 28 contained a potential metaphor. Four more covers contained other rhetorical figures (metonymy and symbol), and only eight out of 28 did not contain any rhetorical device. An important aspect must be commented concerning the potential metaphoricity of an element in discourse; as Steen discussed, we must always consider that the same linguistic component might be metaphorical for ones but not for others, as it is "relative to a group of language users" (Steen 2007: 94). All the decisions concerning our data have been made following the researcher's knowledge of economics discourse, but there is always a degree of disagreement regarding such decisions. Nevertheless, in order to avoid such limitations, an expert on VisMIP was consulted in case of doubt.

Claiming that a given piece of written discourse has a high metaphorical load seems to be easier than doing the same concerning images or multimodal discourse. Considering that more than half of the covers contained at least one metaphor, our study supports the claim that *The Economist* is indeed highly metaphorical, at least observing our data, since 56% of our multimodal corpus contains metaphor, and it reaches 70% of the total if we consider metonymy and symbols as well. As stated in the Introduction, *The Economist* has published several articles on economic metaphors and it has claimed to be metaphorical as well.[4] However, it has done so concerning the articles published weekly on different economic issues, but it has never mentioned the covers or made any reference to multimodal metaphors. Our study, thus, contributes to such claims of metaphoricity and expands them at the same time. Following McCloskey's (1983) words, our study suggests that the discourse of economics is not only "heavily metaphorical", but that this claim can equally apply to written, visual and multimodal instances of economics discourse. Further studies shall continue this line and observe whether the metaphors are found equally in the visual component and in the text that goes along with the image in the cover or if, on the contrary, there is a higher metaphoricity in one of the two modes (written and visual). In any case, the present outcomes can already answer the first research question of our study and validate the first hypothesis, which claimed that *The Economist* is a constant metaphorical container.

5.2 Communicative achievement and multimodality

Concerning the second part of the study, the results will be commented separately and more extensively. To start with, we can claim that there was a high degree of understanding of the three covers, at least in general terms:

---

4 Visit http://www.economist.com/style-guide/metaphors to see an example.

- Concerning the first cover of the interview (cover 3), the majority of the subjects interviewed understood the news that the cover represented, more concretely, 13 out of 17 were right in their interpretation. One student partially understood it and only three did not understand it at all.
- General understanding was also achieved in the second cover of the interviews (Cover 4), since 10 out of 17 comprehended the message, while six of them did it partially and only one did not understand it at all.
- Finally, the third cover (Cover 5) showed the lowest degree of understanding among our subjects, since only eight of them understood the message, six did it partially and three did not understand it.

However, taking those who understood the news entirely and partially as a whole, 14 subjects understood the news of the first cover, 16 the second and 14 the third one. Thus, these results would also validate the second research question, as the covers reach their communicative purpose since most of the subjects, who were not experts on the area whatsoever, understood the message to one extent or another.

If analysed individually, various results are obtained. To start with, while the first cover, containing a clear metaphor, is the one with the highest degree of understanding, such understanding is achieved mainly through the headline more than the visual elements. Nevertheless, the text in this case is one of the longest in the entire corpus and it is very explicative as well, which makes the fact that the interviewees' interpretation lied mainly on it logical. It can be presumed that the message would have also been grasped if the image had been shown separately, but no evidence can be proved on this matter. In any case, the metaphors in the picture were of great help as well, as some of the extractions from the interviews prove (the English translation has been added):

> Female, 19 years old: "La boca es como que está abriendo las puertas a otra recesión" ('It is as if the mouth is opening the doors to another bailout').
>
> Female, 23: "el monstruo sigue ahí y vamos a caer en una más grande" ('The monster is still there and we are going to fall in a bigger one').
>
> Male, 23: "da la sensación de que el animal grande es más poderoso y es como una crisis más grande" ('it gives the impression that the big animal is more powerful and it is as a bigger crisis').

From these extracts, it is observed that, even if the students claimed to have been helped mainly by the headline, they made constant reference to the visual elements (mainly the monster) and they used many metaphorical markers ('it is as if', 'it gives the impression') that indicate they were aware of what each visual component represented.

Concerning the second cover of the interviews, containing metaphor, metonymy and even a symbol (the flag), ten students fully understood the news and six did it too but only partially. Thus, a total of 16 students understood the message and therefore the communicative purpose of the cover was achieved in this case as well. Besides, the subjects recognized that it was mainly the picture in this case that had helped them understand the message, which seems somehow logical as, contrary to what had occurred with the first cover, the headline is very short and the words "the way ahead" need visual support to make full sense and therefore achieve complete comprehension. This, together with the opposite correlation of the first cover, may suggest that the shorter a headline, the more visual support it will need to be understood. The extracts below also reveal that the subjects were also aware of the comparisons being made; besides, they also made use of metaphorical markers, which are important elements for any researcher observing how a subject finally understands the incongruities contained in a metaphorical element:

> Female, 22: "se van a hundir, es como que lucha contra marea, que es lo que dice Merkel" ('He is going to sink, it is as if he is fighting against the tide, which is what Merkel says').
>
> Female, 20: "el remolino es como que se va a meter en algo malo" ('the whirlpool is as if he is getting into something bad').
>
> Male, 23: "va remando a contracorriente; "la tempestad es Alemania" ('He is rowing against the tide; the tempest is Germany').
>
> Male, 20: "lo del tornado expresa que se van a ahogar" ('The tornado expresses he is going to drown').

Finally, the third cover, containing mainly metonymy (the Discobolus standing for the country and the currency standing for the continent) is the one that presents the lowest degree of understanding and therefore the communicative purpose is not fully achieved. Only eight students entirely understood the news and six of them partially did, while three did not grasp the meaning at all. Besides, it is also the cover in which the image (containing the rhetorical devices) causes the lowest degree of interpretation of the cover, regardless of whether that interpretation was correct or not. Instead, the majority of the subjects (nine) confessed it was the headline that had helped them understand the cover, while five confessed having based their conclusions on both the image and the headline and only three used just the image. As occurred with the first cover, this might be due to the extension of the headline, which is quite long, and it would therefore support the aforementioned claim relating the length of the headline to its usefulness as an interpretative tool. The extracts from this part of the interview show more confusion when the subjects tried to interpret the incongruities and deduce the meaning:

> Female, 19: "tirar el disco es tirar el euro, desperdiciarlo" ('throwing the discus is throwing the euro, wasting it')
>
> Male, 22: "sólo entiendo que el euro se refiere a Europa y la estatua, a Grecia" ('I only understand the euro refers to Europe and the statue, to Greece')
>
> Male, 19: "lo que debería ser un disco es un euro" ('what should be a discus is a euro coin')
>
> Female, 23: "es como que el futuro depende de Grecia, está sujetado por ella" ('it is as if the future relies on Greece, it is being hold by 'her'')

5.3 Final remarks and conclusion

Having discussed all the results of both parts of our study, we can claim that all hypotheses but one have been validated, and that, as we assumed, due to the communicative, manipulative and ideological power, discourse devices as metaphor and metonymy are frequently used in the media. Our results therefore support previous studies observing the pervasiveness of these tools in the economic discourse and in the printed media (Alejo González 2011; McCloskey 1983). Considering that more than half of the covers contained metaphors, this serves as an indicator that journalists and cover designers of *The Economist* are aware of their usefulness in the communication process. Moreover, the covers were generally understood, even if in some cases the message was grasped more easily or directly than in others.

In spite of the high degree of comprehension achieved by our subjects, we hypothesized that the metaphors would play an important role and the headlines would be a helpful tool. However, as observed from the results, while the visual metaphors were very useful, the headlines were not simply helpful tools in the comprehension process; on the contrary, they have proved to be equally important. The data under analysis in the interview was very reduced since this was a pilot study, but a relation can be made between the two covers where the subjects signalled the headline as the main interpretative device, since in both of them the headline was considerably long if compared to the other 25 covers. As aforementioned, this may point at a correlation between the length of the headline and the need for visual support. In any case, it also suggests that visual and written metaphors are mutually needed for the highest degree of understanding; therefore, we claim that any cover with a multimodal metaphor will probably reach better understanding by its viewers/readers than another one making use of only one metaphorical mode (written or visual).

To conclude, this study aimed at observing the pervasiveness and the communicative power of visual metaphors in the discourse of economics in general terms and, in specific terms, in the covers of the English publication *The Economist*. For such purpose, we gathered a visual corpus of 28 covers from November 2014 to August 2105 and analysed all of them applying VisMIP method, which follows a step-by-step procedure to make the decision process concerning potential metaphoricity more reliable. The results of this part of the analysis showed that 15 covers out of the total contained metaphors. Other devices as metonymy and symbol were also found. Once the pervasiveness of metaphor was analysed, three covers were selected, and they were shown to 17 university students, who were asked a set of pre-designed questions with the aim of observing differences between the expression and the conceptualization of meaning. The interviews also aimed at examining whether they could understand, at least in general terms, the piece of news behind each cover only by the picture and the headline and to what extent each modality of language was useful in such process. The results revealed that the communicative achievement was not equally achieved in the three of them and that the cover containing a clear metaphor was the one that was best understood, but most subjects recognized it was the headline more than the picture that had conveyed comprehension. In conclusion, this, alongside the varied results obtained, can point at the fact that multimodality is, in all cases, the most practical and useful tool if a metaphor is to achieve its communicative purpose.

This small study was a pilot project that is now being extended and some of the limitations are being solved. For instance, the fact that some of the subjects doubted when they were asked whether it had been the image or the headline that had made them understood the news suggested that a different design of the interviews might be preferred. In addition, future studies may separate the visual elements and the headlines (text) and present them separately in order to observe whether there is a correlation between both in terms of message interpretation and comprehension. Moreover, the cultural background of the subjects is an interesting aspect when dealing with disintegrating a given discourse. For this reason, a possible approach could investigate two different (and larger) groups of subjects trying to understand the covers (for example, university students compared to adults in their 30s or 40s, who are more aware of the economic situation but still not experts on this field). In fact, asking experts on economics to follow the same interview could also provide researchers with interesting outcomes, as they may make use of different resources to explain the covers, leading to different uses of language. Finally, and in relation to this, another future path of research from this analysis could follow an annotation procedure to observe degrees of novelty and conventionality in the covers of *The Economist* and compare them to those used in the economic written language.

Acknowledgements: I would like to thank the Metaphor Lab team at the University of Asmterdam for organizing the Summer School where we were taught about many aspects of metaphor identification, being visual metaphors and the method to identify them one of the contents. Also, I would like to express my thankfulness to Professor Marianna Bolognesi for helping me by answering my doubts concerning some of the steps of VisMIP when I applied it to the covers of this study. Finally, I want to thank my colleague at the University of Castile-La Mancha, D. Eugenio-Enrique Cortés, for his help when collecting the data for this study.

References

Alejo González, Rafael. 2011. The container schema in economics and its discourse. *International Journal of Innovation and Leadership on the Teaching of Humanities* 1 (1). 64–79.

Bolognesi, Marianna, Romy van den Heerik, & Ester van den Berg. 2017. VisMet 1.0: A Corpus of Visual Metaphors. Manuscript under review.

Bounegru, Liliana & Charles Forceville. 2011. Metaphors in editorial cartoons representing the global financial crisis. *Visual Communication* 10 (2). 209–229.

Caballero, Rosario. 2014. Exploring the Combination of Language, Images and Sound in the Metaphors of TV Commercials. *Atlantis*, 36 (2). 31–52.

Charteris-Black, Jonathan. 2000. Metaphor and vocabulary teaching in ESP economics. *English for Specific Purposes* 19 (2). 149–165.

El Rafaie, Elisabeth. 2009. Metaphor in political cartoons: Exploring audience responses. In Charles Forceville & Eduardo Urios-Aparisi (eds), *Multimodal Metaphor*, 173–196. Berlin & New York: De Gruyter Mouton.

Eubanks, Philip. 2000. *A War of Words in the Discourse of Trade: The rhetorical constitution of metaphor*. Carbondale: Southern Illinois University Press.

Forceville, Charles. 1996. *Pictorial Metaphor in Advertising*. London and New York: Routledge.

Forceville, Charles. 2002. The identification of target and source in pictorial metaphors. *Journal of Pragmatics* 34 (1). 1–14.

Gkiouzepas, Lampros, & Margareth Hogg. 2011. Articulating a new framework for visual rhetoric in advertising: A structural, conceptual and pragmatic investigation. *Journal of Advertising* 40 (1). 103–120.

Goatly, Andrew. 2007. *Washing the Brain: Metaphor and Hidden Ideology*. Amsterdam: John Benjamins.

Herrera-Soler, Honesto & Michael White (eds.). 2012. *Metaphor and Mills. Figurative language in Business and Economics*. Berlin & New York: De Gruyter Mouton.

Koller, Veronika. 2004/2008. *Metaphor and Gender in Business Media Discourse: A Critical Cognitive Study*. Basingstoke/New York: Palgrave.

Koller, Veronika. 2006. Of critical importance: Using electronic text corpora to study metaphor in business media discourse. In Anatol Stefanowitsch and Stephan Th. Gries (eds.), *Corpus-based Approaches to Metaphor and Metonymy*, 237–266. Berlin & New York: De Gruyter Mouton.

Koller, Veronika. 2009. Brand images: multimodal metaphor in corporate branding messages. In Charles Forceville & Eduardo Urios-Aparisi (eds.), *Multimodal metaphor*, 45–71. Berlin & New York: De Gruyter Mouton.

Kövecses, Zoltán. 2010. *Metaphor. A practical introduction*. Second edition. New York/Oxford: Oxford University Press.

Lakoff, George & Johnson, Mark. 1980. *Metaphors We Live By*. Chicago: University of Chicago Press.

McCloskey, Deirdre. 1983. The rhetoric of economics. *Journal of Economic Literature* 21. 481–517.

Mouton, N. T. O. (2012). Metaphor and economic thought: A historical perspective. In Honesto Herrera-Soler & Michael White (eds.), *Metaphor and Mills: Figurative Language in Business and Economics*, 49–76. Berlin & New York: De Gruyter Mouton. Applications of Cognitive Linguistics, Bind. 19.

Negro, Isabel. 2011. Metaphor and ideology in the business press: The case of Endesa's takeover. *Miscelanea: A Jounal of American and English Studies* 43. 73–85.

Negro, Isabel. 2013. Verbo-pictorial metaphors in the business press. Paper presented at the 31st Conference of the Spanish Association of Applied Linguistics. University of La Laguna, 10–13 April.

Negro, Isabel. 2015. Pictorial and verbo-pictorial metaphors in Spanish political cartooning. *Círculo de lingüística aplicada a la comunicación* 57. 59–84.

Pérez-Sobrino, Paula. 2016. Multimodal Metaphor and Metonymy in Advertising: A Corpus-Based Account. *Metaphor and Symbol* 31 (2). 73–90.

Phillips, Barbara J. & Edward F. McQuarrie. 2004. Beyond visual metaphor: A new typology of visual rhetoric in advertising. *Marketing Theory* 4 (1/2). 113–136.

Prince, Violaine & Stéphane Ferrari. 1996. A textual clues approach for generating metaphors as explanations by an intelligent tutoring system. In Simon Botley et al. (eds), *Proceedings of Teaching and Language Corpora. Lancaster*, 217–32. University Centre for Computer Corpus Research on Language.

Richardt, Susanne. 2003. Metaphors in expert and common-sense reasoning. In Cornelia Zelinsky-Wibbelt (ed.), *Text, Context, Concepts*, 243–296. Berlin & New York: De Gruyter Mouton.

Robins, Shani & Richard E. Mayer. 2000. The metaphor framing effect: Metaphorical reasoning about text-based dilemmas. *Discourse Processes* 30 (1). 57–86.

Rojo López, Ana María & María Ángeles Orts Llopis. 2010. Metaphorical pattern analysis in financial texts: Framing the crisis in positive or negative metaphorical terms. *Journal of Pragmatics* 42. 3300–3313.

Soares da Silva, Augusto. 2013. O que sabemos sobre a crise económica, pela metáfora. Conceptualizações metafóricas da crise na imprensa portuguesa. [What we know about the economic crisis through metaphor. Metaphorical conceptualizations of the crisis in the Portuguese press]. *Revista Media & Jornalismo* 23 (1). 11–34.
Sopory, Pradeep. 2008. Metaphor and intra-attitudinal structural coherence. *Communication Studies* 59 (2). 164–181.
Šorm, Ester & Gerard J. Steen. 2013. Processing visual metaphor: a study in thinking out loud. *Metaphor and the Social World* 3 (1). 1–34.
Šorm, Ester & Gerard J. Steen. 2018. VISMIP: towards a method for visual metaphor identification. In Gerard J. Steen (ed.), *Visual Metaphor: How Images Construct Metaphorical Meaning*. Amsterdam: John Benjamins.
Steen, Gerard J. 2007. *Finding Metaphor in Grammar and usage: a Metaphorical Analysis of Theory and Research*. Amsterdam: John Benjamins.
Steen, Gerard J. 2011. From three dimensions to five steps: the value of deliberate metaphor. *Metaphorik.de 21*. 83–110.
Vismet Baby corpus documentation, to be found on the website: http://vismet.org/VisMet/.
White, Michael. 1996. *La metáfora en el tratamiento de la crisis monetaria en la prensa británica* [Metaphor use in the monetary crisis in the British press]. Madrid: Universidad Complutense. Servicio de Publicaciones de la UCM, CDRom.
White, Michael. 1997. The Use of Metaphor in Reporting Financial Market Transactions. *Cuadernos de Filología Inglesa* 6 (2). 233–245.
White, Michael. 2003 Metaphor and economics: the case of *growth*. *English for Specific Purposes* 22 (2). 131–151.
Wolf, Hans-Georg & Frank Polzenhagen. 2003. Conceptual metaphor as ideological stylistic means: An exemplary analysis. In René Dirven, Roslyn Frank and Martin Pütz (eds.), *Cognitive Models in Language and Thought: Ideology, Metaphor and Meanings*, 247–275. Berlin & New York: De Gruyter Mouton.
Online articles used from *The Economist*'s website:
http://www.economist.com/style-guide/metaphors. Last consulted on 15/10/2016.
http://www.economist.com/blogs/freeexchange/2011/05/economic_metaphors. Last consulted on 16/10/2016.
http://www.economist.com/blogs/johnson/2011/05/metaphors. Last consulted on 16/10/2015.

Charles Forceville

Developments in multimodal metaphor studies: A response to Górska, Coëgnarts, Porto & Romano, and Muelas-Gil

Abstract: This chapter discusses and reflects on the contributions in the "metaphor analysis in multimodal discourse" part of the current book, and sketches developments and challenges in CMMT (Conceptual Metaphor & Metonymy Theory). Specifically, aspiring multimodality scholars are exhorted to invest time and energy in learning about other modes and media than the one they have been trained to analyze; to familiarize themselves with other theoretical paradigms; to investigate other tropes besides metaphor and metonymy; and to be aware of the crucial importance of genre.

Keywords: conceptual metaphor theory, multimodal metaphor, multimodal metonymy, non-verbal tropes, image schemas, genre

1 Introduction

It is both encouraging and telling that a volume entitled *Current approaches to metaphor analysis in discourse* has a robust section devoted to "Metaphor analysis in multimodal discourse". While for more than a decade since Lakoff and Johnson's (1980) paradigm-changing *Metaphors we live by* the study of conceptual metaphor (and increasingly: conceptual metonymy) was more or less equivalent with the study of its verbal manifestations, nowadays this line of research is complemented by a healthily strong, and growing, body of work analysing visual, gestural, and multimodal expressions of metaphor and metonymy. This broadening of the discipline is excellent news for several reasons. In the first place, Conceptual Metaphor & Metonymy Theory (henceforth CMMT) has provided tools for the analysis of discourses in media that do not draw (exclusively) on the verbal mode, such as cartoons, comics, films, commercials, and music (e.g., Forceville and Urios-Aparisi 2009), but also aid the development of the quickly growing discipline of "multimodality" (e.g., Bateman 2008, 2014; Bateman et al. 2017; Jewitt 2014; Klug and Stöckl 2016; Kress 2010; Kress and Van Leeuwen 2001, 2006; Machin 2014). As a result, CMMT turns truly interdisciplinary. But this

Charles Forceville, University of Amsterdam, Dept. of Media Studies, Amsterdam, the Netherlands.

https://doi.org/10.1515/9783110629460-017

comes at a cost: seriously becoming an interdisciplinary scholar requires becoming an expert in at least two media. Since hitherto the vast majority of CMMT scholars have been trained as linguists, they need to invest time and energy in learning about another medium or at least another mode. If they do not make this effort, they run the risk of making painful mistakes in their analyses because of insufficient awareness of medium-specific and mode-specific affordances and constraints.

But even CMMT linguists wishing to restrict themselves to language will need to develop some familiarity with visual and multimodal manifestations of metaphor and metonymy, at least if they are interested in the cognition aspect of these tropes. What has hitherto not been sufficiently acknowledged is that the affordances characterizing modes other than language enable them to metaphorize in ways that are difficult, or even impossible, to achieve in verbal form (e.g., Forceville and Paling 2018). Fortunately, the four papers in the "Metaphor analysis in multimodal discourse" part of this book robustly build on this awareness.

2 A response to Górska, Coëgnarts, Porto & Romano, and Muelas-Gil

The cartoons by the Polish artist Janusz Kapusta examined by Elżbieta Górska show how profound ideas can be presented in deceptively simple verbo-pictorial form. Górska persuasively argues that "image schemas" such as UP/DOWN, FORCE, BALANCE etc. (Hampe 2005, 2017; Johnson 1987) are crucial to helping us understand the visual part of the cartoons. Undoubtedly, the salient role of strongly embodied image schemas contributes to the cartoons' universal appeal. From a multimodal point of view, it would be an interesting test to see how much of the visual information makes sense even without any verbal text at all. Viewers would definitely have to recognize the recurring protagonist as a "blend" between a Buddha and a chess pawn. The Buddha part suggests the creature's aspiration to, say, achieve wisdom, whereas the pawn part emphasizes its "everyman" character. To understand this blend, one would thus have to be able to both recognize Buddha and pawn (the least valuable and least unique piece in chess) and to know something about their cultural meaning. The cartoon in example 1, incidentally, shows that elements in visuals are by no means always Peircean icons: the interrupted lines, so important in the overall meaning of the cartoon, function in a very different way than the contour lines that make up its "characters". I find it intriguing that in this cartoon the circle is used as a bounded space for "pain" whereas the rectangle is used for "love" – as the accompanying text suggests. This is perhaps somewhat counter-intuitive, as edgy things are conventionally considered negative and harsh ("takete"), whereas round things are positive and soft ("maluma" – see Kennedy 1982: 602). Moreover, while Górska interprets the interrupted lines as cueing "the temporariness of the two states" (Górska 2019/this volume: 283), I submit that the interrupted nature of the lines also suggests that love and pain are permeable – and interact, just as their overlapping does.

The cartoons trigger additional meanings that are attributable to their visual part alone. In example 2 the "line" is not just the instrument that helps the character maintain balance; it is also something that the character firmly "holds on" to (via the GRASP schema, as Górska points out) as if it were a crutch. The character in example 3 strikes me as walking on a relatively less-curved – and hence "wise" – path, avoiding the more curved – and thus "more stupid" – paths that are visible. And in example 4 the figure-ground reversal – the protagonist is "in" his suitcase-full-of-worries rather than carrying it – too, is only conveyed visually.

I fully agree with Górska that "the affordances of the visual mode allow for a straightforward realization of a number of image schemas, namely: the BOUNDED SPACE, CYCLE, LINK, NEAR-FAR, and the PART-WHOLE" (Górska 2019/this volume: 283). As always, the precise meaning of any schema will depend on its interaction with other schemas and with information in other modes (if present) as well as on the genre to which the discourse as a whole belongs. I am not sure, though, that the FORCE schema as theorized in Talmy (1988) cannot be easily represented in visuals, as Górska claims. If the cartoonist had chosen to use speed and movement lines (Forceville 2011a; Kennedy 1982) and "squash and stretch" techniques, this schema, too, could have been rendered exclusively in the visual mode. I note in passing that in *moving* images, optionally supported by sound and music, this can be accomplished even more effortlessly – see Forceville (2017a).

Maarten Coëgnarts is one of a still rare species, a cognitivist *film* scholar who systematically deploys Conceptual Metaphor Theory to discuss the medium in which he is an expert. His central point is that not just creative metaphors (called "image" metaphors by Lakoff and Turner [1989] and "resemblance" metaphors by Grady [1999]) manifest themselves in film, but that structural or "correlation" (Grady 1999) ones do so as well (Coëgnarts 2019/this volume). These latter, he argues, draw heavily on image schemas such as FRONT-BACK, SOURCE-PATH-GOAL, and CENTRE-PERIPHERY. Since live-action film in many respects "copies" whatever it records, it is of course possible to convey image schemas in a film's pro-filmic *mise-en-scène*, and could thereby also occur, for instance, in a theatrical performance. But Coëgnarts's goal here (see also Coëgnarts and Kravanja 2012) is to demonstrate that film in addition has various *medium-specific* opportunities to influence the viewer's perception of this pro-filmic reality, such as framing, camera movement, lighting, and editing. In this chapter he focuses on the pertinence of the CONTAINER schema, discussing two of its manifestations in a scene from Francis Ford Coppola's *The Conversation*. The CONTAINER schema is specifically pertinent to the medium of film, Coëgnarts argues, because every film shot literally *frames* a portion of the filmed scene. The "frame" is thus a container "in" which the contents of what is seen (directly, or indirectly via what a character in the story world sees in a "point-of-view" shot) are made accessible to the film viewer. Necessarily, much of what is portrayed are, in fact, metonyms leading the viewer to construe larger wholes (see Forceville [2009] and Pérez-Sobrino [2017] for other applications of metonymy to the visual and multimodal realm). This framing is not static: different parts of the filmed scene come "into" view by means of camera movements and editing. We are hardly aware of this mechanism as it is not fundamentally different from how human beings perceive (and focus attention on) things in the real world, as Coëgnarts reminds us by his chapter motto that "the most powerful conveyor of meaning is the immediate impact of perceptual form" (Rudolf Arnheim). A second aspect of the CONTAINER schema he discusses is where it partakes in EMOTION IS A FLUID IN A PRESSURIZED CONTAINER, a subtype of the more general EMOTIONS ARE FORCES metaphor (Kövecses 2008), in which a strong emotion (joy, anger, embarrassment) that rises in a person's body is metaphorically understood as a liquid that begins to boil and thereby puts pressure on the pan or kettle in which it is located. Coëgnarts argues that a series of shots in a crowded elevator (itself a "pressurized container") depicting the character of Harry Caul (Gene Hackman) first in medium close-up, then in close-up, then in medium-close-up again, nudges the viewer to perceive Harry's state of mind in terms of an increase, followed by a decrease, of his embarrassment and panic.

It is much more difficult to persuade readers that these filmic choices deserve to be understood in terms of metaphors than in (audio)visual media in which reality-as-we-know-it has been explicitly manipulated, as in comics (e.g., Forceville 2005, 2011a) and animation film (e.g., Fahlenbrach 2017; Forceville and Jeulink 2011; Forceville and Paling 2018). Coëgnarts' interpretation of the shot sequence (carefully designed by the filmmaker, after all) is nonetheless highly plausible. It would be interesting to test his claims experimentally. In the above scene, for example, manipulating the depiction of Harry Caul by showing him only in medium-shots, or only in long shots, should lead test subjects to evaluate the character as *less* embarrassed/panicking than in the original sequence.

Coëgnarts' project (see also Coëgnarts and Kravanja 2014, 2015a) is an important one. On the one hand, his work provides instruments for film analysis that are not part and parcel of cognitivist film scholarship by providing a metaphorical *raison d'être* for certain shot sequences. On the other, he demonstrates how conceptual metaphor studies feed into cognition studies. More generally, combining insights from cognitive linguists and cognitive film scholars (e.g., Bordwell and Thompson 2008; Forceville 2011b; Grodal 2009; Smith 2017; Tan 1996;) offer promising opportunities for synergy.

In a fine chapter (Porto and Romano 2019/this volume), Porto and Romano investigate how a metaphor can "migrate" from one mode to another mode or combination of modes – which they baptize "transmodal metaphor" (see Forceville [1999] for an early example of such a project). They direct their attention to the Spanish 15M movement that over the past decade or so has voiced and embodied the dissatisfaction of many citizens with the consequences of the financial crisis, and with the neoliberal policies in response to this crisis. Specifically, the authors focus on the Madrilenean Mareas protests, showing how the neutral A MASS OF PEOPLE IS A TIDE metaphor acquired specific, and positive, connotations in the context of these protests. Once the notion of the "tide" was firmly associated with the Mareas protests, Porto and Romano show, it became a kind of *topos* or *meme* that could subsequently be used in other, non-verbal and multimodal media as well, such as banners, placards, logos, and posters. Since different groups partaking in the protests had come to be connected with certain colours, visual manifestations of the "tide" could from then on play with this colour symbolism. When the *Solfónica* choir was founded, the central metaphor began to be expressed in the musical mode as well.

Porto and Romano's illuminating case study of the Mareas strikes me as an exemplary demonstration of the concept of transmodal metaphor. The chapter has several other praiseworthy characteristics. For one thing, it shows that metaphor theory can be well combined with critical discourse analysis to engage with politically and culturally charged ideological issues – as was perhaps first demonstrated by Charteris-Black (2004) and has more recently been addressed by Musolff (2016). Related to this, it is encouraging that the authors do not only draw on cognitivist linguistics models, but also benefit from semiotics-oriented approaches, notably the work by Kress and Van Leeuwen. Thirdly, they confirm that making meaning is in various senses a dynamic process. Not only can a given metaphor develop *within* a medium, for instance in language; it is moreover bound to transform and adapt itself to some extent when it migrates to another medium, with its own affordances and constraints, such as visuals, visuals-plus-written texts, or music. Therefore, a given metaphor may in two different media "hide and highlight" (Lakoff and Johnson 1980: 10–13) different aspects of the source domain. Finally, the authors remind us that meaning-making, of course, goes beyond metaphor. Undoubtedly, we "live by metaphors" – but we live by many other things – metonyms, stories, colour symbolism ... – as well.

In her chapter (Muelas-Gil 2019/this volume), Muelas-Gil first analyses 28 covers of the English *The Economist* magazine (November 2014 – August 2015) according to the VISMIP method (Šorm and Steen 2018), charting how many of them can be said to feature a visual metaphor or metonym. She establishes among other things that 15 of the 28 covers sport a visual metaphor. The author goes on to report an experiment with 17 Spanish students "talking-out-loud" about three figurative *Economist* covers. Although not all participants understood the metaphors and metonyms in all three covers, the author concludes that "most of the subjects, who were not experts on the area whatsoever, understood the message to one extent or another" (Muelas-Gil 2019/this volume: 359).

It is commendable that the author expands the repertoire of genres featuring metaphors and metonyms by focusing on magazine covers. There are, however, several methodological issues that counsel caution vis-à-vis her findings. In the first place, Muelas-Gil refers to the (possible) pertinence of "headlines" to the interpretation of the trope at issue, but it was left to the participants to decide for themselves how important these headlines were. As the author herself acknowledges, this is a weakness in the experimental design, since it is impossible to attest whether or not participants based their interpretations (consciously or subconsciously) only on the visuals if they were exposed to the complete visuals-plus-written text. The lack of attention in the experimental design for the relative role of visuals and text has another unfortunate consequence, as it blurs the distinction between visual and multimodal metaphor. If the verbal information in the headline is indispensable for identifying one of the terms (target or source), this would make a metaphor or metonym multimodal rather than visual according to the definition adopted in Forceville and Urios-Aparisi (2009). Šorm and Steen (2013), on whose approach Muelas-Gil bases herself, do not make the distinction, however. As a result, she is not able to distinguish between (monomodal) pictorial/visual metaphor and (multimodal) verbo-pictorial metaphor. Thus, rather than hypothesizing that "the shorter a headline, the more visual support it will need to be understood" (Muelas-Gil 2019/this volume: 360), my suggestion would be that if the headline contains a metaphorical target or source that is *not* also rendered visually, it is much more crucial than if the pertinent metaphorical term is also visualized.

A second thorny issue is that the three alternatives the author proposes (metaphor, metonymy, both) suggest a misleadingly easy manner of categorizing. For one thing, it is not advisable to say that something *is* a metaphor/metonymy or not; it is better to say that it is (not) possible/advisable/imperative to *construe* a metaphor to make sense of the cover as a whole. Construing, or not construing, a metaphor inevitably depends to a considerable extent on an audience's ability to recruit appropriate background knowledge – and the Spanish student participants (some of whom even needed to have the English headlines translated for them ...) are hardly the envisaged readers of *The Economist*. For another, many metaphors are rooted in metonyms or vice versa (see Pérez-Sobrino [2017] for extensive discussion). As a matter of fact, in cover 1, the USB-portal is a metonym for the machine, specifically the computer, while cover 3 presents an image that invites construal not just as metonym but also as the metaphor EURO IS DISCOBOLUS – where "being thrown away" is the key feature mapped from source to target. With reference to cover 2, one might query the verbalization of the metaphor identified. In its discussion no mention is made, for instance, of the metaphor MERKEL IS ROCK. Surely, the scenario (Musolff 2006, 2016) that is presented here is a variety of the POLITICS IS A JOURNEY metaphor, in which if Tsipras "goes ahead," away from the whirlpool, Greece's ship-of-state will crash on the Merkel-rock.

3 The next level

Where should multimodal CMMT scholars go from here? I see various exciting opportunities for novel developments. It is becoming ever more clear that – just as metaphor and metonymy – hyperbole, irony, allegory, antithesis, and probably other tropes, operate first and foremost on the conceptual level – which means that theorization requires analysis of their manifestations both in exclusively verbal and in visual and multimodal discourses. This obliges linguists and rhetoricians to reread the scholars who first defined these tropes – classical sources such as Aristotle, Cicero, and Quintilian – and then refine (and if necessary; redefine) them through the lens of contemporary cognitive scholarship in linguistics, stylistics, film studies, comics scholarship and whatever other disciplines the cognitive approach flourishes in. The reformulations can then constitute the basis for examining the manifestations of the various tropes in different media, taking into account the affordances and constraints of the modes upon which these media draw. This work has, in fact already begun. Cognitivist-oriented proposals have been made for, at least, visual puns (Abed 1994), oxymoron and "pictorial grouping" (Teng and Sun 2002), hyperbole, paradox, and onomatopoeia (Pérez-Sobrino 2017), allegory (Cornevin and Forceville 2017), and antithesis (Tseronis and Forceville 2017). Incidentally, it is important to carefully consider whether/where the list of classic Aristotelian tropes may need to be conflated for their visual or multimodal varieties. (For instance, is it tenable and desirable to distinguish oxymoron, paradox and antithesis in visuals as they are now commonly distinguished in language?) This line of research can be captured in the slogan "from CMT, via CMMT, to CTT," the latter acronym standing for "Cognitive Trope Theory".

Another promising source of new insights is investigating other visual and multimodal genres and subgenres. After all, metaphors (just like any other potentially meaning-generating pattern) may "behave" in slightly or vastly different ways depending on the medium and genre in which they are expressed. Film metaphor, for one, is receiving more and more scholarly attention (e.g., Coëgnarts and Kravanja 2015b; Fahlenbrach 2016, 2017; Ortiz 2011, 2015; Winter 2014). Abdel-Raheem (2019) examines cartoons and op-ed illustrations, bringing to the genre first-hand knowledge of Arabic perspectives, as does Maalej (2015) to university promotion material (for some thoughts on cultural dimensions of visual and multimodal metaphor, see Forceville 2017b). Another intriguing genre is street art. Poppi and Kravanja (2019) focus on Banksy's public art, whereas Asenjo (2018) works on the famous political wall paintings in Belfast. It is to be noticed, incidentally, that in most of this work the discussion of modes partaking in multimodal metaphor is restricted to the visual and the written-verbal mode. Multimodal metaphor research – and multimodal discourse analysis more generally – including the sonic and musical modes is still rare.

In carrying out this highly complex and demanding research, it is crucial to bear in mind that models for identifying tropes should eventually benefit the analysis of visuals and multimodal text rather than the other way round. Put differently, research should in the last resort help solve puzzles and problems in all kinds of discourse, and models are nothing less but also nothing more than tools to achieve this. We should therefore not hesitate, whenever necessary, to adapt models if they are not, or not sufficiently, capable of performing the job of accounting for new textual data. The idea that analysts should first try to exhaustively describe the visuals and text of a piece of discourse, then signal incongruity, and then identify any metaphors, as Negro et al. (2017) propose, is in my view a misguided strategy. As these authors themselves discovered, even having only two raters describe a given picture rarely leads to the same results. The problem is that a picture can potentially be described in an infinite number of ways. I suggest we start at the other, pragmatic end, namely by attesting to what genre a discourse belongs. If we do this correctly, we know what interpretation strategy is called for, since genres trigger expectations as to what kind of meaning is intended. For instance, a commercial advertiser wants to make a positive claim about a product, service, or brand, while a political cartoonist intends to make a critical, preferably humorous, comment on a political situation. As analysts we then, as it were, "backtrack" and observe what visual and verbal information is pertinent to conveying the message. Once we have inventoried this information, and notice that its presentation manifests some sort of incongruity, we can start reflecting whether, and if so, how, it makes sense to label this incongruity "metaphorical" (or metonymical, symbolical, ironical, hyperbolical ...), and/or pertains to odd stylistic features, an intertextual reference, or any of a range of other phenomena. In short, any analysis of any discourse – and hence of any element partaking in this discourse – needs to begin by assessing what sort of information its communicator wants to communicate. Therefore the analysis of tropes must be embedded in a theory of communication and cognition. My candidate for such a theory is relevance theory (Sperber and Wilson 1995; Wilson and Sperber 2012; Forceville 2014, in prep.; Forceville and Clark 2014).

References

Abdel-Raheem, Ahmed. 2019. *Pictorial framing in moral politics*. London: Routledge.

Abed, Farough. 1994. Visual puns as interactive illustrations: Their effects on recognition memory. *Metaphor and Symbolic Activity* 9. 45–60.

Asenjo, Roberto. 2018. The influence of culture in the multimodal murals of Northern Ireland. Warsaw Multimodality Workshop and Masterclass, University of Warsaw, Poland, 7–9 June.

Bateman, John. 2008. *Multimodality and genre: A foundation for the systematic analysis of multimodal documents*. Basingstoke: Palgrave Macmillan.

Bateman, John. 2014. *Text and image: A critical introduction to the visual/verbal divide*. London: Routledge.

Bateman, John, Janina Wildfeuer & Tuomo Hiippala. 2017. *Multimodality: Foundations, research and analysis – a problem-oriented introduction*. Berlin & New York: De Gruyter Mouton.

Bordwell, David & Kristin Thompson. 2008. *Film art: An introduction*, 8th edn. Boston: McGraw-Hill.

Charteris-Black, Jonathan. 2004. *Corpus approaches to critical metaphor analysis*. Basingstoke: Palgrave Macmillan.

Coëgnarts, Maarten. 2019/this volume. Analyzing metaphor in film: Some conceptual challenges. In Ignasi Navarro I Ferrando (ed.), *Current approaches to metaphor analysis in discourse*, 304–320. Berlin & New York: De Gruyter Mouton.

Coëgnarts, Maarten & Peter Kravanja. 2012. From thought to modality: A theoretical framework for analysing structural-conceptual metaphor and image metaphor in film. *Image [&] Narrative* 13 (1). 96–113.

Coëgnarts, Maarten & Peter Kravanja. 2014. On the embodiment of binary oppositions in cinema: The containment schema in John Ford's Westerns. *Image & Narrative* 15 (1). 30–43.

Coëgnarts, Maarten & Peter Kravanja. 2015a. Film as an exemplar of bodily meaning-making. In Maarten Coëgnarts & Peter Kravanja (eds.), *Embodied cognition and cinema*, 17–40. Leuven: Leuven University Press.

Coëgnarts, Maarten & Peter Kravanja (eds.). 2015b. *Embodied cognition and cinema*. Leuven: Leuven University Press.

Cornevin, Vanessa & Charles Forceville. 2017. From metaphor to allegory: the Japanese manga *Afuganisu-tan*. *Metaphor and the Social World* 7 (2). 236–252. DOI: 10.1075/msw.7.2.04cor.

Fahlenbrach, Kathrin (ed.). 2016. *Embodied metaphors in film, television, and video games*. London: Routledge.

Fahlenbrach, Kathrin 2017. Audiovisual metaphors and metonymies of emotions and depression in moving images. In Francesca Ervas, Elisabetta Gola, and Maria Grazia Rossi (eds.), *Metaphor in communication, science and education*, 95–117. Berlin & New York: De Gruyter Mouton.
Forceville, Charles. 1999. The metaphor COLIN IS A CHILD in Ian McEwan's, Harold Pinter's, and Paul Schrader's *The Comfort of Strangers*. *Metaphor and Symbol* 14 (3). 179–98.
Forceville, Charles. 2005. Visual representations of the Idealized Cognitive Model of anger in the Asterix album *La Zizanie*. *Journal of Pragmatics* 37. 69–88.
Forceville, Charles. 2009. Metonymy in visual and audiovisual discourse. In Eija Ventola and Arsenio Jésus Moya Guijarro (eds.), *The World Told and the World Shown: Issues in Multisemiotics*, 56–74. Basingstoke: Palgrave Macmillan.
Forceville, Charles. 2011a. Pictorial runes in *Tintin and the Picaros*. *Journal of Pragmatics* 43. 875–890.
Forceville, Charles. 2011b. The source-path-goal schema in Agnès Varda's *Les Glaneurs et la Glaneuse* and *Deux Ans Après*. In Monika Fludernik (ed.), *Beyond cognitive metaphor theory: Perspectives on literary metaphor*, 281–297. London: Routledge.
Forceville, Charles. 2014. Relevance theory as model for analysing visual and multimodal communication. In David Machin (ed.), *Visual Communication*, 51–70. Berlin & New York: De Gruyter Mouton.
Forceville, Charles. 2017a. From image schema to metaphor in discourse: The FORCE schemas in animation films. In Beate Hampe (ed.), *Metaphor: Embodied cognition and discourse*, 239–256. Cambridge: Cambridge University Press.
Forceville, Charles. 2017b. Visual and multimodal metaphor in advertising: cultural perspectives. *Styles of Communication* 9 (2). 26–41.
Forceville, Charles. in prep. *Analyzing visual and multimodal mass-communication: A pragmatic model* (working title). To be published by Oxford University Press.
Forceville, Charles & Eduardo Urios-Aparisi (eds.). 2009. *Multimodal Metaphor*. Berlin & New York: De Gruyter Mouton.
Forceville, Charles & Marloes Jeulink. 2011. The flesh and blood of embodied understanding: The source-path-goal schema in animation film." *Pragmatics & Cognition* 19 (1). 37–59.
Forceville, Charles & Billy Clark. 2014. Can pictures have explicatures? *Linguagem em (Dis) Curso* 14 (3). 451–472.
Forceville, Charles & Sissy Paling. 2018. The metaphorical representation of DEPRESSION in short, wordless animation films. *Journal of Visual Communication* (published ahead of print 21-9-2018 at http://journals.sagepub.com/doi/10.1177/1470357218797994).
Górska, Elżbieta. 2019/this volume. Spatialization of abstract concepts in cartoons: A case study of verbo-pictorial image-schematic metaphors. In Ignasi Navarro i Ferrando (ed.), *Current approaches to metaphor analysis in discourse*, 279–294. Berlin & New York: De Gruyter Mouton.
Grady, Joseph E. 1999. A typology of motivation for conceptual metaphor: Correlation vs. resemblance. In Raymond W. Gibbs, Jr. & Gerard J. Steen (eds.), *Metaphor in cognitive linguistics*, 79–100. Amsterdam: Benjamins.
Grodal, Torben. 2009. *Embodied visions: Evolution, emotion, culture, and film*. Oxford: Oxford University Press.
Hampe, Beate (ed.). 2005. *From perception to meaning: Image schemas in cognitive linguistics*. Berlin & New York: De Gruyter Mouton.

Hampe, Beate (ed.). 2017. *Metaphor: Embodied cognition and discourse* (239–256). Cambridge: Cambridge University Press. DOI: 10.1017/1108182324.
Jewitt, Carey (ed.). 2014 [2009]. *The Routledge handbook of multimodal analysis*, 2nd edn. London: Routledge.
Johnson, Mark. 1987. *The body in the mind: The bodily basis of meaning, imagination and reason*. Chicago: University of Chicago Press.
Kennedy, John M. 1982. Metaphor in pictures. *Perception* 11. 589–605.
Klug, Nina-Maria & Hartmut Stöckl (eds.). 2016. *Handbuch Sprache im multimodalen Kontext* [*The Language in Multimodal Contexts Handbook*]. Linguistic Knowledge series. Berlin & New York: De Gruyter Mouton.
Kövecses, Zoltán. 2008. Metaphor and emotion. In Raymond W. Gibbs, Jr. (ed.), *The Cambridge handbook of metaphor and thought*, 380–396. Cambridge: Cambridge University Press.
Kress, Gunther. 2010. *Multimodality: A social semiotic approach to contemporary communication*. London: Routledge.
Kress, Gunther & Theo van Leeuwen. 2001. *Multimodal discourse*. London: Arnold.
Kress, Gunther & Theo van Leeuwen. 2006 [1996]. *Reading images: The grammar of visual design*. 2nd edn. London: Routledge.
Lakoff, George & Mark Johnson. 1980. *Metaphors we live by*. Chicago: University of Chicago Press.
Lakoff, George & Mark Turner. 1989. *More than cool reason: A field guide to poetic metaphor*. Chicago: University of Chicago Press.
Maalej, Zouheir. 2015. Mono-modal and multi-modal metaphor and metonymies in policy change: The case of the KSU2030 strategic plan. *Language Sciences* 47. 1-17.
Machin, David (ed.). 2014. *Visual communication*. Berlin & New York: De Gruyter Mouton.
Muelas-Gil, María. 2019/this volume. Visual metaphors in economic discourse: An analysis of the interaction of conventional and novel visual metaphors in *The Economist*. In Ignasi Navarro i Ferrando (ed.), *Current approaches to metaphor analysis in discourse*, 347–365. Berlin & New York: De Gruyter Mouton.
Musolff, Andreas. 2006. Metaphor scenarios in public discourse. *Metaphor and Symbol* 21. 23–38.
Musolff, Andreas. 2016. *Political metaphor analysis: Discourse and scenarios*. London: Bloomsbury.
Negro, Isabel, Ester Šorm & Gerard Steen. 2017. General image understanding in visual metaphor identification. *Odisea* 18. 113–131. DOI: 10.25115/odisea.v0i18.1900
Ortiz, María J. 2011. Primary metaphors and monomodal visual metaphors. *Journal of Pragmatics* 43. 1568–1580.
Ortiz, María J. 2015. Films and embodied metaphors of emotion. In Maarten Coëgnarts & Peter Kravanja (eds.), *Embodied cognition and cinema*, 203–220. Leuven: Leuven University Press.
Pérez-Sobrino, Paula. 2017. *Multimodal metaphor and metonymy in advertising*. Amsterdam: Benjamins.
Poppi, Fabio & Peter Kravanja. 2019. Actiones secundum fidei: Antithesis and metaphoric conceptualization in Banksy's graffiti art. *Metaphor and the Social World* 9 (1).
Porto, M. Dolores & Manuela Romano. 2019/this volume. Transmodality in metaphors: TIDES in Spanish social protest movements. In Ignasi Navarro i Ferrando (ed.), *Current approaches to metaphor analysis in discourse*, 321–345 . Berlin & New York: De Gruyter Mouton.
Smith, Murray. 2017. *Film, art, and the third culture: A naturalized aesthetics of film*. London: Oxford University Press.

Šorm, Esther & Gerard J. Steen. 2013. Processing visual metaphor: A study in thinking out loud. *Metaphor and the Social World*. 3 (1). 1–34.

Šorm, Esther & Gerard J. Steen. 2018. VISMIP: Towards a method for visual metaphor identification. In Gerard J. Steen (ed.), *Visual metaphor: How images construct metaphorical meaning*. Amsterdam: Benjamins.

Sperber, Dan & Deirdre Wilson 1995 [1986]. *Relevance theory*. 2nd edn. Oxford: Blackwell.

Talmy, Leonard. 1988. Force dynamics in language and cognition. *Cognitive Science* 12. 49–100.

Tan, Ed S. 1996. *Emotion and the structure of narrative film*. Mahwah, NJ: Erlbaum.

Teng, Norman Y. & Sewen Sun. 2002. Grouping, simile, and oxymoron in pictures: A design-based cognitive approach. *Metaphor and Symbol* 17. 295–316.

Tseronis, Assimakis & Charles Forceville. 2017. The argumentative relevance of visual and multimodal antithesis in Frederick Wiseman's documentaries. In Assimakis Tseronis & Charles Forceville (eds.), *Multimodal argumentation and rhetoric in media genres*, 165–188. Amsterdam: Benjamins.

Wilson, Deirdre & Dan Sperber. 2012. *Meaning and relevance*. Cambridge: Cambridge University Press.

Winter, Bodo. 2014. Horror movies and the cognitive ecology of primary metaphors. *Metaphor and Symbol* 29 (3). 151–170, DOI: 10.1080/10926488.2014.924280

Subject Index

https://doi.org/10.1515/9783110629460-018

www.ingramcontent.com/pod-product-compliance
Lightning Source LLC
Chambersburg PA
CBHW051555230426
43668CB00013B/1863
9783110764321